SOUTHERN LADY, YANKEE SPY

Also by Elizabeth R. Varon

*We Mean to Be Counted: White Women and
Politics in Antebellum Virginia*

Southern Lady, Yankee Spy

The True Story of Elizabeth Van Lew,

A Union Agent in the Heart

of the Confederacy

ELIZABETH R. VARON

OXFORD

UNIVERSITY PRESS

2003

OXFORD
UNIVERSITY PRESS

Oxford   New York
Auckland   Bangkok   Buenos Aires   Cape Town   Chennai
Dar es Salaam   Delhi   Hong Kong   Istanbul   Karachi   Kolkata
Kuala Lumpur   Madrid   Melbourne   Mexico City   Mumbai   Nairobi
São Paulo   Shanghai   Taipei   Tokyo   Toronto

Published by Oxford University Press, Inc.
198 Madison Avenue, New York, New York 10016

www.oup.com

Oxford is a registered trademark of Oxford University Press

Library of Congress Cataloging-in Publication Data

Varon, Elizabeth R., 1963–
   Southern lady, Yankee spy : the true story of Elizabeth Van Lew, a
Union agent in the heart of the Confederacy / Elizabeth R. Varon.
      p.   cm.
ISBN 019-514228-4 (acid-free paper)
1. Van Lew, Elizabeth L., 1818–1900.
2. Spies—United States—Biography.
3. United States—History—Civil War, 1861–1865—Secret service.
I. Title.
   E608.V34 V37 2003
   973.7'85'092—dc21

                                                      2003009266

9 8 7 6 5 4 3 2 1

Printed in the United States of America
on acid-free paper

FOR WILL

CONTENTS

ACKNOWLEDGMENTS   ix

Map of Central Virginia   xii

Map of Richmond   xiii

PROLOGUE   3

1 *"An Awful Responsibility"*
The Making of a Dissenter, 1818–1860   9

2 *"My Country! Oh My Country!"*
Virginia Leaves the Union   35

3 *"Our Flag Was Gone"*
The War's First Year   52

4 *"The Bright Rush of Life"*
The Making of the Richmond Underground   77

5 *Elizabeth and "The Beast"*
Butler Finds His Spy   107

6 *"This Precious Dust"*
The Clandestine Reburial of Colonel Ulric Dahlgren   135

7 *"The Smoke of Battle"*
Grant Moves on Richmond   153

8 *"A Flaming Altar"*
The Fall of Richmond and Its Aftermath   185

9 *"A Fiery Ordeal"*
The Trials of a Female Politician   216

10   *The Myth of "Crazy Bet"*   242

     EPILOGUE: Van Lew's Ghost   257

     LIST OF ABBREVIATIONS   263

     NOTES   265

     INDEX   305

ACKNOWLEDGMENTS

All authors have their debts; I am more indebted than most. I literally could not and would not have written this book without the expert assistance of a host of skilled research assistants and generous scholars. Vicki Killian of Takoma Park, Maryland, navigated the intricate National Archives and culled a wealth of information. She not only doggedly followed up on every lead I gave her, but also brought to my attention sources that I would have otherwise missed. Kelley Brandes of the Library of Virginia did me a similar service in Richmond. She both tracked down documents that I requested and identified others that I should request. Bill Pugsley worked through a key manuscript collection for me at the University of Texas, Austin. Here in Wellesley, Eden Knudsen devoted three summers to scouring nineteenth-century newspapers on my behalf.

I am also deeply indebted to those scholars who took the time to read and comment on my manuscript. Keith Poulter commented extensively, and incisively, on my first draft, and suggested changes that improved the book immeasurably. Marie Tyler-McGraw, Brent Tarter, and Julie Campbell, dear friends all, brought their expertise on Virginia history to bear on the manuscript. (Julie also shared her house, car, CD collection, and knowledge of Richmond's historical sites and finest eateries on my many research trips to the city.) Melvin Patrick Ely, the toughest critic around, helped me grapple with the difficult prewar sections of my story. And Dorothy Grant graced me with her fascinating insights into Van Lew family lore.

Two historians in particular went far beyond the call of duty and the duties of friendship in assisting me. J. Matthew Gallman and Robert C. Morris sent me valuable documents they had unearthed in their own research projects. I am also grateful to Mike Gorman, whose superb website on Civil War Richmond was a boon to me.

The staffs of a variety of libraries and archives deserve my thanks. It is an honor to have worked on this book, as I did on my previous one, with the wonderful folks at the Library of Virginia, Virginia Historical Society, and Valentine Richmond History Center. The Commonwealth of Virginia should regard these institutions and their keepers as state treasures. Most of all, I am grateful to the interlibrary loan staff at Wellesley College, which responded with promptness and efficiency to each of my seemingly endless requests for material.

Wellesley College provided invaluable institutional support for this project, in the form of sabbatical leaves and research grants; I thank the Dean's Office for its generosity. My research was also supported, in its initial stages, by a summer stipend from the National Endowment for the Humanities. My colleagues and students at Wellesley motivated me by expressing a keen interest in my project, and provided me with much needed reasons to work on something other than Elizabeth Van Lew. I am especially grateful to our department chair of the last few years, Lidwien Kapteijns, for being so understanding and supportive.

Of course this book would not have seen the light of day without the help of my agent, Rick Balkin, and editor, Peter Ginna. They had the imagination to look at my rough book proposal and see in its place a finished book worthy of Oxford University Press.

How can I begin to thank my family? My father Bension, a historian at heart, has shown me how words have the power to enchant. My mother Barbara is in all things my mentor. Her encyclopedic knowledge of the Victorian era and her peerless mastery of the English language are resources I have drawn on again, and again, and again. Her own years of work in the trenches of Virginia civic and political life, and her abiding commitment to making the Old Dominion a better place, helped to draw me, inexorably, toward Elizabeth Van Lew. My brother Jeremy, my colleague in this profession and my fellow author, has buoyed me with his praise and encouragement.

Most of all, I am grateful to my husband Will. He was sure I could write this book even when I had doubts. He made it possible for me to burrow into my basement office or to fly off to Richmond for research secure in the knowledge that our little family would hum happily along in my absence. He read the entire manuscript with perfect care, and knew that I needed him to tell me not only what was broken, but how to fix it. Most of all, he inspired me with his own example—with the excellence of his own work, and with his conviction that we historians have the duty to reach out beyond the confines of our profession.

And so this book is for him.

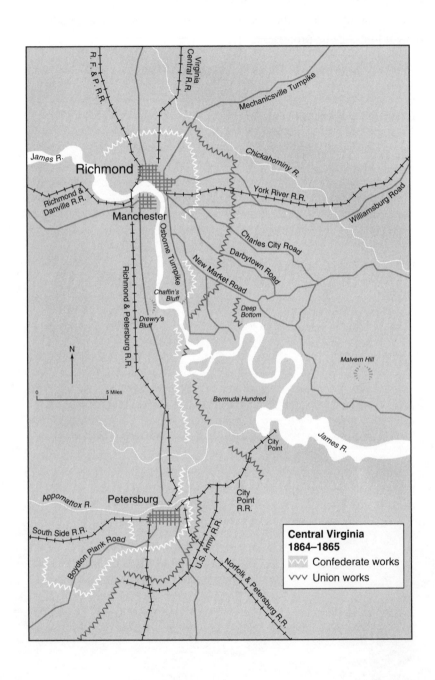

R. F. & P. R.R.

Virginia Central R.R.

Mechanicsville Turnpike

James R.

Chickahominy R.

Richmond

York River R.R.

Williamsburg Road

Richmond & Danville R.R.

Manchester

Osborne Turnpike

Charles City Road

Darbytown Road

Richmond & Petersburg R.R.

New Market Road

Chaffin's Bluff

Deep Bottom

Drewry's Bluff

Malvern Hill

N

Bermuda Hundred

0   5 Miles

City Point

James R.

Appomattox R.

Petersburg

City Point R.R.

South Side R.R.

Boydton Plank Road

U.S. Army R.R.

Norfolk & Petersburg R.R.

Central Virginia
1864–1865

Confederate works

Union works

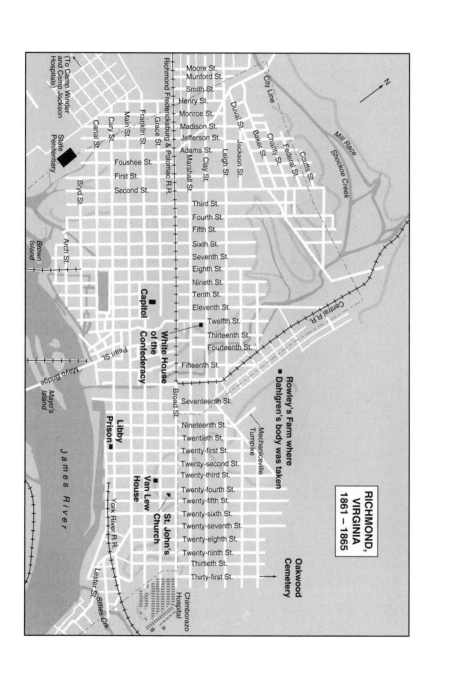

RICHMOND,
VIRGINIA
1861 – 1865

N

James River

Mayo's Island

Brown Island

Mayo Bridge

Pearl St.

State Penitentiary

(To Camp Winder and Camp Jackson Hospitals)

Richmond Fredericksburg & Potomac R.R.

Canal St.
Cary St.
Main St.
Franklin St.
Grace St.

Byrd St.
Arch St.

Foushee St.
First St.
Second St.

Marshall St.
Clay St.
Leigh St.

Moore St.
Munford St.
Smith St.
Henry St.
Monroe St.
Madison St.
Jefferson St.
Adams St.

Duval St.
Jackson St.
Baker St.
Charity St.
Federal St.
Coutts St.

City Line

Mill Race

Shockoe Creek

Third St.
Fourth St.
Fifth St.
Sixth St.
Seventh St.
Eighth St.
Nineth St.
Tenth St.
Eleventh St.
Twelfth St.
Thirteenth St.
Fourteenth St.
Fifteenth St.

Capitol

White House
of the
Confederacy

Central R.R.

Rowley's Farm where
■ Dahlgren's body was taken

Broad St.

Seventeenth St.

Libby
Prison ■

Nineteenth St.
Twentieth St.
Twenty-first St.
Twenty-second St.
Twenty-third St.
Twenty-fourth St.
Twenty-fifth St.
Twenty-sixth St.
Twenty-seventh St.
Twenty-eighth St.
Twenty-ninth St.
Thirtieth St.
Thirty-first St.

Mechanicsville Turnpike

Van Lew
House

▲ St. John's
Church

York River R.R.

Lester St.
Stiltes Crk.

Chimborazo Hospital

Oakwood
Cemetery

SOUTHERN LADY, YANKEE SPY

Prologue

THE HOUSE THAT STOOD ATOP GRACE STREET, IN THE ELEGANT CHURCH HILL NEIGH-borhood of Richmond, still presented an imposing façade, with its stately pillars, wide porches, and sweeping view of the James River below. Yet this was a home that spoke of past glories. Its stucco was chipped and its paint was peeling. Its once magnificent gardens were now overgrown and unkempt. Carriages no longer came calling and servants no longer bustled to and fro. Inside, the dust was thick on the carpets and window-sills. In the drawing room, beneath a large mirror, an elderly lady dressed in black looked down mournfully at the body of her aunt—a small, worn, nearly skeletal figure, laid under a tightly pulled covering. This was the body of Elizabeth Van Lew, who died in the early morning hours of September 25, 1900, at the age of 81.[1]

There were few reminders on that day that Van Lew had been a great heroine of the Civil War. It was here, in her once lively and gracious home, that she had worked so bravely on behalf of the Union cause, hiding fugitive soldiers who had escaped from Confederate prisons, plotting with Union sympathizers, and meeting clandestinely with couriers and spies from the Federal army. Here, Van Lew had spent much of her family's fortune on behalf of Union soldiers and civilians, and ruined her family name in the eyes of her Richmond neighbors. Here, in the darkest hours of the Civil War, Elizabeth had prayed for the deliverance of her beloved Virginia from the tyrannies of secession, slavery, and war. And it was here that her prayers had been answered, when she witnessed the fall of Richmond to the Union army on April 3, 1865.

Just as it had served as a place of refuge for Van Lew and as the nerve center of her political activism during the Civil War, the Church Hill mansion served these functions after the war. Appointed by President Ulysses S. Grant as postmaster of Richmond in 1869, Elizabeth embarked on a

3

pioneering and controversial career as a female politician and representative of the Republican party. For eight long years, until she was stripped of the postmastership in 1877, Van Lew had regularly made the trip from Church Hill to the Custom House Building on Main Street, where the post office was located. In order that she might continue her work even at home, she had converted the library in her mansion into an office. Here, Van Lew had written letters to the Northern press decrying white Richmond's treatment of African Americans; here, she had played host to fellow Republicans and woman's rights advocates Susan B. Anthony and Anna Dickinson; here she confided to her journal her horror at the political attacks that her opponents—Republicans who coveted her office for themselves and Democrats who objected to her racial egalitarianism—had launched against her. In the 1880s and 1890s, with her political career over, Van Lew regarded the Church Hill mansion both as a shelter and a sort of prison. So hostile to her were her fellow white Richmonders that she had no choice but to remain within the walls of her home.[2]

On September 25, 1900, there were few reminders of these struggles and glories; and yet, some telling artifacts remained in the mansion—those Van Lew could not bear to sell or to donate, as she had donated so many of her possessions over the years, to those less fortunate than herself. In the parlor hung a small picture of Ulysses S. Grant as he appeared in the last stages of the war, wearing his general's garb and an expression both tired and purposeful; on the back read the dedication, "For Miss Van Lew, from U. S. Grant, lieutenant general, U.S.A." The parlor also displayed a picture of John A. Andrew, the barrel-chested, handsome former Governor of Massachusetts, whose wire-rimmed spectacles and well-groomed curls lent a thoughtfulness and softness to his face. In the library were two more pictures. One was of Virginia politician John Minor Botts, whose mulish expression reflected his stubborn, self-righteous character. The other picture was of United States Senator Charles Sumner. Disfigured in the brutal caning he suffered at the hands of a proslavery antagonist in 1856, Sumner made a fierce impression, enhanced by his unruly halo of hair. The last of the five political images in the Van Lew mansion was familiar to all Americans—a bust of Abraham Lincoln, placed on top of a table in the library.[3]

How curious, even incongruous, this gallery of portraits was. Botts was an elite slaveholder who opposed the election of Lincoln in 1860 and argued, in vain, for compromise during Virginia's secession debates; during postwar

Reconstruction, he opposed the enfranchisement of African Americans. At the other end of the political arc were Andrew and Sumner. Andrew was an abolitionist and avid Lincoln supporter; Sumner was the leader of the Radical Republican faction in the Senate, and a tireless advocate for racial equality. And then there were Grant and Lincoln, the architects of Union victory, pragmatists both, who embraced emancipation when it became clear that freeing the slaves was the key to Union victory.[4]

These images were perhaps so dear to Van Lew because they represented her own political evolution. Botts had socialized at the Church Hill mansion in its antebellum heyday, and embodied the respectability and prudence of the Whig political elite to which Van Lew's family belonged. Before the war, Elizabeth had idolized him, and shared his hope that Virginia could forge her own solution to the problem of slavery without interference from either radical Northerners or extremist Southerners.[5]

When Virginia's moderate leaders were marginalized by the swift ascendance of the secession movement in the spring of 1861, Van Lew cast her lot with the Lincoln administration and the Union army. Like Grant and Lincoln she embraced the cause of emancipation during the war, and came to see African Americans as vital partners in the struggle to restore the Union. In Grant she found a patron who, while general in chief of the Union forces, solicited her services as an intelligence agent during his Virginia campaign; as president, he then appointed her to the coveted and important office of postmaster of Richmond. She found in Grant, finally, a loyal friend and kindred spirit, whose postwar campaign motto "Let Us Have Peace" seemed to augur Virginia's reintegration into the Union and a new era of sectional harmony. Though Van Lew never met Lincoln, her deepest understanding of the war's meaning echoed his own. Just as Lincoln, by the time of his Second Inaugural, had come to see the sufferings of the war as repentance for the sin of slavery—a cataclysm that would repay with every drop "drawn with the sword" the blood of slaves that had been "drawn with the lash"—Van Lew came to view the war as the instrument of the nation's moral redemption.

The divisive politics of Reconstruction drew Van Lew into fellowship with the Massachusetts politicians Andrew and Sumner. Elizabeth befriended Andrew after the war, as she fought to advance the cause of black civil rights, much as he had done while governor. The bitterness of her own political battles radicalized Van Lew, kindling her admiration for Sumner;

an uncompromising idealist, he envisioned a world without racial discrimination, and accused first Lincoln and then Grant of not doing enough to foster racial justice.[6]

The images in Van Lew's house would have been highly offensive to the elite Southerners of her Church Hill neighborhood; they proudly displayed pictures of Robert E. Lee, Thomas J. "Stonewall" Jackson, Jefferson Davis, and other Confederate luminaries. Lest a visitor conclude that Van Lew's choice of images was evidence of her "Northern" attitudes and allegiances, however, the portrait of Botts served as a reminder not only that Elizabeth had once positioned herself as a political moderate, but also that she clung tenaciously, to her dying day, to her Virginia identity.

On the day of her death, the most significant of Van Lew's possessions— her personal papers—had been gathered and placed on a battered marble table in the drawing room. They were waiting to be claimed by her friend and executor, John P. Reynolds Jr., who had been summoned from Boston to her deathbed but had not arrived in time to bid her farewell. Van Lew had bequeathed to him a tattered and mismatched jumble of documents, running several hundred pages. The condition of the papers reflected the trying circumstances in which Van Lew kept records of her life. Fearing that Confederate detectives might storm her house at any moment, Van Lew had, during the war years, kept her current diary entries at her bedside, where she could easily destroy them if necessary. The finished portions of what she called her "occasional journal" she kept buried in some location that she never disclosed. After the war, when such precautions were no longer necessary, Van Lew gathered together these diary entries and inserted among them newspaper articles she had clipped and saved, reminiscences of wartime events she penned after the fact, and examples of her postwar correspondence with the press and with political associates.[7]

Whatever their disorder, Van Lew's papers were a treasure trove of scintillating descriptions of life in wartime; trenchant analyses of the major political issues of the era; and revealing attempts by Van Lew to address posterity directly, to shape how she would be remembered. Alerted to the news of her death, newspapers from Richmond to Boston rushed to print obituaries, identifying Van Lew as the female spy who had betrayed the South. Deep within Van Lew's papers was a poignant protest against such characterizations. On two sheaths, written decades after the war, Van Lew repeatedly reworked, with accumulating pathos and even anger, one defining statement—her repugnance at being known, in both the North and the South, as a "spy." She wrote plaintively, "I do not know how they can call me a spy serving my own country within its recognized borders. . . . [for] my loyalty am I now to be branded as a spy—by my own country, for which I was willing to lay down my life? Is that honorable or honest? God knows."[8]

This book is an effort to answer Van Lew's questions about her own legacy, and to shape a new public image of her. The discordant labels of "Southern lady" and "Yankee spy" at once described her and constrained her. Behind the labels lies a true story more stirring than fiction, the story of a heroine who deserves to be remembered, first and foremost, as a patriot.

1

"An Awful Responsibility"

THE MAKING OF A DISSENTER, 1818–1860

"FROM THE TIME I KNEW RIGHT FROM WRONG, IT WAS MY SAD PRIVILEGE TO DIFFER in many things from the perceived opinions in my locality. This has made my life intensely sad and earnest. . . . [I became] quick in feeling and ready to resent what seemed to me wrong."[1] In reminiscences penned after the Civil War, Elizabeth Van Lew thus traced to her childhood a keen sense of loneliness and alienation. Her dramatic career as a Union agent and crusader against racism, she seemed to suggest, was foreordained; it was her tragic destiny to play the role of outsider. We must resist the temptation, however, to attribute to Van Lew an uncompromising and consistent moral vision, for the historical record tells an altogether more complicated story. Rather than standing aloof from the conventions of her time, Van Lew grew up in a family that worked tirelessly to assimilate into Richmond society.

Instead of rejecting slavery and the company of slaveholders, the Van Lew family carefully staked out a position on the tenuous middle ground between abolitionism and the proslavery creed. The Van Lews simultaneously held blacks in bondage and lamented the evils of slavery, hoping all the while that through individual acts of kindness, charity, and manumission they could erode slavery gradually, from the inside. It may well be that Elizabeth Van Lew always knew that slavery was wrong. Yet it was only after rising sectional tensions between the North and the South closed off the middle ground, dashing her hope that the white South might reform itself, that Elizabeth looked to the Union army to end slavery and redeem her native region. Van Lew would thus bring to her war work and postwar crusades the special zeal—born of guilt and regret—of a latecomer to the truth.

⌐⌐

Elizabeth Van Lew was born in Richmond, Virginia, on October 15, 1818, the first child of John Van Lew and Eliza Louise Baker Van Lew. Neither of her parents was a native of the South. Her father, born in 1790 in Jamaica, Long Island, was of Dutch stock; his forebears had immigrated to America in the 1660s. Having apprenticed in the mercantile profession in New York, John moved to Richmond sometime in the early 1800s and established a hardware business. Van Lew's mother Eliza was born in 1798 in Philadelphia, Pennsylvania. Eliza's father Hilary Baker was an ardent patriot during the American Revolution and afterward one of the architects of the new Republic—he participated in Pennsylvania's constitutional convention in 1789 and 1790 and then served three terms as Philadelphia's mayor, from 1796 to 1798. Baker also became one of the first members of the Pennsylvania Abolition Society, a highly influential and pioneering antislavery organization, joining it in 1784 and remaining on the membership rolls until his death.[2]

Elizabeth Van Lew was reared on tales of her grandfather's heroism— Hilary Baker died in office in 1798, felled by the yellow fever he had contracted ministering to the sick of the city during an epidemic. In her memoirs Van Lew recalls how the noble spirit of her grandfather was passed on to her mother. As Hilary neared death, he was taken to the outskirts of Philadelphia, where his family had taken refuge from the epidemic. His three-month-old daughter Eliza was placed beside him and "with her tiny fingers outstretched" touched his fevered brow, as if to bid goodbye to the great man. Along with Hilary Baker, a female icon loomed large in the family lore: Baker's sister, Letitia Smith, "was very patriotic during the Revolutionary War," and Elizabeth thrilled to the "interesting stories of her successful labors for the prisoners" taken captive by the British when they occupied New York.[3]

In 1808, Hilary Baker's widow Anna died, and the orphaned Eliza Baker was sent to live with her brother, Hilary Jr. in Richmond. There she met the up-and-coming businessman John Van Lew. The couple were married at St. John's Episcopal Church in the Church Hill neighborhood on January 10, 1818. Richmond's foremost newspaper, the *Enquirer*, duly took note of the wedding, describing John and Eliza, in words that obscured their Northern origins, as "both of this city."[4]

The Richmond in which the Van Lews chose to make their start was a city in transition. In the quarter century from John Van Lew's wedding in 1818 to his death in 1843, Richmond was transformed from a proud but small and provincial port town—a "rugged terrain" of sparse dwellings and "wagon-rutted roads" that would seem little more than a country village to modern eyes—into a productive metropolis that in many ways resembled other major eastern cities.[5]

Richmond staked its pride on its reputation as a political hub. As the capital of Virginia, the state that was "mother" to Founding Fathers Washington, Jefferson, and Madison, Richmond was a mecca for the "veneration of Revolutionary heroes." The city boasted an impressive capitol building, an "imposing Greek edifice" that stood at the center of town; Capitol Square was adorned by a famous statue of George Washington by Jean-Antoine Houdon that civic boosters advertised as one of the city's main attractions. Moreover, Patrick Henry had given his immortal "Give Me Liberty or Give Me Death" speech at Richmond's St. John's Church during the Revolutionary War, and Richmond could claim John Marshall, Chief Justice of the Supreme Court, as a native son. The city's sense of its importance as a keeper of the flame of Republicanism was confirmed when Revolutionary War hero the Marquis de Lafayette chose Richmond as one of the stops on his wildly popular and much celebrated tour of the United States in 1824.[6]

If Richmond embodied the heroic past of Virginia, it also embodied the striving future. Located at the falls of the James River, the city specialized in the milling of grains from the hinterland; in the 1820s and 1830s Richmond's "millers expanded their business interests to naileries, foundries, and cotton and woolen manufactories." The coming of the railroad—in 1836 the Richmond, Fredericksburg, and Potomac (RF&P) Railroad became the first line to connect Richmond to the nascent national rail system along the east coast—accelerated the city's economic development and diversification. Its tobacco factories and iron foundries made Richmond the leader of Southern manufacturing by 1840.[7]

Over the course of the 1820s and 1830s, the city's population nearly doubled, exceeding 20,000 by the time of the 1840 United States census. Shops, saloons, groceries, hotels, and places of entertainment proliferated, and new neighborhoods sprang up, providing Richmond with an "urban, bourgeois culture . . . typical of antebellum American cities." But while a visitor from New York or Philadelphia would have found much that was familiar in Richmond, he or she would have also confronted the inescapable paradox of this Southern town—Richmond's growth and modernization were powered by slave labor. Nearly half of the city's population was African American: the 1840 census counted some 7,509 slaves and 1,926 free blacks.

The political and economic leaders of the city were, overwhelmingly, slaveowners.[8]

The city's traditional elite—the "first families" who could trace their bloodlines to the Revolutionary era heroes of Virginia—guarded their prerogatives carefully, and welcomed into their ranks only those newcomers who possessed all the requisite attributes: wealth, measured in real estate and slaves; gentility, displayed by strict adherence to the codes of gentlemanly and ladylike behavior; taste, evinced by the possession of fine luxuries; and pedigree, which one might possess as a birthright or, as in the case of John Van Lew, marry into, by attaching oneself to a respectable family such as the Philadelphia Bakers.

If we cast our eyes back to the 1820s and 1830s, to Elizabeth Van Lew's childhood, we see abundant evidence that her parents successfully assimilated into Richmond high society. Well-positioned to take advantage of the dynamic economy, John's hardware business, the first such enterprise in the city, thrived. Advertisements for his firm regularly appeared in the Richmond papers; an announcement that the store had just received a shipment of "fine pens and pocket Cutlery, Scissors, Razors, Bowie, Dirk and other Knives, Knives and Forks, with Ivory, Stag, Buffalo and Bone Handles, ALSO Anvils, Vices, Files, &c., of the very best manufacture" conveys the broad range of products the term "hardware" encompassed at the time. John soon counted among his business associates men of the first families of Virginia such as Thomas Randolph of Tuckahoe. Van Lew even played a crucial role in the construction of the University of Virginia, as his firm was one of the principal suppliers of hardware and glassware for the fledgling campus. The secret to John's success was his determination not to live beyond his means or take on too much debt; his rule of thumb, as he confided to a young cousin, was never to extend credit to anyone with whom he was not "personally acquainted."[9]

By 1836 John Van Lew had amassed enough of a fortune to purchase a three-story mansion on prestigious Church Hill, just across the street from Eliza's brother Hilary, who by this time had become a partner in John's hardware business. Located on the 2300 block of East Grace Street, the mansion had been built in 1802 for Dr. John Adams, a physician and one-time mayor of Richmond. As the numerous Mutual Assurance policies John Van Lew took out on the house reveal, he initiated a series of improvements to the residence, rendering it into a showpiece renowned throughout the

"Richmond scarce presents so fine a prospect." *The Van Lew mansion, from a sketch in* Harper's Weekly (LIBRARY OF VIRGINIA).

city. He altered the basic Federal design of the brick and stucco dwelling by adding a dwarf Doric portico on the side of the house that fronted Grace Street and an imposing, two-story Doric piazza on the rear of the house overlooking the gardens. Both of these classical touches were in keeping with the prevailing tastes of the era. On the inside, the house featured an 18-foot-wide central hall and 14 rooms. John Van Lew took considerable interest in how the house was appointed and kept on the lookout during his business travels for furnishings that would improve it.[10]

However impressive the architecture and appointments of the Van Lew mansion, it was the house's felicitous geographic setting that made it so remarkable. Occupying an entire city block, the Van Lew property faced a row of elegant and architecturally diverse homes on Grace Street. The mansion itself was wreathed by elaborate gardens—featuring magnolia trees, hedges of privet and box bushes—that fell gently, in a series of terraces, down the hill behind the house, toward the James River below. The Henrico Agricultural and Horticultural Society, which sponsored a yearly competition to determine the finest garden in the city, frequently awarded top honors to Eliza Van Lew for designing and tending the Church Hill property.[11]

In June of 1843, the editor of the *Richmond Enquirer*, Thomas Ritchie—one of the most influential men in the city—published an evocative and admiring account of his visit to the Van Lew mansion. In an effort to conjure up for his readers the splendid view of the river from the back of the house, he wrote, "Stand upon the portico and cast your eyes over the landscape in front, with all its variations of extensive views and brilliant landscapes. Richmond scarce presents so fine a prospect as the eye takes in from that commanding viewpoint. The river below seems broken into several beautiful

"That commanding
viewpoint."
*The back piazza of the
Elizabeth's Church Hill
home* (VALENTINE RICH-
MOND HISTORY CENTER).

lakes from the apparent conjunction of the islands and the tongues of
land."[12]

Adding to the property's luster was its proximity to the venerable St.
John's Episcopal Church, located just across the street on the corner adjacent
to the Van Lew mansion. Ritchie called St. John's the "classic ground of the
city"—its very heart and soul. The church, where the Van Lew family worshipped, boasted among its parishioners some of the most distinguished
families of the state, such as the Taliaferros, Roysters, and Carringtons. While
the Van Lew mansion itself no longer exists, St. John's has survived to the
present day in nearly pristine form, and by walking its hallowed grounds a
modern-day visitor to Richmond can get a good sense of why Church Hill
was considered the prime real estate in the city—and of why its inhabitants
felt themselves to be the natural nobility of the Old Dominion.[13]

Indeed, it is impossible to overstate the impact that Elizabeth Van Lew's
physical surroundings had on her sense of self. Van Lew spent her youth at the
family's first house, located at the edge of the Church Hill neighborhood, on
I Street between Twenty-Fourth and Twenty-Fifth Streets; when her father purchased the Grace Street mansion in 1836, the family moved a few blocks into the
center of the Church Hill district, and a few rungs up the social ladder into Richmond's elite. To live in such a setting as Church Hill was to inherit a sense of en-
titlement and responsibility. Long after the Civil War, Elizabeth Van Lew would
attest to her belief that during her young adulthood, her family's Grace Street
mansion had been "one of the [most] beautiful homes of the world."[14]

"The classic ground of the city."
Exterior view of St. John's Episcopal Church (VIRGINIA HISTORICAL SOCIETY).

Most of what we know of the Van Lew family's life in this period comes from the pen of Eliza Griffin Carrington, who lived on "Carrington Row" across the street from the Van Lews. Born in 1827 to Eliza G. and Littleberry Carrington, Eliza Griffin had the bluest of blood, by Virginia standards; she was a descendant of Colonel Richard Adams, one of the original inhabitants of Church Hill and a friend of Thomas Jefferson. Her great uncle, Dr. John Adams, had sold John Van Lew the Church Hill mansion in 1836. Late in her life, in the first years of the twentieth century, Eliza Griffin wrote a detailed reminiscence of Elizabeth Van Lew. Describing herself as Van Lew's "most intimate friend," Carrington claimed that the Van Lews "formed a part of Richmond's most select society among whom were the Lees, Marshalls, Robinsons, Wickhams, Adamses, Cabels [sic] and Carringtons." According to Eliza Griffin, John Van Lew's parlors and gardens frequently became the stage for elaborate parties, graced by such celebrities as Chief Justice John Marshall, writer Edgar Allan Poe, and Swedish opera star Jenny Lind.[15]

The sterling reputation of the family testified not only to John Van Lew's success but also to the comportment of his wife, Eliza, who "vied with him in a life of usefulness," recalled Carrington. The Richmond elite demanded of its women that they conform to the idealized image of the "Southern lady." Eliza, petite and elegant at five feet two, with gray eyes and a fair complexion, fit the physical mold of the "lady," and lived up to the exacting behavioral standards as well. The opinion makers of the day—ministers, editors, authors, and politicians—directed women to be pure, pious, and refined. Playing the gracious hostess was but one of the Southern lady's

"Give Me Liberty or Give
Me Death."
*The interior of St. John's
Church, scene of Patrick
Henry's famous speech* (VIR-
GINIA HISTORICAL SOCIETY).

duties. She was expected to be an efficient household manager, a devoted
teacher of moral values to her children, and, in keeping with the precepts
of Christianity and *noblesse oblige*, to extend the hand of charity, or "benevolence," to less-fortunate whites. In Carrington's opinion, Eliza Baker Van
Lew was the very embodiment of this ideal. "Benevolence was her watch-
word," Carrington wrote admiringly of Van Lew's mother.[16]

While their gardens, charity, and moral rectitude marked the Van Lews
as Richmond worthies, it was their slaveholding that revealed how fully these
former Northerners had embraced the customs of the South. By the mid-
1830s, the Van Lew residence was home not only to John, Eliza, Elizabeth,
and her two younger siblings Anna Paulina and John Newton (born in 1820
and 1823, respectively), but also to a corps of African American bondpeople.
The number of slaves working for the Van Lews grew over the years, climb-
ing from three in 1820 to nine in 1830 to fifteen in 1840.[17]

In owning slaves, John Van Lew was also staking his claim in Richmond
society, where slaveholding was a prerequisite for the wielding of political
influence. John, in the parlance of the day, was an "old-line Whig," a former
Federalist who jumped on the Whig bandwagon when that party emerged
to challenge the ascendancy of the Jacksonian Democrats in the mid-1830s.
In Virginia, the Whigs were a coalition of strange political bedfellows—
nationalists such as John, who favored a state-sponsored system of "internal
improvements" such as roads and canals to support commerce and diversify
the economy, and states-rights men, such as Beverly Tucker, who bolted the
Democratic party fearing that Andrew Jackson and his successor Martin Van
Buren were soft in their support of slavery. The Church Hill neighborhood

where the Van Lews lived was a Whig stronghold; John's neighbors Little-berry Carrington and George W. Smith served on Whig campaign committees and the Van Lew mansion hosted parties attended by prominent Whigs such as John Minor Botts, Franklin Stearns, John F. Lewis, and Charles Palmer.[18]

Here, then, was a conventional, prosperous, urbane Southern family—at least, to all outward appearances. However, as Elizabeth's private recollections reveal, there was a disparity between the outer life of the family—the way it performed in public—and its unconventional inner life. In her own brief account of her childhood, Van Lew chose to highlight not her family's wealth, connections, or popularity but its commitment to a life of the mind. "My parents were both intellectual and devoted to books," she wrote, adding that they set aside the large sum of $50 a year to increase the holdings of the family's library. An inventory of Eliza Van Lew's estate reveals that, by the time she died in 1875, she owned some 254 books, covering an impressive range of subjects: the Van Lew library featured contemporary political works, such as the speeches of Whig hero Henry Clay; travel books on France and England; histories such as Gibbon's classic study of Rome; poetry by popular authors such as Lydia Sigourney; and social commentary such as de Tocqueville's *Democracy in America*.[19]

Moreover, Elizabeth Van Lew's recollections conjure up images of her parents' unusually egalitarian marriage, one based on mutual respect and a passion for learning: "Mother had the reading time & when father wd. come home & they had gone to bed, I remember . . . as we slept in the adjoining room, hearing [mother's] delicious rehash of all [she had read] for his benefit." It is exceedingly rare in Southern women's writings from this era to find the adjective "intellectual" bestowed as a compliment by one woman on another, just as it is rare to get such an intimate glimpse into a couple's inner life. There is no question that Van Lew regarded her parents' marriage as out of the ordinary. "I have seen so much misery often in married life," she would muse looking back on her childhood, "that I am thankful for the memory of one true marriage."[20]

The tenor of life in the Van Lew household gave Elizabeth a sense of specialness that she carried into the outside world. According to Eliza Carrington, Van Lew stood out from her school classmates: "Elizabeth Van Lew was a wonderfully intelligent child. At school many a less gifted pupil owed success to her ready aid in mastering the tasks." Eager to provide the best possible education for her talented daughter, Eliza Van Lew had young

Elizabeth sent to Philadelphia in the early 1830s to live with her Pennsylvania relatives and to attend the academy from which Eliza herself had graduated. While there are no surviving records of Elizabeth's experiences in Philadelphia, we can safely surmise that her time in that bustling Northern metropolis contributed to her sense of being different from her peers. More than ten times the size of Richmond, Philadelphia was in the 1830s a hothouse for moral reform societies, most controversial among them those dedicated to the abolitionist movement. Even though she was too young to partake of the city's political life, Elizabeth may well have been exposed to antislavery ideas; one source contends that Elizabeth had a governess in Philadelphia who advocated the emancipation of the slaves. Whether or not this is true, Elizabeth must have felt upon her return home that Richmond looked decidedly smaller and more provincial than it had before.[21]

After receiving her education, a Southern girl was supposed to enter the most glorious epoch of her life—her years as a "belle." During this period of late adolescence, a young woman typically began the highly choreographed dance of courtship. Her family and friends identified potential suitors, whom the belle then vetted at a variety of public events such as dances and at formal, chaperoned "private" visits. Van Lew's prospects for finding a husband were good—not only did she come from a respected family, but she was also attractive. "As a maiden she possessed a delicate physique. Her form was sylph-like, her stature was small," and she possessed fine "social qualities," recalled Carrington. Van Lew dutifully accompanied her family to those places—such as the popular spa White Sulphur Springs—where the elite rubbed elbows and made connections. An 1838 letter she wrote to her cousin Charles Richards from Sweet Springs, a resort 17 miles from White Sulphur Springs, is the only surviving document from Van Lew's young adulthood in which she reveals her personality and concerns.[22]

The letter is animated by Van Lew's adoration for her father John, who was at that time in the throes of a serious, unspecified illness. The medical establishment of the day prescribed rest cures at spas as the remedy for a host of maladies, and urged the ailing John Van Lew to "take the water" at White Sulphur Springs. To Elizabeth's exasperation, the prescription backfired, and her father's condition deteriorated; the family removed in a panic to the less-crowded Sweet Springs resort, which Elizabeth described to her cousin as "one of the dullest places I was ever in." The fact that John began to recover there did not reconcile Van Lew to her situation. "Oh! What a

"Her form was sylph-like."
The earliest known likeness of Eliza-
beth Van Lew (LIBRARY OF VIRGINIA).

mistake it is to send poor invalids from the comfort of home to these com-
fortless spas," she lamented.[23]

Van Lew's letter reveals not only a devoted daughter but also a witty,
affectionate—even flirtatious—young woman who delighted in playing with
language. Among the many drawbacks of life at Sweet Springs, she confided
to Charles, were the legions of mosquitoes. "I am engaged in a continual
and bloody warfare which I hope will end in their extermination. I had the
floor scrubbed today in hopes of drowning them as they were becoming too
impudent and could be seen in great glee jumping about the floor in a style
that seemed to set human nature at defiance." Van Lew also adopted the
coy pose we associate with belles of the Scarlett O'Hara variety, teasing her
cousin: "I am very sorry to hear that a young gentleman one whom I esteem
HIGHLY VERY HIGHLY was loudly intoxicated in Fredbg the fourth of July
remained so all day and disgraced himself at the dinner and ball—but I am
at a loss who to think it is—will you not tell me? I think it must be some
mistake. It could not have been you." Moreover, Van Lew took evident
delight in relating the gossip from the Springs to Charles, describing a col-
orful cast of characters including a Mr. Graves who was suspected of murder,
and a pretty "Spanish girl" whom Van Lew thought was the very kind to
steal Charles's heart.[24]

Given Van Lew's family connections, physical attractiveness, and her

ability to play the role of flirtatious belle, why did she never marry? There
are a number of possible explanations. The first is that the one suitor to
whom she gave her heart as a young woman died before she could marry
him; as Eliza Carrington recalls, "she had an early love—death severed the
tie—here we draw the veil." Van Lew family lore, passed down over the
years to the descendants of Van Lew's brother John Newton, holds that
Elizabeth was actually engaged to be married. John Newton's great-
granddaughter, Dorothy Grant, to this day proudly wears a locket that, she
was told by her grandmother Annie Randolph (Van Lew) Hall, was given to
Elizabeth by this fiance. While we do not know the fate or identity of Elizabeth's lost love, we do know that she had extremely high expectations, a
legacy of her upbringing, of what marriage should be. Perhaps she found it
easier to fantasize about her lost suitor than she did to take a chance on a
lesser man.[25]

More important, even in her teens and early twenties Van Lew displayed
a seriousness and sense of purpose that suitors may well have found un-
becoming. While other young women reveled in the predictable rituals of
courtship, Van Lew threw herself into benevolent work. "Her great heart
carried her on many missions of mercy to the dark and dangerous slums of
Richmond," wrote Carrington. "I, strong and vigorous, have often accompanied her where human pity had to give place to personal apprehension."
In dispensing charity, Van Lew followed the lead of a visible and influential
cadre of female reformers in Richmond. Since the 1810s, these reformers
had worked to bring the benefits of education to poor children, and to
promote piety (through the distribution of Bibles and other religious tracts)
among poor adults. Van Lew was in short very much her mother's daughter,
committed to a life of "usefulness."[26]

In September of 1843, the course of Elizabeth Van Lew's life was forever
altered when her father finally lost his long battle with illness. A long obituary published in the *Richmond Enquirer* bespeaks his standing in the community. A man of "irreproachable character," John "possessed a warm heart
and an open hand. Many are the friends who can testify to the former
assertion: many the poor and destitute who could give evidence in favor of
the latter." The obituary writer went on to imply that while John had not

been a particularly pious man for most of his life, he had on the eve of his demise opened his heart to God: Van Lew had "repeatedly conversed of late with his family on his soul's salvation, . . . and eagerly listened to their instructions as they pointed out to him the way of salvation through the blood of our Lord Jesus Christ." With the help of Eliza and the children, John had met death with "calm composure."[27]

The high esteem in which John Van Lew held his wife and children is clear from his will, a document that provides tantalizing clues about the inner dynamics of the family. John named his wife Eliza as executrix of his estate, bequeathing to her property and powers that far exceeded the customary "widow's third" (the right of a widow to use—but not to sell—one-third of her husband's real estate). Indeed, he granted her ownership over his movable property, such as carriages, furniture, and silver, and his real estate and residences, along with the power to sell them if she deemed it necessary. To each of his three children, Van Lew bequeathed $10,000, specifying in the cases of Elizabeth and Anna that this inheritance should "be free and exempt from the control or use of any husband" either might take. In making this stipulation for each daughter, John Van Lew was protecting them from the "civil death" that the vast majority of antebellum women experienced as adults: by law, a woman upon marriage gave over all her property to her husband, who became the sole legal authority over it. Only a special maneuver like John Van Lew's—the creation of a "separate estate" on her behalf—could protect a woman from losing her property rights when she took a husband.[28]

By far the most significant aspect of John Van Lew's will are its provisions regarding the family's slaves. In the original will, John bequeathed to Eliza "all my slaves and the future increase of the females of them" for the use of his family, and prohibited any public or private sale of them "except such sale as my said wife may choose to make or direct to be made." But John evidently had second thoughts about this arrangement, for he added a codicil that read: "I revoke so much of the bequest in the 4th clause of my will as gives to my wife Eliza Van Lew my slaves and the future increase of them absolutely and I will and direct that my said wife have the use of the said slaves and the said increase of them during the time of her natural life and at her death, that they be distributed in the same manner as is provided in my will for the distribution of the residue of my personal estate." In other words, Eliza had the right to "use" but not to sell—or to free—the slaves;

John had revoked her "absolute" authority over them. After her death, the human property, like John's other property, was to be divided up among the children.[29]

Just why John felt he had to constrain Eliza becomes clear from the actions of the Van Lew women after John's death—actions that register the women's moral qualms about slavery and about the racial status quo. The first of these was Eliza's decision to have a family slave, identified in the church records only as "Mary Jane, a colored child belonging to Mrs. Van Lew," baptized at St. John's on May 17, 1846. While the baptism of a black child in St. John's was not unheard of, it was very rare. None of the Van Lew's other bondpeople received this treatment; indeed, two other Van Lew slaves, Oliver Lewis and William Roane, were baptized in the First African Baptist Church, the preeminent black church in Richmond. The fact that Mary Jane was singled out for baptism in St. John's is the first of many signs that the family considered her special, and privileged her over their other slaves.[30]

The second unconventional action was Eliza's decision to sell off real estate she had inherited from John to a pair of free black women—Mary Ann Rix and her daughter Virginia. In the mid-1830s, John Van Lew had purchased from George W. Adams a goodly number of parcels of land that had originally been part of the estate of Colonel Richard Adams, one of Church Hill's founders. After John's death, Eliza began to sell some of these lots, asking for them the considerable sums—one of the lots of the Adams estate that Eliza sold in 1846 fetched $935—that one would expect for such prime land. On April 29, 1847, however, Eliza closed a deal that seems to have been motivated by something other than monetary considerations: she sold a parcel of the Adams estate, at the intersection of Thirty-Second and I Streets, just beyond the city limits, to Mary Ann Rix for $75. According to the Henrico county "register of free negroes and mulattoes," Rix, a "woman of dark brown complexion," had been born free in 1803. A year and a half after the 1847 transaction, in September 1848, Eliza Van Lew sold the adjacent lot to Rix's daughter, Virginia, a "dark brown woman," age 22, who had also been born free; like the first parcel, Virginia's acquisition cost her $75.[31]

Unfortunately, the historical record is silent on the question of how Eliza Van Lew made the acquaintance of this mother and daughter. But the very fact that they were the only blacks to whom Eliza deeded land, and that she

reserved for them two adjacent lots at prices well below what she was accustomed to charging, suggests that Eliza was trying to help them. Indeed,
Eliza's actions seem to embody the philosophy of "personalism," a term
coined by historian Suzanne Lebsock to describe the "distinct female value
system" that was often at work in nineteenth-century women's monetary
and legal transactions. Rather than being guided by social custom or by
fiscal considerations, Lebsock has argued, women in disposing of their property "indulged particular attachments—they were alert to the special case,
to the personal exception." The Rix women were such exceptions.[32]

The third in a long series of unconventional actions by Eliza was her
playing hostess to a controversial visitor from abroad. In June of 1851, the
Van Lew women welcomed into their home the distinguished Swedish author Frederika Bremer. Recognized now as one of the forerunners of feminism, Bremer made her reputation in the 1840s for the sympathetic depic-
tions of women in her novels. When she embarked on a tour of the United
States in 1849, she found herself besieged by female admirers. But Bremer's
visit was not a mere publicity tour. Instead, the author visited the United
States with the express purpose of meeting its noteworthy women and of
seeing the shameful institution of American slavery, which Bremer ardently
opposed, with her own eyes. She fulfilled both purposes when, toward the
end of her tour, she called upon the Van Lews in Richmond.[33]

We know about Bremer's visit because she described it in her book *Homes
of the New World*, an account of her travels in the United States that was
published in 1853 to widespread acclaim. According to Bremer, she was
"greatly pleased" with the Van Lew women, as "intellect, kindness, and refinement of feeling were evident in their gentle countenances." But it was
Elizabeth who became her special companion. "The daughter, a pleasing,
pale blonde, expressed so much compassion for the sufferings of the slave,
that I was immediately attracted to her," Bremer explains. Elizabeth took
Bremer on a tour of the city, obliging her request to visit a tobacco factory.
Once there, Bremer watched in horror as slaves toiled ceaselessly amid the
"murderous" smells and dirt produced by the tobacco and the machinery
used to roll and pack it. "If these slaves had only any future, any thing to
hope for, to strive for, to live for, any prospect before them, then I should
not deplore their lot—but nothing, nothing!!!" Bremer was keenly aware
that her companion shared her sense of horror. "Good Miss Van L. could
not refrain from weeping," Bremer wrote. Significantly, the two women did

nothing to betray their views to the proprietor of the factory, who cordially gave Bremer a large cake of tobacco as a parting gift.[34]

Bremer's travelogue is the earliest evidence we have of Elizabeth Van Lew's misgivings about slavery and empathy for slaves. Eager to understand the origins of her antislavery sentiments, John Albree Jr., an amateur scholar who wrote a series of essays about Van Lew in the early twentieth century, conducted interviews with relatives and acquaintances of hers. Albree learned from Elizabeth's cousin Anna Whitlock that as a young girl, Elizabeth met the daughter of a slave trader during one of the Van Lews' trips to Hot Springs and heard from her a searing and unforgettable tale. The slave trader had "had for sale a slave mother and her young babe, and . . . when the mother found that she had been sold to one purchaser and parted from her babe, who had been sold to another, the mother's heart broke and she fell dead." Albree was told by Whitlock that the encounter with the slave trader's daughter left a permanent stamp on Elizabeth Van Lew.[35]

Such apocryphal anecdotes are seductive in their simplicity. But they have very little explanatory power. As Bremer's account demonstrates, Elizabeth Van Lew hardly needed outside influences and chance encounters to illustrate for her the nature of slavery. A lifelong resident of Richmond, Elizabeth would have routinely seen slaves doing backbreaking labor and being mistreated by whites. Rather than try to artificially pinpoint a moment at which Van Lew was "converted" to abolitionism, we need to grapple with the question of why the sights she saw moved her to feel empathy for slaves, when most of her fellow Richmond whites were immune to such feelings. Most important, we must ask what Van Lew chose to do about the moral repugnance she felt toward the slave system.

The key to answering both questions lies in the influence of Elizabeth's mother Eliza. For over the course of the 1850s—just as John suspected she might—the widow Van Lew took measures to reduce the family's slaveholdings. Looking back, we can surmise that Eliza had made an uneasy peace with her husband's slaveholding; perhaps she had rationalized that slaves were better off under her benign tutelage than under that of a typical Southern master. After John's death, however, she struggled for ways simultaneously to preserve the family's mantle of respectability and to salve her conscience. Elizabeth would be her mother's student and partner in this struggle.

The Richmond tax rolls and census schedules show that Eliza Van Lew held 21 slaves in 1850, 14 of them living in Richmond and another seven on the family's 36-acre farm in Henrico County. By contrast, the 1860 census and tax records list Eliza as owning only two slaves, both of them elderly women. The records also show that the widow Van Lew employed two free black servants at her Church Hill mansion. Eliza had sold the Henrico farm in 1856, for more than $3,000; the transaction was the last, and the most lucrative, of the numerous sales of family land that Eliza made after John's death. The widow Van Lew had, in other words, made it her practice to convert land into cash.[36]

While census statistics taken alone might seem to make a powerful case that Eliza reduced her slaveholding simply by setting slaves free, other kinds of sources from the period 1850 to 1865 cast doubt on such a conclusion.[37] Richmond officials kept files of "deeds of manumission"—legal documents granting freedom to slaves—and no deeds from the Van Lews are among the extant records. Because many of the records of Richmond's high courts were lost or destroyed in the nineteenth century, the absence of surviving deeds of manumission does not absolutely preclude the possibility that the Van Lews formally freed slaves and registered such deeds. But other silences in the historical record militate against that possibility. The surviving "register of free negroes and mulattoes" kept by Henrico county officials does not identify any freedpeople as former slaves of the Van Lews; nor are there extant petitions from Van Lew's ex-slaves requesting exemption from the 1806 law that required manumitted slaves to leave the Commonwealth within one year of their liberation. None of the Van Lew slaves whose names we know are listed as free people, as they would have been after their manumission, in surviving antebellum census or tax records.[38]

Even more puzzling are the scattered documents that, in direct refutation of the tax rolls and census statistics, identify by name numerous African Americans who served the Van Lews during the late 1850s and war years. The men working for the Van Lews included their butler, William Sewell; Oliver Lewis, who was born in 1825 and baptized at the First African Church in 1843; James and Peter Roane, born in 1833 and 1835, respectively; William Roane, who was baptized at First African in 1856; an elderly man named Nelson Gillum, born in 1800; and two slave men identified in existing records only as Anderson and Bob. Among the women serving the Van Lews were Hannah Roane, mother of James and Peter; Mary Jane Richards, baptized at St. John's in 1846; Judy Johnson, born in 1813; a woman identified only as Caroline, who worked as the Van Lews' cook; Elizabeth Draper, the cook's assistant, whose daughter Maggie Lena Walker would go on to be one of black Richmond's greatest postwar leaders; and Louisa Roane, who was purchased by Elizabeth Van Lew on January 1, 1863—the very day Lincoln promulgated the Emancipation Proclamation—in order that she could be together with her husband Peter Roane.[39]

What was the status of these individuals? Tantalizing evidence suggests that Elizabeth and her mother bypassed the formal legal procedures for freeing their slaves and instead made informal, private, and even clandestine arrangements with them. Such arrangements may have served to circumvent two formidable obstacles that stood in the women's way—John Van Lew's will and the 1806 Virginia law that forced newly freed slaves to leave the Commonwealth within one year or be reenslaved. According to John Van Lew's codicil, it will be remembered, neither Eliza nor Elizabeth had legal authority to free the slaves whom John had possessed. Moreover, John's will articulated his desire that those slaves remain in the family as long as Eliza lived. As for the 1806 law, the only way an ex-slave could win exemption from it was to undertake the daunting task of appealing to the court or legislature—since many such appeals were denied, to manumit a slave was potentially to exile him or her from friends and family in Virginia. This law, that unlike John's will, would apply even to slaves Eliza and Elizabeth acquired on their own and held in their own name, might well have prevented the Van Lew women from issuing public deeds of emancipation.[40]

Caught within this web of legal limitations, the Van Lew women pursued a number of different strategies to disentangle themselves and their slaves. One of these strategies was to permit slaves to "hire themselves out." The practice of hiring out, that emerged before 1800 partly as a solution to manpower shortages faced by Richmond's nascent industries, generally "entailed leasing slave workers to individuals or businesses for cash or payment in kind." The hiring-out system quickly expanded and evolved, with many slaves being permitted by their masters to find their own employers and to keep a small percentage of their earnings; such earnings could and did, in many cases, permit slaves eventually to purchase their own freedom. As it became more common for slaves to hire out their own time, it also became more common for them to "live out," that is to find their own quarters, away from the master's residence. Slaves who were given leave by their owners to strike favorable employment contracts had "all the appearance of free men," historian Luther Jackson has written.[41]

The Van Lews participated in the system of hiring out, employing slaves belonging to others and permitting their own slaves to earn wages. In 1852, for example, Eliza Van Lew hired a woman named Caroline to serve as the family's cook for a year. In 1857, a young man by the name of Cornelius Goodhall was deeded to Elizabeth Van Lew by his owner, Judith Wright. Judith Wright was illiterate, elderly, and close enough to the Van Lews to entrust Elizabeth with a special mission—at the time of Wright's death, the deed stipulated, Elizabeth was to hire Goodhall out "so long as may be necessary to raise sufficient funds to send [him] to some free state or other place where he may enjoy the privilege of freedom." That Wright chose Van Lew to exercise the "discretion" and "sound judgment" required for such a task speaks volumes. At least some of Van Lew's acquaintances were privy to her antislavery views and felt that she had the experience and connections to help a slave buy his freedom and settle in the North. Since Goodhall himself was a congregant at the First African Baptist Church, he may have heard about Elizabeth from one of the Van Lew slaves who attended services there. When exactly Goodhall became a free man is not clear. But we do know that he stayed in Richmond rather than heading North; Goodhall is listed in the 1870 census as a 36-year-old, Virginia-born African American residing in the Madison Ward of the city. It may have been family ties that kept Goodhall in Richmond, as he had a wife named Mary and a child, Betty Carter, in the city.[42]

In the spring of 1861, Eliza Van Lew was fined $10 by the Hustings Court for permitting "her slave Anderson to go at large and hire himself out." Slaves were required to have passes from their masters whenever they moved about the city, and Anderson had been caught with a pass that was out of date. Anderson, like the hired slave Caroline, appears in the historical record only fleetingly, and we may never know whether these two were working to buy their freedom as Cornelius Goodhall was. But together the three stories furnish one possible answer to the question of what became of the slaves who appear in the 1850 census but are invisible in the 1860 one—some of them may have been hired out by the Van Lew women, resided away from the Church Hill mansion, and therefore eluded the census takers.[43]

While the practice of hiring out was a relatively acceptable way to give slaves a measure of freedom, the story of Mary Jane Richards demonstrates that Eliza and Elizabeth found decidedly more risky ways to circumvent the slave system. Mary Jane was, as we have seen, the girl the Van Lew women singled out for baptism in 1846. Sometime in the early 1850s, they sent her North, to Princeton, New Jersey, to receive an education, in order to prepare her to go to Liberia to serve as a missionary. Richards had, in all likelihood, accompanied Elizabeth on one of her regular visits to Northern friends and family and then stayed on after Elizabeth returned to Richmond. Given that Richards is listed in American Colonization Society (ACS) records as a Presbyterian, she probably attended the school for African Americans run by free black Presbyterian and former missionary Betsy Stockton.[44]

The colony of Liberia had been established in 1822 by the American Colonization Society, an influential national reform society, based in Washington, D.C., and pledged to repatriating free blacks in Africa. Mired in controversy throughout its long history, the ACS was a coalition of divergent interests—it drew support from opponents of slavery who thought that to provide a haven for freed blacks was to advance the cause of gradual emancipation, but it also drew support from racist slaveholders who simply wanted to rid the country of free blacks altogether and therefore to render the institution of slavery immune to their influence. While often derided by modern-day scholars for lacking the moral courage of true abolitionists—who demanded an immediate and wholesale rather than gradual and piecemeal end to slavery—colonizationists were in their day a force to be reckoned with. They included within their ranks such national luminaries as Harriet Beecher Stowe, Henry Clay, and Abraham Lincoln.[45]

That the Van Lew women chose to affiliate with the colonization movement and to put Mary Jane in its hands is extremely revealing, for it shows that far from openly repudiating Richmond society and attacking slavery, Eliza and Elizabeth were still, in the late 1850s, working within the customs and rules of their locality, or at least trying to give the appearance of doing so. The colonization movement had boasted the support of some of the Commonwealth's most eminent men, such as Chief Justice John Marshall and former United States presidents James Madison and John Tyler. Many Virginia slaveholders practiced "selective manumission," giving freedom to favorite individuals not to strike a blow at the institution of slavery but rather to reward good behavior. Moreover, to send such an individual to Liberia to do missionary work could be justified as an effort to "christianize the heathen." Although once a mainstream cause in Virginia, by the late 1850s, colonization had come under considerable fire from proslavery whites who saw it as another species of abolitionism; conservative colonizationists, represented by the Virginia Colonization Society (VCS), defended the scheme by reiterating that its goal was free black removal. Meanwhile antislavery colonizationists, such as Elizabeth Van Lew, sidestepped the proslavery VCS and surreptitiously reached out for support and guidance to the parent organization, the American Colonization Society.[46]

Van Lew's correspondence with officials of the ACS allows us to see what her neighbors and acquaintances could not—namely the deep attachment she had to Mary Jane Richards. In the year leading up to Mary Jane's departure, Elizabeth had tried to educate herself about Liberia, frequently writing to ACS officials to request copies of the newspaper, the *Liberia Herald,* and the organization's journal, the *African Repository.* Having finished her studies in New Jersey, Mary Jane embarked for Liberia from New York on December 24, 1855, aboard the *Lamartine,* along with some 55 other black emigrants and the white missionary Reverend J. W. Horne and his wife. They arrived on the African coast on January 24, 1856, having lost only one passenger, a child, to sickness during the voyage. From 1855 to 1859, Elizabeth repeatedly wrote letters to ACS officials asking that they forward money and boxes of necessities to Mary Jane. Van Lew had good cause to be concerned about Mary Jane's material well-being—living conditions in Liberia were harsh, so harsh indeed that many Northern free blacks attacked colonization as an immoral and impractical deportation scheme. Upon arrival, emigrants typically battled "acclimating fever," an ailment that made them vulnerable to a host of other illnesses. They faced danger not only in the form of disease but also from the sporadic warfare that raged between the colonists and indigenous Africans hostile to their incursions.[47]

By September of 1859, Mary Jane Richards had had enough of Liberia. While traveling in Philadelphia and Brooklyn, Elizabeth Van Lew wrote to the Reverend Anthony D. Williams, one of her ACS allies, that Mary Jane's letters were "imploring and beseeching" Elizabeth to bring her back to the United States. Williams was an African American emigrant who had gone to Liberia in 1824 from Petersburg, Virginia, to work as a missionary; after Liberia became an independent republic in 1847, he held a series of offices in the new government. Elizabeth's letters to Williams are deferential and yet insistent. In consultation with her brother John, Elizabeth explained, she had agreed to try to bring Mary Jane home to the United States. "If anything should happen to [Mary Jane] or in case of her death we should feel very badly on account of keeping her in Africa much against her will," Van Lew confided. Elizabeth went on to apologize that Mary Jane had "conducted herself improperly" in Liberia, blaming such (unspecified) bad behavior on the disagreeable climate. Using hindsight, we can surmise that Mary Jane's unhappiness had something to do with the fact that she was in the throes of early adolescence (she was a mere 14 the year she arrived in Africa). Van Lew hoped that Williams would arrange for Mary Jane to travel home "comfortably not in the steerage," and promised that she and John would pay for the expense of the passage as soon as Mary Jane arrived.[48]

Fully aware that a request to return a freed black into the arms of her former master was an unconventional one, Van Lew reassured Williams that she would not "reproach or upbraid [Mary Jane] on her return." "I will feel less anxiety about her and would rather have her here," Elizabeth explained, adding, "I will try to do the best I can by her—as I would be done by." In the next few lines of her letter, Elizabeth threw conventionality to the wind and poured her heart out: "I would like [Mary Jane] to come as soon as possible—I do love the poor creature—she was born a slave in our family—& that has made me always feel an awful responsibility—Oh Mr. Williams how responsible a thing is life!"[49]

Williams evidently came to Van Lew's aid. On March 5, 1860, after a 125-day passage, the ship *Caroline Stevens* arrived from Liberia and docked in Baltimore, with Mary Jane Richards on board (against Van Lew's wishes, Mary had traveled in steerage, not in a first-class cabin). Upon receiving word that Richards had made it safely to the United States, Elizabeth Van Lew sent for her, and Mary Jane returned to Richmond. The former slave was back in the land of slavery.[50]

As Van Lew must have known well, Richards's very presence in Richmond contravened the law: a black who had left Virginia to be educated in the free states was not permitted to return to the Commonwealth. On August 20, 1860, some five and a half months after her return to the United States, Richards was arrested by a nightwatchman named Wasserman for "perambulating the streets and claiming to be a free person of color, without having the usual certificate of freedom in her possession." This was a serious charge. Considered by whites to be "at best an anomaly and at worst a danger to a well-ordered slave society," free blacks existed in a kind of "legal limbo" between citizenship and slavery; a free black caught without a pass could find himself auctioned back into bondage to the highest white bidder as punishment for breaking the law.[51]

Richards was brought before the Mayor's Court, where she claimed, according to the newspaper account of the proceedings, "that her mother was a slave belonging to Mrs. Van Lew of this city, and that she, the daughter, was sent to the North by Mrs. VL, to be 'highly educated,' and after receiving her education, was sent to Liberia, from whence she returned, on a visit to this country, a few weeks ago, and came to Richmond at the instance of Miss Van Lew." At the time of her arrest, Mary Jane went on, the Van Lew women were vacationing at the Springs and therefore unable to vouch for her. Richards was committed to jail. Eliza Van Lew was summoned before the Hustings Court, on September 10, to answer the charge that she had let her slave "go at large," without the required pass. While no record exists of what Eliza told the judge, we can surmise from the court's findings—Eliza was fined ten dollars and Mary Jane was returned to her possession—that the widow Van Lew affirmed that Mary Jane was indeed her slave and not a free person of color. The *Richmond Whig* found Eliza's story suspect, noting pointedly that Liberia was "a strange place, by the way, for *a slave* to go to or come from."[52] But Eliza's reputation in the community evidently inclined the judge to see her as credible.

The most bizarre and revealing aspect of Mary Jane Richards's brush with the law is that she used two aliases, initially telling her captors she was named Mary Jane Henley and then Mary Jones; while the *Whig* wrote that "her real name is Mary J. Richards," the Hustings Court opted to identify her as Mary Jane Henley. This use of aliases is significant because it suggests that Richards was the same person as the "Mary Jones" who appears in the 1860 census as a free mulatto woman, age 24, living in the Van Lew mansion; the same as the free black Mary who married Wilson Bowser on April 17, 1861; and the same as Mary Jane Henley, who on February 9, 1863, was issued a new registration as a "free person of color," having claimed that she had "lost the old one."[53] The use of aliases also suggests that Mary Jane was consciously trying to stay one step ahead of the authorities. Years after the Civil War, when Mary J. R. Richards was working to teach freedpeople in St. Mary's, Georgia, she was interviewed by Reverend Crammond Kennedy, secretary of the American Freedmen's Union Commission, a Northern benevolent organization. She made a striking revelation to him that corroborates the unlikely story of her return to the Van Lews: after arriving from Liberia, Richards told Kennedy, "she went to Richmond, and while appearing as a slave, was in the secret service of the U.S."[54] Whether Richards had ever been given a formal, *de jure* freedom by the Van Lews, we may never know. But Eliza and Elizabeth were clearly partner to her subterfuge.

The remarkable notion that some Van Lew slaves were given a secret freedom but opted to stay on in Richmond, and remain in service to the family, finds support in other sources. According to the reminiscences of her confidante, Eliza Carrington, Elizabeth exercised her independence as a single woman, not bound by her father's will or by a husband's authority, to purchase nine slaves and then to liberate them. Of these nine, Carrington names only one, Judy Johnson, and she reveals nothing of the date or circumstances of the acts of manumission. Census records permit us to place Johnson in Richmond in 1870, working as a washer of clothes. Carrington uses the story of Johnson to make the case that strong bonds of affection existed between Van Lew and the blacks she freed. When Elizabeth lay dying in 1900, Carrington recalls, it was Johnson who kept a vigil at her bedside, as nurse and companion. We can identify a second of the nine slaves as Louisa Roane, who was purchased by Elizabeth in 1863 and was the spouse of Van Lew slave Peter.[55]

Carrington's portrait of Elizabeth as an emancipator in her own right finds some confirmation in Van Lew family oral traditions; Van Lew's niece, Annie, would tell her own descendant, Dorothy Grant, that Elizabeth freed some slaves but gave them the option of staying on to work for the family, and that the offer was accepted, particularly by elderly blacks. Annie, like Carrington, imputed the slaves' decision to their affection for the Van Lews. When Annie attended Elizabeth Van Lew's funeral in 1900, so she would later tell Dorothy, the woman who had served as her childhood "mammy" was present to mourn Elizabeth's passage. The lore surrounding Maggie Lena Walker, one of Richmond's greatest civic leaders and heroines of the late nineteenth and twentieth centuries, represents yet one more piece of the puzzle: Walker's mother Elizabeth Draper Mitchell, according to the received story, had been freed by the Van Lews before the war but chose to stay on and work for the family as a cook's assistant.[56]

Two more pieces of evidence suggest that a kind of mutual dependence, and even affection, bound Elizabeth Van Lew to her family's former slaves. The famed abolitionist orator Anna Dickinson visited Van Lew in Richmond ten years after the Civil War and was struck to find that "nearly all of her old slaves are about her," some of them employed in the mansion itself and some in the post office where Elizabeth was postmaster. Van Lew, in an interview with the *Richmond Enquirer* in 1877, told the story of one such ex-slave: he had gone through the lines to General U. S. Grant's army during the war, and become the body servant to Grant's aide-de-camp Orville Babcock, only to return to Richmond, and to work in the Church Hill mansion for Elizabeth Van Lew, after the Confederacy fell.[57]

The record of the Van Lew women's slaveholding, then, is fragmentary, complex, and surprising. Taken together, the various scraps of evidence suggest that at least some of the blacks who worked for the Van Lews had been given a partial or secret freedom. Elizabeth and her mother thus did not practice overt abolitionism but rather led a kind of double life—their outward conformity to social conventions masked their inner doubts about slavery and the unusual tenor of their relationships with individual African Americans. The women's willingness to socialize with and to compromise with slaveholders was no mere act, but rather a reflection of deep attachments—both personal and professional—that the Van Lew family had to the Richmond elite. The Van Lew women counted slaveholders such as John Minor Botts and Charles Palmer among their close friends, and depended financially on the business of slaveholders. Eliza repeatedly sold real estate to an unsavory man named Bacon Tait, who operated a private slave jail in Shockoe Bottom.[58]

Had Elizabeth and her mother found it impossible to live in slavery's midst they could well have done what hundreds of other white Virginians did in the antebellum period—migrated to the North. A recent study has shown that nearly half of all Virginians who left the Commonwealth opted to resettle in the free rather than slave states. The Van Lews certainly had exposure to the world beyond Richmond. Elizabeth and her mother frequently visited Philadelphia, where they had a ready-made social circle (indeed Elizabeth's sister Anna had married a Philadelphia doctor and settled there). Elizabeth even had the privilege of embarking, chaperoned by Eliza, on a tour of Europe in 1855. But no matter how far afield they wandered, the mother and daughter Van Lew always returned home to Virginia.[59]

Their commitment to residing in Richmond reflected both a fealty to John Van Lew's efforts to establish the family there and a deep responsibility that Elizabeth and her mother felt for their black dependents. To leave the

South, Elizabeth seems to have believed, would be to abdicate that responsibility, and to lose the small measure of authority she had to ameliorate the conditions of individuals such as Cornelius Goodhall, Mary Jane Richards, and Judy Johnson. We can see from hindsight that such a belief was self-serving, for it justified the Van Lews' continued access to black labor power. Indeed, it seems likely that the Van Lew women influenced their black charges to stay on in Richmond with promises that they would be safer under the protective umbrella of the family than they might be on the outside.

Elizabeth and her mother, then, stubbornly refused to relinquish the middle ground—to heed all of the numerous signs that warned them that it was not possible to preserve their world and simultaneously to reform it. Knowing as we do that the Civil War would soon bring emancipation, it is all too easy to condemn the Van Lews' defense of the middle ground as complacent, shortsighted, and conservative. But we should be more humble in our judgments. Elizabeth Van Lew's hopes for a peaceful, gradual compromise solution to the problems of slavery and sectionalism were shared by most of her fellow citizens on the eve of the secession crisis; so too did most Americans feel a gnawing uncertainty about how to define their own political and moral obligations.

What made Elizabeth truly unusual among the legions of Americans who doubted slavery was her devotion to the South. Even as elite Southern whites abdicated the middle ground and staked out proslavery terrain, Van Lew refused to turn her back on her native city and region and to seek refuge in the more congenial political climate of the North. Identifying more and more with the dissenters and the disfranchised among Southerners, and particularly with African Americans, Van Lew during the period 1859 to 1861 elaborated a systematic critique of the proslavery position and, at the same time, renewed her commitment to remain in Richmond. Thus it was not Van Lew's abolitionism but her lifetime of overtures to, negotiations with, and silent subversion of the Southern elite—her years of practice at giving the appearance of conformity even as she harbored secret hopes and plans—that prepared Elizabeth for her courageous work as a spy.

2

"My Country! Oh My Country!"

VIRGINIA LEAVES THE UNION

"THINK OF A COMMUNITY RUSHING GLADLY, UNRESTRAINEDLY, EAGERLY, INTO A bloody civil war! Imagine how the spirit of evil reigned," wrote Elizabeth Van Lew of Virginia's secession from the Union in 1861. Watching in horror as her state joined the ranks of the newly proclaimed Confederacy, she felt profoundly betrayed. "One day I could speak for my country, the next was threatened with death. Surely madness was upon the people!"[1] For Van Lew, secession was a repudiation by white Virginians of their own heritage and political traditions. However deep her moral qualms about slavery, Van Lew had been able to reconcile herself to life in slaveholding Richmond so long as she could work with like-minded people to ameliorate the conditions of blacks, quietly chip away at the slave system, and have her political viewpoint represented by moderate politicians. In Van Lew's eyes, the secession crisis, beginning with John Brown's raid in 1859 and culminating when Virginia joined the Confederacy in 1861, brought about the end of representative government in her native state—the end of reasoned deliberation and the foreclosing of real debate.

Van Lew's sense of bitterness and disorientation was made all the more acute because secession represented, for unconditional Unionists such as herself, a sudden reversal of fortune, an abrupt change of course that displaced them from the political majority. Well into the 1850s, Unionism had predominated in Virginia, owing to both economic realities and the political culture of the state. Although it contained more slaves than any other state, antebellum Virginia also boasted more cities than any Southern state and was the industrial hub of the region. The economic diversity within the state was reflected in its political life. Two-party competition, between the Whigs and Democrats, flourished in antebellum Virginia, with the Whigs attracting men like John Van Lew who looked favorably on the "Market Revolution"— namely government-sponsored economic growth, in the form of new banks, canals, railroads, and industries, and the tariffs needed to protect them. While the Whig party foundered in the mid-1850s, its successors, the Know-Nothing Party and Constitutional Union Party, attracted former Whigs who believed that the economic interests of the Commonwealth would be served by closer links with the Northern states. These parties kept a tradition of political opposition alive in Virginia, even as the Democrats, championing agrarianism and states rights, achieved a one-party stranglehold over the Deep South.[2]

Cutting across the divide between political parties was a regional fault line within Virginia, dividing the lowland eastern counties from the western counties that lay astride the Blue Ridge mountains. While the eastern economy was based on slave labor and plantation agriculture, western counties were characterized by small farms, few slaves, and close economic ties to the neighboring free states of Ohio and Pennsylvania. Western yeoman farmers, who tended by a small margin to favor the Democratic party, had long resented the political dominance of the eastern planter and mercantile elite; eastern counties had disproportionately high numbers of representatives in the state legislature and had passed high taxes and restrictive property qualifications, among other measures, over the objections of western men. Many of the small slaveholders and nonslaveholders in the western part of Virginia viewed secessionism as yet another ploy by the eastern elite to impose its political will on the beleaguered yeomen.[3]

Though various forms of economic self-interest undergirded Virginia Unionism, so too did deeply ingrained political traditions. Virginians across the political spectrum took pride in the Old Dominion's reputation as the "mother of all states." Many believed that it did not befit such an illustrious state to follow the lead of radicals in the North and Deep South; instead Virginia should lead the way, fostering a nationalism true to the founding vision of native sons Washington, Madison, and Jefferson. The majority of Virginia Whigs and Democrats, eastern and western, agreed that the founders had envisioned a slaveholding republic, and thus Virginia's leading Unionist politicians championed the constitutionality of slavery even as they repudiated the doctrine of secession. In the 1850s, the Whig John Minor Botts was the standard bearer of Richmond Unionism, positioning himself as a mediator between the sectional extremes of Northern radical abolitionism and Deep South disunionism, and fancying himself heir to his political idol, the "Great Compromiser" Henry Clay. "This government is the greatest and best which the world has ever seen. Why then, dissolve it?" Botts declared, in a concise summary of his political philosophy.[4]

Secessionists, then, faced an uphill battle in Virginia, as they had not only to appeal to the economic and political interests of a diverse electorate but also to undermine the strong sentimental attachment that most Virginians had to the Union. Following the lead of militant "fire-eaters" in the Deep South states, a small cadre of Virginia disunionists pressed their case in the 1850s, deliberately laying the groundwork for Southern independence. Long before the South was ready to heed the call to outright secession, these fire-eaters struck a nerve among Southern whites by advocating that the region achieve a kind of cultural independence from the North—that Southerners rally together in using literature, education, and the press to counter the abolitionist charges of Southern backwardness and immorality. As antislavery sentiment grew more popular in the North, disunionists responded by playing on the racial solidarity and racial anxieties of Southern whites—they demonized Northerners as proponents of race equality, "race mixing," and race war; threatened that the North would impose industrial "wage slavery" on independent white Southern farmers; and contended that the political party system no longer protected and served Southern interests. The Democratic party, which had long positioned itself as the guardian of "Southern rights," was destined, so secessionists predicted, to lose power to the ascendant antislavery party of the North, the Republicans.[5]

To the shock and dismay of Elizabeth Van Lew, it was the secessionists who found themselves ascendant in Virginia, as a dramatic series of events bolstered their claims and seemed even to fulfill their prophecies. On October 16, 1859, John Brown led a small band of followers to Harper's Ferry, Virginia, where they seized the Federal arsenal in the hopes of enlisting the slaves in the surrounding countryside to rise up against their masters. When the local militia failed to restore order, the United States Marines, under Colonel Robert E. Lee, arrived on the scene and captured Brown. The would-be emancipator was tried in a county court in Charlestown, Virginia, and sentenced to death. On December 2, John Brown was hanged. Contemporary observers and modern historians alike have marveled at how Brown's raid dramatically transformed public opinion in Virginia. Although a failure, the raid gave gleaming salience to an argument the secessionists had long been making—namely that Northern abolitionists, backed by the Republican party, were conspiring to invade the South and to foment race war there.

These fears were stoked when Brown became a martyred hero in the North, the subject of laudatory legislative resolutions, editorials, prayers, poems, and public meetings. Prominent politicians in Virginia such as Governor Henry Wise seized on Brown's martyrdom as proof that the Northern people could no longer be reasoned with.[6]

Elizabeth Van Lew's remarkable reflections on the secession crisis of 1859 through 1861, which she penned from memory at various times during and after the Civil War, reveal that she viewed the South's rejection of the Union not as a detached outsider might but rather as an insider, shocked to see madness descend upon her "own" people. The secession crisis itself radicalized Van Lew, gradually disabusing her of the notion that one could compromise with slaveholders and with slavery. "There is no denying the fact our people were in a palpable state of war from the time of the John Brown raid," Van Lew's analysis begins. "Henry A. Wise was Governor of Virginia, and he did everything to keep up excitement, thinking, perhaps, to use his zeal as a stepping stone to popularity and the presidential chair." While Van Lew "never thought John Brown right," she was nonetheless horrified at the mob mentality that she believed had seized her fellow white Virginians: "Our people required blood, the blood of all who were of the Brown party. They thirsted for it; they cried out for it. It was not enough that one old man should die." For Van Lew, the lust for revenge that she perceived contravened Christ's teachings that people should have sympathy for all God's creatures, "however sunken, however sinning."[7]

As a member of the elite, Van Lew had access to the prominent politicians in whose hands the fate of Virginia rested. During the summer of 1860, as the momentous presidential election campaign geared up, Van Lew vacationed at White Sulphur Springs where she met secessionist leaders James Pettigru and Edmund Ruffin and was privy to discussions among male politicians. "The Dissolution and reconstruction of the Union was the daily talk at the Springs," she wrote; from such talk she learned that the range of acceptable political positions was fast narrowing. "People were if anything more morbid than ever on the subject of slavery, and I heard a member of the Virginia Legislature say that anyone speaking against it, or doubting its divinity, ought to be hung. Yes, hung, as certainly and as truly as he would be for murder." One sympathetic state senator went so far as to make a chilling confession to Van Lew: "[he] told me that the members of the senate did not dare to speak as they thought and felt, that they were afraid, that is, if they did not think pro-slavery or pro-South." Van Lew assured the agitated politician that she would not betray his trust.[8]

The presidential election campaign of 1860 was essentially two separate contests, with Republican Abraham Lincoln facing off against Democrat Stephen Douglas in the North, and states-rights candidate James Breckenridge, from a breakaway faction of the Democrats, facing off against John Bell, of the "Constitutional Union" Party, in the South. (Lincoln, who did not campaign in the South, had negligible backing—less than 1 percent of the electorate—in Virginia). The Van Lews favored Bell, as he promised to preserve the Union and commanded the support of former Whigs such as John Minor Botts. The campaign itself was bitter. Botts, who took to the stump for Bell, could not disguise his contempt for Breckenridge; the Southern Democrats, Botts charged, were intent on reviving the transatlantic slave trade and were willing to sacrifice the Union for the sake of their own economic aggrandizement. Botts was equally adamant in his denunciations of Northern abolitionists, who "agitated" the slavery question for "their own purposes." But he was not ready to write Lincoln off as an abolitionist. If Lincoln became president, and took measures to openly threaten slavery, Botts would seek constitutional remedies and solutions first. It was cowardly of would-be secessionists, he argued, to "run before a blow [was] struck." Breckenridge backers in Richmond, for their part, heaped invective upon Botts, charging that he was "ostensibly for Bell, [but] really for Lincoln" and that his Unionist stance was cowardly and traitorous.[9]

The 1860 election proved to be a Pyrrhic victory for the Constitutional Union party. Although the Bell ticket won Virginia by a small margin, Lincoln prevailed, on the strength of his Northern support, in the national contest. To the dismay of Virginia Unionists, Lincoln's election only gave added momentum to the burgeoning secessionist movement. Southern nationalist fire-eaters such as Ruffin argued that Lincoln's victory represented the North's repudiation of the Constitution and its determination to invade the South and dismantle slavery. The rapid secession of the seven lower Southern states strengthened the hand of Virginia's extremists: disunion was no longer an abstract possibility but a reality, and Virginia's fate, so the fire-eaters argued, lay with her sister states to the South. The prospects for reconciliation dimmed further as compromise measures failed in Congress and as Northern legislatures denied the right of secession and expressed their willingness to "coerce" the seceded states back into the Union.

When the Virginia General Assembly convened in January of 1860, it arranged for the election of delegates to a special state secession convention to be held in February. The results of that election were deceiving. While Unionist delegates outnumbered secessionist ones, the plurality of seats went to undeclared "moderates" who, as the ensuing debates would reveal, were closer in philosophy to the secessionists than to the compromisers. Virginia's acrimonious and dramatic secession convention would, in other words, lay bare a new political fault line—one dividing erstwhile "conditional Unionists," who regarded secession as a viable last resort should the Federal government not meet Southern demands, from "unconditional Unionists," namely people such as Elizabeth Van Lew who rejected secession altogether.

Van Lew was among the many "ladies" who thronged Mechanic's Hall in Richmond to witness the proceedings. Elite women had long been accustomed to playing the role of spectator at political functions. Beginning in 1840, the Whig party had appealed to women to turn out for partisan rallies, speeches, and parades. Although females could not vote, the Whigs reasoned, women could and did exercise influence on how men cast their ballots; moreover, elite women were considered repositories of moral virtue, and their endorsement could represent a moral seal of approval. After initially showing a distaste for such partisan appeals to women, the Democratic party eventually adopted the same tactics as the rival Whigs. It became standard fare in the electoral battles of the 1850s for each party to claim that it had the ladies on its side. Just as political parties had competed for women's support, so too would the contending factions in the 1861 showdown: Unionist politicians and opinion makers argued that because women loved harmony and peace, they were in favor of a reconciliation between North and South, while secessionists argued that women wanted to avoid the moral taint of association with the radical Republican party and therefore favored joining the Confederacy.[10]

During the first stage of the secession convention, lasting from February 13 to March 9, it looked as though a coalition of outright Unionists and undeclared moderates might be able to forge a solution to the crisis. To Van Lew's disappointment, the "bold and true" Unionist leader John Minor Botts had been passed over by voters in eastern Virginia and was not among the delegates to the secession convention. But she gladly invested her faith in the western Virginians who now assumed the mantle of leadership among the Commonwealth's Unionists. Most prominent among them was George

W. Summers, a longstanding advocate of gradual emancipation, whose "aristocratic bearing" commanded the respect even of his political enemies. The crux of the Unionists' argument was that Lincoln did not pose an "immediate menace" to the South and that he could be negotiated with; indeed, Summers had initiated the idea of holding a "peace conference" in Washington, D.C., to hammer out a compromise.[11]

The peace conference convened on February 4, 1861, and continued even while Virginia's secession convention was meeting. As historian Daniel Crofts has explained, the stakes could not have been higher: "Heightened expectations that a satisfactory Union-saving formula could be agreed upon ... made Unionists hostage to the success of the peace conference. Should it deadlock ... Unionists would find themselves in a difficult position." Chaired by ex-President John Tyler of Virginia, the conference drew delegates from fourteen free states and seven slave states (none of the states that had already seceded sent delegates). In three of the slave state delegations—those of Virginia, North Carolina, and Missouri—Southern rights supporters were in the majority; the Old Dominion's five-man delegation consisted of Unionists William C. Rives and Summers, and Southern rights men Tyler, James A. Seddon, and John W. Brockenbrough. Positioning themselves as mediators, Southern Unionist delegates at the conference generated a proposal designed to reassure proslavery secessionists. Congress and the territorial legislatures, it was suggested, would be prohibited by constitutional amendment from interfering with slavery in existing states and territories below the old Missouri Compromise line of 36° 30'. Unfortunately, the proposal did not satisfy the states' rights delegates, who wanted protection for slavery not only in territories currently held but also in those territories "hereafter acquired." Nor did the compromise please Republicans, who felt that it went far beyond the Missouri Compromise by explicitly restricting the Federal government from taking action against slavery below the 36° 30' line. The resolution passed, by a very slim margin, on February 27, and was submitted to Congress for its consideration. Back in Virginia, secessionists railed against the compromise proposal, calling it "an attempt to cheat, swindle, and defraud the South." The proposal fared no better in Washington, D.C., where it fell short of the two-thirds Senate majority needed to make it law. The overtures of Virginia's Unionists had failed.[12]

Hard on the heels of that failure came Lincoln's momentous inaugural address of March 4, in which he called secession the "essence of anarchy" and pledged that the laws of the Union would be "faithfully executed in all the States." This pledge was widely interpreted by Virginians as a declaration that Lincoln would use coercion to restore the seceded states to the Union. Now in damage-control mode, Virginia Unionists sent representatives such as legislator Joseph Segar to meet personally with Lincoln and extract reassurances that he was committed to peace. Although such reassurances were tendered, they were drowned out in the secessionist clamor. "The Inaugural Address of Abraham Lincoln inaugurates civil war," the *Richmond Dispatch* fumed. "The Demon of Coercion stands unmasked."[13]

Watching from the gallery as the delegates to the Richmond convention debated, Elizabeth Van Lew understood that momentum within the convention was shifting, and that the Unionist coalition was reeling. "Mr. Summers spoke the truth in vain, and so did others," she wrote. For "the secessionists grew bold and more imprudently daring." With her characteristic insight, Van Lew observed that "the doctrine of secession seemed to gratify an innate feeling of pride" among her fellow Southerners. Southern nationalists argued that dependence on the North was a form of unmanly submission; only independence would permit the region to assume its rightful place in the world. Van Lew captured the gist of the secessionist appeal when she wrote, "Drunk with . . . license our Southern leaders firmly believed in the power of cotton to rule the world. It had clothed and fed them, was it not necessary to clothe and feed all nations!"[14]

Would-be Confederates consolidated their gains during the second phase of the convention, which stretched from early March until early April. In the aftermath of Lincoln's inauguration, secessionists exceeded Unionists in the ardor and enthusiasm of their campaign for popular support; round-the-clock rallies, stump speeches, and meetings, coupled with rousing press coverage, gave secessionists control of the streets well before they had control of the convention itself. One of the primary goals of their campaign was to win the allegiance of women. In an effort to gratify female pride, secessionist politicians and journalists declared that because women's patriotism was even purer and stronger than men's, the "ladies" had all embraced the Confederacy. By making the claim often enough, such opinion makers reasoned, they could make women believe it was so. Secessionist papers delighted in printing such fare as the anonymous "Sentiments of a Virginia Matron." Defending slavery as sanctioned by the Bible, the "matron" declared that

Southerners were "compelled to withdraw from a people who deny us what we are entitled to." "Beware!" was her message to the Lincoln Republicans.[15]

Unionists had difficulty countering such rhetoric, for by late March there was no longer a pro-Union organ in Richmond: the once-reliable *Richmond Whig* fell into the hands of secessionists, who bought up the paper's stock and then fired its Unionist editor and replaced him with a disunionist. Thus, when a handful of ladies presented a wreath and poem to Unionist delegate John B. Baldwin on March 23, 1861, the press easily wrote the act off as an aberration. The gesture to Baldwin, the *Enquirer* contended, was "instigated by . . . *Northern ladies*" and therefore did not reflect the sentiments of real Virginians. To Van Lew's palpable disbelief, the secessionists' unrelenting campaign for female support proved effective. Elizabeth was appalled to see "well dressed ladies of the highest education walk up and down the Capitol square asking 'Do you think the state will go out today for if it does not, I cannot stand it any longer?' " Secession flags began to "flaunt from the house tops and from the windows." As far as Van Lew could tell, "very few ladies . . . were for their Country [the United States], very few."[16]

From Lincoln's inaugural on, the debates inside the convention hall and outside it were dominated by the Fort Sumter issue. The fort, which lay in Charleston Harbor, South Carolina, was occupied by a small Federal garrison, a thorn in the side of the Confederacy. Well into March, Lincoln's secretary of state William Seward reassured Southern Unionists that the Federal government would evacuate rather than reinforce the fort. This conciliatory pledge permitted Virginia's Unionists to maintain their dominance, however tenuous, of the Richmond convention.[17]

The Lincoln administration's "hands-off" policy, however, proved politically untenable, as key Republicans came to see concessions as fruitless and confrontation as inevitable. To quote Daniel Crofts: "The hard-line Republican critics of a hands-off policy contended . . . that a coercive policy offered the only chance of holding the Union together because a hands-off policy would never bring back the seceded states. . . . Seward and southern Unionists saw war as the greatest danger to reunion, while hard-line Republicans saw fear of war as the greatest danger to reunion." By the end of March, Lincoln had come to accept the logic of the hard-liners. He did agree to one last meeting with a representative of Virginia's Unionist delegation, John B. Baldwin, on April 4, but it came to naught; indeed that very day Lincoln

made up his mind to send supplies to the beleaguered Federal garrison at
Fort Sumter.[18]

~

Lincoln's fateful decision marks the end of the second stage of Virginia's
secession drama and the opening of the last act. As early as April 3, rumors
of the resupply effort were rife in Richmond; on April 8, they were officially
confirmed. The reply of the Confederacy was swift and decisive. Intent on
striking a blow before the relief expedition reached the fort, and on pre-
empting any independent action by rash South Carolinians, the Confederate
cabinet authorized the bombardment of the federal outpost. On April 12,
1861, with the supply ships approaching the harbor, the Confederate military
trained its guns on the Fort Sumter and opened fire. The Federal garrison
surrendered after 34 hours of punishing bombardment. On April 15, Lincoln
issued a proclamation calling on the states of the Union, Virginia included,
to furnish 75,000 troops to "coerce" the seceded states back into the national
fold.[19]

Van Lew, like so many other commentators at the time, recognized the
firing on Fort Sumter as the point of no return for Virginia and the South.
The people of Richmond were "jubilant" at the news from South Carolina,
she wrote. The entire nation looked to see which way Virginia would go,
and "the holding of the Convention at Richmond made that city the focus,
the soul, the centre of treason." For most of the convention delegates, Lincoln's call for troops lent a stark clarity to the choice that faced them: now
that fighting had erupted, they had simply to choose which army to join.
Secessionists moved in for the rhetorical kill, branding Northerners as the
"haters" and "insulters" of the South and characterizing Confederates, by
contrast, as the "brethren," the metaphorical kin, of Virginians.[20]

On April 16, the day after the convention received word of Lincoln's call
for troops, the galleries of the convention hall were cleared and the delegates
went into secret session. A revolutionary spirit gripped the state capital. Not
far from the legal convention, an extralegal "Southern Rights Convention,"
with some 200 hard-line secessionists in attendance, convened in Metro-
politan Hall and called for immediate secession. The brainchild of former
governor Henry Wise, the convention was intent on wresting the state government out of the hands of current governor John Letcher, and, if neces-

sary, seizing and imprisoning Unionists such as Summers. Wise and Letcher not only represented rival factions of the state's Democratic party, but also antagonistic personalities. While Wise was vociferous and passionate, Letcher was by nature calm and conservative, and "obsessed with law, order, and Union." Wise was embittered by Letcher's election as governor in 1859, and determined to recapture control of the state's Democratic party. When Letcher refused to take orders from Wise's fire-eaters, and have state troops seize the Federal armory at Harper's Ferry and Federal navy yard in Norfolk, Wise and his cabal ordered volunteer militia companies under their control to initiate such actions. By the end of the week, Southern rights forces had seized control of Virginia's principal Federal military installations.[21]

Van Lew rightly regarded the "spontaneous" meeting of fire-eaters as an "Intimidation Convention," determined to carry the state out of the Union "at all hazards." Because the Unionist press had obtained copies of the Southern rights cabal's "secret" circular urging secessionists to seize control of the state, Van Lew was aware that Wise's cadre "had its agents at work" throughout Virginia, sowing fear and hatred. Even as he orchestrated this extralegal bid for power, Wise asserted his authority within the legal convention that was now facing its moment of truth. On April 17, Wise made an impassioned speech to the convention delegates. A renowned orator, he shouted at the Unionists that they must now decide whether to kill their own kin. Wise placed his pistol on the podium in front of him, and dared his foes to come forward and shoot him for treason.[22]

With Wise's harangue still ringing in their ears, the delegates voted down, by a tally of 79 to 64, a compromise proposal by Robert Scott, that would have postponed the vote on secession for another month. On April 17, 1861, the Virginia convention passed an ordinance of secession, by a vote of 88 to 55. By the time of the May 23 popular ratification vote, secessionists had captured a definitive majority, garnering 141,837 votes to the Unionists' 43,089. "There is now no middle course," the *Enquirer* intoned in the wake of ratification. "He who is not for us is against us; and the man who sympathizes with the Lincoln government or withholds his aid from Virginia in her hour of trial is a recreant to our venerable mother and a traitor to the allegiance which he owes her."[23]

The secessionists had won, but had they won fairly? For Van Lew, the answer was no. In Elizabeth's analysis, the secessionists triumphed not only because of their powers of persuasion—the ways they had so cannily appealed to Virginians' pride and so deviously stoked their fears of the North—but also because of their practice of coercion. Men who had, earlier that winter, been loyal to the Union went over to secession because they were "intimidated" by the fire-eaters, made to fear not only for their political futures but for their lives. "One gentleman, who signed the ordinance of secession," Elizabeth recalls, "told me he thought that if he had not done so, the streets of Richmond would have run with blood." If John Minor Botts had been a member of the convention, she opined, "he would have been assassinated." After the passage of the ordinance, Confederates "cried out for the blood of Summers and Carlisle [sic]" and other Unionists delegates; "the Union members of the convention . . . fled for their lives."[24]

Elizabeth's evocation of the oppressive political atmosphere in Virginia is echoed in the reminiscences of other Unionists. John F. Lewis, a convention delegate from Rockingham County and family friend of the Van Lews, voted against secession on April 17 despite the fact that he had been told frequently by members of the convention that he would "never leave Richmond alive" if he did not sign the secession ordinance. He then fled the city with other west Virginia delegates. Intimidation played a role in the ratification vote, as well. Unionists faced the threat of social ostracism, humiliation, or even worse. James Sharp of Charles City County, who would serve as one of Van Lew's secret couriers during the war, was told by his neighbors that he "would not be respected" if he didn't vote for secession; he opted to sit out the ratification election. Horace Kent, a Richmond intimate of Botts's, who would one day funnel money into Van Lew's underground, also refrained from casting a ballot in the ratification election, because he could not vote for secession and "didn't dare to vote against it." Kent had heard that men who voted against secession were "followed through Capitol Square, hooted [at] & stoned." Joseph Segar, the pro-Union state legislator who would after the war serve as the attorney for many of Van Lew's fellow secret service agents, did not vote at all in the May ratification election. Fleeing Richmond on April 19, he took refuge in Washington, D.C., and when he ventured back home to Hampton, Virginia, on May 23, he "found the county in a state of extraordinary excitement." His wife, children, and friends told him that he was not safe and entreated him not to go to the polls and vote, for he would "probably [be] shot down" if he tried.[25]

The threats of secessionists, then, were potent enough to frighten many brave men into silence or flight. But Elizabeth Van Lew refused to be intimidated. Even as the terrible events of April 1861 sapped the resolve of Virginia's Unionist men, Van Lew felt strangely energized. "What a memorable day was the 17th of April 1861," she would write years later, looking back on those turbulent times. "How can I describe my feelings when on my way down town, looking towards the Capitol, I saw the flag of treason floating over it. . . . I never did remember a feeling of more calm determination and high resolve for endurance over me than at that moment." How can we account for Van Lew's determination and resolve? Most of the elite whites in her social milieu had proven susceptible to secessionist arguments or threats while Van Lew had remained immune to them. From what sources did Van Lew's unconditional Unionism derive?

Historian Stephen V. Ash has persuasively argued that unconditional Unionism among whites in the Upper South had three principal "wellsprings." The first was connections to the North: a "significant proportion" of Southern Unionists were immigrants from the North who "took a more detached and skeptical view of Southern rights agitation than did their Southern-born neighbors." The second wellspring was partisan affiliation: former Whigs, with their penchant for economic modernization, formed the political backbone of antisecession forces in the South. The third wellspring was social standing: "plain folk" from nonplantation regions, such as Unionists in western Virginia, had longstanding social resentments against the planter class and rejected secession as an elitist gambit.[26]

However illuminating, Ash's categories of analysis have limited relevance for Van Lew's case. The Northern origins and Whiggish inclination of Van Lew's family help explain why she opposed secession but do not, by themselves, explain why she vowed to stay on in Richmond and take the fight to the Confederacy. To plumb the depths of Elizabeth's commitment to the Union, we must return to two themes discussed earlier—the distinctive culture of her family and the evolution of her views on slavery. It was not simply the Van Lew's "northernness" but their particular heritage that emboldened Van Lew. Her maternal grandfather Hilary Baker, it will be recalled, was one of the "founding fathers" of the state of Pennsylvania, and his sister Letitia Smith was a bona fide heroine of the Revolutionary War. Elizabeth had been raised to believe that membership in such an illustrious lineage brought with it burdens—namely, the responsibility to uphold the principles, and live up to the example, of one's ancestors. As the eldest of John and Eliza's children, Elizabeth seems to have felt this responsibility especially keenly; once her father died, she saw herself as assuming the burden of helping her mother run the family and the household.

As historian Marjorie Spruill Wheeler astutely observes in her book on the first generation of Southern woman's suffragists, who in the 1890s were themselves heirs to Van Lew's struggles for political influence, "personal characteristics, including courage and confidence, even stubbornness, always play a role in an individual's decision to work for a reform . . . and continue working for it against such strong opposition and with so little success."[27] Van Lew certainly possessed the characteristics of courage, confidence, and stubbornness in large quantities. If the courage was inspired in part by the example of her ancestors, the confidence was born of the guidance and nurturing of her parents John and Eliza, who gave Elizabeth the tools—the books, the instruction, and the encouragement—she needed to develop her natural intellectual gifts. The stubbornness, it seems, came not from Eliza, who by all accounts was a gentle, giving soul, but from John, who had come to Virginia with so little and had doggedly established himself among the first rank of Richmond high society.

Van Lew's upbringing and temperament, then, were important wellsprings of her Unionism. But the most important source of all was her growing conviction—one that deepened during the years 1859 to 1861—that the system of slavery was poised to destroy the very Union she had been raised to revere. Van Lew's fragmentary and episodic personal papers contain her extensive ruminations on slavery, and virtually all of these reflections on the subject she frames as an answer to what she calls "the most deeply interesting of questions"—namely why secession took place. In keeping with her family's legacy to her, Van Lew felt a keen responsibility to fully understand disunion and explain it to the coming generations. As she groped for ways to make sense of the "madness" that descended on her community, Van Lew came at last to confront the slave system fully. Secession represented for Van Lew, in other words, both a catastrophe and an epiphany.[28]

Van Lew's critique of slavery, forged in the firestorm of secession, was a cost accounting of the price white Southerners paid to maintain the system of human bondage. Slavery, she attested, had made Southern whites antidemocratic, coercive, intellectually backward, and dangerously self-righteous and arrogant. Echoing the rhetoric of Lincoln's Republican party, which laid the blame for sectional strife on a "Slave Power Conspiracy" of elite Southern masters, Van Lew wrote, "Slave power is arrogant—is jealous, and intrusive—is cruel—is despotic." Until the secession crisis, she had taken refuge, as so many "gradualists" did, in the notion that time was on the side of slavery's opponents—that "slave power was losing [its] strength before the increasing influence of honest and enlightened free labor."[29]

But secession illustrated just how far slavery's partisans were willing to go to maintain their power. Watching helplessly as moderate Virginia politicians, such as John Minor Botts and George W. Summers, were ushered off the political stage, Van Lew concluded that "slave power crushes freedom of speech and opinion." She was appalled to see how quickly the press and the pulpit were co-opted by the disunionists. Men in positions of power, such as the editors of the *Enquirer* and *Dispatch*, "found exciting occupation" in whipping up a popular frenzy, and the clergy, "relying on the protection afforded by their gowns," called slavery a "Christianizing institution" and encouraged Southerners to become drunk on the "odor of our own sanctity." The "Origin of Secession" Van Lew was convinced, lay in the "false teaching—false preaching—[and] corrupt press" of the "slave power."[30]

The young Southern men who became caught up in secession mania Van Lew regarded as pitiable dupes. When she asked a group of soldiers from South Carolina who had come to Virginia why they took up arms, they replied "Mr. Lincoln had said he was coming down to take all our negroes and set them free." How did they know this was true, Van Lew inquired? "The newspapers said so," they answered, confirming for Van Lew the dangerous power of the proslavery press over public opinion. Upon meeting two young Virginia men who were "in tears" because they had been pressured into enlisting in the Confederate army, Van Lew concluded that "slavery takes away a man's moral courage" and replaces it with "brute valour" and arrogance, such as undergirded the popular boast that "one Southern man could whip five hundred Yankees."[31]

Van Lew's sense of disbelief at secession was compounded by the fact that some of the members of her inner circle and extended family in Richmond chose to embrace the Confederacy. Her sister-in-law Mary—the wife of John Newton Van Lew—supported secession. So too did members of her uncle William A. Baker's family. Elizabeth's cousin John Van Lew McCreery, who had spent part of his childhood living in the Church Hill mansion, served the Confederacy as a soldier in the Richmond Howitzers.[32]

In arguing that the elitist slave power constituted a threat to the very foundational principles of the Union—namely, to majority rule and freedom of expression—Van Lew was articulating a position that had won widespread acceptance in the North; even whites who were not sympathetic to the slaves had come to accept the Republican party's charge that despotic Southern slaveholders were the enemies of democracy. But Van Lew's analysis of the secession crisis went beyond an assessment of slavery's political implications for whites. She also confronted its injustices to blacks.

Van Lew's estrangement from proslavery whites in Richmond deepened her empathy for and even identification with the city's blacks. Slavery disfigured whites, she came to acknowledge, because whites disfigured blacks; Van Lew's journal became the refuge where she could name, record, and lament the white practice of cruelty. "Looking upon slavery as it really is," Van Lew explicitly repudiated the Southern position that abolitionists had exaggerated slavery's evils. "What is more absurd than the idea that 'Uncle Tom's Cabin' could be an exaggeration!" she wrote. "No pen, no book, no time can do justice to slavery's wrongs, its horrors." And yet Van Lew tried to summon her pen to conjure up acts "too horrid to believe." Blacks were, she confided to her journal, punished "for any little thing, misdemeanor or stubbornness." "They would be placed in a coffin with holes over their face to breathe through," for entire days. They were "whipped almost to death . . . The blood would be in puddles where they were whipped." The whipper would draw his fingers through the lashes of the whip "as if milking to rid it of the blood." Like abolitionists had long been doing, Van Lew acknowledged Northern complicity in the racial status quo—the "negro whips were made of the North's cowhides," she noted, and "sent south."[33]

In such journal entries, Van Lew not only echoed the abolitionists' moral critique of human bondage but also their assertion that slavery was a national sin for which whites would eventually be forced to atone. Tantalizing evidence suggests that Van Lew may have been influenced by the blacks working in her household to adopt this framework of sin and redemption. Not long after secession, Van Lew remembers, one of the family's servants predicted the downfall of the Confederacy, telling her, " 'You will see. . . . They shall fall down slain. That is the fulfillment of prophecy.' " Van Lew recorded the words in her journal, followed by a brief and empathetic postscript: "So said with clear eye and bright hope, the intelligent colored man, William Roane, that called us owners." Van Lew shared this "bright hope" and looked to the Union army to fulfill Roane's prophecy. During the war, we will see, she would arrange for the flight of some of her slaves while enlisting others into her work on behalf of the Federal soldiers.[34]

From the time of the secession crisis on, Van Lew's observations about slavery and racism were consistently accompanied by the refrain "what I write I can prove." Now that Virginia's descent into political madness had precluded the possibility that moderates could peacefully reform the region from within, Elizabeth began to fashion a new role and self-image—that of truth teller and chronicler. Her position as someone who knew slaveholder society intimately privileged her—indeed required her, so she reckoned—to record the truth about it. "Free countries have no such scape goats as our poor slaves," she explained, from her vantage point as a Southerner, "and they don't understand us."[35]

Van Lew's appropriation of the prophetic power to see what others could not is cogently expressed in her reflections on the events of April 19, 1861. That day, just two days after the convention had passed the ordinance of secession, Van Lew received the news that a bloody clash had taken place in Baltimore, as Union troops en route from Massachusetts to Washington had fought with a secessionist mob, leaving four soldiers and twelve civilians dead. "War in all its reality was upon us," she wrote. Secessionist Richmond gloated at reports that the "Federal troops coming through Baltimore had been attacked and repulsed." Van Lew remembers in particular "one man whose eyes flared with the red light of hate." It was "awful to see, to feel, to face."[36]

Just before dark, Van Lew staggered home, on the arm of a friend (perhaps Eliza Carrington). "I could scarcely walk for the bitter, blinding tears. My country! Oh, my country! These tears were my feeble offering in atonement for the blood shed in Baltimore." That night Van Lew stood in her family's garden and watched a pro-Confederate torchlight procession snake its way through the city. She alone, or so it seemed, knew what Southern arrogance had wrought: "Such a sight! . . . the multitude, the mob, the whooping, the tin-pan music, and the fierceness of a surging, swelling revolution. This I witnessed. I thought of France and as the procession passed, I fell upon my knees under the angry heavens, clasped my hands and prayed, 'Father forgive them, for they know not what they do!' "[37]

3

"Our Flag Was Gone"

THE WAR'S FIRST YEAR

"OUR BEAUTIFUL CITY PRESENTS THE APPEARANCE OF AN ARMED CAMP," A RICH-
mond correspondent wrote to the *Baltimore American* on April 25, 1861,
remarking on the "multitude of volunteers" who descended on the Confederate capital, tendering their services to the "Cause." The *Richmond Enquirer*
likewise marveled at the rapid mobilization, confessing to its readers that
"companies continue to arrive so very rapidly . . . that we find some difficulty
in keeping pace with them." Among the first volunteers to arrive were troops
from South Carolina; by the end of April hundreds of Carolina soldiers were
thronging makeshift encampments at locales such as Richmond's Old Fair
Grounds. The press described them as "invincible and heroic"—as "perfect
gentlemen, in every respect." No wonder, then, that the South Carolina men
soon became "great favorites with the fairer portion of Richmond," the
Enquirer observed.[1]

Indeed, Richmond women such as Sallie Ann Brock delighted in the
arrival of the South Carolina soldiers. "Admiring crowds of ladies" met the
troops when they arrived at the railroad depot, Brock remembers, eager to
"get a sight of the heroes of Fort Sumter." Countless female admirers attended the festive evening dress parades of the soldiers, and sallied forth to
the fair grounds to bring the troops the uniforms, tents, and other supplies
that they had lovingly made. In so serving their men-at-arms, Richmond's
women were fulfilling the mandate that the city's opinion makers carefully
spelled out for them. Female patriotism was defined in Confederate rhetoric
as a set of obligations women had to their menfolk—the obligation to urge
men to enlist and the obligation to do "benevolent" work on behalf of the
soldiers, such as making provisions and tending the sick. Richmond news-

papers were full of praise for Confederate women, casting them as patriotic exhorters who nerved men for the test of battle and as "ministering angels," whose devotion would sustain the weary, the heartsick, the wounded. Fealty to the Confederacy was a new civil religion, and women were to be exemplars of piety. Of the numerous Richmond ladies making articles of clothing for the soldiers, the *Richmond Dispatch* intoned, they "have demonstrated their faith by their works. All honor to them." The *Dispatch* also noted approvingly that the "ladies of Church Hill" were working in concert to aid the troops, not only by giving them supplies but also by nursing those soldiers who fell ill.[2]

These early days of the war were a time of high spirits for Confederate women but also a time of high anxiety. From the very outbreak of hostilities, rumors were rife that the Federals planned to invade Richmond. On April 21, for example, a rumor that the United States gunship *Pawnee* was heading up the James to shell Richmond threw the city into a panic; "the women," the Confederate diarist Sallie Brock remembers, "pale and trembling with affright, clung to their sons and husbands, wherever they could." Although the dreaded attack never materialized, the episode revealed how unprepared—logistically and psychologically—Richmonders were for the taste of battle.[3]

In this tense atmosphere, with Confederate women struggling both to suppress their fears and to channel their hopes into constructive activities, Elizabeth Van Lew began a new chapter in her double life. In keeping with their determination to bring honor to Church Hill, the Confederate ladies of Van Lew's neighborhood asked Elizabeth and her mother to join them in making shirts for the South Carolina troops. The Van Lew women refused. This act of defiance was met with a stern reaction; the Van Lews received "personal threats" of an unspecified nature, warning them that such a refusal was not acceptable. Elizabeth and her mother quickly took measures to dispel the taint of disloyalty. Rather than make common cause with their neighbors, however, the Van Lew women made their own gesture, venturing to the Old Fair Grounds to bring some books and flowers to the South Carolinians mustered there. While the press had described the troops as "perfect gentlemen," Elizabeth Van Lew found them to be "of the very humblest class and deplorably ignorant." It was not noble courage but base conformity to social pressure that motivated the young men, Van Lew observed in her journal. She yearned to tell them "be not like dumb driven

cattle" going willingly to their slaughter pens. But, knowing full well that
the eyes of her community were on her, Van Lew kept silent. "I dared not
speak the truth to them."[4]

The Van Lew women's trip to the Old Fair Grounds had the intended
effect of lifting the pall of suspicion from them. Though ostensibly for the
comfort of the Southern soldiers, the gesture added much "to *our own comfort*," Van Lew explains.[5] But this new kind of double life, with the stakes
so very high, had only just begun. For the next four years, Van Lew would
make a series of public displays intended to divert Confederate suspicion
while she prayed, hoped, and worked for the Union. As Confederates tight-
ened the noose of punitive measures against Unionists—threatening them
with deportation, sequestration of property, imprisonment without trial,
conscription, and even execution—Van Lew's ruses to shield her secret life
would become more inventive and more daring. Daily she would struggle
not only with the sharp fear of being exposed but with numbing realities of
alienation. When Confederate Richmond rejoiced, Van Lew despaired; when
her community despaired, she privately rejoiced.

⌐

The first major clash of arms in Virginia—and first cause for Confederate
celebration—was the Battle of Bethel Church, a rebel victory that took place
on June 10, eight miles west of Hampton, Virginia. While the *Enquirer*
crowed that the "brilliancy of the battle [was] well calculated to appeal to
every sentiment of patriotic pride," Van Lew had a very different reaction.
"From this battle I saw young men returning and heard them tell how men
had tossed the dead Yankees into pits, in any fashion as 'creatures too exe-
crable to touch,'" she recalled with palpable horror. Van Lew was especially
disgusted by Richmond ladies' displays of bloodthirstiness. Contrary to their
image as ministering angels, Confederate women demanded of their menfolk
"Kill as many Yankees as you can for me" and yearned for some relic of
Confederate victory—"Mr. Lincoln's head, or a piece of his ear"—Van Lew
confided to her journal.[6]

Even as she excoriated the Southern rebels, Van Lew repeatedly used the
term "we" when characterizing Confederate actions; she wrote of one of the
young men lost in the battle, the Confederate Private Henry L. Wyatt, that
"we made a great hero of him." Such uses of the first person plural are

significant—sometimes they seem purposeful, and give a sarcastic edge to Van Lew's reflections, and at other times instinctive, revealing how psychologically difficult it was for Van Lew to cast off a lifetime's habit of identifying with the South.[7]

The atmosphere in the city changed dramatically as news arrived of the first major battle of the war, at Bull Run/Manassas on July 21. This, too, was a Confederate victory, but a terribly costly one, the bloodiest battle America had ever witnessed. Some 387 Confederates were killed and 1,582 wounded; more than a quarter of the Confederate soldiers in the fight were Virginians. The battle gave Richmond a new hero to worship—the victorious General Thomas J. "Stonewall" Jackson—and seemed to many a confirmation of the South's martial superiority. But other Confederates, such as the prolific diarist Mary Chesnut, saw the battle as a Pyrrhic victory. "It lulls us into a fool's paradise of conceit at our superior valor . . . and will awake every inch of [Northern] manhood."[8]

Soon hundreds of wounded men streamed into Richmond. "Almost every house in the city was a private hospital, and every woman a nurse. . . . There arose from the hearts of every Southern soldier a hearty 'God bless the women of Virginia!' " declared Sallie Brock of her countrywomen's efforts. Among the new battle-shaken inhabitants of the city were more than 1,000 Union prisoners, including some prominent civilians: New York Congressman Honorable Alfred Ely and lawyer Calvin Huson Jr. (Ely's former opponent for a seat in Congress) had, like so many other misguided civilians, gone to Manassas hoping to witness a great Union victory, only to fall into Confederate hands. With existing city and county prisons already overflowing, Brigadier General John H. Winder, inspector general of military camps for Richmond, converted a series of tobacco factories in the neighborhood of Main and Twenty-fifth Streets—Ligon's Factory, Howard's, and Harwood's, to name but a few—into military prisons.[9]

Thanks to the publication of numerous reminiscences by Union prisoners, we know a good deal about conditions in these makeshift facilities. In keeping with the normal, peacetime differences between the status and rights of officers and those of enlisted men, the two groups of soldiers were accorded glaringly different treatment during the war. Officers, along with civilians such as Congressman Ely, were separated from enlisted men; the first floor of Ligon's was reserved for officers and civilians, as was the entire Howard's facility. Officers and civilians received three meals a day (compared to one or two for enlisted men) and were permitted, if they had managed to smuggle money or other valuables into prison, to supplement their rations by purchasing additional foodstuffs. Such items were brought into the facility by black cooks and attendants who could be hired by prisoners to wait on them and to run errands. Moreover, officers and civilians benefited from the services of enlisted prisoners, who were required to do cleaning and other menial chores for their superiors.[10]

According to accounts by Ely and others, officers and civilians also enjoyed the privilege of courteous treatment from General Winder and of contact with the outside world. Ely recalls being treated by Winder "with the utmost kindness and respect," while Union officer Michael Corcoran later wrote that Winder did all in his power to make the prisoners "as comfortable as possible." Winder allowed Ely to receive newspapers (that the egotistical congressman scoured for mentions of his own name) and to be called on by a host of elite visitors, including John Letcher, governor of Virginia, and Martha Haines Butt, a popular novelist. Winder extended no such courtesy to enlisted men.[11]

Among those elite visitors was Van Lew, who cannily won the trust of Confederate officials by pretending to be loyal to the "Cause." In the summer of 1862, Van Lew visited Lieutenant David H. Todd, overseer of Federal prisoners at the converted factory complex (and half-brother of First Lady Mary Todd Lincoln) and offered her services as a hospital nurse for its wounded Union prisoners. Todd refused Van Lew's request, prompting her to go over his head to Confederate Secretary of the Treasury Christopher G. Memminger. She found him "alone in his office" and "begged him" for permission to visit the incarcerated Federals; he looked at her "sternly" and explained that such Yankees were not worthy of the ministrations of a "lady" such as herself. Manipulating the association of "ladyhood" with piety, Van Lew deftly changed the subject to Christianity, praising Memminger for a speech she once heard him deliver at a religious convention. "His face relaxed with a smile." Pressing her advantage, Van Lew went on: "If we wish 'our cause' to succeed" she told Memminger, "we must begin with charity to the thankless." Van Lew thus reassured him that it was her fealty to the duties of ladyhood, and not disloyal sentiments, which motivated her request. Memminger accepted her at her word, giving her a note of introduction to General Winder.[12]

Winder, who would repeatedly hold Van Lew's fate in his hands over the course of the war, has been one of the more controversial figures in Confederate history. A Maryland native and West Point graduate, Winder had a distinguished career of nearly 40 years in the United States army before tendering his resignation in 1861 to join the Confederacy. Like so many others from the Upper South, Winder watched his family divide over secession—one of his sons, William Sidney, joined the Confederate army while the other, William Andrew, became an artillery captain for the Union. Early in the war Winder was reviled in the Confederate press for his leniency to Union prisoners of war and for his lack of zeal in rounding up Southern Unionists. As we shall see, his reputation would undergo a sea change. In his capacity as provost marshal general of Richmond (1862 through 1864) Winder would earn the enmity of Southern civilians, and as warden of Andersonville Prison in Georgia (1864 through 1865), he would come to be feared and reviled by Union soldiers. Indeed, by the end of the war, Winder was widely regarded as one of the most tyrannical of Confederate leaders.[13]

When Van Lew first entered Winder's makeshift office on Bank Street in the summer of 1861, she beheld a stout, stern, gray-haired man of 61 years of age, with an imposing "aura of command." She was "most politely and kindly received" by Winder, and after sizing him up, Van Lew decided to use the technique of flattery, complimenting Winder on his regal mane of silvery hair before making her request. She left with a note granting her permission to visit Union prisoners and bring them "books, luxuries, delicacies, and what she may please." "How joyful was I to be put in communication with what to me was most sacred," she recalls. "Federal soldiers in prison and in distress!"[14]

Van Lew was right to assume that the Union prisoners were in distress. For although those incarcerated early in the war fared considerably better than those who would later endure the horrors of Andersonville and other infamous Confederate prisons, the lot of Richmond's first wave of inmates—officers, civilians, and enlisted men alike—was nonetheless a difficult one. The converted tobacco warehouses in Richmond were simply not designed to accommodate so many people. The more than 500 men at Ligon's had to share one well for bathing; under such unsanitary conditions—and at the height of a searing Richmond summer—vermin and fever spread rapidly. For months, the men slept on the floor without blankets or pillows; in October the authorities finally provided them with straw and cotton coverlets. Understandably, prisoners also suffered from boredom and

"Federal Soldiers in Prison and in Distress!" *A Harper's Weekly* sketch showing Winder, Todd, and their "rebel prisons" (LIBRARY OF VIRGINIA).

homesickness. In order to alleviate the problems of demoralization, Congressman Ely, the senior prisoner at Howard's, presided on July 25, 1861, over the founding of the "Richmond Prison Association"; its official seal consisted of a ring of lice around a circle and the motto "Bite or Be Damned." The Association set up debates, card games, sing-ins and "various expedients . . . to kill time," remembered captive Michael Corcoran; not surprisingly, "Home, Sweet Home" was the inmates' favorite tune.[15]

On the same July day that the Richmond Prison Association was formed, Van Lew and her mother visited the "helpless" men who had been captured at Bull Run, bringing "a little chicken soup and cornmeal gruel" to prison for their relief; they even succeeded in winning the "kindly feeling" of prison commandant David Todd by plying him with "ginger cakes & buttermilk." The Van Lews in all likelihood also lent a hand in furnishing supplies to wounded Federal prisoners who had been taken to makeshift hospitals, where they were at the mercy of enemy surgeons. "The entire stock of lint and bandages" for wounded Union soldiers from Manassas, prisoner William Harris wrote, was "furnished by the Unionists of Richmond."[16]

With so many Confederate men in need of women's assistance, the Van Lew women's ministrations to Union prisoners came under new scrutiny. Elizabeth was explicitly warned not to "show sympathy for any of those prisoners" by a so-called gentleman who shook his finger in her face and threatened harm to her family. By the end of July, Van Lew and her mother had earned themselves a very public chastisement. An article in the July 29, 1861 issue of the *Richmond Enquirer* reported:

> Two ladies, a mother and a daughter, living on Church Hill, have lately attracted public notice by their assiduous attentions to the Yankee prisoners confined in this City. Whilst every true woman in this community has been busy making articles of comfort or necessity for our troops . . . these two women have been expending their opulent means in aiding and giving comfort to the miscreants who have invaded our sacred soil, bent on raping and murder, the desolation of our homes and sacred places, and the ruin and dishonor of our families.
>
> . . . The largest human charity can find ample scope in kindness and attention to our own poor fellows. . . . The Yankee wounded have been put under charge of competent surgeons and provided with good nurses. This is more than they have any right to expect, and the course

of these two females . . . cannot but be regarded as an evidence of sympathy amounting to an endorsation [sic] of the cause and conduct of
these Northern Vandals.[17]

The *Enquirer* meant to convey in no uncertain terms that the rules by which
elite women such as Van Lew had long abided had changed—the dispensing
of charity, long considered the duty of the true Southern lady, had become
so politicized that giving it to the wrong kind was regarded by the press as
treasonous. Nor could the Van Lew women's wealth and status insulate them
from criticism. The *Richmond Dispatch* followed up the *Enquirer*'s article,
calling the Church Hill ladies "Yankee offshoots, who had succeeded by
stinginess, double-dealing and cuteness to amass out of the credulity of
Virginians a good, substantial pile of the root of all evil." If the Van Lews
were not careful, they would be "exposed and dealt with as alien enemies
to the country." The press had refrained from identifying the Van Lews by
name this time, but would not, so the articles implicitly warned, show such
delicacy in the future.[18]

It is instructive to contrast these public chastisements with the treatment
accorded another lady who sought to aid the Union prisoners—Northerner
Fanny Ricketts. Upon hearing that her husband, Captain James B. Ricketts,
commander of Ricketts's Battery, had been killed at Bull Run, Fanny made
her way from Washington, D.C., to Richmond to claim his body, only to
discover that he was badly wounded and incarcerated at Ligon's. She stayed
on in Richmond to tend his wounds until he recovered and was permitted
to go home in a prisoner exchange in December of 1861. While Ricketts
met with some public scorn, she also earned considerable admiration from
Confederates. As Sallie Brock remembers it, Fanny Ricketts's plight "called
forth the deepest sympathies from many of the ladies of Richmond," who
recognized in her a "faithful and devoted wife," doing for her husband what
any "true woman" would do. The Van Lews merited no such sympathy, for
their actions on behalf of Union prisoners could not be construed, and
excused, as service to their own menfolk.[19]

The divergent attitudes toward Ricketts and Van Lew reflected two warring conceptions of women's nature and duty. One was the longstanding
and resilient notion that women, in times of war, should be classed (like
children) among the "innocent"—since they were subordinate to men, they

were not politically culpable. Seen in this light, Fanny Ricketts's act of devotion to her husband was apolitical and innocent, as were the actions of Confederate female patriots who made similar sacrifices for their own menfolk. The other notion was of recent vintage, the fruit of antebellum controversies over female abolitionism and the nascent woman's rights movement—the idea that women were autonomous political actors who were accountable for their actions. In the eyes of the Richmond press, as well as some of the city's inhabitants, the Van Lew women embodied the threat of female autonomy. (The fact that Elizabeth was a spinster and Eliza a widow only reinforced this perception.) The presence of Unionist women in Richmond not only belied the press's repeated claim that Southern females were solidly Confederate but also raised a troubling specter: that of women defying male leadership and community pressure to make independent political judgments. Unionism on the part of Southern women was, in other words, a threat not only to the political order but to the social order.

Dealing with that threat proved to be a vexing problem for the Confederacy. Even as the press was poised to stigmatize Van Lew and her mother as "alien enemies," military and political authorities were hesitant to define women in those terms. On August 8, 1861, the Confederate Congress passed an Alien Enemies Act that compelled males—but not women—over 14 who were not citizens of states in the Confederacy to swear an oath of allegiance to the Confederate government or, after a 40-day grace period, suffer the fate of deportation. In exempting women from taking the oath, the Alien Enemies Act presupposed that women were both politically innocent and subordinate to men; they would follow the lead and suffer the fate of their menfolk, in whom was vested the choice of declaring fealty to, or being exiled from, the Confederacy.[20]

The first major blow the war dealt to the doctrine of female innocence was the arrest and incarceration of Confederate spy Rose O'Neal Greenhow on August 23, 1861. A popular Washington, D.C., hostess—and an ardent secessionist—accustomed to entertaining prominent Union politicians at her mansion, Greenhow was recruited by General Pierre Gustave T. Beauregard's adjutant, Colonel Thomas Jordan, to gather information about Federal military plans. Greenhow rose to the challenge, and on the eve of Bull Run, provided Jordan and Beauregard with a warning of the upcoming Federal advance into Northern Virginia. Although Greenhow's admirers have long

claimed that this information was crucial to the Confederate victory, recent
scholarship has demonstrated that her intelligence contributions to the Bull
Run campaign were only marginal.[21]

In the wake of the battle, Greenhow persisted in ferreting military secrets
out of her many influential friends in the Union capital, and passing such
secrets on to the Confederate authorities. Allan Pinkerton, whose successful
detective agency had recently been converted into the Union's first secret
service operation, was charged with breaking up the Greenhow spy ring;
after weeks of surveillance, his men arrested Greenhow at her Washington,
D.C., home. She remained under house arrest there, along with her daughter
Little Rose and two of her female couriers, until January of 1862, when she
and Little Rose were transferred to Old Capitol prison.[22]

Though the women never met, Greenhow's story is integral to Van Lew's,
not only because Rebel Rose was the first of the "Big Five" (Belle Boyd,
Antonia Ford, Pauline Cushman, and Van Lew being the other four) of
female spies who would eventually gain legendary status, but also because
Greenhow's arrest changed the way women were regarded on both sides of
the Mason-Dixon line. Northern opinion makers recognized Greenhow's
arrest as a turning point. The *New York Herald* editorialized: "In this struggle
of life and death the government cannot stand upon technicalities or gal-
lantries. . . . It must meet this rebellion at all points and in all its disguises,
and strip it of its false pretences wherever they can be detected."[23]

In the South, Greenhow became an instant "cause celebre." To Confederates, Greenhow's imprisonment was proof of growing Federal ruthlessness
toward civilians. On the issue of Greenhow's innocence or culpability, the
Confederate press was determined to have it both ways. Newspapers praised
her devotion to the cause of secession and at the same time cast her as a
helpless victim. The editors of the *Richmond Dispatch* thundered, a mere
month after making veiled threats against Van Lew, "Nothing is so hideous
in the tyranny inaugurated at Washington as its treatment of helpless
women. In all civilized countries, the name of woman is a protection
stronger than a shield of iron. None but savages and brutes make war upon
the defenceless sex. It has been reserved to Yankees to make this a war upon
women."[24]

Time and time again over the course of the war, Confederate newspapers,
politicians, and military leaders would attempt to seize the moral high
ground on the issue of the treatment of women. But as Van Lew herself

surely noted, there was already a gap—one that would grow ever bigger—between the South's claim of civility and realities in Richmond. Even as they condemned Yankee treatment of Southern women, Confederate authorities in the late summer and fall of 1861 took measures to expose and punish dissenting women. In August the first Union woman suspected of espionage was imprisoned in Richmond. She was a Mrs. Curtis, from Rochester, New York, who had been arrested by a rebel picket in Falls Church, Virginia, and sent by General Johnston at Manassas south to Richmond. After a brief incarceration there, she was released and sent home, where she promptly told her story to New York newspapers. As she saw it, she had been imprisoned simply because she had angered Johnston and Winder by openly expressing her scorn for secessionists. Richmond newspapers reprinted the story, as a sort of cautionary tale. Mrs. Curtis, the *Dispatch* noted, was a "strong minded female" and "advocate of woman's rights"—in other words, she was no lady, and therefore did not merit civil treatment.[25]

On August 30, the Confederate Congress escalated its campaign against Unionists. With the Alien Enemies Act under fire from those who felt that deportation was not punishment enough for those who refused to pledge their allegiance to the cause (and that deportees might spirit military secrets from the South to the North), the Congress passed a Sequestration Act, authorizing the seizure and sequestration of property belonging to alien enemies. Unlike the initial alien enemies act, which had targeted only men, the sequestration act applied more broadly to women as well as men. The new law served initially as a form of intimidation: the Confederate government was slow to work out the details of its provisions and to initiate sequestration proceedings. But over the course of the war, the sequestration act would be used as the pretext to divest Union men and women in the South of their property; Confederate agents would ultimately seize $500,000 worth of property from aliens in Richmond.[26]

Van Lew refused to be intimidated by the press's warning to her and by the other signs of danger. Instead, she adapted her behavior to keep her detractors off balance. According to the reminiscences of her friend Eliza Carrington, Van Lew "visited the hospitals and ministered unto the Confederate soldiers," thereby reassuring her community of her benevolence. Even as she made such gestures, Van Lew, in August and September of 1861, dramatically stepped up her own work on behalf of Union prisoners. Ever attentive to the special burden that enlisted men carried, the Van Lew women extended their charity to common soldiers as well as to officers and civilians. Union Private Lewis Francis was among their beneficiaries. Wounded at Bull Run, Francis was taken to Richmond where he suffered the amputation of his leg. After a stint in the prison hospital, he was jailed in one of the converted tobacco warehouses, where, as he has testified, "I should have perished for want, but a lady named Van Lew sent her slave every other day with food, and supplied me with clothing until January." While the identity of this particular slave is unknown, this passing reference is nonetheless very revealing: the collaboration of their slaves and servants was instrumental to the Van Lew women's Union activism, and we should recognize that much of what Elizabeth and Eliza "did" for Federal soldiers— providing food, clothing, and contact with the outside world—was in fact done by the blacks in their service.[27]

In the middle of September of 1861, the war literally breached the walls of the Van Lew mansion. Calvin Huson, one of the civilians imprisoned at Howard's, grew desperately ill. His friend and fellow politician Alfred Ely despaired as fever wracked Huson's body and drained his strength. After numerous petitions and pleas to General Winder and the physician in charge of prisoners, Edward Higginbotham, Ely finally won for Huson release from the prison and transfer to a private residence—that of Eliza and Elizabeth Van Lew. The ailing Huson was moved to the Van Lew house on October 9, and briefly rallied. He told Ely that "he would give one hundred dollars if his family could see for one moment how comfortably situated he was, and the care the [Van Lew] ladies took of him." But on October 13 Huson began a rapid decline. Eliza and Elizabeth "became frightened at his hard breathing" and called for help, but to no avail. On October 14, Elizabeth Van Lew took her carriage to Howard's, where she tearfully informed Ely that Huson was dead.[28]

According to Ely's memoirs, the Van Lew women had, during Huson's stay at their house, "more than once listened to unpleasant remarks . . . for giving 'aid and comfort' to a 'Black Republican enemy.' " Under such circumstances, they decided not to have a large funeral service that might attract publicity and reprisals; on October 15, the Van Lews, Ely, the Reverend John F. Mines of Bath, Maine, and a handful of others buried Huson quietly at Church Hill cemetery. When the modest ceremony was over, Elizabeth "placed a bunch of roses upon the exile's grave."[29]

Having attracted suspicion by nursing Huson, the Van Lew women felt it necessary after his death to somehow defuse public hostility. Elizabeth first attempted to call on Jefferson Davis himself, to ask for protection for her family against the threats and insults of those who regarded the Van Lews as treasonous. Davis "was in a cabinet session," Elizabeth recalls, "but I saw Mr. Josselyn, his private secretary, who told me I had better apply to the Mayor." Just what Van Lew intended to tell Davis and what she did tell his secretary is unclear, but we can presume that she took the same tack as she had in her dealings with Memminger: she argued that her ministrations to the likes of Huson were motivated by a female benevolence entirely appropriate for a Christian lady. The very fact that Van Lew would appeal directly to Davis reveals both her personal confidence and her conviction that she rightfully retained all the prerogatives of her social class.[30]

Protection from the mayor never materialized, so the Van Lews chose an inspired gambit: taking in Captain George C. Gibbs, who had replaced David Todd as head of the tobacco-factory prison complex, and Gibbs's family as boarders in the Van Lew mansion. Elizabeth did not care much for Gibbs ("He was not a man of much intellect & untidy," she opined), but regarded him as a "great protection"—how could the Van Lew women possibly be carrying on any disloyal activity, she hoped her neighbors would reason, when they had a Confederate commandant living in their midst?[31]

Some three weeks after Huson's death, Van Lew received dire news about the fate of Union prisoners. On November 9, under orders from Confederate Secretary of War Judah P. Benjamin, a grim ceremony took place in the officers' quarters at Howard's prison—Alfred Ely was compelled to draw lots to identify Federal officers marked for death should the Union authorities move to execute captured Confederate officers and seamen, of the Confederate privateers *Savannah* and *Jefferson Davis*, imprisoned in New York and Philadelphia. The status of those Southern prisoners had long been a subject of heated debate. The men of the *Savannah* had been captured by the Yankees on June 4, 1861, and those of the *Jefferson Davis* on July 22. The Lincoln administration, refusing to recognize the sovereignty of the Confederacy, opted to treat the prisoners as civilian criminals, charging them with the capital offense of piracy and locking them up in civilian jails. In October of 1861, the sailors were tried. The New York jury deadlocked and a retrial was

set; the Philadephia jury rendered a verdict of "guilty." Shortly after he
learned of the results of the trials, President Jefferson Davis retaliated, ordering the War Department to select 14 high-ranking Union prisoners of
war, one for every captured privateersman, to be incarcerated as "convicted
felons." They were to remain in prison until the Confederates were released.
One Union man would be put to death for every Confederate prisoner
executed. Six of the Union men chosen by lottery were sent to Confederate
prisons in the Deep South, while the remainder were transferred to Henrico
County Jail in Richmond, confined in an 11-by-17 foot cell. There they
would remain until Lincoln relented in February of 1862, revoking the
threatened death sentences of the Confederates and prompting Davis to
return the Union captives to the military prisons.[32]

Remarkably, Van Lew seems to have been one step ahead of the Confederate authorities. One of the hostages, Captain George W. Rockwood of
the Fifteenth Massachusetts, remembers arriving at the Henrico County
Jail: "as we went up-stairs and entered the cell, a basket of hot rolls sat on
a bench inside, sent by Miss Van Lew, the Union prisoners' friend in Richmond. The jailer seeing it uttered an exclamation of anger, saying: 'Well,
you may keep that, but it is the last you will get here.' " Despite the jailer's
vow, the stream of Van Lew charity did not dry up. Major Paul Joseph Revere of the Twentieth Massachusetts recorded in his diary that on January
10, 1862, Elizabeth sent the soldiers some books, an offering he found
"very acceptable, as our stock was quite limited." Sometime after these famous prisoners had been relocated, Van Lew and a friend would visit the
Henrico Jail; in her journal she describes the hostages' cell poignantly as a
"small room with a close double barred window set in a thick wall letting
in a sad light to make darkness visible." It was, for her, a "relic" of Confederate "cruelty."[33]

Revere was not the only inmate grateful for Van Lew's ministrations; in
her scrapbook—an album covering the years 1845 to 1897 and containing
74 pages of newspaper clippings, correspondence, and other documents that
Elizabeth gathered and preserved over the course of her life—are carefully
pasted two letters of thanks from two Union captives. On January 29, 1862,
Colonel William Raymond Lee of the Twentieth Massachusetts sent Van Lew
a picture of his daughter, a token of his gratitude for Van Lew's "constant
kindness." The following day, Colonel Alfred M. Wood of the 144th New
York sent her a few lines of verse: "Dear Lady, though we've never met/Your

kindness I shall ne'er forget/Though I your face may never see/My heart will ever grateful be."[34]

The fact that Rockwood, Revere, Lee, and Wood single out Elizabeth for praise, rather than mentioning Eliza Van Lew as well, signals that the paths of mother and daughter had begun to diverge. Although Eliza had accompanied Elizabeth on her early visits to prisoners, by the winter of 1861 through 1862 Elizabeth had come out from under her mother's shadow. For the remainder of the war, the Van Lew daughter and not the matriarch would assume primary responsibility for planning and executing the family's Union activities—Elizabeth would represent the family in delicate negotiations with Confederate officials; deploy the family's resources, slave labor included, to aid the Union war effort; and come to symbolize, in the eyes of Union soldiers, the existence of a loyalist population within the city.

This division of labor reflected the fact that Elizabeth was both physically stronger and the more confident and daring of the two women. And it had other merits, as it deflected suspicion from Eliza. In her capacity as ostensible household head, the widow Van Lew conspicuously offered refuge for hungry and wounded Confederates. "For humanity's sake, the Confederate *private* ever found a friend" in Eliza's home, Elizabeth recalls. Such a show of support for the boys in gray was both consistent with Eliza's benevolent nature and politically pragmatic—even as Elizabeth risked her reputation by advocating on behalf of Union men, Eliza worked to preserve the family's mantle of respectability. The notion that Eliza was a sort of decoy for Elizabeth finds confirmation in the recollections of M. A. Revere, kin of the Union officer Paul J. Revere; Mrs. Revere visited the Van Lews after the war, and learned that Eliza had secretly "helped Bet day and night" in her Union work and yet never committed "any offense that could be taken hold of" by the community. Elizabeth's brother John Newton played a similar game; he, too, aided Elizabeth while maintaining the façade of Confederate loyalty. So well did he keep up this act that in the spring of 1862 he was one the "intelligent gentlemen" empaneled to serve on the jury in the murder trial of a Confederate guard accused of killing a fellow guard.[35]

Over the course of the war's first winter—a particularly harsh one by Richmond standards—Elizabeth Van Lew not only extended her charity to the condemned Union officers at the Henrico County Jail, but also kept up her work on behalf of those soldiers imprisoned and hospitalized elsewhere in the city. She took some comfort in the friendship of Fanny Ricketts, whom she was permitted to visit. But Van Lew was reminded just how precarious such privileges were when on January 23 she received a note from Assistant Surgeon Owen B. Hill informing her that Dr. Edward Higginbotham, surgeon in charge of the prison hospitals, had rescinded her permission to take food to wounded Union captives and that thereafter "nothing to eat [was to] go into the Hospitals except that furnished by the Commissary of the Post." Hill admitted that he thought Van Lew's charity would be good for the prisoners and that he was sorry he could not be of aid to her. Elizabeth and a few friends (her journal does not name them) went to Assistant Secretary of War A. G. Bledsoe to lobby to have the permission restored; Van Lew brought along an ample portion of the custard she was accustomed to providing sick prisoners, to prove it "innocent." Bledsoe proved sympathetic, noting that Confederate prisoners in Washington, D.C., were allowed to receive donations of food from Southern sympathizers and that Higginbotham had no right to refuse Van Lew's contributions; he sampled the custard (it was to his liking) and vowed to make the ladies' case before General Winder. Not content to take Bledsoe's word, Van Lew wrote a short letter to Confederate Secretary of War Judah P. Benjamin, asking for "permission to send the sick some nourishment daily." The letter was forwarded to Winder, who restored to Van Lew the privilege of visiting the prisoners.[36]

Winder's repeated acts of forbearance toward Van Lew have prompted much speculation. Why would he let a suspected Union sympathizer have contact with the enemy? Van Lew herself called Winder "easily imposed upon and credulous" and boasted to M. A. Revere that she could "flatter almost anything out of Winder, his personal vanity [was] so great." Moreover, Van Lew was the beneficiary of an ongoing feud between Winder and Higginbotham; the two men hated each other, Van Lew observed, and the general not only overturned the doctor's order but had him arrested for "taking precedence in rank."[37]

More important, Winder's respectful and even helpful attitude toward Van Lew is consistent with his comportment toward elite Union men and women during the first stage in his tenure in Richmond, before the declaration of martial law in March 1862. During 1861, Winder and his detectives had shown no hesitation in imprisoning suspected Unionists. But they had concentrated their efforts on rounding up "undesirables"—poor, disorderly, physically or mentally feeble men. As William Harris, a Union soldier imprisoned in Richmond recalled, civilians locked up for suspected Unionism prior to March of 1862 were a motley crew: "Young boys, scarcely old enough to know what Union means, old men, ragged, unshaven, filthy... nearly all are afflicted with incipient consumption, brought on by want of proper raiment... [and] ignorant of the charges against them." According to Harris, wealthy and influential Union men were rarely incarcerated and if so, only for brief stints in which they shared the relatively endurable quarters of jailed Union officers.[38]

Unionist ladies seem to have enjoyed an even greater degree of immunity than gentlemen did from proscription by Winder. Prison reminiscences by Alfred Ely, Harris, and others testify to the kind ministrations of nameless "Union ladies" who were permitted to visit them or send them food, flowers, and other such supplies. In late February of 1862, the *Richmond Enquirer* quoted the claim of George W. Walker, a paroled Union soldier, that there were "very numerous" Union women in the city tending Federal soldiers in the hospitals and prisons; Walker revealed nothing of the women's identities or backgrounds. In the first year of the war, elite Southern women's benevolence to Union soldiers did not arouse much disapproval among Richmonders. The leading Richmond dailies decried this public indifference and official leniency toward Unionists, and bitterly criticized Winder for "looseness... in regards to suspicious characters."[39]

Walker's claim notwithstanding, Van Lew cast the first year of the war as a time of relative isolation, during which her Unionist circle was very small. Ironically, it was only once the Confederacy ratcheted up its efforts to expose Unionists that Van Lew was able to identify potential allies outside of her immediate family and old friends.

The immunity of influential citizens to arrest and detention was compromised in the wake of Jefferson Davis's inauguration on February 22, 1862. After a midwinter lull in campaigning by both the Federal and Confederate armies, the war machines geared up again, with dire consequences for the Confederacy. The successful invasion of Tennessee by General Ulysses S. Grant, culminating in the fall of Forts Henry and Donelson in mid-February, was the first of a series of Confederate reverses in the Western theater. "The timid will begin to croak, the half-hearted to quail and suggest submission, the traitourous to agitate," predicted Confederate clerk Robert Kean about the changes the news from Tennessee would bring in Richmond. More ominous still for Virginians was the threat posed by the formidable forces of General George McClellan—his Army of the Potomac was some 100,000 strong and poised to make good on his promise that he would advance "on to Richmond." Richmonders knew that the gentle breezes of spring would herald the onslaught of the Federal army. Though his had been the most insistent of all Confederate voices in condemning Yankee treatment of civilians, newly inaugurated Confederate president Jefferson Davis decided to take an unprecedented measure for the "effective defense" of areas vulnerable to Yankee incursions—namely the suspension of the writ of habeas corpus. As of midnight, March 1, 1862, Richmond and the surrounding area within a ten-mile radius fell under martial law. The Richmond press applauded Davis's action. "We must give the authorities our cheerful and uncomplaining trust," averred the editors of the *Enquirer*.[40]

Davis placed the job of enforcing martial law squarely in the hands of Winder, appointing him provost marshal general and instructing him to establish a military police force to rid Richmond of traitors and spies. Confederate Richmonders had reason for alarm—ever since the Federal successes in Tennessee, Unionists in Richmond had seemed to multiply and become more brazen. "On the walls of buildings at various street corners were read such inscriptions as these: 'Union Men to the Rescue!' 'Now is the time to rally around the Old Flag!' 'God Bless the Stars and Stripes!' . . . and many other taunts, that convinced us we had traitors among us," wrote Sallie Brock.[41]

A devoted soldier well aware of the increased pitch of Union activity, Winder moved quickly to fulfill his new mandate. He may have derived added zeal for the work of rounding up civilians from the knowledge that his brother William, a proslavery, anti-Lincoln lawyer in Philadelphia, was languishing as a Federal prisoner in Boston, Massachusetts, having been arrested for nothing more than the crime of disloyalty to the Union. In January of 1862 William was offered his freedom should he take an oath of allegiance to the United States; he refused, and remained in jail until November of 1862. Embittered by such evidence of Federal "despotism" and evidently eager to prove his Richmond critics wrong, Winder was about to cast off his reputation for leniency.[42]

On the morning of March 2, General Winder's men arrested one of the *eminences grises* among Virginia's politicians, John Minor Botts. The moment

was humiliating to say the least: soldiers surrounded Botts's home and literally dragged him out of bed and into custody. Botts, as we have seen, had
been a leading advocate of sectional reconciliation—and the political idol of
Elizabeth Van Lew. A few hours later, the authorities collected a second
suspected Unionist ringleader, Franklin Stearns. A Northerner by birth and
open Union sympathizer, Stearns was regarded by Confederates as the worst
sort of scoundrel: while others were sacrificing for the "Cause," Stearns was
making a small fortune selling liquor to Confederate soldiers. The *Examiner*
railed that Stearns had "by means of his whiskey . . . done more to disor-
ganize our army than all the balance of the Yankee nation put together."
The *Richmond Dispatch* urged his execution.[43]

In targeting Botts and Stearns, Winder's men were evidently acting on a
tip—on February 28, 1862, the Honorable W. S. Ashe had sent a letter to
Jefferson Davis warning him that there were "designing men in this City
plotting treason against our Government." "Mr. Botts and a Mr. Stearns
have been supposed to be at the head of this treasonable band," Ashe continued. Their "immediate apprehension" and imprisonment would, he recommended, "destroy the scheme in embryo." Accepting this logic, Winder's
men threw the two men into McDaniels Negro Jail, soon to be dubbed
"Castle Godwin" (after prison commander A. C. Godwin). The authorities
then proceeded to round up dozens of other suspects, including ice dealer
Burnham Wardwell, carpenter William Fay, grocer John M. Higgins, and
import-export merchant Charles Palmer. By mid-March, Castle Godwin
held 28 men accused of disloyalty.[44]

Some of those who were targeted, such as Burnham Wardwell, attracted
suspicion because of their "Yankee" origins (he was a native of Maine);
others had explicitly taken actions that antagonized the Confederates. Fay,
a native of Massachusetts and business associate of the Van Lews, was outspoken in his disloyalty, prompting the *Richmond Examiner* to brand him a
"loud-mouthed Union ranter." Higgins, a native of Ireland, had called attention to his Unionism by extending help to Federal prisoners, particularly
fellow Irishman Michael Corcoran. Palmer, though a native Virginian and
eminence grise in his own right (he was in his early sixties), had run afoul
of the authorities by trying to visit Botts in prison and by arguing for his
release.[45]

There is evidence that most of the men rounded up in the March 1862
sweep were, in fact, dedicated Unionists. But did they constitute, as the

Confederates charged, a conspiracy to overthrow the government? Was there, at this early stage in the war, an organized Richmond underground? The answer is no. It should come as no surprise that Botts, Stearns, Palmer, Wardwell, and others strenuously denied the charges against them. More revealing however is that even after the war, when it would have been politically advantageous for such men to claim to have headed up a Union conspiracy, none did. Botts in his 1866 book *The Great Rebellion*, written with the express purpose of staking his claim as a Unionist hero, protests his innocence and that of the other men arrested in March of 1862, casting them as victims of repressive martial law. Moreover, he is at pains to note that while Stearns and Palmer were his dear friends, many of the other incarcerated Unionists were "strangers" to him.[46]

The conclusion that the charges of conspiracy against Botts and other prominent Unionists were trumped up is further borne out by the Confederacy's own handling of their cases. Those detainees with friends in high places—Confederate friends—were able to secure an expeditious release from prison. Charles Palmer was vouched for by his son William P. Palmer, the highly respected captain of one of the companies of the Richmond Howitzers, and discharged on March 6. Botts wrote to his friend Elizabeth Van Lew from prison, asking for her advice; he settled on a strategy of having women intercede on his behalf. Botts had his advocate, legislator John B. Baldwin, forward to Secretary of War George W. Randolph notes from Botts's daughter and other female relatives protesting the authorities' unfair treatment of him. When the court-martial heard Botts's case on April 25 it agreed to the request that Botts be released on parole and allowed to rejoin his family on his Culpeper estate, provided he remain there for the duration of the war and refrain from speaking out for the Union. Franklin Stearns, for his part, had his team of lawyers lobby the secretary of war to expedite his hearing so he could be released to go and see his ailing wife; he was examined by a court-martial in late April but as "nothing to his prejudice was elicited by the examination," he too was set free. The Confederate government would go on to pay Stearns tidy sums to rent buildings in his possession and convert them into hospitals.[47]

Predictably, Unionists who were less well connected had longer and more difficult stays in prison. Wardwell and Fay were among the dozens of Richmond civilians who languished at Castle Godwin for months only to be transferred to the even more dismal Salisbury Prison, in North Carolina, in

May of 1862. Philip Cashmeyer, a Winder detective who crossed over to the Union side later in the war, testified in the fall of 1865 that "several hundred Union (citizen) prisoners were confined [at Salisbury] during the year 1862, very many of whom died. Colonel Godwin, former provost-marshal of Richmond, was in command during the period these prisoners were confined. His treatment of them was unkind and severe." Sarah Wardwell, Burnham's wife, wrote to Confederate official John G. Williams complaining that conditions in Salisbury were so poor as to endanger the health and even the life of her husband; her complaint was forwarded to the secretary of war but not acted upon.[48]

Winder's March sweep was intended to have a deterrent effect on Unionism in the city, to frighten potential fifth-columnists into silent submission. Frighten them it did—from March 1862 on Elizabeth Van Lew and her mother Eliza lived in terror of being arrested themselves—but they chose not to submit. Rather the arrests seem to have had unanticipated consequences, as they brought Unionists together who may not have known about each other before. Thanks to detailed press coverage of the arrests, well-to-do Unionists such as Van Lew were able to learn the names and identities of working-class loyalists, who lived outside of the elite circle of social and business contacts. Later in the war, Van Lew would find some of her most important co-conspirators among men—Wardwell and Higgins, among others—who had been arrested and exposed as loyalists in the spring of 1862 and subsequently released.

If Winder's crackdown was an ominous sign that the era of official leniency toward Unionists had come to an end, another one appeared when Castle Godwin welcomed its first female inmate. Anne E. Scott of Leesburg, in Northern Virginia, was arrested there in early March, charged with crossing the Confederate lines and communicating with the enemy. The *Examiner* described her as a "rather fine looking lady" and reported that she occupied her own room on the ground floor of the prison. She seems not to have been a committed Unionist of the Van Lew sort—in late April she took an oath of allegiance to the Confederacy and was released. But her arrest nonetheless signaled the Confederate government's determination to make examples of female traitors.[49]

Most ominous of all for Van Lew was the discovery by Winder's men of an actual Federal espionage scheme in Richmond. Ever since Bull Run, Richmonders had been paranoid about the threat of Union spies. Ironically,

Confederate fears of Union treachery had been stoked by the rumors of
Rose Greenhow's exploits; if the Union capital could so easily be infiltrated,
why not the Confederate capital? "Spies were there who for gold were ready
at any moment to deliver the city into the hands of our enemies," wrote
Sallie Brock, giving voice to a widespread fear.[50]

Confederate fears were largely unfounded, at least in the early months of
the war. As Edwin Fishel demonstrated in his detailed study of Union intelligence in the period 1861 to 1863, the Federals were embarrassingly slow
to establish a foothold in Richmond. Federal intelligence operations initially
fell under the aegis of Allan Pinkerton's private detective agency. During the
summer of 1861, Pinkerton's men were too consumed with monitoring the
activities of Greenhow's ring in Washington, D.C., to do any data gathering
in the South. The few Pinkerton "plants" in Richmond at that time were
tracked so closely by Confederates as to be rendered ineffective.[51]

In mid-October of 1861, the Federals scored their first intelligence coup
when Timothy Webster, the "star performer" of Pinkerton's detective force,
infiltrated Richmond. A 40-year-old native of Britain, Webster posed as a
secessionist courier from Baltimore to the Confederate capitol. Though
Confederate clerk John B. Jones was suspicious of the "mysterious" letter
carrier and refused to give him a pass authorizing travel around the Confederacy, Webster obtained his pass from Winder, in return for a favor—
Webster carried letters to and from Winder's son William in Washington,
D.C. (William, to his father's severe disappointment, had remained loyal to
the Union.) Webster gathered data on Richmond's earthwork batteries, ord-
nance capabilities, and regimental strength, and returned safely to the
North; a second and third mission to Richmond from November to mid-
December, and Christmas day to January 30, proved equally fruitful. Webster returned to Richmond in February, but fell ill with inflammatory
rheumatism.[52]

Webster convalesced at the Monument Hotel in Richmond, waited on by
a Hattie Lawton, a Pinkerton operative who was posing as his wife, and John
Scobell, an African American agent posing as Webster's servant. Lawton had
been one of the Pinkerton detectives who arrested Rose O'Neal Greenhow
back in August. Eager to ascertain the status of his trusted agents, Pinkerton
sent two more operatives, Pryce Lewis and John Scully, to track Webster
and Lawton. Lewis and Scully were themselves tracked by Confederate counterintelligence agents. After receiving a tip from a Confederate civilian who

recognized the two men as the very same Pinkerton agents who had searched his Washington, D.C., home early in the war, Confederate authorities arrested and jailed Lewis and Scully, and found them guilty of espionage by court-martial. Under threat of execution the two men fingered Webster, won a reprieve, and were released. On April 3, Webster and Lawton were imprisoned at Castle Godwin (where Lawton shared a room with Anne E. Scott, the other female inmate); Scobell was not suspected of being an agent and was therefore released.[53]

While Webster and Lawton awaited word of their fate, the Confederate government passed a groundbreaking law with dire implications for Unionists: the conscription act. The measure compelled all white men between the ages of 18 and 35 to join the military for three years, unless they practiced an occupation—nursing, teaching, and iron work, for example—that brought exemption from service. In Richmond and elsewhere in the South, conscription agents took special pleasure in targeting Unionists; what better way to compel a man's loyalty than to force him into the army? Elizabeth Van Lew would feel the reverberations of this policy, as her brother John became the prey of conscription officers in 1864.[54]

On April 29, 1862, Timothy Webster became the first American to be hanged as a spy since Nathan Hale. Webster was taken from his Richmond jail to Camp Lee, a former parade grounds, now the site of a holding pen for prisoners and of a substantial wooden scaffold. According to the *Richmond Examiner*, the good people of Richmond found Webster so contemptible that they did not even bother to turn out to witness the execution; "on the trees and high places . . . commanding a view of the gallows there may have been as many as two hundred persons," the paper reported, "but these were for the most part negroes and boys." Webster's "wife" (Lawton) exhorted Webster to "die like a man!" and he did. The first time the trap door on which he stood was sprung, the rope around Webster's neck slipped and he fell to the ground. As his captors rerigged the rope, Webster uttered his last words: "I suffer a double death. Oh, you are going to choke me this time." They did. The body hung half an hour, and then was cut down; "the detectives present cut up the fatal rope," the *Examiner* concluded, "and "stuffing it in their pockets, followed the body."[55]

Van Lew kept a close watch on Webster's fate. After the hanging, Van Lew requested of Confederate authorities that the "poor agonized" widow Webster be permitted to stay at the Church Hill mansion. The request was denied, and Lawton languished in Castle Godwin for a year, before being released in a prisoner exchange. During her captivity, Lawton maintained her cover as Webster's wife and refused to be sent North as a disloyal person, claiming that she was a Southern woman who desired only to return to her native Maryland.[56]

In the eyes of Allan Pinkerton, Webster's chief in the secret service, Lawton perfectly fulfilled the mandate of female patriotism. In a chapter of his memoirs entitled "A Woman's Devotion and a Patriot's Heroism," Pinkerton tells the story of the last meeting of Lawton and Webster, as the latter awaited his execution. "Tears filled the eyes of the faithful woman," Pinkerton writes of Lawton, "as she gazed at the pale and emaciated form of the heroic patriot." Not surprisingly, Confederates saw Lawton quite differently. Hoping to tap into some of the same feelings of sympathy that Confederate authorities had shown toward Fanny Ricketts, Lawton called on First Lady Varina Howell Davis to plead for Webster's life, but to no avail. The Richmond press similarly had no sympathy for Lawton, reviling her as "nothing more nor less than a common and notorious prostitute."[57]

Timothy Webster's death brought to a close the first chapter of Elizabeth Van Lew's Civil War experience. She faced a stark reality. To maintain the façade of loyalty was to preserve one's freedom. But should that façade slip, revealing a heart true to Old Glory, a Unionist could expect deportation, the seizure of his or her property, prolonged imprisonment—or death.

4

"The Bright Rush of Life"

THE MAKING OF THE RICHMOND UNDERGROUND

THE MONTHS AFTER TIMOTHY WEBSTER'S EXECUTION SAW ELIZABETH'S HOPES RISE and fall with the fortunes of George McClellan's ill-fated army. McClellan's threatened campaign had begun to materialize in early March, as a Federal fleet transported his men from the outskirts of Washington, D.C., down the Potomac and Chesapeake Bay to Fort Monroe, a Federal outpost on the tip of the York River Peninsula. There the army massed until it reached some 100,000 soldiers and set about laying siege to the much smaller Confederate forces, consisting of 17,000 men, assembled at Yorktown. Thanks in part to overestimation of Confederate strength by McClellan and Pinkerton (and to the dramatic flair of opposing General John B. Magruder, who paraded his troops through a clearing over and over to make the Yankees believe that they faced a sizeable foe), McClellan believed himself outnumbered, and to the exasperation of Lincoln, delayed launching a frontal assault against the enemy. Only after Confederate General Joseph Johnston—well aware that *he* was outnumbered—evacuated Yorktown did McClellan's army begin to move north along the peninsula toward Richmond.[1]

The two armies faced off in the first major battle of the Peninsula Campaign on May 31, at Seven Pines five miles outside of Richmond. The battle was a strategic draw, the most important consequence of which was the replacement of the injured Joe Johnston by Robert E. Lee. While McClellan waited for reinforcements, Lee planned an assault against the invaders. Richmond held its breath, knowing full well that a momentous clash was imminent. "How long is this to last? We are in hourly expectation of a battle," Elizabeth wrote on June 20, 1862. She and her mother diffused the tension by fantasizing that the Federal commander would fight his way to their doorstep: "Mother had a charming chamber, with new matting and pretty curtains, all prepared for Genl. McClellan, and for a long time we called [it] Genl. McClellan's room," she wrote. A Unionist woman boarding with the

Van Lews—a milliner by the name of Miss McGonigle—confirms Van Lew's story; McGonigle saw the McClellan room prepared "even to the water drawn for the bath."[2]

Adding to the tension of those June days was the revelation, from the lips of Captain Alexander of Castle Godwin, that Elizabeth had "been reported several times"—in other words, that suspicious Confederates had accused her of improper attention to the Union prisoners. In what was now a familiar routine, the Van Lew women deflected such charges by conspicuous acts of Confederate sympathy; they entertained young men from the Richmond Howitzers and other prominent citizens. They even opened their doors to a mysterious young man whom Elizabeth feared was trying to entrap them into admissions of disloyalty. "We were kind and polite and he took tea with us," she explains in her June 21 journal entry, adding, "We have to be watchful and circumspect—wise as serpents—and harmless as doves, for truly the lions are seeking to devour us."[3]

On June 25, Lee began his offensive, crossing the Chickahominy River to confront Federal troops in the battle of Oak Grove, the first of the contests that came to be known as the Seven Days Battles. The Federals sustained heavier casualties than the Confederates and Lee followed up this tactical victory by mounting an attack against Federal troops at Mechanicsville, a crossroads village six miles north of Richmond. Richmond civilians anticipated a showdown, and on the morning of June 26, wrote John Jones, "hundreds of men, women, and children were attracted to the heights around the city to behold the spectacle." Rather than wait out events at home, Elizabeth set out on a daring adventure that reveals how confident she was in her powers of deception. On the blistering hot afternoon of June 26 she, along with friends, Eliza G. Carrington and an unnamed friend referred to only as "commodore," rode northeast out of Richmond to visit the recently acquitted Unionist John Minor Botts and his family, who were staying at a farm they owned in Hanover County. The route to Hanover took Elizabeth along the Mechanicsville Turnpike—directly toward the day's fighting and toward the Confederate pickets who enforced a stringent domestic passport system. Confederate guards were posted at major crossroads, demanding of citizens government-issued passports confirming their identities and granting them leave to travel. Among the effects in Van Lew's scrapbook is a pass issued to her friend Eliza Carrington on March 25, 1862, good for 60 days, and signed by none other than Provost Marshal Godwin; we can surmise that Elizabeth possessed similar paperwork.[4]

By posing before Confederate pickets as loyal Southerners and producing the requisite passports, Elizabeth and her friends were able to make it to Botts's farm and to return safely that evening. At the end of her momentous day, Elizabeth confided the sights and sounds of her outing to her diary: "The excitement on the Mechanicsville Turnpike was more thrilling than I could conceive. Men riding and leading horses at full speed; the rattling of their gear, their canteens and arms; the rush of the poor beasts into and out of the pond at which they were watered. The dust, the cannons on the crop roads and fields, the ambulances, the long line of infantry awaiting orders. . . . We found Mr. Botts and family listening to the roar of the artillery. The windows rattled. The flash of the bursting shells could be seen. The roar, too, of musketry could be plainly heard. The rapid succession of guns was wonderful."

Elizabeth was acutely aware that her visit to Botts symbolized a dramatic break with her former life and with the conventions that had governed female life in peacetime. "No ball could ever be so exciting as our ride this evening," she wrote with palpable exhilaration. "I realized the bright rush of life, the hurry of death on the battlefield!"[5]

Unfortunately for the Van Lews and other Unionists who awaited liberation at the hands of McClellan, the week of the Seven Days Battles (June 25 to July 1) witnessed a series of Union reversals culminating in the Federals' retreat. Confederate Richmonders were grateful that the Yankee invasion had been repulsed but heartbroken by the cost of victory. The Seven Days Battles had produced frightful carnage, with the South sustaining 20,000 casualties to the Union's 16,500. Sarah Pryor, a general's wife who reluctantly went to work tending the wounded, captured the defiant yet somber mood of Confederate Richmonders in her reminiscences: "Each of the battles of those seven days brought a harvest of wounded to our hospital. I used to veil myself closely as I walked to and from my hotel, that I might shut out the dreadful sights in the street,—the squads of prisoners, and, worst of all, the open wagons in which the dead were piled. Once I did see one of these dreadful wagons! In it a stiff arm was raised, and shook as it was driven down the street, as though the dead owner appealed to Heaven for vengeance."[6]

Van Lew's vivid observations on the aftermath of the battle reveal both her sympathy for injured soldiers and her growing contempt for "Confederate matrons" such as Pryor. "Tents were put up in the streets and in the hillsides in the thickly settled parts of the city. In these were put most of the patients suffering from gangrene and some who had been considered hopeless cases," Van Lew wrote in her journal. "The largest and finest stores on Main Street were used as hospitals and filled with rooms of cots and beds in which were lying the poor wounded men. The weather was very warm, the doors were open and no curtain or screen shielded them from the gaze of passers by.... So sickeningly fetid was the atmosphere that we could not sit in our grounds [at the Church Hill mansion]."[7]

About the activities of Confederate women in the aftermath of the Peninsula Campaign, Van Lew had no words of empathy, only ones of derision. "Women were ultra in 'patriotism,'" Van Lew reflected. "They had collections and many other ways of making money. At the corner of Ninth & Broad streets a bazaar was kept for the benefits of the rebel interest where were sold fancy works, pictures, any thing sent, and a lady of the Mount Vernon association superintended it, walking around and expatiating and dilating in treason to the hearts content of the most ultra." The irony of the scene at the bazaar was surely not lost on Van Lew—the Mount Vernon Association had been founded in 1854 with the twin purposes of preserving George Washington's estate and promoting harmony between the North and South. No manifestation of female "benevolence" irked Van Lew more than the activities of the "Ladies Aid and Defense Association," founded by elite women in the spring of 1862 to provide for the construction of a gunboat to defend the James River. Members solicited donations of iron, lead, and brass, in the form of pots, pans, jewelry, and other personal property, to be sent to the Tredegar Iron Works and melted down. In light of the carnage that "ultraism" had brought to Richmond, Van Lew found the gunboat association to be "something supremely ridiculous."[8]

Although she derided their efforts as misguided and trivial, Van Lew shared with many of the Confederate women of Richmond a profound desire to be useful, and to make common cause with other civilians. Just as Confederate citizens ratcheted up their war work in the summer of 1862, so, too, did Richmond Unionists. Indeed, it was in the immediate aftermath of McClellan's failed conquest that the various, discrete groups of Unionists in the city began to coalesce into a formal network and to work in concert. Already acquainted with members of the old Whig elite such as Botts, Stearns, and Palmer, Van Lew broadened her circle to take in men from outside her social milieu.[9]

Palmer and Botts were the crucial links between Van Lew and the men who would become her trusted deputies. We can establish that during the summer of 1862, Palmer was in contact with Frederick William Ernest Lohmann, himself the central figure in a community of German Unionists in Richmond. Lohmann, who was 35 years of age when the war began, ran a grocery business and restaurant in the New Market district connecting Sixth and Seventh Streets with Broad and Marshall. His brothers Eberhard, Herman, and John, all carpenters by trade, were also Unionists, as was fellow German Christian Burging, who ran a saloon next to F.W.E.'s establishment. The fact that none of these men owned slaves is consistent with historian Klaus Wust's observation that many laboring-class German immigrants "disliked the institution of slavery"; having "left Germany to get away from perennial political troubles," they opposed secession as a slaveholders' ploy that threatened the order and stability of their adoptive country. Unfortunately for the likes of the Lohmanns and Burging, they were a minority within a minority—recent scholarship has established that the majority of Richmond's ethnic Germans supported the Confederacy. For most German immigrants in the Virginia capital—even those who had a distaste for slavery—believed in white supremacy and saw the Republican party as a threat to the racial hierarchy.[10]

Rivaling F. W. E. Lohmann in importance in the nascent Unionist network was William S. Rowley, who early in the war made the acquaintance of John Minor Botts and impressed the venerable politician with his loyalty to the United States government. Rowley was a native of New York who rented a farm on the outskirts of Richmond; he was 45 years old when the war began. Like the Lohmanns and Burging, he did not own slaves. Rowley would soon emerge as Van Lew's favorite deputy. She describes him in a postwar letter to President U. S. Grant as "the bravest of the brave, and the truest of the true," and a *"character"*—a man of "rare perception and wonderful intuition." Thanks to the survival of two photographs of Rowley among Van Lew's papers, we know him to have been lean of frame, kind and serious in countenance, and graced by an unfashionably long beard (but no mustache) that gave him the look of an Amish man.[11]

"The bravest of the brave."
Van Lew's coworker and confidante,
William Rowley (NEW YORK PUBLIC
LIBRARY).

White Unionists in Richmond, in other words, fell into distinct categories—elite former Whigs from the slaveholding class, who would bankroll
the operations of the loyalist underground, and men of the commercial or
laboring classes, predominantly nonslaveholders of immigrant or Northern
background, who would bear the brunt of the physical dangers and risks in
fulfilling the underground's missions. Significantly, most of the men in both
categories were husbands and fathers. Rowley, for example, was married to
a fellow New Yorker, Catharine, and had three sons, ranging in age from
nine to fifteen at the war's outset; all of the Lohmann brothers were married
and had children. These men, in other words, had a great deal to lose, as
their activism potentially put their families in harm's way. The fact that they
chose to stay in the South and court danger rather than flee to the North
bespeaks their commitment—and that of their families—to maintaining an
identity as Virginians and to redeeming the Old Dominion for future
generations.[12]

As early as the summer of 1862, these Richmond Unionists were deep in
danger, collaborating to undermine the Confederate prison system. The Peninsula Campaign was a grim turning point in treatment of prisoners of war.

As Lee and McClellan battled on the outskirts of Richmond, thousands of Union prisoners were herded into the city; by July 9, the inmate population exceeded 5,000. Confronted with such unprecedented overcrowding, Confederate officials stepped up their security measures, restricting civilian access to the jails and intimidating inmates with brutal displays of force. Gone were the days when Elizabeth could openly visit Union prisoners or extend aid to the likes of Calvin Huson; gone were the days when individual acts of charity could alleviate suffering and soothe the conscience. The Richmond underground had to adapt, and it did. Elizabeth and her fellow loyalists developed an intricate system for helping the prisoners—and for facilitating their escapes.[13]

Richmond Unionists faced a set of determined and ruthless foes. Heading up the recently established Libby Prison, a warehouse on Cary Street, between Twentieth and Twenty-first Streets, just six blocks from Van Lew's mansion, was Major Thomas Pratt Turner, a man whose "utter depravity," wrote one prisoner, "seems to have gained a full and complete expression in every lineament of his countenance." Libby soon became horribly overcrowded, with more than 100 men crammed into each of the six rooms that comprised its upper floors. Like the inmates at other prisons in the city, those at Libby had to deal with scarce rations, poor ventilation, the absence of furniture, blankets, and eating implements, inadequate lighting, and the threat of quick reprisals from guards who relished the opportunity to shoot anyone (indeed the guards called it "sporting for Yankees") who got too close to the windows or otherwise violated regulations. "To 'lose prisoners' was an expression much in vogue," Van Lew wrote, "and we all understood that it meant cold blooded murder."[14]

Incarcerated Federal soldiers were not the only ones who felt the wrath of Libby's keepers—free and enslaved African Americans who worked at the prison were preyed upon; "the flogging of the negroes that worked at Libby was an every-day occurrence," a Federal officer who had been an inmate later testified. Dick Turner, Major Thomas Pratt Turner's second-in-command, was the designated "negro-whipper" of the prison and never missed an opportunity to enforce his power. "As many as six negro women [were] stripped and whipped, at one time, for having passed bread to [Union] soldiers as they marched through the street."[15]

As badly as the denizens of Libby fared, the inmates of Castle Thunder—deserters, political prisoners, and disorderly soldiers—were worse off still.

"Their trembling
comrades."
*Exterior view of Castle
Thunder, prison for disloyal
civilians* (LIBRARY OF
CONGRESS).

Established in March of 1862 to house the overflow of inmates from Castle
Godwin, Castle Thunder, a converted tobacco factory, adjoined by a second
smaller factory and warehouse at the intersection of Cary and Eighteenth
Streets, soon became notorious as a hellhole. The flogging of prisoners was
a common occurrence, as was the use of other forms of corporal punishment, such as hanging inmates by their thumbs, and "bucking" them, a
humiliating torture described by prison warden Marion C. Riggs as "passing
a split across the elbows and tying them beneath the thighs, after the manner
of a calf going to market." The commandant of the prison, Captain George
W. Alexander, was a "desperate brigand looking villain," according to Van
Lew—dressed in black, "black whiskers flowing in the wind," with his fierce
boarhound Nero at his side. Alexander seemed to relish meting out pain.
Equally contemptible was Alexander's right-hand man, John Caphart, a filthy
"tottering giant" the sight of whom "made humanity sick," Van Lew wrote.
His "heavy club" was his "unfailing companion," and so quick was he to
use it on prisoners that he was dubbed "Anti-Christ" by Union soldiers and
sympathizers. Van Lew lingers in her memoirs over an incident revealing
the depths of Caphart's cruelty. Having heard the jailer referred to frequently
as "Anti-Christ," a black woman who passed him in public, "innocently
thinking it was right . . . and wishing to display a great deal of her African
politeness," called Caphart "Mr. Anti-Christ" to his face. This was "too much
for his ill nature to tolerate," Van Lew recalls, so "up went the old club &
out belched the usual oath" and he beat the woman mercilessly while she

cried out "Oh please Mr. Anti-Christ don't beat me; what have I done Mr. Anti-Christ?"[16]

The only means by which prisoners at Libby and Castle Thunder could hope to mitigate the cruelty of their captors was by plying them with bribes, in the form of Confederate money or especially precious United States "greenbacks." All comers to Libby were upon their arrival forcibly divested of their dollars by Confederate officials and guards. Those few lucky men who were able to conceal any of their money during this "thieving process" were able to obtain—for a brief while until their funds ran out—exorbitantly priced articles of food and clothing exchanged on a prison black market, and the privilege of receiving gifts from well-wishers on the outside. Civilians who sought to visit Libby and Castle Thunder had to apply to the provost marshal for permits. Winder was at this stage in the war stingy with such permissions, reserving them for ministers and others whose characters and motives seemed unimpeachable. Richmond loyalists, then, faced a formidable challenge: how could they funnel goods and money into the prison system?[17]

Despite her efforts to manipulate Winder, Van Lew was never permitted to enter Libby prison. So she devised a series of expedients for gaining access to Union soldiers. According to the testimony of General George H. Sharpe, Van Lew "influenced rebel surgeons to send [imprisoned Union] men to the hospitals," where she was permitted to visit them and provide them with food. "She alone went from cot to cot where lay a sufferer in blue," Sharpe observed, while other Richmond ladies only attended the men in gray. Van Lew was for a time able to convey messages and money to hospitalized prisoners through her trusty custard dish, which had a secret chamber inside it. But early in 1863, Thomas Pratt Turner sent Van Lew a note requesting that she desist from providing meals for the injured, arguing fallaciously that "abundant and palatable food is prepared for the patients at the hospital," and—in an unwitting understatement—that meals from the outside had a "tendency to subvert the consistency of prison rules and discipline."[18]

Fortunately for Van Lew and her co-conspirators, the ranks of the clergy, like those of the medical authorities, included some prominent individuals who were sympathetic to Union sufferers, if not to the Union cause. These included the Reverend Thomas Moore of Richmond's Second Presbyterian Church. Moore succeeded in winning access to Libby and Castle Thunder, and he took money from Van Lew and other well-to-do Unionists, such as merchant Horace Kent, to the prisoners there.[19]

In another move intended to play on rebel heartstrings, the underground even called on the skills, sympathy, and bravery of its youngest members. Burnham Wardwell's "little sons" repeatedly visited Union prisons and came home "with military buttons from the soldiers jackets" as souvenirs. As Wardwell recounts, the young daughters of his dear friend and fellow loyalist William Fay made their own appeal directly to the prison authorities: on at least one occasion, the "little girls" went to the one of the Confederate prisons, "trembling, blushing, tears flowing down [their] young cheeks with little packages of *food* in hand asking permission to feed starving men." They were dressed "just as well as a loyal father could dress" them, with "Aprons as white as a loving Mothers hands could make them."[20]

Efforts to spark some human sympathy in the hearts of rebel doctors, ministers, and guards only went so far, however. Appeals to Confederate greed and self-interest proved far more effective. The wealthiest members of the underground—the Van Lews and Kent and Palmer, among others— bankrolled bribes, and thereby motivated certain Confederate guards and officials to pass goods furnished by the Richmond underground on to the prisoners. "[O]ur officers and men felt the effects of [Van Lew's] care," Union General George Henry Sharpe wrote in 1867: "For one [she obtained] additional food, for others raiments and bedding, for some a few hours a week more in the open air. . . . Not only clothing and bedding, but even furniture was sent in to prisoners." The Van Lews "put their hands on whatever of their patrimony they could realize and expended it in what substantially was the service of the U.S. government," Sharpe testified. Even Van Lew's enemies would acknowledge her sacrifices. Major J. W. T. Hairston, Commander of Confederate State Prisons in 1861 and 1862, declares in his reminiscences of the war that Van Lew "expended her entire fortune in ameliorating the hard lot of the prisoners." Although no figures survive to detail exactly how much money the Van Lews spent during the war, and although the family did retain the Church Hill mansion and assorted properties, as well as valuable silver, furnishings, and other belongings after the war, anecdotal and census evidence supports Sharpe's and Hairston's contention that wartime sacrifices depleted the family's patrimony. The 1860 census valued Eliza and Elizabeth's personal estate at a total of $37,000; by 1870, the figure had dropped to $15,000. Indeed, Elizabeth's main preoc-

"Our officers and men felt the effects of her care." *Libby Prison, whose inmates Van Lew devoted herself to aiding* (LIBRARY OF VIRGINIA).

cupation after the war would be that of earning a living to support her family.[21]

Bribery could not only win for prisoners better treatment and access to goods from the outside, but it could also, on rare occasions, facilitate their escape. Newspaper articles and soldiers' reminiscences tell the stories of Confederate guards who looked the other way as Federal inmates slipped out of Libby and into the night. One such Union fugitive who made it safely home, John F. Hill of the Eighty-ninth Ohio regiment, revealed that a good number of the guards had noble motives for their betrayal of the Confederacy—the desire to feed their hungry families (a difficult thing, he noted, on a rebel soldier's pay) and disdain for the "Cause." "I can truthfully say," Hill wrote, "that one third of the soldiers that guarded us [at Libby] were good Union men, but had been dragged into the rebel ranks." Most Union soldiers, however, attributed the treachery of Confederate guards simply to "blind cupidity."[22]

The successful bribing of the guards was only the first of a series of dangerous steps a would-be fugitive had to take. Once out of the prison he

needed both luck and expert assistance—Unionist friends to help him ne-
gotiate foreign terrain, provide him passes (forged or obtained by bribing
Winder's clerks) through Confederate lines, and furnish him food and shelter. Thanks to Northern newspaper accounts, we know that as early as August of 1862, Richmond Unionists were engaged in this risky business of
spiriting escaped inmates out of the Confederacy. That month in the *New
York Herald*, four Union men—Lieutenant F. Murphy, Captain J. M. Oakley,
Lieutenant Willliam Riddle, and a Richmond loyalist named David Mc-
Avery—related the details of their flight from the officer's prison on Eighteenth Street. Formerly Talbott and Bonn's factory, this prison had been
fitted up to take the overflow from Libby. On the morning of August 7,
tearing a board off the rear of the warehouse and eluding sleeping sentries,
the men escaped to an alley near Eighth Street, where they hid for the day
and night. On the eighth, they "visited a house occupied by a lady of the
most thorough going Union sentiments, who furnished us with food and
clothing. We also met other Union friends here, who did everything in their
power to aid our escape." The Unionists provided the prisoners with disguises and with forged exemption tickets, which represented the prisoners
to be employees on government contract works. Once out of the city limits,
the prisoners relied on the kindness of unidentified black Unionists, who
provided them with raiment and informed them of the position of the cavalry search party that was tailing them. After a harrowing passage along the
"Mataponic River," the escaped inmates made it to Northern lines. Two
other Union officers who attempted escape at the same time—a Colonel
Hatch and a Lieutenant Masters—seem not to have availed themselves of
the help of Richmond Unionists and were quickly recaptured and incarcerated at Greanor Prison.[23]

Successful breakouts had reverberations far beyond the prison walls.
Every escaped prisoner was a potential source of intelligence for the Federals—indeed the aforementioned Lieutenant Murphy and his fellow fugitives, who "through means of numerous Union sympathizers [in Rich-
mond]" were "kept thoroughly versed in all facts known to the public there,"
duly reported to Union officials at General McClellan's headquarters what
they could about Confederate fortifications and troop dispositions. A month
after the escape of Murphy and his comrades, the Richmond underground
aided another fugitive, Colonel Adolphus Adler, who related his story to the
New York Times. A Hungarian native and veteran of Garibaldi's Italian cam-

paign of 1859, Adler had been pressed into service in the Confederate army early in the war. When Adler resigned in August of 1861 he was imprisoned in Castle Godwin as a "suspicious character." Having bribed the guards, on August 8, 1862, Adler walked out of the prison in a disguise and "hastened to the house of a Union man of his acquaintance—and there are many in Richmond—and remained hidden for two days. . . . Warned by his host that the Government detectives were on his track, he changed his hiding place in the night, and managed, by shifting his domicile in the same way, re-peatedly, to remain secretly in Richmond for eight days." With the help of two blacks, he made his way to the railroad depot and hid in one of the cars, which spirited him away from Richmond to Staunton at the head of the Shenandoah Valley. From there he made his way on foot to Northern lines, providing "leading military men" reports based on his "intimate knowledge of the rebel organization, plans &c."[24]

While neither the Murphy party nor Adler revealed to the press the iden-tities of their Unionist benefactors or of any Confederate colluders, we can establish without a doubt that Van Lew's house was the principal place of refuge for prisoners in the city. Thanks to the story of escapee Captain William H. Lounsbury, we can also establish that the most important Con-federate colluder was none other than Erasmus Ross, clerk of Libby prison. A nephew of Unionist Franklin Stearns, Ross had—at Van Lew's urging—obtained the position of clerk of Libby prison, and was responsible, among other duties, for keeping track of the inmates through daily roll calls. Ross, of course, played the role of ardent rebel to the hilt; "he never called the rolls without swearing at us and abusing us," remembered Lounsbury, one of Libby's unfortunate denizens. Accordingly, Lounsbury felt nothing but dread when one evening Ross struck him in the stomach and said " 'You blue-bellied Yankee, come down to my office. I have a matter to settle with you.' " As soon as the pair were in the office, Ross wordlessly directed Louns-bury to a Confederate uniform hidden behind a counter, which the Yankee prisoner hastily donned. Lounsbury then walked out the door and ran across the street to a vacant lot, only to be intercepted by an emissary from Van Lew: ". . . a colored man stepped out and said, 'Come with me, sah, I know who you is,' and he took me to Miss Van Lew's house on Church Hill."[25]

Once he was at the Church Hill mansion, Lounsbury was in all likelihood concealed in a secret chamber in the attic that the Van Lews prepared for such fugitives. Van Lew's niece Annie left an account of her own discovery

"I followed her on tiptoe
to see what she was
doing."
*The entrance to the secret
room in Van Lew's attic*
(VALENTINE RICHMOND HIS-
TORY CENTER).

of the secret chamber—Annie once saw Elizabeth "going upstairs with a
plate of food" and "followed her on tiptoe to see what she was doing."
Elizabeth opened the attic door and Annie "crept after her"; when Van Lew
moved a box and panel concealing the room "a man's head appeared." The
fugitive was "about to cry out" with surprise but Annie "put her finger to
her lips to warn him" and then the little girl slid quietly away, her aunt
Elizabeth none the wiser. Later, as Annie remembers the dramatic episode,
she sneaked back upstairs to talk to the mysterious man and he chided her,
saying "if your Aunt had caught you what a spanking you would have got."[26]

Thanks to Elizabeth's discretion, and to that of her kin and her servants,
the Church Hill mansion proved a safe way station on the perilous journey
beyond Confederate lines. Lounsbury recalls how Elizabeth prepared him
for the next stage in his flight: "Miss Van Lew told me the roads and where
to take to the woods to escape the pickets and to go down the James River,
and I could, perhaps, before morning reach a place of safety where I could
escape to our troops." Lounsbury, of course, succeeded in his escape and
lived to tell the tale. According to the memoirs of Colonel David B. Parker,
who learned of Van Lew's exploits while he was a superintendent of the
mails for the Army of the Potomac, and stationed at General U. S. Grant's
headquarters at City Point, Virginia, Lounsbury was but one of many beneficiaries of Van Lew's system: "Miss Van Lew kept two or three bright, sharp
colored men on the watch near Libby prison," writes Parker, "who were
always ready to conduct an escaped prisoner to a place of safety." As we
shall see, such places included the homes of Unionists Arnold B. Holmes,
John H. Quarles, Abby Green, Burnham Wardwell, and William Rowley, as
well as the Van Lew mansion.[27]

"A place of safety."
Interior of the secret room
(VALENTINE RICHMOND HIS-
TORY CENTER).

Remarkably, African American Unionists not only came to the aid of Federal soldiers who had breached the walls of Confederate prisons—blacks also communicated with those still on the inside. The black men and women doing menial labor in the prisons and subject to the brutal treatment detailed above proved to be courageous and resourceful allies to the Unionist underground. After the war, two former Libby inmates would reveal to interviewer John Albree that "nearly every Sunday" Van Lew had walked down Church Hill and then turned and strode along the street in front of the Libby, "never looking toward the prison" lest she betray her interest in its inhabitants. African American laborers, at great risk to themselves, alerted the prisoners as to the meaning of Van Lew's ritual: "The negroes who came in to scrub would say 'That is Miss Van Lew. She will be a friend if you can escape.' " Just how Elizabeth made the acquaintance of these "negroes" is not clear; it may be that the blacks who worked for the Van Lew family at the Church Hill mansion vouched for Van Lew's trustworthiness and enlisted fellow African Americans in Unionist activism.[28]

While we can only speculate as to the identities of the men Van Lew posted outside of the prison (William, James, and Peter Roane, Oliver Lewis, Nelson Gillum, and Anderson are all possibilities), we can recover the stories of two intrepid African American men—one who worked on the inside of Libby and one who helped Libby escapees once they had left Richmond. These two will have to represent the countless other black Unionists whose names are unrecorded. The Richmond underground's principal African American contact within Libby was Robert Ford. Ford was a Northern free black who served as a teamster in the quartermasters' department of the Union army in the Shenandoah Valley. He was captured by the Confederates on May 22, 1862, and sent to Libby prison, where he was made to serve as the hostler to warden Dick Turner. He remained in Libby until July of 1864, when he successfully escaped to Union lines. During his incarceration, a postwar Senate report shows, Ford was "very serviceable to the Union prisoners, affording them information, and aiding their escape from prison." Ford's main partner in this subterfuge was white loyalist Abby Green. Green, who had been born and educated in New Hampshire and settled in Richmond before the war, evidently put one of her own black servants in touch with Ford, and that way was "fully apprised of every thing that transpired" in Libby prison; as we shall see, Green and Ford would undertake heroic measures on behalf of Union POWs during the "great escape" from Libby in 1864.[29]

Just as stirring as Ford's case is the story of William H. Brisby. A free black farmer who owned 50 acres of land in New Kent County, the industrious Brisby was also a skilled blacksmith, wheelwright, and fisherman. When the war broke out, Brisby soon earned a reputation as one of the most prominent Union men in his county. As his neighbor Warren Cumber testified, Brisby "carried Union prisoners through the rebel lines at the risk of his life and took them in a boat to Yorktown to the union lines." Brisby possessed the requisite passes to travel in and out of Richmond, and went into the heart of the city to pick up would-be fugitives. Brisby drove a cart for this risky work: fugitives would "have to lie down in the cart" and Brisby would "cover them with something," and then leave Richmond after dark. One night, while Brisby and his friend Thomas Fox were waiting in Richmond for some refugees to meet them, they were arrested. Fox was let go but Brisby was thrown in Castle Thunder, and when nothing could be proven against him, he was released. Like so many other loyalists, Brisby was undeterred by this brush with the law and went right back to work helping Unionists flee the Confederacy. By the end of the war he had helped more than 100 persons through the rebel lines.[30]

While the collusion of supposed Confederates like Erasmus Ross and the steadfastness of African American Unionists such as Robert Ford and William Brisby made it possible for a steady trickle of Union inmates to flee Libby and other Richmond prisons, other kinds of "insiders" furnished Van Lew and the fugitives with strategic information. David Parker contends that Van Lew had a "trusty Union man" who was a clerk in the Adjutant-General's Department at Richmond, where "he had access to the returns showing the strength of the rebel regiments, brigades, divisions, and corps, their movements, and where they were stationed." Sharpe confirms that Van Lew extracted information directly from members of the Confederate bureaucracy itself, noting that she had "clerks in the rebel war and navy departments" in her confidence.[31]

Escapees were a source not only of military intelligence for the Union but also of propaganda against the Confederacy in the midst of a bitter war of words over which side was more barbarous to its captives. The first round in that war of words—the controversy over Lincoln's handling of Confederate privateersmen captured in the summer of 1861—had culminated by July of 1862 in an uneasy truce between the two governments. A cartel, modeled on the agreement between the United States and Britain during the War of 1812, was established requiring each side to parole prisoners of war and send them to their own lines, to await formal release when an equivalent number of men was made available for release by the enemy. A complex scale was devised to assess the relative worth of the various ranks (e.g., one colonel was worth fifteen privates) and a series of detention camps were established to house and process the parolees. Though the exchange system functioned to reduce—albeit temporarily—the prison populations in places such as Richmond, it was characterized from the start by a spirit of distrust and suspicion that prevailed on each side. Reports from released prisoners in the Northern press revealed that the parole process itself came with risks—one soldier freed in August related that he and his comrades had undergone a strenuous and circuitous march from Richmond to the exchange point, Aiken's Landing, on which 20 of his comrades had died from exhaustion. The fact that Union officers Oakley, Murphy, et al. had found captivity so intolerable that they chose the risks of flight rather than trust the Confederates to abide by the cartel was powerful testimony to the dire condition of Union prisoners in the South. For the duration of the cartel, Northern newspapers such as the *New York Times* featured a steady stream of reports from parolees and escapees alike on the "outrages against civilization" perpetrated by the Confederate prison system, stoking enmity and prompting public calls for Union reprisals against Confederate prisoners.[32]

The time and money Van Lew and her compatriots expended on behalf of the Union prisoners of the city was, in other words, well spent, as it yielded military and political dividends for the Union. Equally important were Van Lew's efforts to sustain the morale of the Unionist civilians of the city. By acts of charity to "many families of plain people," according to George H. Sharpe, the Van Lew family encouraged their fellow Unionists to "remain true to the flag"; such acts of charity included hiring lawyers to represent Unionists who were arrested and tried for disloyalty. Indeed the Van Lew family quickly came to embody in the eyes of the Richmond's loyalists a spirit of defiant self-sacrifice. "I was informed in Richmond by the plain union people that the Van Lews marketed as regularly for Libby Prison, as they did for their own house," Sharpe would write in 1867.[33]

One of the Unionist civilians aided by Van Lew was a Philadelphian identified by Elizabeth as Miss McGonigle. McGonigle had settled in Richmond about a year before the war broke out and taken charge of a millinery shop. Like other Northern transplants, she was intimidated and harassed by secession enthusiasts. When she was threatened after refusing to walk under a Confederate flag that her neighbors had hung out, McGonigle "sought out Miss Van Lew" for protection." Van Lew took McGonigle in, to bide her time until Elizabeth could arrange for her passage North. According to Van Lew's own reminiscences, she treated McGonigle "like a lady," giving her the best room in the house and "servants to wait on her." After a few months, Van Lew arranged for McGonigle and several other Unionist civilians to make the perilous journey through the Confederate pickets, and toward Washington, D.C.[34]

The Van Lews were not alone in their generosity. Others of Richmond's elite Unionists saw fit to ameliorate the conditions of their poorer compatriots. Charles Palmer, undeterred by his imprisonment on charges of disloyalty, proceeded upon his release in the spring of 1862 to arrange for the distribution of precious greenbacks to "deserving and necessitous" Union families. His go-between in this effort was F. W. E. Lohmann. Lohmann had not yet attracted the suspicion of Confederate authorities, despite the fact that he, as early as 1862, was conducting his own pro-Union operation: along with friend Christian Burging, Lohmann conveyed Unionist civilians and Confederate deserters desperate to flee the South to the Rappahanock and Potomac Rivers so that they could proceed to cross over to Northern lines. By the spring of 1863 they had hastened some 28 families on their way to the North, relying on Lohmann's durable horses and wagons to travel as much as 60 miles in a single day. Sometime during 1863, Lohmann would begin collaborating with William Rowley, the latter testified, in "getting Union men and prisoners out of the Confederacy." Van Lew likely relied on one of these men to spirit McGonigle to the North.[35]

The Unionist network mobilized to help African Americans, as well as whites, flee the Confederacy. Van Lew's niece Annie recollects that sometime early in the war, Elizabeth arranged for the Van Lew butler, William Sewell, and his wife and children, to go North. According to an interview Hall gave in 1910, "Van Lew managed to get [the Sewells] through, but I don't know how. . . . The family had an awful hard time in getting north . . . it was very much like 'Uncle Tom's Cabin.' One of the children was called Eliza, and she had to ford the river, and it was almost identical with the story." The Sewells' flight ended in freedom—the family was soon "settled and had a comfortable home" in one of the Northern states. A second credible source, Dr. Emily Chenault Runyon, who was Van Lew's physician in 1900, likewise testified that Van Lew "helped runaway slaves." William Brisby, who aided Libby escapees, made even more extensive efforts on behalf of black civilians; indeed he specified that the majority of the Unionist refugees he assisted were "colored people" fleeing slavery. Brisby may well have assisted civilians in Van Lew's circle to leave Richmond.[36]

Just as escaped prisoners were a source of intelligence for the Federals and of bad press for the Confederates, so too were fugitive civilians and slaves. Union newspapers regularly featured stories on Southern civilians who had sought refuge in the North, seeing their flight as evidence that the Confederate regime was repressive and that there was a strong undercurrent of loyalism beneath the Confederate tide. The *Brooklyn Times,* for example, ran the statements of a lady and her two daughters who left Richmond in mid-August; the women opined that "the Union feeling is much stronger in Richmond than has been supposed. There are many enemies to the cause of secession there who get together quietly, and talk over the state of the country. They all long for the time when the old flag shall again float over the city." Perhaps the most influential of such refugees from the Confederacy was William Henry Hurlbut. A native of Charleston, South Carolina, who had repudiated his native region, embraced the antislavery creed, and become an editor for the *New York Times*, Hurlbut went South in June of 1861 for an interview with Confederate Secretary of War Judah P. Benjamin. After the meeting in Richmond he went to Charleston and then to Atlanta, Georgia, where he was arrested on suspicion of being a Union spy. He was eventually conveyed back to Richmond and imprisoned there until January of 1862, when he was released and kept under surveillance.[37]

From then until his August 1862 escape, he resided with a Unionist family in Richmond, and befriended the Van Lews, Charles Palmer, and William Fay (who was back in Richmond after his stint in Salisbury prison), with whose aid he effected his flight. A note written by Hurlbut on the eve of his escape reveals that he regarded prominent Richmond lawyer F. J. Cridland as a potential ally to the underground—Hurlbut asks Cridland to permit John Van Lew to read "any papers, periodicals, &c" that Hurlbut might be able to send to Richmond after his flight. By August 21, Hurlbut had, with the help of the underground, made his way out of Richmond and safely reached Washington, D.C., where he related to military authorities what he knew of the rebel forces. He shortly thereafter began a regular column in the *New York Times*, entitled "Fifteen Months at the South," in which he argued that Unionism was on the rise there, evidence of "the tendency to distintegration . . . manifesting itself behind the gleaming array of Southern bayonets allied for war."[38]

While Van Lew, Palmer, Lohmann, Rowley, Fay, and others worked on behalf of Federal prisoners and Unionist civilians in 1862, their compatriot Samuel Ruth worked on a different front, at the most improbable and risky of the underground's activities. As superintendent of the Richmond, Fredericksburg, and Potomac Railroad, which ran from Richmond through Henrico, Hanover, and Caroline counties to a terminus five miles south of Fredericksburg, Ruth was in charge of a vital supply line of Robert E. Lee's army. Conveniently, the terminal of the RF and P railroad stood at Eighth and Broad Streets, not far from the New Market; as historian Meriwether Stuart has put it, Ruth "did not have far to go, if he wished to enjoy the food and *Gemutlichkeit* [good cheer] of the Lohmann restaurant, or to consult its host on some problem connected with their secret service." Naturally, Ruth would have been divested of his important position had he not masqueraded as an ardent Confederate. But beneath the veneer of loyalty to the rebellion Ruth masterminded a series of schemes—ones he hoped were undetectable—to reduce the efficiency of the railroad and thus slow the movements of Lee's army. The painstaking research of Stuart has established that Ruth's trains inexplicably ran much more slowly than they could have when transporting Confederate brigades during the spring campaigns of 1862. Others of Ruth's management decisions, such as tardiness in repairing key bridges, his reducing the number of railroad employees, and giving priority to private freight over military supplies, likewise inhibited the operations of the railroad in 1862. These machinations prompted Robert E. Lee to accuse Ruth in January of 1863 of operating the railroad "without zeal or energy." But Ruth proved adept at deception, making sure that periods of poor performance by his railroad were interspersed with periods of evident efficiency, and that powerful Confederate friends, such as the RF and P's owner Peter V. Daniel Jr., remained convinced of Ruth's devotion to the "Cause."[39]

Although Richmond's loyalists labored assiduously for the Union during the summer and fall of 1862, the Federal high command still refrained from attempting to recruit spies and scouts from among them. As we have seen, during McClellan's tenure as head of Army of the Potomac, spymaster Allan Pinkerton had relied for his intelligence gathering on "plants"—such as the ill-fated Lewis, Scully, Webster, and Lawton—who entered Richmond under disguises or assumed identities. McClellan's successor Ambrose Burnside made a promising move in appointing the able John C. Babcock to replace Pinkerton as head of his secret service, but then squandered Babcock's talents and failed to establish contact with local Unionists in Fredericksburg, during the failed Federal campaign that culminated in a devastating defeat for the Union in December of 1862. Burnside's replacement by Joseph Hooker in January of 1863 led to an immediate shake-up of Federal intelligence operations. George Henry Sharpe, a New Yorker described by one intelligence historian as "the personification of a swashbuckling nineteenth-century spymaster," was named deputy provost marshal general and chief intelligence officer. Along with assistants Babcock and John McEntee, Sharpe revolutionized Union intelligence gathering, organizing a new Bureau of Military Information that would practice "all-source intelligence"—the Bureau gathered together, interpreted, and provided comprehensive reports for Hooker on the information brought to it by sources such as the cavalry, balloonists, and Signal Corps. For all his innovations, Sharpe was slow to depart from his predecessors' practice of using Northern agents rather than Southern Unionists as spies. In March of 1863 Sharpe dispatched an agent named

Joseph H. Maddox to be his "listening post" at Richmond. Maddox's performance was disappointing; there is no evidence that he made contact with the Richmond underground, and secrets he promised to "worm out" of the Confederate government never materialized. Maddox would work in isolation as the only Federal intelligence agent in Richmond for almost a year, until the Federals finally saw fit to recruit Van Lew and her compatriots.[40]

The Richmond underground, then, spent the better part of 1862 and 1863 improvising, working without direction or compensation from the Union army. The efforts of Van Lew and others on behalf of prisoners became much more urgent and hazardous as Confederates lashed out against Lincoln's emancipation measures, the prison cartel broke down, the inmate population grew dramatically, and conditions within the prisons deteriorated. The news that Lincoln had issued a preliminary emancipation proclamation on September 22, 1862—declaring that slaves in states still in rebellion on January 1, 1863, shall from then on be "forever free"—fell like a "firebrand into rebeldom." The *Richmond Enquirer* frothed that the edict ordained "servile insurrection" and called Lincoln a "savage" given to the "darkest excesses." The Virginia legislature passed a resolution granting immunity to any person who killed any parties found on the "sacred soil," armed or unarmed, aiding to carry out the "fiendish purposes" of the proclamation. In other words, it gave leave to Confederate citizens to hunt down and murder antislavery Unionists. A few months later, Lincoln brought to life the Confederacy's worst nightmare when he issued his final, confirmatory Emancipation Proclamation on January 1, 1863, declaring free all slaves in states, or parts of states, still in rebellion. The proclamation exempted from its terms two areas under Union control—in southeastern Louisiana and eastern Virginia—that had elected representatives to the United States Congress in 1862, and also exempted all of Tennessee and the counties slated to make up the new state of West Virginia. Contrary to the enduring myth that the proclamation only applied to areas controlled by the Confederacy, slaves were immediately freed in parts of nine Southern states that were occupied by Union troops but not included in the above exemptions; moreover, some Union commanders in Tennessee ignored that state's exemption and freed slaves there anyway. Understanding well both the practical and symbolic impact of the proclamation, Virginia's governor John Letcher spoke for his fellow Confederates when he declared before the state legislature that Lincoln's actions ended any hope for sectional reconciliation: "The alliance between us is dissolved, never, I trust, to be renewed at any time, or under any conceivable state of circumstances."[41]

Scholarly studies of Southern Unionism suggest that for the region's loyalists, the issuance of the emancipation proclamation represented a crossroads—should they embrace the new antislavery war aims of the North, and potentially be accused of promoting "servile war," or should they disavow the North's radical turn and accept the Confederacy as the lesser of two evils? To be sure, Lincoln's proclamation disillusioned many Unionists, who felt that it was a betrayal of his initial promise that the war was to be waged conservatively—for national restoration, not abolitionism. In East Tennessee, for example, the president's measure caused a schism among loyalists, with Unionist partisans such as T. A. R. Nelson concluding that "the Lincoln administration now posed a greater threat to Southern rights than the Confederacy." Significantly, Lincoln's antislavery edict produced no such attrition in the ranks of the Richmond underground. While neither Van Lew nor her compatriots have left us reflections on the Emancipation Proclamation itself, their actions speak volumes—rather than scale back their activism, Richmond's loyalists stepped it up. The underground's most daring and important work for the Union was still to come.[42]

Lincoln's proclamation reverberated through the Confederate prison system, as it prompted reprisals that crippled the already shaky exchange cartel. In response to the preliminary proclamation, Jefferson Davis decreed that captured black soldiers would not be exchanged as POWs but would instead be treated as runaway slaves and remanded to the Southern states to be enslaved, and that white officers captured while leading black troops would be charged with fomenting slave rebellion and executed. After the confirmatory proclamation, Davis extended this retaliatory measure by asserting that "all commissioned officers of the United States that may hereafter be captured by our forces in any of the States embraced in the Proclamation"—not only those leading black troops—would be punished as "criminals engaged in exciting servile insurrection." When the Confederate Congress approved these measures, Union Secretary of War Stanton called an end to all exchanges of Confederate officers; by June of 1863 official exchanges of commissioned officers had ground to a virtual halt.[43]

With the exchange system in shambles, prisons in Richmond were soon groaning with POWs; the arrival of some 3,500 Union prisoners in the wake of the rout of the Federals at Chancellorsville in May of 1863 burdened the system to the breaking point. Belle Isle, a prison camp established on a tract of land in the James River in the summer of 1862, was designed to hold 3,000 captives. The cartel had temporarily emptied it of inmates in the fall of 1862, but by the fall of 1863, Belle Isle had more than 6,300 prisoners and by early 1864 some 8,000. With the cessation of the exchange of officers in 1863, Libby prison too became appallingly overcrowded, holding as many as 4,221, more than 700 prisoners crammed into each room (compared to 100 at the pre-cartel peak). Men were "obliged to huddle on their haunches" one inmate would later recall, "like so many slaves on the middle passage." Rations were paltry. One Union surgeon testified of the hunger he witnessed at Libby, "I have seen an officer, standing by the window, gnawing a bone like a dog." Boxes of food and clothing that were sent to Richmond by Northern civilians, the United States Sanitary commission, and the Federal government were withheld, a practice Van Lew derided in her journal: "The commissaries had the beef sent to the prisoners from the United States and withheld it from them, giving them our beef, and Confederate coffee was substituted for real coffee—the officers, surgeons, stewards etc. using the latter. The sick prisoners are suffering for covering, and dying, it is said, of dysentery, but in reality of starvation." For Van Lew, the Confederates' treatment of these Union prisoners was but another species of the domination white Southerners exercised over slaves. For Southerners were "a people practised in prisons," she wrote bitterly, "aye, slave prisons and jails of the most loathsome and degraded character! Prison houses, in which no eye of justice but God's ever looks, always full of innocent victims, sold for convenience, for avarice, for lust."[44]

Meanwhile, conditions had become so desperate at Castle Thunder, where Unionist civilians and Confederate deserters were incarcerated, that the Confederate government in April of 1863 appointed a special committee of the House of Representatives to conduct an investigation into the treatment of prisoners there, particularly charges that George W. Alexander, in his fondness of corporal punishment, was guilty of "gross cruelty" to the inmates. While a majority of the committee acquitted Alexander, some members of it believed him to have abused his power. As in the cases of Belle Isle and Libby, the population of Castle Thunder far exceeded capacity—by mid-

1863 some 3,000 prisoners were detained in a space intended to hold 1,400. Among them were hundreds of African American prisoners, most of whom, historian Mark E. Neely Jr. has argued, were runaway slaves whom the authorities would try to return to their masters.[45]

For those deemed the worst offenders against the Confederacy, Castle Thunder was a place to await the gallows. Van Lew's narrative of the war is punctuated with vivid and chilling entries on the execution of Union spies by the Confederates. On September 25, 1863, a year and a half after the hanging of Timothy Webster, Union spy Spencer Kellogg Brown was executed in Richmond. Van Lew's journal entry on the subject reveals how she struggled to draw inspiration from his death. Kellogg, as the condemned man was known, was an antislavery Kansan who had done espionage work in Tennessee for U. S. Grant, only to be captured and sent to Richmond. According to Van Lew's account of Kellogg's last day, "He was an educated gentleman, sustained by firm Christian faith, and went to the gallows glorying in his fate and in being worthy to die for his country. On the way to the place of execution, followed by the crowd to see him die, he looked towards them, and then asked one who accompanied him, 'did you ever pass through a tunnel under a mountain? My passage, my death, is dark, but beyond all is light and bright.' This language is not exactly remembered, but it was beautiful. He spoke of the flowers and of glory."[46]

Castle Thunder was the hellish holding pen not only of captured male slaves and of male spies, but also of approximately 100 women, charged with treason, disloyalty, disaffection, demoralization of the soldiers, and a host of minor offences; most of them, following the precedent set in the case of "Mrs. Timothy Webster" (Hattie Lawton) were sent North after their imprisonment. The most celebrated of these female inmates were those who were arrested for posing as men. One Margaret Underwood, for example, followed her Confederate sweetheart into service by donning male attire and mustering into his company as a substitute. While Underwood faded into obscurity after her release and banishment to the North, another female soldier who was detected and imprisoned at the Castle, Madame Loreta Janeta Velasquez, made her way to Chattanooga after her release and served as a spy for the Confederacy; she went on to write a postwar memoir, *Woman in Battle*, and become something of a legend.[47]

Equally notorious among Castle Thunder's inmates was Dr. Mary Walker, a rare female surgeon for the Federal army whose insistence on wearing bloomers rather than petticoats added to her reputation as a curiousity. Union soldier Reuben Bartley, a Libby inmate, wrote of his memorable encounter with Walker. As he and some fellow inmates were being marched through the streets of Richmond, to be transferred to a new prison, they passed Castle Thunder and "saw on the balcony a Female surgeon belonging to our south western army . . . accompanied by a few other union Ladies captured in the Shenandoah Valley." The women seized the opportunity to express solidarity with the men in blue: "They told us to be of good cheer our day was coming. One of them opened out a fan and on one side was the stars & stripes." Walker, after a three-month stay in the Castle, was released on exchange for a Confederate officer. She went back to work as a contract surgeon for the United States army.[48]

More obscure are the stories and fates of the scores of female prisoners charged with disloyalty or of being "suspicious characters." Confederate prison records reveal that male civilians incarcerated for disloyalty were overwhelmingly nonelite—laborers, farmers, boatsmen, coachmen, artisans, and the like. Fragmentary evidence in newspapers such as the *Richmond Enquirer* suggests that female inmates were, likewise, people of modest means. One Laura J. Johnson, described by the *Enquirer* as "haggard, weary and ragged," had tried to follow her fiance's battalion from North Carolina to Virginia, only to run out of money. After running afoul of Confederate guards for not possessing a pass, she was sent to the Castle. Fanny Mathews, to give a second example, was a widow "living on the proceeds of a small grocery store"; the cause of her incarceration, according to the *Richmond Enquirer*, was a charge of treason. While the presence of so many women in Castle Thunder might seem to indicate that Confederate officials had gotten over any squeamishness they initially felt at imprisoning women, two telling episodes involving Richmond women—the Richmond Bread Riot of April 1863 and the arrest of Mrs. Pat Allan in July of 1863—reveal that the authorities continued to see women through the lens of social class, and that wealth brought with it a measure of political protection for women.[49]

The famous Richmond Bread Riot of 1863 was working-class women's response to intense suffering and deprivation brought on by a seeming conspiracy of dire events. The winter of 1862 through 1863 was an especially brutal one, with unusually low temperatures and heavy snowfall; snow blanketed the city as late as March 19–20, making roads virtually impassable. Basic foodstuffs were in short supply and prices were exorbitant, with flour at $40 a barrel, turkeys $15 apiece. In order to feed and equip the starving soldiers, the army "impressed" or seized the food and matériel of civilians; the military was legally required to pay a "fair price" for such goods but more often than not failed to properly compensate civilians for it. Elizabeth notes in her journal that horses were especially vulnerable to seizure by the army; "frequently not a horse was to be seen on the streets, except those in Government employ." The Van Lews devised clever expedients to dodge the impressment agents, hiding their horse first in the smokehouse and then in their very residence: "[we] spread straw upon the study floor, and he accepted at once his position and behaved as though he thoroughly understood matters, never stamping loud enough to be heard."[50]

For those lacking the resources of the Van Lews, subsistence itself was a challenge. Cash was hard to come by and wages could not keep pace with inflation. Women clamored for factory jobs at places like the Tredegar Iron Works, though the wages were inadequate ($2.40 a day) and the work dangerous. On March 13, 1863, an explosion at the Confederate ordnance lab on Brown's Island took the lives of at least 45 and injured 23 others, including a nine-year-old girl who had been among those workers filling cartridges with gunpowder.[51]

With the threat of famine hanging like a dark cloud over the city, a group of 200 to 300 women convened on April 1, at Belvidere Hill Baptist Church on Oregon Hill, to share their grievances and make a plan for ameliorating conditions; the meeting was presided over by Mary Jackson, the wife of a sign painter with one son in the Confederate army. The women chose from among their ranks a committee to go to Capitol Square the following day to call on Governor Letcher himself, and make the case that they deserved to obtain food from the government storehouses at the same low prices the government paid civilians when it impressed goods from them. On April 2, when the committee reported back that their meeting with Letcher had proven fruitless and that he had ushered them out empty handed, the crowd of women became enraged, and made its way out of Capitol Square down Main Street, shouting out a battle cry of "Bread!" James Craig, a Scots Unionist who lived on Main Street and saw the riot firsthand, fled the city shortly afterward and upon making it to Union lines offered the following account to Colonel George Sharpe: "Armed with axes and hatchets, and the ringleader Mrs. Jackson with a pistol, they commenced an attack on the provision stores and with the help of some blacks carried off the flour, bacon&c. An attack was also made on clothing and shoe stores. . . . The city guard was ordered on the ground and Mayor Mayo read the riot act. . . . Governor Letcher then made his appearance and addressed them saying, that the proceedings were disgraceful to the Southern Confederacy." Only when Jefferson Davis himself arrived on the scene with a detachment of Confederate troops, and warned the rioters that if they did not disperse in five minutes they would be fired upon, did the crowd break up.[52]

The response of the Confederate authorities, press, and elite to the riot reflect a distinct lack of empathy for the poor, a virulent sexism, and deep anxiety about the machinations of the "secret enemies" of the South. Confederate officials quickly went into damage control mode: the city council ruled that the riot was motivated by "devilish and selfish motives" and the War Department ordered that neither the telegraphs nor newspapers send out word of the riot for fear of humiliating the Confederacy and stoking further acts of opposition to it. Forty-seven individuals were arrested and processed through the Mayor's Court at city hall; at least twelve were convicted. The press described the accused in most negative of terms—Mary Jackson was, according to the *Richmond Examiner*, "a good specimen of a forty year old Amazon, with the eye of the Devil" and her fellow rioters "prostitutes, professional thieves, Irish and Yankee hags and gallows birds from all lands." This motley crew had been incited to riot, the *Examiner* went on, by "emissaries of the Federal Government." "For sometime past the Northern press has teemed with intimations of some wonderful secret machinery which was at work to overthrow the South. This is what they meant." Northern newspapers countered this charge by arguing that the riot was the work not of outside agitators but of respectable Southern women who had been driven to desperation by a government criminally insensitive to their needs.[53]

What role if any the Richmond underground had in the riot, and the degree to which the rioters had Unionist sentiments, is unclear. We can safely surmise that Van Lew felt a keen sympathy for the rioters, as her journal entry for January 1864 contains the following lament: "Alas for the suffering of the very poor! Women are begging for bread with tears in their eyes, and a different class from ordinary beggars. . . . There is a starvation panic upon the people." The *Richmond Examiner* found it suspicious that many of the those who were arrested for rioting were able to employ counsel during their trials and then to post bail; given Van Lew's documented generosity to poor Unionists it is plausible that she and the Richmond underground furnished money to help defend and win the freedom of some of the accused rioters.[54]

A few months after the riot, the issue of women's loyalty and accountability was again being debated in Richmond, as the case of Mary Caroline Allan hit the newspapers. Mary was a Cincinnati-born woman, who by virtue of her marriage to Patterson Allan, had become a member of one of the wealthiest and most respectable families in Richmond. She was arrested on July 18, 1863, charged with treasonable correspondence with the enemy: she had allegedly written letters to parties in the North, most notably the Reverend Morgan Dix of New York, brother of Union General John A. Dix, divulging the identities of Northerners who supported the Confederate cause and conveying observations on military movements and other strategic matters. Richmonders thronged the courthouse for the duration of her protracted trial, which received painstaking coverage in the city's dailies. In deference to her social position and entreaties from her husband, General Winder refrained from incarcerating Allan in Castle Thunder and instead had her detained in the St. Francis de Sales convent of the Sisters of Charity. Under the headline "HER WEALTH TOO MUCH FOR CASTLE THUNDER," the *Richmond Examiner* fumed that Allan's having chosen to "prostitute [her] position to the basest of crimes" and did not deserve special treatment. But the *Examiner's* attempt to prosecute Allan in the court of public opinion proved ineffectual. She was ably defended by her two highpowered attorneys—George W. Randolph and James Lyons—who cast sufficient doubt on her authorship of the letters that Judge James D. Halyburton freed her on a $100,000 bail bond, and sent her to the Allan family plantation in Goochland County to wait for a retrial that, thanks to endless postponements, never took place.[55]

It was not only in Richmond that elite Southern women used their social standing as a political shield. Thomas G. Dyer's recent study of Atlanta, Georgia, has revealed that a Unionist secret circle—remarkably similar in its composition and activities to the Richmond underground—was at work on behalf of Union prisoners there. Dyer has found that while the Atlanta press was quick to condemn female Unionists who catered to Federal prisoners, the Confederate authorities were "unprepared for the complicity of women," especially elite ones, in Unionist activities and therefore ineffectual at putting a stop to them. Two women of the Atlanta secret circle—Cyrena

Stone and Mary Hinton—were arrested in August 1862 and brought before a military court. Though each one was in fact a devout Unionist, Stone, because of her family's respectability, was treated with deference by the court and exonerated while Hinton, who lacked social connections, was interrogated harshly and kept under surveillance for the rest of the war.[56]

The disposition of Allan's case and the Stone/Hinton episode shed light on why Elizabeth Van Lew herself was not ensnared by Confederate authorities and sent to Castle Thunder for her treasonous activities in 1862 through 1863. Elizabeth was not only protected by her own skills at deception—she was also insulated by the ideology of Southern nationalism itself. Confederate authorities remained constrained by their own propaganda, which posited that elite Southern ladies had a natural and unimpeachable devotion to the "Cause" and that disloyalty was a disease that only afflicted the riffraff. Moreover, Southern officials feared that heavy-handed treatment of elite women suspected of Unionism would be a public relations nightmare—undercutting the case Jefferson Davis and others made that the Confederacy abided by the rules of "civilized warfare" while the Yankees had degenerated into savagery toward civilians. Perhaps it is fitting that Union General Benjamin "the Beast" Butler—in Southern eyes, the embodiment of Yankee "barbarity" toward Confederate ladies—would be the first military official on either side to recognize just how potent a force Elizabeth Van Lew's patriotism was.

5

Elizabeth and "The Beast"

BUTLER FINDS HIS SPY

BY DECEMBER OF 1863—THE MONTH IN WHICH HE FIRST MADE CONTACT WITH Elizabeth Van Lew—Benjamin Butler was the Union man most loathed by the Confederacy. He owed this notoriety to a series of actions, dating back to the first year of the war, that seemed calculated to strike at Confederate morale and to imperil Southern civilians. In May of 1861, while in command of Fort Monroe on the Virginia coast, Butler had—without fully appreciating the consequences of his actions—initiated a sea change in Union policy regarding slavery. When three slaves who escaped their sentence of hard labor on Confederate fortifications made it to Butler's lines, he dubbed them "contraband of war" rather than returning them to their Southern masters. Butler was no abolitionist; indeed he was an ardent Democrat, who had wanted Jefferson Davis to be that party's candidate in the 1860 presidential election. His seizure of the slave "contrabands," as all fugitive slaves who made it to Union lines would soon be known, was entirely pragmatic—why should enslaved blacks be permitted to labor for the Confederacy when they could be doing so for the Union? Butler's "confiscation" of these slaves inspired Congress's own first Confiscation Act of August 1861, which authorized the Union army's seizure of slaves used for Confederate military purposes, and paved the way for the North's eventual embrace of emancipation as a "military necessity." For Confederates, confiscation itself was an outrage, an abrogation of the rules of civilized war.[1]

Butler had more "outrages" in store for the South. In April of 1862, following Commodore David Farragut's capture of New Orleans, Butler was named commander of the Union occupying forces in the crescent city. He soon earned the wrath of its Confederate occupants by cracking down on insurgent sentiment, ordering the execution of a rebel who tore down the American flag and the arrest of the mayor and his recalcitrant cronies. He also defied the exchange cartel by refusing to release prisoners in New

Orleans who had been paroled. But the coup de grace was Butler's General Order No. 28, or "Woman Order." On May 15, 1862, he decreed that any Confederate woman who "by word, gesture, or movement" insulted Union soldiers would be "held liable to be treated as a woman of the town plying her avocation"—regarded, in other words, as a prostitute. Butler defended this measure, as he had confiscation, on pragmatic grounds. Complaints were pouring in from his soldiers that Southern ladies sneered, shrieked, and spit at them, avoided them on the streets for fear of "contamination" and even emptied chambers of water onto them from the balconies above. Butler feared that any effort to round up and arrest such ladies would "be a source of perpetual turmoil" and even cause riots, so he issued his Order No. 28 as a deterrent, intended to put a stop to such insolence and make arrests unnecessary. Butler would later write in his memoirs that his gambit was a total success, that "all the ladies in New Orleans forebore to insult our troops because they didn't want to be deemed common women."[2]

Needless to say, Southerners did not accept the notion that the order was a well-intentioned deterrent. Instead, the Confederate authorities and press raised a howl against Butler, reading his order as an "instigation to the violation of the women of New Orleans." Butler had gone far over the line. Jefferson Davis thundered that Butler's actions in New Orleans rendered him a "felon, deserving of capital punishment. I do order that he be no longer considered or treated simply as a public enemy but as an outlaw or common enemy of mankind, and that in event of his capture the officer of the capturing force do cause him to be immediately executed by hanging." Civilians seconded this plea; Butler wrote wryly in his memoirs: "a reward of ten thousand dollars was offered for my head; and a gentle, soft-hearted little Southern lady published that she wanted to subscribe her mite [contribute money] to make the reward sixty thousand dollars, so that my head would be sure to be taken." Criticism was not restricted to the South; Northern newspapers such as the *New York Times* took issue with Butler's measure, and the British Parliament felt compelled to condemn it.[3]

Historian Drew Faust has shown that Butler's infamous order revealed that the war had transformed women's roles and status; Butler "held women accountable for their actions in the public sphere" and did not permit them to claim political immunity on the grounds of gender, class, or race. He recognized that their partisan displays had "substantive meaning."[4] While Butler's willingness to punish women for their political disloyalty has occa-

"A reward of ten thousand dollars
was offered for my head."
Benjamin "the Beast" Butler (LIBRARY
OF CONGRESS).

sioned much comment from scholars, his willingness to reward them for
their loyalty has largely gone unnoticed. The infamous Beast would be a sort
of patron saint for Elizabeth Van Lew.

Butler's recruitment of Van Lew had its origins in a daring prison break that
the Richmond underground facilitated at the close of 1863. On December
8, two Union soldiers—"Captain Harry S. Howard" (the alias for Harry
Catlin, a scout for Butler's army) and John R. McCullough, an assistant
surgeon for the First Wisconsin Infantry (captured at Chickamauga)—escaped from the hospital of Libby Prison. McCullough, as he would later
reveal to the Northern press, had been sent to the hospital for a minor
illness and was visited shortly after his arrival by a "young lady of the city,"
bearing a bag of what purported to be fine Virginia tobacco. The lady was
Josephine Holmes, daughter of Unionist Arnold B. Holmes. At the bottom
of the bag McCullough found a note with the words "Would you be free?
Then be prepared to act. Meet me tomorrow at—." The next day Holmes
again visited the hospital and whispered to McCullough a plan for his escape;
she told him that he might arrange to have a single comrade join him.[5]

Josephine Holmes, although a mere 15 years of age, was acting as a representative of the Richmond underground. Like many other prominent loyalists, the Holmes family had both Northern and Southern roots—Josephine's father Arnold was a native of Virginia, but he had married a Pennsylvania woman, Elmira. Before the war, the couple lived for a time in Ohio, where Arnold plied his trade as an engineer, and where Josephine was born. By the time of the 1860 census the Holmeses had moved to Philadelphia, Pennsylvania; they seem to have returned to Arnold's native state and settled in Richmond on the very eve of secession. It may be that the Holmes's Philadelphia connections formed the basis for a friendship with the Van Lews.[6]

On a day Josephine Holmes had appointed, McCullough resorted to a risky and unseemly gambit, one that other prisoners had tried in the past— he pretended to be dead. With the help of Howard and three other inmates, McCullough was laid out as a corpse, covered with a blanket, and conveyed to the dead house (a makeshift morgue on the hospital grounds), where he lay, as still as he could, from midday until dusk. While their comrades distracted the guards with a sham fight, McCullough and Howard passed out of the hospital and proceeded to a place designated by Holmes; she "told them to follow her at a distance, keeping in sight her white handkerchief." She in this way led the fugitives to the house of her father, Arnold; at about midnight on the eighth Burnham Wardwell came to the Holmes house and conveyed McCullough and Howard to the home of William Rowley, where they would find refuge for ten days. Rowley, with the help of Unionist railroad superintendent Samuel Ruth, procured for them—for the tidy sum of $3,000 Confederate dollars—passes to enable them to exit the city, while Unionist ladies fashioned suits for them out of rebel blankets to serve as disguises. Rowley then led the two men through the Confederate lines to the Potomac river, from where they proceeded to the provost marshal's office in Washington, D.C. The Washington press reported the dramatic tale, and by January 28, 1864, the story of McCullough and Howard's escape had hit the Richmond papers. An article in the *Dispatch* lamented that "The 'Union people' of Richmond, who made the suits of clothing and obtained passports for McCullough and Howard, will rejoice to learn of their successful journey" and asked, leadingly, "By the way, are not some of them [the Union people] known to the detectives?" Alarmed that deceased Yankee officers so often came up missing, the prison authorities created the office of "dead-house keeper"; "after this the dead were under surveillance as well as the living," remembers Libby inmate Willard Glazier.[7]

While Confederate Richmond fretted about secret enemies, the Union high command at last established contact with them. After arriving safely in Washington, D.C., Howard reported to General Butler at Fort Monroe. Butler had been recalled by Lincoln from his New Orleans post in December of 1862; a year later Lincoln yielded to pressure from Butler supporters—particularly Radical Republicans who saw Butler as a convert to their cause, thanks to the general's contraband policy and his support for enlisting blacks as Union soldiers—and gave the embattled Butler a new post. On November 2, Butler was placed in charge of the Department of Virginia and North Carolina; from his headquarters at Fort Monroe he would preside over an extensive swath of Union-occupied eastern Virginia—including the peninsula between the York and James Rivers up to Williamsburg and the coastal cities of Norfolk and Portsmouth—and direct the operations of the Army of the James against Richmond. To his credit, Butler immediately recognized the utility of recruiting Richmond insiders to provide him with strategic information.[8]

On December 19, 1863, shortly after Howard and McCullough made it to Union lines, Butler wrote a confidential letter to Charles O. Boutelle of the United States Coast Survey Office in the Federal capital. Boutelle, a native of Massachusetts, was a highly respected topographical engineer; as commander of the steamer *Chancellor Bibb,* he had rendered Butler "most effective aid" in 1861 on the Union fleet's journey from Hatteras to New Orleans. Just how Boutelle knew Van Lew remains a mystery. Butler's letter began: "My Dear Boutelle, You will find enclosed a letter from a dear friend of yours in Richmond. I am informed by the bearer that Miss Van Lieu [sic] is a true union woman as true as steel. She sent me a bouquet, so says the letter carrier." Although Butler does not explicitly identify the "letter carrier," both the timing of the exchange and the fact that Butler would later refer to this unnamed letter carrier as "doctor" strongly suggests that it was John R. McCullough who served as Van Lew's emissary and who revealed to Butler the extent of the Richmond underground's operations. Butler, for his part, wrote Boutelle to confide a plan: "Now, I much want a correspondent in Richmond, one who will write me of course without name or description of the writer, and she need only incur the risk of dropping an ordinary letter by flag of truce in the Post Office, directed to a name at the

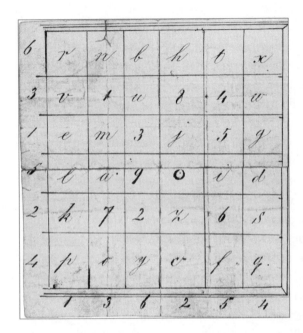

"I much want a correspondent in Richmond."
Cipher that Van Lew used to encrypt her dispatches
(NEW YORK PUBLIC LIBRARY).

North. Her messenger thinks Miss Van Lieu [sic] will be glad to do it." (By mutual agreement between the two warring governments, "flag-of-truce" boats took civilians and correspondence back and forth between the South and the North.) Butler went on to ask Boutelle whether it was safe to send a man to Van Lew to ask her to take on the role of correspondent. He could offer Van Lew money as an inducement, Butler pointed out, but "from what I hear of her I should prefer not to do it, as I think she would be actuated to do what she does by patriotic motives only."[9]

Boutelle evidently offered Butler the reassurances he sought, for Butler's next move was to send H. S. Howard back to Richmond to seek out Van Lew. Sometime in January of 1864 Howard arrived at William Rowley's house, where he had been secreted after his prison break, and there he formally recruited Rowley and Van Lew as Federal agents. He delivered to Van Lew what appeared to the uninitiated to be a letter from one "James Ap. Jones" to his "dear Aunt"; in reality, when acid and heat were applied to the letter a second missive, in invisible ink, became visible. The letter was addressed to "My dear Miss" and read, "The doctor who came through and spoke to me of the bouquet said that you would be willing to aid the Union cause by furnishing me with information if I would devise a means. You can write through Flag of Truce, directed to James Ap. Jones, Norfolk, the letter being written as this is, and with the means furnished by the messenger who brings this. I cannot refrain from saying to you, although personally unknown, how much I am rejoiced to hear of the strong feeling for the Union which exists in your own breast and among some of the ladies of Richmond." At Rowley's house Howard instructed Van Lew on the use of a "peculiar kind of ink and writing materials"—including a cipher so that she could encrypt her messages—that would permit her to write letters to Butler. Remarkably, the key to Van Lew's secret cipher—a square chart for converting letters and numbers into code—survives among her papers. According to the recollections of her niece Annie, Elizabeth "always carried [the key] in the case of her watch." Dispatches "were written with a colorless liquid which was kept in a small bottle and looked like water but which with the application of milk came out perfectly black."[10]

Van Lew would henceforth serve not only as Butler's chief correspondent in the rebel capital but as the head of his spy network. William Rowley would later testify that Howard employed him "to act as a spy upon the enemy which I did reporting to one Miss Elizabeth Van Lew." It has repeatedly been claimed in modern treatments of Van Lew that even as she was enlisted by Butler, she was simultaneously in the service of Major General George Meade, funneling him information while assuming the code name "Babcock."[11] Such claims rest on a slender foundation, namely the survival in Van Lew's papers of a February 4, 1864, letter from Meade to "Mr. Babcock" asking "Have you any information showing over what roads the enemy move their supply wagons from Battlefield?" To draw the conclusion that Van Lew *was* Babcock is to overlook the fact that John C. Babcock, Sharpe's right hand man in the Bureau of Military Intelligence, reported directly to Meade; indeed, Babcock's own papers reveal that Meade routinely wrote letters addressed to him, as "Mr. Babcock," with queries similar to that found in the February 4, 1864, letter in Van Lew's possession. It strains credulity to suppose that the bureau would have created needless confusion by giving Van Lew a code name that was the real name of a real spymaster! Moreover, the dispatches Van Lew sent and received, unlike the Meade missive, were encoded. Finally, historians Edwin Fishel and William B. Feis have established that Meade's Army of the Potomac did not make contact with Van Lew until the spring of 1864. In short, it is probable that the February 4 note from Meade was intended for John C. Babcock, and fell into Van Lew's hands later. Butler, and not Meade, was responsible for mobilizing Van Lew's network.[12]

The arrangement between Butler and the Richmond underground was quickly imperiled, as Howard was captured on his way back to Fort Monroe and imprisoned at Castle Thunder. By now a master of escape, Howard found, after two weeks of confinement, a way out of Castle Thunder and once again relied on the assistance of Rowley and Ruth to reach Union lines. The two men furnished Howard with some $1,200 to enable him to bribe Confederate officers for passes out of the city; procured for him the assistance of a railroad engineer to take him Hamilton Crossroads; and arranged for a guide to take him from there to the house of a Unionist named "Silverson" (Isaac Silver) on the Rappahanock. As Ruth would later put it in a postwar claim for remuneration, "in accomplishing all this I was, of course, subjected not only to considerable expense, but also incurred a great deal of risk."[13]

Meanwhile, Van Lew's first intelligence dispatch—written in code and invisible ink on a seemingly innocent letter from "Eliza A. Jones" to her "Uncle"—made its way to Benjamin Butler. The January 30, 1864, dispatch warrants a full transcription here:

> DEAR SIR:
>
> It is intended to remove to Georgia very soon all the Federal prisoners; butchers and bakers to go at once. They are already notified and selected. Quaker knows this to be true. Are building batteries on the Danville road.
>
> This from Quaker: Beware of new and rash council. Beware! This I send you by direction of all your friends. No attempt should be made with less than 30,000 cavalry, from 10,000 to 15,000 infantry to support them, amounting in all to 40,000 or 45,000 troops. Do not underrate their strength and desperation. Forces could probably be called into action in from five to ten days 25,000, mostly artillery. Hoke's and Kemper's brigades gone to North Carolina; Pickett's in or about Petersburg. Three regiments of cavalry disbanded by General Lee for want of horses. Morgan is applying for a 1,000 choice men for a raid.[14]

The dispatch was hand delivered to Butler on February 4 by a messenger Van Lew had sent North with the help of a guide arranged and paid for by Arnold Holmes. According to Butler's transcription of their exchange, the messenger—whom the general referred to only as "my boy"—had been staying at the Van Lew home and had volunteered to act as her emissary. "Miss Lizzie told me . . . to tell you of the situation of the army," the messenger began. He went on to reveal that the primary source of Van Lew's troop estimates was Charles Palmer, and that it was Palmer's opinion that "Richmond could be taken easier now than at any other time since the war began." The messenger also conveyed the advice of "Quaker," who thought that the best way to execute a raid on Richmond to rescue the prisoners was to make a diversionary feint on Petersburg and then attack the Confederate capital from the west. When queried by Butler about the identity of this "Quaker," the messenger said only that his mysterious informant did "not wish to be known by any other name." According to scholar Meriwether Stuart, "Quaker" may well have been the code name for Rowley, who was a Dunkard—a member of a dissenting sect that Rowley's contemporaries might have confused for the Quakers—and who had by his own admission "an urge to self-concealment." And the "boy" messenger, Stuart has surmised, was in all probability Rowley's son Merritt.[15]

Van Lew's dispatch together with her messenger's elaborations confirmed what Butler already suspected—in order to deal with the overcrowding of the Richmond prisons, the Confederacy was going to ship inmates from Belle Isle and elsewhere to a new facility at a far remove from the battlegrounds of Virginia and from potential rescue operations by the Federal Army: the soon-to-be infamous Andersonville Prison, in Georgia. Butler immediately sent Van Lew's report to Secretary of War Stanton with the appeal "Now, or never, is the time to strike." The controversial general proposed to "make a dash with 6,000 men," the first purpose of which, as he would later state in his memoirs, was "to release the large number of prisoners [in Richmond]." The liberated prisoners would make, Butler reckoned wishfully, a "very great addition to our force" and aid his army in the second object of the "dash"—"to capture the Confederate Cabinet and Mr. Jefferson Davis." Stanton's ready endorsement of this heady scheme testifies both to the trust the Union high command reposed in Van Lew's network and to how efficacious the loyalists had been in keeping the North apprised of conditions in the rebel capital; thanks in good part to the Richmond underground, the desperate state of the Union prisoners was well known to the Northern press and citizenry, and President Lincoln and his administration were under enormous public pressure to take action on behalf of the suffering inmates.[16]

Butler delegated the execution of the important mission to Brigadier General Isaac J. Wistar. Having received intelligence that Bottom's Bridge—that crossed the Chickahominy 12 miles east of Richmond—was being guarded by a mere 20 Confederate pickets and that there were practicable fords on either side of it, Wistar opted to send a cavalry brigade to take the bridge and hold it until he could send the infantry through. Wistar's instructions to Colonel S. P. Spear of the Eleventh Pennsylvania Cavalry reveal that the Union high command was falling into the very trap Van Lew's dispatch had cautioned them against—that of "underrating" the Confederates. With more than a touch of hubris, Wistar told Spear that if he took Bottom's Bridge as planned, Union forces would be able to enter Richmond and "destroy the navy-yard ... attend to the Libby Prison ... seize the bridge to Belle island, liberating the prisoners ... capture Jeff. Davis at his residence ... destroy the Tredegar Iron Works and numerous public buildings, factories and store-houses adjacent"—all in about five hours![17]

To insure that Wistar's charge went well, Butler asked General Sedgewick, filling in as head of the Army of the Potomac for the ailing George Meade, to arrange a diversionary demonstration of troops on the Rapidan River to draw Confederate forces away from Richmond. Sedgewick intially demurred, thinking Butler's plan "childish"—a hastily planned raid would spoil the Union chances for a surprise attack in the future. In response to pressure from his own superiors, Sedgewick relented, and issued orders for the First Corps to demonstrate at Raccoon's Ford and the Second Corps at Morton's Ford, on the Rapidan. "The whole thing was very sudden, all round, and none of *our* fish," complained Colonel Theodore Lyman, a staff officer at Meade's headquarters. On February 6, the Federal divisions sallied forth, only to be met in force by Confederate Lieutenant General Richard Ewell's Second Corps of the Army of Northern Virginia; after sporadic skirmishing, the Federals withdrew on February 7.[18]

Unfortunately, the diversion was in vain, for Wistar's action was from the start an abject failure. At 2:50 A.M. on February 7, 1864, Federal troops reached Bottom's Bridge, only to find some four batteries of Confederate artillery and three regiments of infantry waiting there to fend off the "surprise" attack. The rebel force had already destroyed the bridge itself, blocked the road with felled trees, and dug extensive earthworks and rifle-pits. "Owing to the peculiar darkness of the night," Wistar later reported, "it was impossible to attack until daylight"; when the sun came up the Federals made a charge on the bridge by the only approach, a "long causeway flanked on either hand by an impassable marsh," and were repulsed, with a loss of nine killed and wounded. Knowing that without Bottom's Bridge their "object of surprising the city must necessarily be defeated," Wistar's troops began their ignominious withdrawal toward Fort Monroe.[19]

A disappointed Butler wrote his superiors that Wistar's "brilliantly and ably executed movement" had failed "only from one of those fortuitous circumstances against which no foresight can provide": a Yankee deserter, William Boyle, had tipped the Confederates off about the Federal advance. According to the *Richmond Examiner*, Boyle's tip "obtained consistency from a number of circumstances, and impressed the authorities to such a degree that a disposition of forces was made to anticipate the supposed designs of the enemy"; civilians interrogated by Wistar's men confirmed that some 16 hours before the standoff at Bottom's Bridge, the Confederates had begun making preparations to repulse the Federal dash. One of the "circumstances" that may have lent credence to Boyle's information was the fact that on January 29, 1864, the Confederates had captured three men—Burnham Wardwell, John Hartwell, and James Hines—trying to pass from Richmond to Union lines. According to a letter from R. C. Shiver, at Major General Wade C. Hampton's headquarters in King and Queen County, to Secretary of War Benjamin, the Confederates were as early as January 29 in daily expectation of an enemy raid from Yorktown against Richmond; the three captured men were, Shiver averred, "making their way to the enemy doubtless with information concerning this Raid." While Butler was eager to lay the failure of the raid at the feet of the uncooperative General Sedgewick and the traitorous deserter, the Richmond loyalists who called for the raid might have noted that Butler himself disregarded their estimate that some 45,000 troops would be required for a successful raid and Quaker's advice that the Federals mount their attack from the west, rather than the east, of the city.[20]

While the imprisonment of her close associate Wardwell and the failure of Wistar's raid were setbacks for Van Lew, neither event weakened her resolve to aid the suffering Union inmates. Indeed, as Butler planned his ill-fated bid to rescue the prisoners from the outside, Van Lew and her fellow loyalists had laid the groundwork for a very different kind of prison break. Isaac Wistar was surely incredulous—and maybe a little embarrassed—when on February 14 two of his pickets brought him some stunning news from Richmond: more than 100 Union officers had just escaped from Libby by digging a tunnel under the street![21]

⌐⌐

The story of the Libby breakout is breathtaking and unforgettable. The engineers of the scheme were Colonel Thomas E. Rose of the Seventy-seventh Pennsylvania Infantry, who had been taken prisoner at the Battle of Chickamauga, and Major Andrew G. Hamilton of the Twelfth Kentucky Cavalry, who had been captured at Jonesboro, Tennessee, in September of 1863. Both were from the start obsessed with devising a means of escape, and made as thorough a study as possible of the layout of Libby. Essentially, Libby was a rectangular box divided into three stories and partitioned from east to west into three sections. The six rooms on the upper floors housed inmates, while the three ground floor rooms served special purposes: the west room was an office and sleeping quarters for Confederates, the middle room was a cooking and dining room for use of the prisoners during the daytime, and the east room was the prison hospital. Below the three ground floor rooms were three cellars, equal in dimensions to the rooms above them, and separated by thick walls. The east cellar was used for storing commissary supplies such as straw. The middle cellar was subdivided, one section containing horrific cells for the confinement of troublesome prisoners and the other a space for workmen such as carpenters. The west cellar was subdivided into quarters for black prisoners and into a cooking room. Rose and Hamilton concluded that the most promising route of egress was through one of these three cellars of Libby. One afternoon on which each man had surreptitiously made his way into basement to do a little reconnaissance, the two met up and made a pact to collaborate. After conceiving and then aborting at the last minute a plan to escape through the door in the middle cellar by overpowering the sentinels there, Rose and Hamilton focused their attention on the east cellar, known because of the hordes of vermin that lived there as "Rat Hell."[22]

They soon concluded that the only way to go in and out of Rat Hell without detection was to cut a hole in the back of the kitchen fireplace in the middle ground floor room that would lead eastward into the cellar below the hospital; the fireplace was shielded by three large cooking stoves. With the help of a few officers—including Major George Fitzsimmons of the Thirtieth Indiana Infantry, Captain John Gallagher of the Second Ohio Infantry and Captain I. N. Johnston of the Sixth Kentucky Infantry—whom they had taken into their confidence, Rose and Hamilton began the nerve-wracking nocturnal work of chiseling through the fireplace diagonally to the cellar below; fortunately both Hamilton and Gallagher had been house builders by trade and knew their way around bricks and mortar. After some two weeks of digging, the men gained access to the east cellar; "It seemed as though half the battle had been won," Hamilton later wrote, "although in reality our labors were barely commenced."[23]

Determining that the best course of action was to begin their tunnel in the southeast corner of the cellar and to dig in the direction of a large sewer that passed down Canal street, Rose and Hamilton laid in some necessary supplies—a wooden spittoon in which to convey dirt out of the tunnel, some bits of candle, and some large chisels—and recruited some more officers to join in their plot. The party's first attempt was a near disaster: the tunnel the men so arduously dug was flooded by the canal that ran alongside the sewer, nearly drowning Rose. A second plan, to dig a route to a smaller sewer that ran into the main sewer, also ended in failure as the new tunnel passed under a brick furnace, and partially caved in under the weight. The weary party's third effort went no better: they tried to access a small wood-lined sewer that led from the kitchen to the main sewer, only to find that it was lined with immovable oak plank that rendered it too narrow for a man to pass through. The men had worked 39 nights for nothing, and were in the depths of despair. As Frank Moran, one of the officers who would eventually succeed in escaping, has written: "most of the party were now really ill from the foul stench in which they had lived so long. The visions of liberty that had first lured them to desperate efforts under the inspiration of Rose and Hamilton had at last faded, and one by one they lost heart and hope and frankly told Colonel Rose that they could do no more."[24]

Hamilton and Rose proved immune to despair. Sometime in late January, about a month into their fruitless labors, the men conveyed to Elizabeth

Van Lew, via prison hostler Robert Ford, Unionist Abby Green, and their connections, word of their efforts to escape. Indeed, Ford was the vital link between the prisoners and the outside world, and was instrumental to their planning, as he conveyed to them information about the network of safe houses in the city. Elizabeth's account of the Libby outbreak reveals that she and her family "knew there was to be an exit, had been told to prepare, & had one of our parlors or rather end rooms—had dark blankets nailed up at the windows & gas had been kept burning in it—very low day and night—for about 3 weeks. We were so ready for them, beds prepared in there." While Elizabeth and her mother fitted out the house to receive their fellow patriots, Hamilton and Rose struggled to turn the fortunes of the would-be escapees. Whether or not Elizabeth already knew about the planned escape when she sent her January 30, 1864, dispatch to Ben Butler is not clear. It may be that her knowledge of Rose's plans lent an urgency to her call for a Union cavalry raid on the city—if Butler's army could rescue the prisoners, they would not have to run the risk of rescuing themselves.[25]

After a careful examination of the northeast of the cellar, the two men hatched a new plan—they would tunnel under a vacant lot on the east side of Libby, a distance of some 50 to 60 feet, to an endpoint behind a board fence in a yard between two buildings that abutted the vacant lot. Rose and Hamilton assembled a party of 15 comrades willing to renew their struggle to escape; it included Captain Terrence Clark of the Seventy-ninth Illinois Infantry, Major Bedan McDonald of the One Hundred and First Ohio Infantry, and Lieutenant John C. Fislar of the Indiana Light Artillery. In addition, the tunnelers had their "silent partners"—men such as Lieutenant Colonel Harrison C. Hobart and Lieutenant John Sterling, who did not participate in the digging but knew it was going on and furnished the tunnel party supplies such as candles. Clark and McDonald successfully broke through the cellar wall on the first night and thereafter the men worked in shifts: "Usually one man would dig, and fill the spittoon with earth; upon the signal of a gentle pull, an assistant would drag the load into the cellar by the clothes-lines fastened to each side of this box, and then hide it under the straw; a third constantly fanned air into the tunnel with a rubber blanket stretched across a frame, the invention of the ingenious Hamilton; a fourth would give occasional relief to the last two; while a fifth would keep a lookout." The diameter of the tunnel averaged a little over two feet, and the longer the tunnel got, the more difficult it was to convey air to the digger;

the breathless tunnelers had also to contend with the din of 'hundreds of rats squeal[ing] all the time while they ran over the diggers almost without sign of fear." I. N. Johnston, who as we shall see got to know the tunnel better than any other man, wrote that it was "more like a grave than any place can be short of a man's last narrow home."[26]

In the eyes of Rose's men, as formidable a challenge as digging the tunnel itself was the challenge of disguising from the Confederate prison authorities the absence of the five inmates who were daily at work in the cellar. The 1,200 prisoners were counted twice a day, at about nine in the morning and four in the afternoon. Not knowing that Libby clerk Erasmus Ross was a member of the Richmond underground, the tunnelers attributed his tendency to overlook missing prisoners to his gullibility and incompetence. Rose's men believed they hoodwinked Ross with a primitive ruse: when the clerk counted the prisoners, five of those who had been among the first counted ducked down and ran toward the foot of the ranks so as to be counted again, in the place of their absent co-conspirators; this according to Moran was enough to "dethrone the reason of the puzzled clerk."[27]

The work of concealing the tunnel operation became decidedly more difficult when a small-scale prison escape prompted the Libby authorities to ratchet up their scrutiny of the inmates. On January 29, Major E. L. Bates of the Eighteenth Illinois Infantry and Captain John F. Porter Jr. of the Fourteenth New York Cavalry broke out of Libby; while Bates was recaptured, Porter, with the help of Richmond Unionists, made it to safety. "Impudence was the trump card" of Porter's escape, according to a detailed account provided by Albert D. Richardson, a Northern journalist who was an inmate at Castle Thunder. Very simply, Porter disguised himself, by shaving his beard, darkening his eyebrows and donning civilian clothes he had somehow obtained, most likely in collusion with Ross. Porter then "walked out of the prison in broad daylight, passing all the sentinels, who supposed him to be a clergyman or some other pacific resident of Richmond." For nine days, the fugitive was secreted by a "Union lady" in Richmond, as he bided his time waiting for the right opportunity to reach Union lines. At the end of that time he obtained a passport from a rebel officer and started out for the Army of the Potomac. He arrived in Washington, D.C., on February 14, 1864, just in time, according to Richardson, to claim the hand of his fiancee. "He was an enterprising bridegroom," Richardson concluded wryly.[28]

A few months after the escape, in April, Porter would reveal to the Northern press that the "Union lady" who had provided him with refuge was Mrs. John H. Quarles. Her husband, a Northerner transplanted to Richmond, accompanied Porter to Union lines and promptly enlisted in the Union army under an alias. According to Porter, the rebel authorities caught wind of this subterfuge and soon after the escape "confiscated [Quarles's] property and turned his wife and children out of doors." Somehow, Mrs. Quarles and her children—ranging in age from four months to four years— were able to flee from Richmond and make it to New York, where Porter came forward to publicize the brave refugee's "great distress" and to ask the Northern public to extend kindness and charity to her. After the war, it would come to light that a second Union lady, Abby Green, had likewise helped Porter in his escape, communicating with him while he was imprisoned—again through Robert Ford—and informing him of where to find a safe house once he had broken out. Green eluded the notice of the authorities and remained in Richmond, where, as we shall see, she would play a vital role in the tunnel escape of the Libby officers.[29]

In the wake of the Porter incident, Libby prison clerk Ross was directed not simply to count the prisoners but to undertake tedious roll calls, whereby each prisoner was required to answer to his name while stepping between a line of guards. This innovation left in the lurch the two prisoners—the aforementioned B. B. McDonald and I. N. Johnston—who happened to be digging in the cellar that day. Upon being informed by his fellow inmates that the guards were on the lookout for him, McDonald chose to give himself up, and pleaded that he had missed roll call because he had fallen asleep in the upper west room. Johnston by contrast remained hidden in the cellar, where he was brought food and drink by his fellow tunnelers, one of whom, Lieutenant Fislar, had circulated the story that Johnston had successfully escaped the prison. When it became clear that Johnston's health was endangered by the "sickening air, the deathly chill, [and] the horrible, interminable darkness" of the tunnel it was arranged that each night Johnston would creep upstairs and sleep among the prisoners, and return to the tunnel at the break of day. With the prison guards determined to account for absentees, the escape party desisted from daywork on the tunnel but "continued the nightwork with unabated industry." According to Captain James Wells of the Eighth Michigan Cavalry, those inmates who had been let in on the escape scheme began to "put themselves in readiness for the

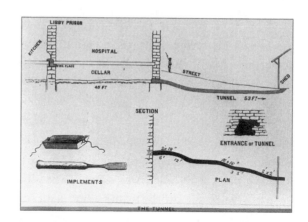

"Visions of liberty."
*The tunnel under Libby,
from a sketch made by a
prisoner there* (LIBRARY OF
VIRGINIA).

exodus," building their strength through "persistent . . . physical exercises"; "my comrade and myself once walked a distance of twenty-two miles around the room in a single day," Wells remembers.[30]

As the first week of February drew to a close, Rose and his compatriots came to the conclusion that the tunnel had traversed the requisite distance to the tobacco shed on the opposite side of the street, and sent a man down with instructions to break ground once he reached the end of the tunnel; unfortunately this experiment revealed that the passage was still too short: the digger had broken through in the open lot, perilously close to the sight lines of the nearby sentinel. Rose was called upon to repair the breach and while doing so he placed an old shoe at the point of exit; "the day afterward he looked through the prison-bars and saw the shoe lying where he had placed it, and judged from its position that he had better incline the direction of the tunnel slightly to the left." Deep in the night on February 8, after heroic exertions by Rose in particular, the men finally reached the point they desired, inside the tobacco shed, with a board fence concealing the tunnel opening from the east-side sentinels. While the tunnelers were tempted to seize the moment and leave at once, they decided to wait until the following night, so that a fresh and early start could be made. According to the reminiscences of Hamilton, "It was decided that each of the fifteen in the digging party should choose a friend to go out with him, and when the thirty had passed through the hole its entrance was to be closed by [Lieutenant Colonel] Hobart." Hobart was to lead out a second escape party the following night.[31]

"The ninth of February was a long day, and long to be remembered; never was my anxiety so great as for the setting of that day's sun," I. N. Johnston has written of the day of the great escape. "Dreary hours I feared that the cup of happiness, now so near our lips, would be rudely dashed away." Taking along bread and dried meat and whatever civilian clothes bribery, collusion, and the good offices of the Richmond underground had made available, the first escape party commenced their flight at about 7 P.M. As Hobart remembers it, "In order to distract the attention of the guard a dancing party with music was extemporized in the [cook room] . . . as the guard were under orders to fire upon a prisoner escaping, without even calling him to halt, the first men who descended into the tunnel wore that quiet gloom so often seen in the army before going into battle. It was a living drama; dancing in one part of the room, dark shadows disappearing through the chimney in another part, and the same shadows reappearing on the opposite walk." Unfortunately, the plans Rose, Hamilton, Hobart, and others had made for an orderly egress of the prisoners soon fell apart. Close to 9 P.M., as the first of the escapees were spotted from the prison windows by inmates who had caught wind of the drama unfolding in the cellar, hundreds of men began to clamor for the privilege of joining the escape party. Descending to the kitchen, which was by now supposed to be off limits to inmates and was pitch dark, these men accosted Hobart, who despite his brave efforts to restore order, could not keep them at bay. The best he could do was get them to promise that after he and the last of the party had passed out, the rope by which they descended through the chimney to the basement would be pulled up for one hour, to give the fugitives a fighting chance. After the hour had passed the rope and chimney and tunnel would be "free to all in the prison." A free *for* all ensued. Willard Glazier, one of those who struggled in vain to get out, has written that "the weak had to step aside, or rather, they were pushed aside without apology. No respect was shown to rank or justice. . . . There was no standing aside for betters." Some wily prisoners resorted to crying wolf, calling out "Guards! Guards!" to get their fellows to scurry back upstairs while they themselves made for the tunnel. This stampeding to and away from the tunnel continued until the morning of February 10, when those who remained behind covered the opening in the chimney and returned to their quarters.[32]

Libby officials were baffled and horrified to discover, at the daily morning count of inmates, that the "number of the prisoners fell alarmingly short"—

a total of 109 were missing. Prison commandant Major Turner initially assumed that the night guard had been bribed into duplicity, and accordingly
arrested and consigned to Castle Thunder the officer of the guard and the
sentinels who had been on watch. But a careful inspection of the prison by
Turner and Lieutenant LaTouche soon disclosed the tunnel; they sent a
"small negro boy" through it and watched in amazement when he emerged
at the terminus of the subterranean route. Confederate authorities immediately dispatched couriers in every direction to spread word of the escape
and doubled the number of pickets posted on the roads and bridges leading
toward the peninsula and the "embraces of Butler the Beast," as one Confederate newspaper put it. Early in the day on February 11 four escapees
were recaptured a few miles below the city; within a few days 48 others
would be rounded up and returned to prison, including tunnel mastermind
Colonel Thomas Rose himself. These unfortunate men were placed in irons
in "narrow and loathsome" cells, on bread and water rations. Even those
Libby inmates who were not part of the escape party felt the wrath of Turner
and the other prison officials, who in their anger and embarrassment were
"extremely insulting in their conduct toward the prisoners" in the weeks
after the breakout, reducing their rations, and rifling through and confis-
cating their meager stores of personal property—such as "beautiful speci-
mens of bone work" that the prisoners had whittled—and generally sub-
jecting them to constant scrutiny. "The whole thing was shameful," recalled
inmate Neal Dow.[33]

Sadly, but not surprisingly, Turner was especially barbarous in his treatment of prison worker Robert Ford, whom he suspected of complicity in
the escape. He whipped Ford "nearly to death," meting out "500 lashes."
This torture, Abby Green would later testify, the heroic Ford "bore without
ever betraying certain other persons who had aided in concealing said prisoners after their escape."[34]

The story of the escape hit the Richmond dailies on February 11, and
soon crowds of curious onlookers were visiting the "Great Yankee Wonder,"
as the tunnel, which was placed on exhibition, was called. The newspapers
naturally gloated over the recapture of certain of the Yankee fugitives—"big
fish" such as Rose—and lamented the fact that other escapees seemed to
have slipped permanently through the Confederate net. The press and prison
officials alike were especially keen on the recapture of Colonel Abel D.
Streight of the Fifty-first Indiana Infantry. For Confederates, Streight had

been at once the most reviled and most feared of Libby's inmates. He had made his name leading a raid on Rome, Georgia, in May of 1863; though the raid failed and resulted in his capture, the Confederates charged him with intimidating and destroying the property of innocent civilians. Streight's conduct in prison did nothing to repair this reputation. According to Libby inmate Albert D. Richardson, Streight "talked to the Rebel authorities with imprudent, but delightful frankness. More than once I heard him say to them: 'You dare not carry out that threat! You know our Government will never permit it, but will promptly retaliate upon your own officers, whom it holds.' " In August of 1863 Streight penned, on behalf of his fellow prisoners, a scathing assessment of conditions in Libby, especially of the "semi-starvation" of the inmates, and sent this protest to the Confederate secretary of war James Seddon; "Humanity cannot contemplate such [treatment] without feelings of deepest horror," Streight declared. While overtly protesting through official channels, Streight covertly schemed to get out. He bribed a guard in December of 1863 hoping thereby to effect his escape only to have the sentinel betray him. After this failed attempt, the tunnel success was a kind of revenge for the Indiana colonel. Richmond officials "would rather have lost half the prisoners around the city than the 'hell-hound' Streight," inmate Joseph Ferguson opined in his memoir of Libby days. The press, for its part, was convinced that Streight and the others who evaded the Confederate search parties were "laying up in the houses, or hiding-places, provided for by the disloyal element to be found in and around Richmond."[35]

The press was right—many of the escapees did find refuge with Unionists, white and black. Indeed, on the night of February 9, a handful of the fugitives—evidently following instructions that had been smuggled into the prison—made their way to Van Lew's house, and stealthily knocked on the door to the servants' rooms on Twenty-fourth Street. Van Lew's driver answered the door and heard the escaped prisoners' pleas to gain entrance to the hiding rooms that Van Lew and her mother had so carefully prepared some three weeks earlier. But because Elizabeth Van Lew was away from the house that night, her servant turned the callers away, fearing that they were Confederates in disguise sent to trick and expose the Van Lews.[36]

What would prompt Van Lew to be away from home at such a critical moment, and therefore to miss the chance to provide a safe haven for the prisoners? Nothing less than a family emergency—one that was, ironically, exacerbated by the Libby escape. On the very night of the breakout, Elizabeth was helping her brother John evade Confederate authorities. Earlier that February, John had been drafted by the Confederate army, had deserted, and had gone into hiding with a loyal family, biding his time for a chance to flee to Union lines. On the night of the ninth, knowing that a Libby escape plot was in the works but not knowing that the moment of truth was at hand for Rose et al., Elizabeth Van Lew donned a disguise—"coarse clothes—with a sunbonnet on my head & basket on my arm"—and went to visit the "kind family" that was secreting her brother. This was not the only instance in which Elizabeth so masked her identity: her cousin Anna Whitlock remembered seeing Van Lew "dress up in disguise with cotton stuffed in her cheeks" on other occasions.[37]

Though the family she visited on February 9, 1864, was poor, Van Lew wrote in her journal, they had extended her brother every comfort possible. She spent an anxious night with them, "a strange nervousness or present-ment" filling her mind all the while. On the morning of February 10, Van Lew's driver came to the house with supplies for John and his hosts—and with the revelation that the Libby prisoners had effected their escape and that he and the other servants had felt it prudent to turn those claiming to be fugitive prisoners away from the Van Lew house.[38]

This revelation greatly distressed Van Lew—both because she was con-cerned for the well-being of the Libby men and because she immediately perceived the implications of the breakout for her brother: the Confederates would shore up their pickets and redouble their vigilance along Richmond's outskirts, making it impossible for John, himself a fugitive deserter, to make it safely to Union lines. "As desperate situations sometimes require despic-able remedies," Van Lew wrote in her journal, she went straight to General Winder's office, passing along the way Confederate soldiers scanning the city for escapees. Winder received her "kindly," listening to her pleas that John was suffering from some sort of debilitating injury and therefore not fit for service. The general met with John the following morning and after trying in vain to obtain for him a medical exemption settled upon a workable plan of action, telling John "Mr. Van Lew I wish you to choose your company—choose the 18th VA Regt.; that is mine & I can protect you." John Van Lew reported for duty and by liberal generosity to his fellow soldiers (providing them with whiskey) he won over the "friendly feeling of the company." From February to May John was largely permitted to attend to his own business; it was not until May of 1864 that he was ordered to the field. As historian Meriwether Stuart has written, Van Lew's story of how she saved her brother from active service "would seem incredible, were it not confirmed circumstantially by the muster rolls of Company C and by the medical records found in the compiled military service record of John Van Lew." Van Lew's journal reveals that in her dealings with Winder she was still casting herself, as she had early in the war, as a pro-Confederate elite lady, full of compassion for the suffering men on both sides. Elizabeth and her mother went so far in this ruse as to invite Winder and his wife and daughter to dinner, during which Elizabeth "attempted to talk Southern Confederacy" as best she could, even as Mrs. Winder made a series of comments that suggested, so Elizabeth avers, that the general's wife "had a strong feeling for the U.S. gov."[39]

Maneuvering on John's behalf, Van Lew struggled to hide the fact that she was "torn with anguish" at the news that so many of the Libby refugees were being rounded up by the Confederates. On February 15, 1864, nearly a week after the breakout, Elizabeth finally got the chance to meet four of the escapees—including none other than the infamous Streight. The men had been aided in their flight from Libby by Abby Green, the same intrepid Union lady who had helped John F. Porter escape, in disguise, in late January. Through Robert Ford, Streight had contacted Green a few days before the tunnel was finished and she had conveyed back to him directions on how he and his comrades could reach her once they had exited the prison. On the fateful night of February 9, Streight and three other escapees—Major Bedan B. McDonald, Captain William Scearce, and Lieutenant John Sterling—proceeded to the home of a loyal African American woman; she promptly went off and brought to them Abby Green, who piloted them to a place of safety on the outskirts of town—a property owned by the Unionist John Quarles, who had, as we have seen, absconded with John F. Porter. Presiding over and evidently boarding at the Quarles's house was Lucy A. Rice, who, like Green, had long been in communication with the inmates at Libby. The men were concealed and cared for by Rice for more than a week: "She kindly gave up her rooms to the escaped prisoners, and made purchases of under clothing for them, also provisions for their subsistence,"

A. C. Roach, an associate of Streight's, wrote. Elizabeth's account of these events suggests that she did not know Green or Rice personally before the breakout—she refers to Abby Green as "a Mrs. Green" and makes it clear that Rice was not in the Van Lew's social circle—but that Green and Rice, like the escapees themselves, knew by reputation of Van Lew. The fugitives requested to meet Van Lew, and on February 15, Lucy Rice came in her own carriage to Church Hill, picked up Elizabeth, and took her to a "humble house on the outskirts of the city." (If Elizabeth had taken her family's own, more ostentatious horse and carriage into this neighborhood, they would have "create[d] an excitement.") Rice, who despite her poor health, gave the men every comfort and consideration, instantly won Elizabeth's admiration. It is very likely that Elizabeth provided pecuniary assistance to Rice, enabling her to make the necessary purchases for the prisoners; according to Union Colonel D. B. Parker, a colleague of Van Lew's after the war, the various safe houses in Richmond were "supported by [Van Lew's] means."[40]

Elizabeth's wartime journal features a detailed evocation of the moment she met the Libby escapees: "I followed Mrs. Rice into the house, the front door of which opened into the parlor or sitting room, and I found myself in the presence of the four fugitives. I was so overcome with terror for them that I quite lost my voice for some time." But the men's solicitous demeanor soon put her at her ease. As she recalls the scene, "I was particularly de-lighted with the man who made the tunnel—Col. McDonald, I think, was his name. Broad shouldered and kind hearted, an honest, true, genial looking man; it was a pleasure to take the hand which had worked so faithfully, so hard, to deliver himself and fellow prisoners. He put in my hand the chisel with which alone he made the passage." Elizabeth was also relieved to see that Streight in particular "seemed in good condition." She told him frankly that there was "particular enmity towards him" among Confederates because of allegations that he had commanded a black regiment. Streight responded that he had not done so but that he "would have had no objection." In what we should interpret as a token of respect, Streight asked Elizabeth Van Lew her "opinion of the cause of [the] war." Her instinct was to quote the party line of her political hero, John Minor Botts—that "Democracy [by which Botts meant the reckless Democratic party] was the whole and sole cause" of the war. The conversation soon turned to lighter matters; Elizabeth and the four men "had a little laughing and talking" and then she bade them farewell, and "God help You." Lucy Rice took her home. As the two women were not sure they could trust their carriage driver, they paid him a "round sum in Confederate dollars" for his silence.[41]

Somehow, the Union underground managed to send word to the Yankee army that Streight and company were at Rice's; on February 15, the same day that Van Lew visited Rice, Union Brigadier General Isaac Wistar sent instructions to his chief of staff reading: "Colonel Streight is concealed in Richmond, but at large. His friends desire the papers to state his successful arrival here, for obvious reasons. Please arrange it immediately with the Associated Press agent." The instructions were followed, and on February 16, 1864, the *New York Times* printed an "official dispatch" from Benjamin Butler declaring that "Col. STREIGHT, with seventeen others [of the escapees] are safe." Taking this bait, the *Richmond Sentinel* reported on February 20 that Streight had arrived safely at Fort Monroe.[42]

Despite Federal efforts to throw Confederates off the scent of Streight and the others, Van Lew rightly sensed that it was not safe for her to visit the men again. Tipped off by the carriage driver or some other suspicious observer, several military detectives soon visited and searched the sanctuary; they found nothing incriminating, as Rice had cleverly hidden the men somewhere on the premises. According to Richmond hospital matron Phoebe Yates Pember, the authorities as of February 19 had placed a guard around the Van Lew mansion, as well; to Pember's consternation, however, the "Confederate government was too delicate minded to search the premises."[43]

Though Van Lew did not dare call on Rice again, she was able, presumably through black intermediaries, to send messages to Streight and his fellow fugitives. In the days after the meeting at Rice's house, Elizabeth "felt troubled" about her response to Streight's query on the origins of the war. So she penned a letter to him, inscribing her true feelings—her conviction that slavery was the "whole and sole cause" of the war. The note elaborated on this theme: "Slave power crushes freedom of labor. Slave power is arrogant—is jealous, and intrusive—is cruel—is despotic—not only over the slave, but over the community, the State. Slave power was losing this strength before the increasing influence of honest and enlightened free labor. I think this is one of the most deeply interesting of questions, but I cannot enter into it now. It is a vast field in which I have gathered many facts. I have thought and felt deeply on this subject. I would be glad to speak with you, but the time is not now." Elizabeth ended the note by cautioning Streight not to attempt to contact her, "unless you want to have my head taken off by the powers that be." In all likelihood, Van Lew had initially concealed her true feelings from Streight because she knew that her view was controversial and that most Union soldiers were not abolitionists—they were fighting for the Union and the principle of majority rule, not for the salvation of the slaves. That she felt so compelled to set the record straight, and the words she chose to do so, reveal a great deal about Van Lew's self-image as a Southern Unionist: as one who knew the "facts," she was honor bound to educate Northerners.[44]

Elizabeth's note never made it to Streight, for he and his fellow fugitives soon embarked on a 13-day trip to Union lines; "their safe arrival, after many days of suffering and wandering, gladdened our hearts," Van Lew wrote. While the Richmond press applauded the recapture of dozens of Libby men, the Northern press celebrated the flight to safety of dozens of others. The *New York Herald* of March 1 announced the arrival of Streight, Searce, McDonald, and Sterling in Washington, D.C.; a few days later Streight and others testified before the House Military Committee on the "horrors of rebel captivity." Streight had been so impressed by Van Lew that he erroneously told the press after the war that Van Lew had secreted him in Richmond during his flight from Libby.[45]

In the months following the breakout, Northern readers thrilled to learn details of how the small bands of fugitives who had fanned out over the Virginia countryside made it to Union lines; "the perils and sufferings through which they passed form one of those exciting episodes which war only can produce," noted the *New York Herald*. While the men followed many different roads to freedom, most did not tarry in Richmond as Streight did, but rather sought immediately to pass through the fortifications around Richmond and cross the lower Chickahominy in the hopes of falling in with the cavalry detachments Butler had dispatched to search for the fugitives. In the many interviews, articles, and reminiscences by these Libby men, one theme stands out—the heroism and patriotism of black Unionists who came to the timely aid of the escapees. Lieutenant Colonel Harrison C. Hobart, for example, tells of how he was secreted and fed by a black family, and piloted round the Confederate pickets by a "sharp, shrewd" African American guide; "if good deeds are recorded in heaven this slave appeared in the record that night," he declared. Lieutenant Charles W. Earle was likewise concealed by an African American family; he remembers how "a guard of colored people" was posted around the hiding place as the fugitives were "thoroughly warmed and well fed" and provided with directions for the next stage of their perilous trip. Captain I. N. Johnston's memoirs tell of how a brave "negro sentinel" had watched over him and his fellow Union men while they rested and then guided them for four miles on their journey to freedom; a white man pretending to be a Unionist, by contrast, had tried to hand them over to the Confederates. The experience gave the soldiers a new perspective on the very theme of racial difference; in a scenario that reversed the antebellum order in which slave runaways had relied on the kind offices of sympathetic whites, white men were the ones being hunted down. "We contrasted the duplicity—nay, almost perjury, of the civilized white man who had betrayed us into the power of our enemies, with the fidelity of the African slave who had proved so kind and true, and felt that under the dark skin beat a nobler heart," Johnston concluded. For pro-emancipation journals such as the popular *Harper's Weekly*, which in March of 1864 featured an article on how escaping Union officers were "succored by slaves," the courageous conduct of blacks in the great escape from Libby prison was proof—just as the battlefield heroism of African American regiments was—that black Unionists deserved the respect and gratitude of white Northerners.[46]

What then, ultimately, was Elizabeth Van Lew's contribution to the "great escape?" Although Elizabeth missed the chance to provide shelter for the escaped men, it is safe to say that the Libby break could never have happened without her. Since the very beginning of the war, Elizabeth had symbolized, more than any other single individual, the existence of an abiding and active Union sentiment in Richmond. It was thanks largely to her money and connections that the lines of communication between inmates and the outside world had stayed open. Prisoners could and did nourish their spirits on stories of successful escapes and fire their hopes on rumors that just outside the prison walls were true hearts eager to embrace them. Unionists such as Abby Green and Lucy Rice knew they could count on Van Lew's generosity to sustain them. While hers was only one of many safe houses in the Richmond area, Van Lew was, in Union Colonel D. B. Parker's words, the "guiding spirit" of the band of brave men and women, white and black, who aided runaway soldiers.[47]

"How the eye of hope grows dim." *Belle Isle Prison* (LIBRARY OF VIRGINIA).

However impressive the Libby breakout was—and however good for Northern morale—it did little to soothe the fears or calm the soul of Van Lew. She knew all too well that the escapees represented but a tiny fraction of the seething, suffering masses of prisoners in Richmond, who with each passing day of the brutally cold winter were slipping closer to death. In a move that suggests that Van Lew had persuaded the Confederates of her innocence in the Libby affair, the authorities permitted Elizabeth, under "strict surveillance," to visit the perimeter of Belle Isle Prison, on the James River, on February 27, 1864. She was traumatized by what she saw:

> It surpassed in wretchedness and squalid filth my most vivid imagi-nation. The long lines of forsaken, despairing, hopeless-looking beings, who, within this hollow square, looked upon us, gaunt hunger staring from their sunken eyes. The crowds within this little space, the wretched, smoky, tattered tents, the holes in the ground, and men lying on the ground, some without a thing over or under them, some picking the vermin off their legs, some looking for them in their clothing, and the prospect to render doubly wretched their wretchedness, within a few, very few steps . . . the newly made graves of their late companions.

... Oh, ground of unopened graves, how the eye of hope grows dim and the heartbreaks look on you. For this month-extended, hope deferred, despairing prison house! Oh weary, longing, dying eyes—day of deliverance, will you never come?[48]

On the very day Van Lew penned this lament, General George Meade of the Army of the Potomac officially sanctioned a new raid for the deliverance of the Union inmates of Richmond. The spectacular failure of the plan would confront the Richmond underground with its greatest challenge and inspire its most dramatic feat.[49]

6

"This Precious Dust"

THE CLANDESTINE REBURIAL OF COLONEL ULRIC DAHLGREN

"EVERY AVAILABLE MAN WAS CALLED OUT. THERE WAS AN AWFUL QUIET IN THE streets; the heavy silence was oppressive." Such was the atmosphere of dread in Richmond on March 1, 1864, as Confederates clashed with Union raiders on the outskirts of the city. The city's motley home defense brigade—an ill-trained group of civilians, including clerks, factory workers, politicians, merchants, school boys, and elderly retirees—was mustered into five battalions and made its way to the battle front. Even some of Van Lew's fellow loyalists were swept up in the drive to defend the city. "I drove out in the afternoon and I saw all the militia drilling, among them Northerners, and some I know to be Unionists," Van Lew remembered. "So potent is fear to blind conscience!"[1]

Once again Van Lew's hopes for the liberation of the city were dashed. Richmond's defenders had the bravery and resourcefulness to repulse the Yankee advance. Only later would Van Lew learn the details of the abortive raid; once again Union bad luck and ineptitude, as much as rebel heroics, had prevented the men in blue from taking advantage of Richmond's vulnerability. As Van Lew concisely reported in her journal, "The body of [Union] men under Col. Dahlgren rapidly approached the city, when through the treachery of a guide, he failed to form a junction and cooperate with Col. [sic] Kilpatrick. [Kilpatrick] was forced to deviate from his course and make his way to the peninsula" and the safety of Federal lines. Meanwhile, Dahlgren, after facing off against Richmond's local militia, attempted a retreat of his own. But it took a tragic turn. The colonel "fell into an ambush, was fired upon and killed."[2]

While it was clear to Van Lew and her contemporaries that something had gone desperately wrong in the Federal army's execution of this raid on Richmond, the origins and motivations of the Dahlgren/Kilpatrick mission, and its implications, were bitterly debated during the war, and are debated still, to this day. Was the mission a plot to assassinate Jefferson Davis, as the indignant Confederates alleged? Or a noble bid to liberate Federal inmates from the "Bastiles" of rebeldom, as Van Lew believed? So, too, has the grisly aftermath of the raid been cloaked in controversy, for Dahlgren's death gave rise to a train of bizarre and macabre events. Van Lew and the Richmond underground arranged, at great risk to their entire covert operation, for the disinterment and reburial on Unionist soil of fallen raider Ulric Dahlgren. But why, and to what end? To examine the "Dahlgren affair" is to gain insight not only into the psyches of Van Lew and her fellow fifth columnists but also into the ways that nineteenth-century people coped with and understood death itself.

The operation endorsed by Meade on February 27, 1864, was every bit as ill-conceived as Wistar's dash earlier that month had been. The proposed raid was the brainchild of the brash Brigadier General H. Judson Kilpatrick, who had earned the moniker "Kill-cavalry" in recognition both of his bravery and recklessness. Hoping that his much-celebrated performance in Stoneman's raid of May 1863—during which Kilpatrick's unit had destroyed Confederate depots, bridges, warehouses and other resources on the outskirts of Richmond—would lend him credibility, "Kill-cavalry" had pitched his idea for an attack on Richmond directly to President Lincoln on February 12. Lincoln had ample reason to be seduced by the plan. Not only was it yet another way to counter charges that the administration was not doing enough for the prisoners, but Kilpatrick's men could also disseminate Lincoln's December 1863 promise of amnesty to Southerners who repudiated secession and declared allegiance to the Union. Meade, for his part, was skeptical of Kilpatrick's "desperate" scheme but felt that the dire condition of prisoners in Richmond warranted taking such risks. Meade's communication to Kilpatrick on the eve of the raid made quite clear who was responsible: "No detailed instructions are given you, since the plan of your operations has been proposed by yourself, with the sanction of the President and the Secretary of War."[3]

The plan itself called for a carefully orchestrated joint action by Kilpatrick on the one hand and his compatriot Colonel Ulric Dahlgren on the other: an advance detachment of 460 men under Dahlgren was to assail the city from the south while Kilpatrick and some 3,000 troops attacked Richmond from the northwest. Kilpatrick was reposing a great deal of trust in Dahlgren: the two commands would be unable to communicate with each other until they reached the perimeter of Richmond. "Kill-cavalry" evidently regarded Dahlgren, a headstrong and handsome young man of 21 years of age, as a protégé; though Dahlgren had lost his right leg at Gettysburg, he hankered to get back in the action, and he saw the proposed raid as chance for glory. If the raid were to succeed, the colonel wrote to his father, Rear Admiral John A. Dahlgren, it would be "the grandest thing on record." The ensuing events would indeed bring Ulric Dahlgren notoriety, but not the kind of which he had dreamed.[4]

As far as Kilpatrick was concerned, the raid started promisingly enough. Setting out on February 28, he and the main body of Union troops proceeded, on schedule, in their southeasterly trek, meeting little Confederate resistance and destroying railroad tracks and other rebel resources as they went. On the twenty-ninth Kilpatrick sent a jaunty note to General Pleasonton that he would double the $5,000 bet he had made that he would enter Richmond. By midday on March 1, Kilpatrick had reached fortifications a mile from the city. But then things took a turn for the disastrous. The Confederate garrison opened artillery fire on Kilpatrick's men, and Kilpatrick lost his nerve. Worried about the fact that Dahlgren's party was nowhere in sight, Kill-cavalry ordered his men to retreat. According to historian Samuel J. Martin, the fate of Dahlgren was only one of the concerns that sapped Kilpatrick's will to fight: "Perhaps for the first time Kilpatrick saw the futility in his plan to free the Federal captives. Even if he passed through the barricade up ahead into the capital to open the doorways to Libby and Belle Isle, what could he do then? He had made no provisions for feeding and arming the prisoners or transporting them to safety. Kilpatrick could only assemble the men into a herd and drive them north like a drove of cattle, while the Rebels circled and sniped like wild Indians at his slow-going column. The most likely result would be his own capture and imprisonment." Quailing at this prospect, Kilpatrick fell back and considered his options. Just as he was on the brink of generating a new plan to salvage the operation, his men were set upon near Mechanicsville by the cavalry of Confederate Major General Wade Hampton, who had been tipped off about the raid early on February 29 and had been trailing Kilpatrick ever since. Hampton's attack snuffed out the last embers of resolve in Kilpatrick and his Union force slunk back to Butler's lines at New Kent Court House on the Peninsula.[5]

What of Dahlgren? Unbeknownst to him, his part of the joint action was compromised from the start. Setting out one hour in advance of Kilpatrick,

Dahlgren believed that the first part of his mission—fording the Rapidan and proceeding to Spotsylvania Court House—went well. In reality, Confederate scouts captured two of Dahlgren's men who were bringing up the rear, and dutifully tipped off Wade Hampton's headquarters about the Federal movements, thus laying the groundwork for Hampton's March 1 ambush of Kilpatrick. Dahlgren's troops proceeded south, reaching Frederick's Hall station on the Virginia Central Railroad on February 29 and then making their way to the James River, whose banks they reached on March 1. They had hoped to cross the river at Dover Mills, only to find recent heavy rains had rendered the ford impassable. Convinced that he had been led astray by the African American guide, Martin Robinson, whom the Bureau of Military Intelligence had assigned to the operation, Dahlgren ordered the man to be summarily executed, in a move that would taint Dahlgren as a rash and bloodthirsty man. The colonel had his own reins used to hang the poor Robinson.[6]

Unable to ford the James and attack Richmond from the south as planned, Dahlgren's troops rode east, approaching Richmond above the James. Once on the outskirts of the city, the Federal horsemen encountered strong resistance from the Confederate home guard. Dahlgren assessed the situation as hopeless and ordered a retreat to the northeast to join up with Kilpatrick's columns. But Dahlgren's retreat proved even more ill-fated than Kilpatrick's had. Groping their way through hostile terrain, under rebel pursuit in the darkness of night, Dahlgren and some 90 of his men got separated from the rest of his command. While the larger segment of the command, under Captain John F. B. Mitchell, Second New York Cavalry, managed to reach Union lines, Dahlgren's segment was trapped. On March 2, rebel cavalrymen and home guardsmen under the leadership of Lieutenant James Pollard, Ninth Virginia Cavalry, ambushed Dahlgren's raiders in King and Queen County near Walkerton. The young colonel was killed and all but 21 of his troops captured.[7]

As his counterparts Butler and Wistar had after the Bottom's Bridge debacle, Kilpatrick went into damage-control mode, writing Pleasonton on March 3 that while he "failed to accomplish the great object of the expedition," he had "destroyed the enemy's communications at various points on the Virginia Central railroad; also the canal and mills along the James River, and much other valuable property." But Kilpatrick's efforts to interpret the outcome of the raid were soon overshadowed by the shocking allegations coming out of Richmond. The true intentions of the Yankee raiders, so the Confederate high command and press charged, were revealed in documents—dubbed the "Dahlgren papers"—found on the deceased colonel's corpse. The papers had been discovered, in one of those remarkable Civil War accidents that strains credulity, by a 13-year-old member of Richmond's Home Guard, one William Littlepage. In the immediate aftermath of the Confederate ambush and Federal retreat, Littlepage had, in a grisly but common ritual in these desperate times, searched the Yankee dead for valuables. He was undoubtedly disappointed that his search of Dahlgren's corpse turned up only a notebook, letters, and some loose papers. But Littlepage dutifully passed the documents along to a trustworthy adult, his teacher Edward Halbach. Upon examining the papers, Halbach realized that Littlepage had happened upon a propaganda goldmine. The teacher, for his part, handed over the papers to the Confederate high command, which in turn passed them along to the press. According to stories that ran in the various Richmond dailies beginning on March 5, the "Dahlgren papers" contained "indisputable evidence of the diabolical designs of the enemy."[8]

What the press was so indignant about were papers purporting to be Dahlgren's instructions to his men on the eve of the raid. One document was an address on the stationery of the "Headquarters Third Division, Cavalry Corps," signed by Dahlgren, and reading: "We hope to release the prisoners from Belle Isle first, and having them well started, we will cross the James River into Richmond, destroying the bridges after us and exhorting the prisoners to destroy and burn the hateful city; and do not allow the rebel leader Davis and his traitorous crew to escape." A second unsigned document was even more explicit, stating that Richmond "must be destroyed and Jeff Davis and Cabinet killed." For Confederates, these words were confirmation of the case that Davis and the high command had long been building: the Yankees were barbarians, too ignoble and cowardly to abide by the rules of war. Ironically, the Confederate press bolstered Kilpatrick's own claim that the raid, though ultimately a failure, had been highly destructive. "The depredations of the last Yankee raiders, and the wantonness of their devastation equal anything heretofore committed during the war," stated the *Richmond Examiner*, in order to suggest that the raiders had been poised to carry through on their murderous plan.[9]

One of the Union soldiers captured during the raid, a signal officer of Dahlgren's named Reuben Bartley, has left a detailed memoir revealing just how the raiders were regarded by the Confederate civilians of Richmond. Many prominent citizens came to see the prisoners for the sole purpose of insulting and reviling them in person. One of the visitors, Mrs. Seddon, wife of the Confederate secretary of war, took palpable pleasure in calling the inmates "*Thieves. Murderers. Fiends. Hell Monsters. Assassins.* and such polite epithets as the Ladies of the F. F. V.s [First Families of Virginia] only use to designate Union soliders," Bartley recalled. She then threatened that she would "use all the influence she possessed to have the whole party Hanged and if she could not have us hanged she would have us put into a dungeon and starved to death." The Richmond press was "equally violent." Some writers were for "blowing us from cannon, some for burning us with turpentine and oakum." All agreed, Bartley noted, that "we must be summarily executed."[10]

Now it was time for a different kind of damage control on the Federals' part. Receiving copies of the Richmond papers on March 6, General Meade ordered an investigation. When Kilpatrick testified that neither he nor Dahlgren had ever issued the orders imputed to them by the rebel papers, Meade in turn wrote Robert E. Lee that the United States government had never sanctioned "the burning of Richmond and the Killing of Mr. Davis and cabinet, nor any other act not required by military necessity and in accordance with the usages of war." The Northern press naturally accepted Meade's view of things, and lionized Dahlgren as a heroic martyr. "The rebels pretend to have found papers on Colonel DAHLGREN'S body, directing the massacre of Davis and all the officials in Richmond," reported *Harper's Weekly*, but Dahlgren had really enjoined his men to uphold the standards of civilized warfare and to "allow no thought of personal gain to lead them off." His career "affords another illustration, beautiful and significant, of that sturdy and courageous manhood which these troublous latter days are maturing as the hope of the Republic."[11]

It is not surprising, of course, that the two contending sides should cherish such diametrically opposed assessments of Dahlgren and his mission; nor is it surprising that historians of the affair have long struggled to ascertain which view of things—the Union or Confederate—accords with the facts. The historian's role as detective has been more difficult than usual where Dahlgren is concerned because of the nature of the physical evidence. In late March, Confederate Secretary of State Judah P. Benjamin sent photographs of the Dahlgren papers to Confederate minister John Slidell in Paris, whose charge it was to circulate the damning documents in Europe and thus taint the image of the Lincoln administration. These photographs were rendered into lithographs in England for distribution abroad. But a set of these lithographs made its way back into the United States into the hands of Rear Admiral John A. Dahlgren, the heartsick father of the slain Union colonel, and he quickly determined that the lithographs exonerated his son: the name Dahlgren was misspelled, with the "l" coming before the "h." The rear admiral went public with this find in August of 1864, stating explicitly in a front-page article in the *New York Herald* that the Dahlgren papers were a "bare-faced atrocious forgery."[12]

The first challenge faced by scholars of the Dahlgren affair, then, has been to reckon with the forgery charge; since none of the original documents have survived, the photographs and lithographs have had to stand on their own. Civil War historian James O. Hall has painstakingly argued that the misspelling of Dahlgren's name in the lithographs was a mistake by the lithographer, who attempted to touch up and reformat the photograph and in so doing transposed two letters. The second challenge facing historians has been to put Dahlgren's notorious orders within the context of Union strategic thinking. This challenge has been taken up by Stephen Sears, who has made a persuasive case that "Both circumstance and logic point to Secretary of War Stanton as authorizer of the dark premise of the Kilpatrick-Dahlgren raid. . . . The idea of liberating the maddened prisoners and exhorting them to carry out the death sentences and pillaging was a masterstroke of rationalization and perfectly in character for the secretary of war."[13]

Scholars have done much to establish, then, that the Dahlgren papers were real, and that they were not a strategic aberration but in keeping with Federal aspirations—at work in the Butler-Wistar raid as well—to strike a blow at the rebel nerve center. To understand the meaning of the Dahlgren affair for Richmond's Unionists, however, we must put aside the certitude that comes with hindsight and remember that Van Lew and her cohort believed Dahlgren to be innocent of the charges laid against him. In her account of the raid and its aftermath, Van Lew declares, in keeping with the rear admiral's August 1864 revelation to the press, that "the pretended order of Dahlgren as given by the Rebel Press spelled his name wrongly, which is of course, proof present that he never signed it." She concludes that "said paper [Dahlgren's order] was prepared in Richmond . . . to irritate and inflame the Southern people." For Van Lew, what was shocking about the Dahlgren affair was not the conduct and plans of the Dahlgren and his men but rather the barbarous treatment by the Confederates of the Union colonel's corpse.[14]

⚊

Written sometime after the war, Van Lew's account of the Richmond raid and its aftermath takes up more space than any other single episode in her personal narrative. In keeping with her self-image as truth teller, Van Lew attempts to sift through the rumors that swirled around the raid and to establish a factual narrative. She is at pains, for example, to explain why Dahlgren was killed by shots to his back. He was not felled, as some reports claimed, while in cowardly retreat; rather, his horse had whirled around at a sudden flash of light. According to "those who were present," Van Lew wrote, "nothing could have been more gallant and daring than his bearing . . . he led his men with his own face to the foe!" In the days that followed Dahlgren's demise, the inner circle of Richmond Unionists would put their own courage to the test.[15]

The morning after Dahlgren fell, the Confederates buried him where he was killed, in a "slashy, muddy hole about two feet deep." On March 6, the day after the story of his inflammatory orders hit the Richmond papers, the body was disinterred and brought to the York River Railroad Depot in the capital, where, according to the *Richmond Whig,* "large numbers of persons went to see it." Accounts of the state of the corpse in the Richmond dailies fell like a thunder clap on the city's Unionists. The *Whig* reported that "It was in a pine box, clothed in Confederate shirt and pants, and shrouded in a Confederate blanket. The wooden leg had been removed by one of the soldiers. It was also noticeable that the little finger of the left hand had been cut off. Dahlgren was a small man, thin, pale, and with red hair and a goatee of the same color. His face wore an expression of agony. About two o'clock, P.M., the corpse was removed from the depot and buried—no one knows, or is to know where." For the press, Dahlgren, who had sought to "ravage . . . defenseless woman and innocent childhood," had met a fitting end: "it would seem something of the curse he came to bestow upon others lighted upon his own carcass," the *Richmond Examiner* opined in defense of the Confederate ravaging of the colonel's corpse.[16]

To Van Lew, the "outrages" committed on Dahlgren's "inanimate body" were yet more shadows of slavery. "The forged papers said to have been found on Colonel Dahlgren's body had maddened the people," she wrote, and "Southern people, when maddened, who have been used to giving way to wrath with violence on negroes, stop not at trifles." Stirred to the depths by the indecent treatment of Dahlgren, Van Lew vowed "to discover the hidden grave and remove his honored dust to friendly care."[17]

To fathom why Van Lew and her compatriots would take on myriad risks to exhume and rebury Dahlgren, when such an act admitted of no strategic or political benefit for the Union cause, we must inquire into mid-nineteenth-century cultural representations of death and dying. As historian Drew Gilpin Faust has explained, Americans of the Victorian era strove to achieve a "good death," believing that "how one died . . . epitomized a life already led and predicted the quality of the life everlasting." A "good death" was one defined by the dying person's serene comportment in the final hour, to connote his or her preparation for God's grace and the better life to come, and by the presence of family around the deathbed. The Civil War confronted Americans on both sides with the challenge of adapting the peacetime ideals of the "good death" to the stark realities of wartime—of brutal and sudden death, far from one's family. "Soldiers, chaplains, military nurses, and doctors conspired to provide the dying man and his family with as many elements of the conventional 'good death' as possible, struggling even amidst the chaos of war to make it possible for men—and their loved ones—to believe they had died well," Faust asserts; she demonstrates, for example, that condolence letters were constructed to make families "virtual witnesses to the dying moments they had been denied." It is in the light of these influential notions of the "good death" that we must assess the Richmond underground's actions in the Dahlgren affair. Van Lew and her co-conspirators would attempt nothing less than to constitute a symbolic family for Ulric Dahlgren, and to render, after the fact, his wretched death into a good one.[18]

Dahlgren was buried by the Confederates in Oakwood Cemetery on Richmond's eastern outskirts, a young sapling serving as his headstone. The Confederate officer in charge of the interment, Lieutenant Colonel John Wilder Atkinson, had received an order directly from Jefferson Davis not to divulge the burial spot to anyone. Van Lew deputized some of her most trustworthy agents to endeavor to find the body, knowing that such a quest was "perilous in no small degree." The Richmond underground succeeded in this seemingly impossible mission only because of the interposition of a courageous African American man, whose name has been lost to history. As Van Lew has written, the body would have never been discovered "had not a negro been out in the burying ground at midnight and saw them bringing Dahlgren." The man concealed himself behind a tree and when the Confederates left the scene he marked the spot of the grave. Thanks to the resourcefulness of F. W. E. Lohman, who took it upon himself to make discreet inquiries around town, the existence of this witness to the Dahlgren's burial soon came to light.[19]

Lohmann's next move was to approach Martin Meredith Lipscomb, the man in charge of seeing to the burial of deceased Federal soldiers in the city of Richmond. A native Virginian and a bricklayer by trade, with the reputation of being somewhat erratic, Lipscomb was engaged at this very time in one of his repeated and fruitless bids for elected office: he was a candidate—albeit a distinctly unpopular one—for the office of mayor. Lipscomb had been offended that the powers that be had bypassed him, taking the burial of Dahlgren out of his hands and delegating it to Atkinson. Lohmann called on Lipscomb's house on Franklin Street, to attempt to enlist his aid in inducing the African American witness to the burial to reveal the spot. Whether or not Lohmann suspected Lipscomb of having a grudge against his superiors or even of harboring Union sympathies is unclear. But according to Lipscomb's own recollections, Lohmann appealed to his sense of decency—not to Unionism or to any mercenary motives—with tales of how Dahlgren's poor father was crazy with grief that his son had not received a proper burial. Lohmann assured his would-be collaborator that the plan to rebury Dahlgren was "all for humanity sake." Lipscomb responded with a pledge of support and a chilling warning: "I told Lohman I was his man and if he deceived me I would certainly kill him before I would be exposed or disgraced."[20]

Aided by Lipscomb, Lohmann persuaded the black cemetery worker to point out where in Oakwood Cemetery Dahlgren lay; Lohmann, in consultation with Elizabeth Van Lew, then set about making all the "necessary arrangements" for the exhumation of the corpse and its removal to a "place of safe keeping." The night they chose for the grim and dangerous work of opening the grave was April 6; the men entrusted with the ghoulish task were Lipscomb, F. W. E. Lohmann, and his brother John A. Lohmann.

While storm clouds, howling winds, and thunder claps so often serve as portents of doom in fictional graveyard scenes, for the three intrepid Union men, the fact that the night of April 6 was a cold and stormy one was a good omen. "Even the elements [were] favoring us," Lohmann has written, knowing that the dreadful weather would keep at least some of their enemies inside. Shrouded by the darkness, their hearts in their throats, knowing that the punishment for the act they were about to commit would surely be their own deaths, the Lohmann brothers and Lipscomb approached the cemetery in a mule-drawn wagon (Rowley had tried in vain to secure a horse) and then proceeded to grope their way to the gravesite. With the assistance of "an old negro gravedigger," the three men, as fast as they possibly could, disinterred Dahlgren's coffin. They had then to perform the nauseating job of opening the casket and examining the body, to confirm its identity; discovering that the corpse was missing its right leg below the knee, they knew it to be the slain Union colonel. The body was transferred to the mule-drawn wagon, and conveyed to Rowley's residence, where it was hidden in an outbuilding, "a kind of seed or work shop," according to Van Lew. There the faithful Rowley kept a vigil over the corpse all night long.[21]

The following morning, the Lohmann brothers brought to Rowley's farm a metallic coffin that had been procured by Lipscomb. "Some idea may be formed of the difficulty encountered in obtaining the metallic coffin," Lohmann reported, "when it is reported, beyond fear of denial, that at that time there were only two in the city of Richmond." The next stage in the plan was to convey the corpse, in the new, superior coffin, to a place more secure than Rowley's. But before the transfer was undertaken, the inner circle of Unionists participated in a ritual that was hazardous and, for them, profoundly significant: Charles Palmer, Franklin Stearns, Elmira Holmes (wife of Arnold B. and mother of Josephine), S. J. Wardwell (wife of Burnham), Almond E. Graham, Elizabeth Van Lew, and her mother Eliza convened at Rowley's farm to view the body and pay their last respects. Graham was a Vermont-born stencil cutter whose inclusion in this ritual is the earliest evidence of his affiliation with the Richmond underground.[22]

As we have seen, Palmer, Stearns, and Burnham Wardwell (S. J.'s husband) had already done turns in Confederate prisons on suspicion of disloyalty, and the Van Lew mansion had recently been under surveillance in the wake of the Libby breakout. Why, then, would these Unionists risk drawing Confederate attention to the secret concealed at Rowley's house? Again, the ideal of the "good death" holds the key to understanding what was at stake for Van Lew and her friends. Her loyalist circle, by coming to see Dahlgren's corpse, were serving as a substitute family for him. The role of the family in a "good death" was not only to provide a comforting presence but "to assess the state of the dying person's soul," as Faust has put it. Since the Unionists had not borne witness to Dahlgren's last hour, since they had no last words or dying gestures to interpret, they tried literally to "read" his body for signs about his spiritual state at the moment of his death. Van Lew relates the scene: "Gentle hands and tearful eyes examined his breast to see if there was any wound there, but nothing of the kind could be perceived. The body, except for the head, was in a perfect state of preservation, fair, fine and firm the flesh. . . . The comeliness of the young face was gone, yet the features seemed regular and there was a wonderful look, firmness or energy stamped upon them." That Van Lew "read" the body differently than the Confederates had—the *Whig*, it will be recalled had declared that Dahlgren's corpse wore an expression of "agony"—speaks volumes. Both readings were premised on the assumption that the look on the deceased's face was a window into his conscience. The state of Dahlgren's body only confirmed for Van Lew that he was a brave and noble man who had been grievously wronged.[23]

The party of mourners who gathered around Dahlgren on April 7 made one last ritual gesture—they cut off some locks of his hair to be preserved as a memento and conveyed, via the underground, to his father—before the body was prepared for the next stage in its perilous journey to a proper resting place. Van Lew's journal provides a detailed account of what came next. The Unionists transferred the corpse from the rough-hewn pine box into the metallic one, "the lid of which was sealed on with a composition improvised by F. W. E. Lohmann, as there was no putty to be found in Richmond." The coffin was then placed in Rowley's wagon, carefully concealed by "young peach trees packed as the nursery men pack them." With F. W. E. and John A. Lohmann, who had lighted out on foot in advance of the wagon serving as guides, Rowley "took the driver's seat" and conveyed the wagon along the Brook Turnpike toward his destination, the farm of fellow Unionist Robert Orrock Jr. In his way lay a formidable obstacle—Confederate picket posts that had recently been shored up to protect Richmond from Yankee raiders.[24]

Van Lew's account captures the high drama of Rowley's encounter with the pickets. It was a moment in which the fate of the entire Richmond underground hung in the balance: "If one [of the pickets] had run his bayonet into this wagon only a few inches, death would certainly have been the award of this brave man [Rowley], and not only death, but torture to make him reveal those connected with him—his accomplices." Knowing full well the stakes, Rowley put on a command performance. As he approached the picket, he "let fall the reins with the appearance of perfect indifference." The lieutenant at the post ordered a guard to examine the wagon. Fortunately, a diversion appeared in the form of a second wagon making its way down the opposite side of the road, and the guard, "seeing Mr. Rowley at leisure," proceeded to search the other wagon first. When the guard got round to Rowley, the clever loyalist engaged him in an exchange about peach tree cultivation. By this time, as Van Lew relates it, another cart had come up requiring examination; when the guard was done he returned to Rowley "and the conversation was resumed in reference to peach trees." After this pattern had been repeated again and again, Rowley had succeeded in "cementing friendship" with the ineffectual guard. "It would be a pity to tear those trees all up, when you have packed them there so nicely," the Confederate picket would tell Rowley as he sent him on his way. "At any rate your honest face is guarantee enough for me."[25]

Once through the picket post, Rowley was reunited with the Lohmann brothers, who climbed aboard the wagon and provided navigation; somewhere near the Yellow Tavern, the wagon left the turnpike and proceeded about ten miles west, to Orrock's farm, near Hungary Station—a stop on the Richmond, Fredericksburg, and Potomac Railroad—in Brookland Township, Henrico County. Orrock was a Scotsman by birth, whose family had come to America in the mid 1850s. While it is unclear whether he had actively aided the underground before collaborating in the Dahlgren affair, he was certainly part of the social web of Virginia Unionism—his brother-in-law was Fredericksburg loyalist and Samuel Ruth associate Isaac Silver and his neighbor was German immigrant Chistopher Bolton, one of the Unionists who had been rounded up by Winder in the spring of 1862 and incarcerated at Salisbury Prison. It was F. W. E. Lohmann, likely at the urging of Bolton or Ruth, who arranged for Orrock to be the guardian of Dahlgren's remains. It was not only his connections but also the location of his farm that recommended Orrock: located near the very railroad run by

Ruth, in a neighborhood full of immigrants (many of whom worked as miners in the coal pits west of the railroad station), Orrock's farm was at a safe remove from Richmond but in "easy communication," as Meriwether Stuart has put it, with the city's loyalists.[26]

Upon reaching Orrock's, the first task that fell to the Lohmanns and Rowley was to finish digging a grave for Dahlgren, work that the Scotsman himself had begun. They placed the coffin in it, and were aided in filling the grave by two mysterious female Unionists whom both Van Lew and S. J. Wardwell describe only as "German women." According to Meriwether Stuart, one was probably Augusta Bolton, the wife of Christopher, and the other Mrs. Orrock (Van Lew wrongly believed the Orrocks to be of German descent). Appropriately enough, given Rowley's experience in the wagon, a peach tree was planted over the grave. "The two Lohmanns then returned home in the wagon," Van Lew has written, "and every true Union heart, who knew of this day's work, felt happier for having charge of this precious dust."[27]

As if exhuming and reburying Dahlgren was not challenge enough, Van Lew and her compatriots next took it upon themselves to inform the grieving Admiral Dahlgren of their feat. Ever since the first reports of his son's death had broken, the admiral had been assiduously lobbying General Butler to arrange for the return to the family of the corpse. Butler in turn submitted an official request to the Confederate agent of exchange, Robert Ould, asking pointedly, "Would it not be desirable to prevent all supposition that your authorities countenance such acts [as the mutilation of the corpse] by delivering the remains to the bereaved family?" By March 23, the Confederates had relented, and promised that the body would be delivered into Union hands at the next flag-of-truce boat. Not privy to these negotiations, the Richmond underground had gone ahead with their own plan for Dahlgren's exhumation. On March 29, Admiral Dahlgren went to Fort Monroe in the hopes that the exchange boat arriving on that day would bear his son's remains; he was bitterly disappointed when he found that the Confederates had reneged on their promise. Sometime shortly after his return home to Washington from Fort Monroe, Admiral Dahlgren recalls, "an entire stranger called and hinted at some information, which he said had reached him, to the effect that the remains of Colonel Dahlgren had been found and removed by some friends to a place of safety, but that great secrecy was necessary, to avoid the search of the rebel authorities." A series of telegrams that the admiral received from Ben Butler on April 17, 20, and 21 confirmed the "stranger's" remarkable story. The remains were, Butler wrote, "in the hands of devoted friends of the Union, who have taken possession of them in order that proper respect may be shown to them." Butler implied that the underground would convey the remains to him at Fort Monroe "at a time which I trust is not far distant." Butler could not, he carefully explained in his telegram to Admiral Dahlgren, ask the Richmond Unionists to give the body directly over to Confederate Commissioner Ould, in order for him to send it home by flag-of-truce, because "that will show such correspondence with Richmond as will alarm [the Confederates], and will redouble their vigilance to detect my sources of information."[28]

Butler had good reason to want to protect his fledgling intelligence network. Amazingly enough, even as they orchestrated the Dahlgren reburial, Van Lew and her agents had stepped up their espionage work for Butler. An encoded message that Butler, in the guise of "Uncle Thomas Ap. Jones," sent to Van Lew, or "his dear niece," on March 4 reveals that Van Lew had sent Quaker and Wardwell to him with intelligence reports; Butler replied with a promise to reimburse Van Lew for money she spent on messengers and informants and with a request for information about the "rebel rams" and Confederate strategy regarding North Carolina. On March 15, Union scouts from Meade's Army of the Potomac received a detailed intelligence message from Herman Lohmann, who "came by direction of Union citizens in Richmond—Mr. Charles Palmer—Mr. John H. Van Liew [sic]—Franklin Stearns—Mr. Lohman—Mr. Graham & others." Lohmann reported that "the enemy are making large preparations for the capture of Norfolk," with Longstreet to lead the attack and a feint to be made on Williamsburg. He also revealed that there was "nothing in Richmond except Home Guards & the men in Batteries & a cavalry force of 1500 men which are being called in for service about the city." George Meade conveyed the report up the chain of command to Halleck. A week later, on March 22, Butler sent encoded messages to Rowley and to Van Lew. Rowley's was delivered by a messenger bearing $50,000 in Confederate money that Rowley was instructed to use in recruiting more agents; "employ none only those you know to be faithful, brave, and true," Butler cautioned.[29]

Even as Rowley searched for new recruits, two veterans of the underground were retiring from service. After aiding in the Porter escape and
great escape from Libby, Abby Green had fled Richmond for Baltimore; on
March 25, 1864, she was paid $200 "For Secret Service rendered" by a clerk
of the war department. Lucy Rice did not make out so well. She, too, made
her way North after the great escape. The early days of April, 1864 found
her in Baltimore, penniless, and in need of aid. The *Baltimore American* ran
a series of notices asking for donations for her support, noting that in hiding
Streight and company, Rice had "subjected herself to a risk that can only be
comprehended by those who understand the vindictiveness of the Richmond
authorities." By the end of the month, Rice had headed to Washington, D.C.,
to plead her case to the authorities; in early May she was paid $100 out of
the war department's secret service fund.[30]

Such sums seem paltry indeed given the risks secret service entailed. Butler's March 22 letter to Van Lew was a study in risk taking. It contained a
message from Burnham Wardwell to Philip Cashmeyer—a special detective
in Winder's office—that Van Lew was to copy and convey on Butler's and
Wardwell's behalf. Wardwell, by the spring of 1864, had ensconced himself
at Butler's camp as a sort of unofficial aide, consulting Butler on the "character, standing, and rebel or union proclivities of many men who came
through from Richmond on various pretexts." When a deserter came to the
Federal lines from the Confederate capital claiming to have useful information, for example, Butler called on Wardwell evaluate the man's reliability.
Wardwell evidently suggested to Butler that Cashmeyer should be sought
out as an ally.[31]

The message passed through Van Lew implored Cashmeyer to meet
Wardwell at New Kent Court House "on business of lifelong importance to
you and your family." Cashmeyer had just undergone, on March 9, a harrowing arrest and imprisonment in Castle Thunder on charges of "holding
treasonable intercourse with the enemy." Having accompanied Yankee prisoners on the flag-of-truce boat to City Point, Cashmeyer was seen handing
a package to a Union prisoner; it was soon discovered that the package
contained some letters, written in his native German, and a "number of
special orders from Gen. Winder's Department." Cashmeyer defended himself, arguing that the package was intended for his wife in Baltimore, to
convey to her his "importance as a Confederate official." The Confederate
authorities eventually accepted this alibi, and after chastising Cashmeyer for

his "indiscretion" reinstated him in his position in General Winder's headquarters.[32]

Knowing full well that Cashmeyer himself was already under suspicion, Van Lew nonetheless audaciously conveyed the Butler/Wardwell message to him. She called on Cashmeyer at Winder's office, sometime after his reinstatement as a detective there, and handed over the potentially incriminating letter; "As he read the message he turned deadly pale," she remembers. "However, he recovered himself and following us out begged me to be prudent and never to come again, saying he would come to see me." Judging from the fact that he never betrayed Van Lew as a spy and that he served in the immediate aftermath of the war as a Federal detective with the likes of the Lohmann brothers, we can surmise that Cashmeyer accepted the offer, tendered that March, to join forces with the Richmond underground.[33]

Coming in the midst of the underground's perilous efforts to recruit more agents, the Dahlgren reburial had the effect of serving notice to Butler and the Union high command just how devoted and skillful the Richmond loyalists were. Of course, the discovery that the body had been stolen from its "secret" site at Oakwood Cemetery served notice to the rebels as well. As the *Richmond Examiner* reported on April 14, the Confederates, in compliance with Union requests, had recently "opened [the grave] under the direction of the officials who interred the remains, but the grave was empty— Dahlgren had risen, or been resurrected, and the corpse was not found." For Christians, the religious overtones of the corpse's disappearance made it all the more eerie and unsettling. Lieutenant Colonel John Wilder Atkinson, the Confederate officer who had been in charge of the Oakwood burial, referred to Dahlgren's disappearance from the grave as the "great resurrection." With the humiliating great escape from Libby still fresh in the public's mind, the great resurrection was deeply disquieting to Confederate Richmond, for it disclosed the presence of a loyalist resistance able not only to spy, smuggle, and bribe, but apparently to work miracles.[34]

However it may have impressed the Union high command and alarmed Confederate Richmond, the reburial of Dahlgren is most significant for what it represented to Van Lew and her fellow loyalists; after all, they did not know when they undertook their ghoulish mission that Dahlgren's absence from his Oakwood grave would so soon be discovered. In honoring the slain colonel's "precious dust," Van Lew and her compatriots were not only rendering a bad death into a good one; they were enacting a ritual, one of many they enacted, to sustain their own morale. We have already seen that Van Lew made gestures that were perhaps needlessly risky but served as emblems of hopefulness, such as her preparing rooms in her house for General McClellan back in 1862 and for the Libby escapees in 1864. Even small acts of defiance could bring great psychic relief to the beleaguered Unionists. When Jefferson Davis called one of his "Fast Days," for example, to unite the Confederate public in religious observances and prayerful entreaties for victory, Van Lew and her family "always tried to have a little better dinner than usual." "We learned to look on these days as memories of good," Van Lew wryly notes in her journal, for "they were generally followed by some Federal success." Loyalists knew that it was extremely dangerous to congregate together but they did anyway—they needed to, to keep their spirits up. As Van Lew has written in the 1864 portion of her journal, "When the cold wind would blow in the darkest and stormiest nights Union people would visit one another. With shutters closed and curtains pressed together how we have been startled at the barking of a dog and drawn nearer together the pallor coming over our faces & the blood rushing to our hearts." Together, Van Lew and her friends would sit around a map and trace the progress of the Union armies, all the while "glorying in [the] Federal leaders." Elsewhere in the South, small bands of intrepid Unionists took great risks to commune with one another; in Atlanta, loyalists gathered at the home of Cyrena Stone to view the small American flag she had secreted away and to sing, ever so softly, the "Star-Spangled Banner" and other patriotic tunes. For Southern Unionists such as Van Lew, resistance to the Confederacy was not primarily a strategic or political matter, however valuable the military intelligence loyalists provided or salutary their impact on public opinion. Rather, resistance was first and foremost a moral responsibility. Seen in this light, the Dahlgren reburial looks not so much like an act of brazenness and bravado, but as the solemn fulfillment of a profound obligation.[35]

7

"The Smoke of Battle"

GRANT MOVES ON RICHMOND

"THE EXCITEMENT IS GREAT THROUGHOUT THE CITY, AND MANY ARE THE RUMORS," Van Lew wrote in her journal on May 6, 1864, as Union and Confederate forces held each other in a death grip on a battlefield called the Wilderness, north of Richmond in Spotsylvania county. The clash augured the coming of the legions of U. S. Grant, the newly named general in chief of all Union armies. With Lincoln's blessing, Grant had conceived, earlier that spring, a strategy for breaking the stalemate in the eastern theater of war and bringing the Confederacy to its knees. Mobilizing the Union's superior manpower and matériel, Grant would strike multiple, simultaneous blows at the rebels: Meade's Army of the Potomac would take on Lee, while Ben Butler's army moved up the James River to threaten Richmond from the south; Franz Sigel would occupy Confederate forces in the Shenandoah Valley to keep them from reinforcing Lee. Meanwhile, in the Deep South, Sherman was to challenge Johnston's army in Georgia while Nathaniel Banks was to take the vital port of Mobile, Alabama, and then move north to join forces with Sherman. In both the Virginia and Deep South theaters, in other words, coordinated assaults by Union forces were to trap the Confederates in a vise. Revealing which campaign he thought was most important—and offering Meade a guiding hand and protection from interference from Washington, D.C.—Grant chose to make his headquarters with the Army of the Potomac.[1]

Two years earlier, during McClellan's doomed Peninsula Campaign, Van Lew had thrilled to the sounds of the nearby battles. Now, as a new spring offensive began, Van Lew was too war weary to rejoice. "It seems to me we have suffered past all excitement," she declared, speaking for her fellow Unionists. "Nothing elates me. I have a calm hope, but there is much sadness with it." That sadness deepened as reports came in from the Wilderness; in two days of savage fighting, the Union had incurred a staggering 18,000

"Yearning for deliverance."
*U. S. Grant, on whom Van Lew's
hopes rested* (LIBRARY OF CONGRESS).

casualties and the Confederacy 10,800. "The burning woods . . . consumed
many Yankees lying there," Van Lew wrote in reference to the brush fires
that burned countless wounded men alive; "Oh death and carnage so near!"[2]

In the days that elapsed until Van Lew's next journal entry, on May 14,
1864, the slaughter intensified, as Grant's and Lee's armies shifted from the
Wilderness southeast to Spotsylvania Court House; May 12 witnessed the
particularly hellish engagement at the "bloody angle," in which each side
suffered about 7,000 casualties. Even as that battle raged, Union Major General
Philip H. Sheridan's cavalry left Spotsylvania behind and headed south,
slashing its way to the very outskirts of Richmond before turning east and
then south again toward Butler's army. The raid left Confederate cavalry
legend J. E. B. Stuart dead in its wake, and resulted in the destruction of
Confederate supply depots, rolling stock, bridges, and track, as well as private
property. Meanwhile, Ben Butler's Army of the James was continuing its
advance toward Richmond, clashing repeatedly with the Confederates at
Drewry's Bluff, a James River fort a mere seven miles from the capital.
Butler's advance was prompted in part by information he received from Van
Lew. As Butler recalled, in early March 1864 one of his "confidential scouts"

(probably Wardwell) had "been at Richmond some weeks and brought me a letter from my correspondent there, Miss Van Lieu"[sic]; the dispatch stated that since most of Richmond's troops had been sent to help Lee, the city was lightly garrisoned and the time was ripe for a Federal attack.[3]

Van Lew was awakened by the sound of cannons on May 14, and passed the time on the rooftop of the family's mansion, straining to make out details of the not-too-distant fighting. Her journal entry for that day is the rare passage in her surviving papers that identifies, by name, the African American servants on whom she so depended. Every morning it was her habit, Van Lew reveals, to turn to her trusted Mary for information: "I say to the servant, 'What news, Mary?' and my caterer never fails!" Van Lew also singles out Uncle Nelson for mention; as the artillery boomed, she asked Nelson if he could distinguish the Yankee guns from the Confederate ones, to which he replied "Yes Missis, them deep ones." Both anecdotes were deployed by Van Lew to support the broader assertion that "most generally our reliable news is gathered from negroes, and they certainly show wisdom, discretion and prudence which is wonderful." As if to underscore how deeply she identified with these black Unionists, her May 14 entry likens the condition of Unionists to enslavement—in a seemingly endless "captivity," she and other true patriots dragged their "lengthened chain," all the while "yearning for deliverance."[4]

Tragically, deliverance was once again deferred, as Butler's offensive ground to a halt. On May 16 General P. G. T. Beauregard launched a Confederate counterattack on Butler's army, driving the Beast back to a narrow tract of land between the James and Appomattox Rivers; after throwing up formidable entrenchments in Butler's path, so completely did Beauregard have Butler bottled up that the rebel general was able to send reinforcements to Lee's army north of Richmond. With Butler neutralized, and Franz Sigel disgraced for botching his mission in the Shenandoah Valley, Grant and the Army of the Potomac were on their own in the quest to vanquish the resilient "Marse Robert." His determination and confidence somehow intact despite the costly reverses in Spotsylvania County, Grant again went on the offensive, initiating a series of flanking movements along the Confederate right, to the southeast. By May 27, the date of Van Lew's final surviving journal entry for that spring, Lee had countermarched his troops to Ashland, 15 miles north of Richmond. Van Lew realized that the two armies were "on the eve of fearful bloodshed." A young man of her acquaintance "turn[ed] deadly pale when ordered to join General Lee," she wrote. " 'I would as soon go into the crater of a volcano,' said he."[5]

The battle that ensued when Grant tried to break Lee's line of defense at Cold Harbor, a crossroads just ten miles northeast of Richmond, was volcanic in its heat and destructiveness. With the Confederate defenders well entrenched, taking, as historian James I. Robertson has put it, "maximum advantage of every ravine, stream, and tree line," the surging Union troops were cut to pieces, thousands falling dead or wounded in the first few minutes of the attack. Grant would later write "I regret this assault more than any one I have ever ordered."[6]

Sometime in the immediate aftermath of the battle, Grant's headquarters were visited by none other than John Van Lew, Elizabeth's brother. With the Confederates intent on forcing him at last into battlefield duty, John had fled Richmond and set out for Union lines. John's flight necessitated the closure of his hardware store and made the financial status of the Van Lew family more precarious. Federal army scout Judson Knight remembers meeting John at Cold Harbor, and trying in vain to recruit him as a Union scout. John demurred, and announced his intention of making his way to Philadelphia. But before he departed, John did pass on some important information: "I will tell you something that may be of value to you," Van Lew confided to the Union scout. "If you can ever get into communication with my mother or sister, they are in a position where they might furnish you with valuable information." Knight would soon receive ample confirmation that the Van Lew women were a priceless asset to the Federal cause, as he took on the role of chief military scout for intelligence head George Sharpe. At the same time that John took flight, William Rowley, too, was coming under scrutiny, as his neighbors reported to the Confederate authorities that he was "a Union man who was shirking out of their service." Rowley was arrested and forced to join a rebel Ambulance committee; it was only after pleading that he, as a Dunkard, was a conscientious objector—and after paying the $500 exemption fee—that Rowley was released from the rebel service.[7]

In the wake of the Cold Harbor disaster, Grant decided that the best course of action was to join forces with Butler's army and take the vital rail junction of Petersburg, 23 miles south of Richmond, thereby cutting off the rebel capital from its lines of supply. To that end, Grant dislodged his vast army from Cold Harbor and moved it south, across the James River. This daring gambit entailed, Grant biographer Jean Edward Smith has explained, "breaking off contact with a powerful opponent along a seven-mile trench line, with rebel revetments sometimes no more than forty yards away; stealthily withdrawing across the Chickahominy swamps to a crossing site on the James during which the army would be vulnerable to attack; and crossing a powerful tidal river half again the width of the Mississippi below Vicksburg." Miraculously, the march "went like clockwork"; Grant's crossing of the James, Smith argues, was the tactical breakthrough that "set the stage for Lee's ultimate defeat."[8]

But that defeat was still a long way off. For four days, June 15 to 18, Federal forces probed at Petersburg's defenses, but despite the great advantage the Union had in manpower, the Yankee army was outmaneuvered and held in check by rebel forces under General Beauregard. Decimated by 64,000 casualties since the spring campaign had opened, Grant's army settled in for a siege. It would stand poised at the gates of Petersburg all summer, fall, and winter and into the war's final spring.[9]

During these last seasons of the war, the Richmond underground would shift its focus away from the plight of the city's prisoners and devote itself instead to furnishing the Federal armies with military intelligence. With Grant in charge of the eastern theater, Ben Butler was eclipsed as the primary patron of Van Lew's network by Colonel George H. Sharpe, intelligence chief for the Army of the Potomac (Sharpe was promoted to brigadier general in February of 1865). Sharpe had an excellent rapport with Grant, and was in constant contact with the general in chief at City Point, the James River landing town that served as "military capital of the United States" during the last year of the war. Sharpe initially placed liaison officers, Lieutenant John I. Davenport and Lieutenant Frederick Manning, with Butler's Army of the James to oversee army correspondence with the Union spy ring, but soon decided to preside personally over the army's exchanges with the Richmond agents. Sharpe testified that he established contact with Van Lew "soon after our arrival at City Point"—sometime, that is, in late June of 1864. According to Van Lew's own recollections, Sharpe quickly proved to be a superior boss to Butler: "As the war advanced and the army closed around Richmond, I was able to communicate with General Butler and General Grant, but not so

"A swashbuckling nineteenth-century
spymaster."
*George H. Sharpe, whose agents con-
nected Richmond and City Point*
(LIBRARY OF CONGRESS).

well and persistently with General Butler, for there was too much danger in
the system and persons. With General Grant, through his Chief of Secret Service, General George H. Sharpe, I was more fortunate."[10]

That Van Lew was able to communicate "well and persistently" with
Grant and Sharpe is easily established; each man testified to the effectiveness
of Van Lew's intelligence gathering in postwar encomiums to her. By contrast, the exact nature of her spy tradecraft—the who, what, when, and
where of her operations—has been more elusive, so careful was her network
to conceal itself from the gaze of outsiders during the war. Fortunately,
sources do exist that permit us access to the inner workings of the Unionist
underground. The best of these are claims for recognition and remuneration
filed by Unionists before the Committee on War Claims and the Southern
Claims Commission in the postwar decades; when supplemented by reminiscences and correspondence by the principal players in the drama, such
sources constitute a paper trail leading from Van Lew's mansion to Union
headquarters at City Point and beyond.[11]

Van Lew's espionage role is better characterized as that of "spymaster"
than "spy." While she continued to carefully mine contacts she had among

"They might furnish you with valuable information." *Scouts and guides of the Army of the Potomac, on the eve of Grant's Virginia campaign* (LIBRARY OF CONGRESS).

the Confederate elite and in the government, her principal function was not to gather intelligence and convey it but rather to receive the queries and directions of the high command; deploy her corps of Unionist agents (also referred to as couriers and scouts) to gather information; sort out and interpret what they brought back to her; and then draft the reports that would be sent by courier on to Union headquarters.[12]

We have already seen how intrepid Unionists William Rowley, Burnham Wardwell, and Arnold Holmes made the transition from efforts on behalf of Unionist civilians and Federal prisoners to serving as agents for Benjamin Butler. As Sharpe geared up his operations, a new network of intelligence runners sprang into action. Their roster included William Fay, John Hancock, D. W. Hughes, and James Duke of Henrico County, and Alexander Myers, Charles Major, James Sharp, Major Marable, Lemuel Babcock, Charles Carter, and Sylvanus Brown of Charles City County. Moreover, the network included at least a few of Van Lew's African American servants and servants of the Carrington family as well. These individuals carried dispatches to Federal army scouts, such as Judson Knight, at five stations on the way from Richmond to City Point. One of the stations was a 12-acre vegetable farm the Van Lews owned about a quarter of a mile below the city of Richmond, along the Osborne Turnpike near the James River. The farms of James Duke in Henrico County and Lemuel Babcock and Alexander Myers in Charles City County may have been others of the five rendezvous points. The preferred overland route in and out of Richmond for Van Lew's couriers was to take the Charles City road, which snaked its way east and then south of the city to the banks of the James, directly across from City Point; when that or the other major roads were closed to civilian traffic, agents had to bushwhack their way on foot along the 35-mile stretch from the rebel capital to Federal headquarters.[13]

Van Lew's agents were a diverse and intriguing lot. William Fay, as we have seen, had been one of those arrested and sent to Salisbury prison in March of 1862. After his release he resettled for a time in Richmond. But by June 1 of 1864, he had decamped from the rebel capital and made it to Union lines, where he served, according to Federal officer George F. Clark, "ostensibly as a Carpenter but really [was] engaged as a secret agent." Fay evidently made the perilous journey back into Richmond numerous times; one Union courier revealed in a postwar claim that he "carried dispatches from General Sharpe to the union people in Richmond . . . [such as] Mr. Fay & Miss Van Lew." Fay not only transmitted military intelligence but also correspondence between John Van Lew in Philadelphia and Elizabeth on Church Hill. Another of the Richmond loyalists sent to Salisbury in 1862, John Hancock, also tendered his services to the Union in 1864. A machinist of English birth, Hancock was described by one Confederate commentator as "a jolly, Rollicking fellow, having wonderful facial expression and great powers of mimicry."[14]

Rivaling Fay and Hancock in importance were Richmond machinist D. W. Hughes and Henrico farmer James Duke. Hughes had done a five-month stint in Castle Godwin for suspected disloyalty in 1861 and served time in Castle Thunder as well. Refusing to be intimidated, he seized the opportunity to join the Union espionage team in 1864; "[I] sent all the information I could through the lines to Colonel Sharpe," he has testified. Hughes in turn recruited his longtime friend James Duke, a Henrico County farmer who lived on a tract of 125 acres five miles southeast of Richmond, between the Charles City and Darbytown roads. Like so many other Unionists who were hounded by the conscription agents, Duke had four sons conscripted by the rebel army but he "got them all out & across the lines & safe to the North." He also "helped Union men & Union soldiers across the lines" and "took care of & secreted deserters & prisoners," this in collaboration with Elias Nuckols, a Richmond Unionist who eventually took up residence at City Point and practiced his trade, carpentry, for the Union

army. Most important, Duke "carried dispatches to Colonel Sharpe," Judson
Knight, and others. Hughes would take the secret messages from Richmond
to Duke's place and Duke would carry them on. In praise of his friend's
skill and efficiency, Hughes would vouch after the war that Duke gave "important despatches 8 or 10 times that I know went through from what I
afterwards heard from Colonel Sharpe."[15]

These men of Henrico County worked closely with a group of Unionists
in neighboring Charles City County. Among them was Alexander Myers,
identified by James Duke as a "very prominent Union man . . . in the secret
service," who accompanied Duke through the lines many times and at whose
house Duke often stopped during his scouting missions. Living some four
miles from Myers, a little east of Malvern Hill, was his fellow scout James
Sharp, a Scotsman described by his friends as devout and honest; though a
"sterling Union man," Sharp had avoided detention by the Confederates
because his neighbors deemed him "inoffensive and not likely to do any
harm." Not quite so fortunate were agents Charles Major and Major Marable; boyhood friends, these Charles City farmers were always perilously
close to being caught in the Confederate net. Major had been conscripted
into the Confederate army and, like John Van Lew, chose to desert and head
for Union lines. Unlike Elizabeth's cautious brother, however, Charles Major
signed on as a scout for the Federal army. Marable, for his part, had done
time in Castle Thunder in 1863 for "helping a man named Morris through
the lines" but chose nonetheless to risk reimprisonment by running dispatches for General Sharpe. Charles Major would later say of Marable, "[I]
trusted nobody & talked to nobody as I trusted & talked to him."[16]

A mile from Charles Major's farm lived Lemuel Babcock, a Vermont
native who had his share of brushes with the Confederate authorities. Knowing full well that his pro-Confederate neighbors considered him a "Yankee
rascal," Babcock joined a "Home Guard of old men" to divert suspicion.
The ruse did not work. In 1862 he was arrested by the County Sheriff for
"reading abolishionary [sic] papers" to local blacks; he was released when
he explained that he had simply been "reading sermons to the colored people
at night." (News of this chilling arrest quickly made the rounds to other
Unionists such as Charles Major.) Fearing that Confederates were determined to find an excuse for detaining him, Babcock sent his wife through
the lines to New Hampshire; sure enough, he was subsequently arrested for
being a "suspicious character." By making a Confederate guard drunk,

Babcock escaped his captors as they tried to take him to Richmond. Soon after that he joined Sharpe's secret service. According to James M. Humphreys, who was a scout for the Army of the James under Butler, Babcock's "house was considered the headquarters of the Scouting parties of the Union Army."[17]

Perhaps the most productive of all Elizabeth Van Lew's couriers was a native Virginian, Charles M. Carter. Carter, "whom [Colonel George] Sharpe once took pains to meet between the lines, lived in Charles City County, beyond the Chickahominy; that suggests that his cover was supplying farm products to Richmond." Whatever the pretense, Carter frequently made his way into Richmond to meet Van Lew in person and receive her instructions.[18]

An excellent window into how Van Lew oversaw and deputized this band of agents is provided in a postwar deposition by James Duke. He relates the details of a particular mission: "On one occasion when I was going through the lines for Miss Van Lew ... she gave me a package of papers for James Sharpe [sic] and Charles Carter who lived a mile from Sharpe. They were both represented to me as being sound Union people during the war. I started to go, and on reaching the Chickahominy found it so high I could not cross, and the bridge being carried away I returned to Richmond and gave the papers to Miss Van Liew [sic]. She said I would have to go again in a few days if neither of them [Charles Carter or James Sharp] came to Richmond in the mean time. I went to see her again soon and found Mr. Carter had been to see her. I rode her horse when I made the trip to the river."[19] Van Lew had at her disposal, then, a devoted group of white men willing to take her orders without question, many of whom had already run afoul of the Confederate authorities and who knew that to get caught was to be branded as "repeat offenders."

Marvel as we should at the courage of these men, we should be all the more awestruck at the risks incurred by the African American members of Van Lew's espionage operation. Free blacks in Richmond, Henrico County, and Charles City County were essential to Union intelligence gathering. For example, about a mile from Lemuel Babcock, near Wilcox's Landing on the James, lived an African American farmer named Sylvanus J. Brown. A confidante of Babcock's, Brown possessed a pass to go into Richmond to sell goods at the market; under such pretense he "carried a good many persons white and colored from Richmond in [his] cart and helped them to escape to Union lines." His experience at aiding fugitives made Brown an ideal recruit for Sharpe's spy network, and indeed Brown proved willing and able, carrying "letters to Union men and women" in Richmond. Brown also accompanied a Union army scout on a dangerous reconnaissance mission, taking him "across the Chickahominy Swamp and by the rebel camps in the night close up to Richmond to see the position of the Confederates." According to Brown's postwar claim, the Confederate authorities came to suspect him of treachery and offered a reward in the Richmond papers to anyone who would capture Brown "dead or alive."[20]

The Van Lew family's own slaves again and again demonstrated devotion to the Union cause and fearless resourcefulness in coming to its aid. Much of what we know about the spy work of Van Lew's servants comes from postwar newspaper reports. In 1869, in its coverage of Van Lew's appointment as postmaster, the *Richmond Dispatch* asserted that military intelligence had been "conveyed to the Union army by Miss Van Lew's male slaves, in whose clothes were sewed up the communication intended for General Grant." In 1883, David B. Parker, who ran the postal service of the Army of the Potomac, conducted an interview with the *New York Tribune* (reprinted in the *Dispatch*), revealing "How Miss Van Lew and Other Richmond Citizens Aided General Grant." According to Parker,

> ... every day two of her trusty servants drove into Richmond [from the Henrico farm] with something to sell—milk, chickens, garden-truck, etc. These negroes wore great, strong brogans, with soles of immense thickness, made by a Richmond shoemaker. ... They never wore out of Richmond the same shoes they wore into the city in the morning. The soles of these shoes were double and hollow, and in them were carried through the lines, letters, maps, plans, etc. which were regularly delivered to General Grant, at City Point. The communication was kept up at our end—by means of a steam launch, which used to land a scout—usually Kearney—on the opposite side of the James early in the night. Before daylight he would communicate with Miss Van Lew's messenger and return to our side of the river.

Another postwar account has a trusted Van Lew servant carrying dispatches to Grant in dummy egg shells hidden among real eggs; the same source

"The Military Capital of
the United States."
*A view of the James River
from City Point* (LIBRARY OF
CONGRESS).

credits the black seamstress of the Carrington family as relaying secret messages to Grant hidden among the paper patterns she carried with her dress
goods. Unfortunately, since none of these sources cite wartime documents
or identify relevant individuals by name, we can only speculate as to the
identities of Van Lew's assistants. Various scraps of evidence establish that
the slaves William, Peter, and James Roane, Oliver Lewis, Uncle Nelson,
Anderson, and Bob, worked for the Van Lews during the war and therefore
may have been the couriers alluded to the newspaper accounts.[21]

The Van Lew slaves were deeply implicated in Elizabeth's double life,
aiding her in making a show of loyalty to the Confederacy even as they
worked secretly for the Union. Elizabeth had a cousin—the son of Eliza Van
Lew's brother W. A. Baker—in the Confederate army and stationed at Chaffin's Farm, an expanse of cleared and cultivated fields south of Richmond
on the James; the Confederate earthworks that girded the region constituted
the outer defenses of the Confederate capital. In July of 1864, that soldier
fell ill with typhoid fever, and the Van Lew women, along with Eliza Carrington, were permitted by the Confederate Provost Marshal Isaac Carrington to visit him. A week after the visit, on July 12, 1864, "Bob & Oliver, svt
of E. L. Van Lew" were granted permission to go to Chaffin's Farm, presumably to pick up the ailing soldier and bring him back to Richmond. Anna
Whitlock, the soldier's sister, reveals that the Van Lew women cared for him
at the Church Hill mansion, and that he died there. Elizabeth's own reminiscences credit William Roane with having cared for the sick Confederate
soldier. Roane paid a terrible price—he contracted typhoid fever from his
patient and died, "a martyr to the war," as Elizabeth put it. In the pages of
her journal, Elizabeth unflinchingly accepted the responsibility for Roane's
death. "God forgive us," she wrote.[22]

The most fabled—and most elusive—of Van Lew's African American co-workers is the mysterious Mary Elizabeth Bowser. Very little hard evidence exists to corroborate the stirring stories of her heroism. Evidently, rumors began circulating after Van Lew's death that during the war she had planted an African American servant as a spy in the very inner sanctum of the Confederate White House. An article published in the *Richmond Evening Leader* in July of 1900 as Van Lew lay dying told the story of how one of Van Lew's "maids, of more than usual intelligence, was sent by her mistress to Philadelphia to receive a superior education and then given her liberty and sent to Liberia." Van Lew, "feeling that a trusted, educated employee would be convenient to have around," sent for this charge. She came back to Richmond, was arrested (presumably for breaking the law that forbade blacks to return to Virginia after having left the Commonwealth to be educated in the free states), and brought before a judge. In her defense, she "declared that she had never been given her freedom but had only been permitted to go away on a visit." She was then given into the keeping of her former mistress, Eliza Van Lew. This same mysterious slave—whom the newspaper did not name—was planted, so the article revealed, by Van Lew in the Confederate White House, where in her guise as a domestic servant she really gathered intelligence for the Union spy network.[23]

This story, in virtually the same words, appears as well in a "biographical sketch" of Van Lew by John P. Reynolds Jr., the executor of her estate. Reynolds was the nephew of the late Colonel Paul Revere, a soldier whom Van Lew had aided during the war. Reynolds's sketch is an unpublished typescript appended to Van Lew's personal papers. Whether he was the source of the *Richmond Evening Leader* article or was merely parroting it is unclear. It is clear, however, that the story circulated widely enough to prompt a response from none other than Varina Davis, Jefferson Davis's widow, in 1905. Davis wrote to Isabelle Maury, regent of the Confederate White House museum, that she never "had in [her] employ an educated negro 'given or hired' by Miss Van Lew as a spy" during the war. "My maid was an ignorant girl born and brought up on our plantation," Davis continued, "who would not have done anything to injure her master or me." She concluded with an aspersion against Van Lew herself: "that Miss Van

Lew may have been imposed upon by some educated negro woman's tales
I am quite prepared to believe."[24]

Notwithstanding this disavowal, and the sheer improbability of the Davis's
hiring a black servant who had lived in the North and had been arrested by
the Richmond authorities, the story took on new life when John Reynolds
purportedly ascertained the identity of the White House spy. In 1910, at the
request of a man named William Gilmore Beymer who was preparing an
article on Van Lew for *Harper's Monthly,* Reynolds interviewed Van Lew's
niece, Annie Randolph (Van Lew) Hall, and asked her if she remembered
the name of the servant who had worked for Jefferson Davis; she confidently
identified the African American spy as "Mary Elizabeth Bowser." Hall described Bowser as one of Van Lew's "favorite" slaves, a housemaid who
waited on the family, and indicated that sometime before the war, Elizabeth
had freed Mary. "Mary had gone north," Hall continued, "then she came
back." Whether she had come back at the request of Elizabeth, Hall did not
know. As Hall recollected, during the war Mary "sort of disappeared from
Miss Van Lew's house," and it was during this "disappearance" that she was
"working for the Jefferson Davis's."[25]

When asked if she had knowledge of anything that Bowser had reported
from the Davis White House, Hall replied "No, I don't know of anything.
Of course I was just ten when the war was all over, and they wouldn't let
the children know what was going on." Hall was unsure of Bowser's postwar
fate, though she recalled that Mary Elizabeth married after the war, and that
the husband's name may have been Carter. She lived after her marriage,
according to Hall, in Stamford, Connecticut. Unfortunately, the one piece
of unimpeachable primary source evidence—the April 1861 St. John's marriage record announcing the wedding of Van Lew servant Mary and Wilson
Bowser—that corroborates the existence of a Mary Bowser also calls into
question Hall's claim that Mary did not wed until after the war. No records
of a Mary Elizabeth Carter residing in Connecticut have come to light.[26]

Despite this thin evidentiary foundation, Reynolds passed the name
"Bowser" on to Beymer, who made the information public in his 1911 article
on Van Lew for *Harper's Monthly.* According to Beymer, "The Van Lews had
owned a negro girl of unusual intelligence; several years before the war she
had been given her freedom, sent North, and educated at Miss Van Lew's
expense. This young woman, whose name was Mary Elizabeth Bowser, was
now sent for; she came, and for a time was coached and trained for her

"Time has effaced the answers."
The White House of the Confederacy, where Van Lew is rumored to have placed an agent (LIBRARY OF CONGRESS).

mission; then, in consummation of Miss Van Lew's scheming, she was installed as a waitress in the White House of the Confederacy. What she was able to learn, how long she remained behind Jefferson Davis's dining-chair, and what became of the girl ere the war ended are questions to which Time has effaced the answers."[27]

Most everything that has been written about Bowser since then has drawn upon, and embellished, this Beymer article. Van Lew herself never mentions a "Mary Elizabeth Bowser" in her extant papers.[28] Given the paucity of surviving information on Bowser, we must entertain the possibility that Van Lew's educated servant/spy was, in fact, Mary Jane Richards. As we have seen in chapter one, it was Mary Richards whom the Van Lews sent north to be educated, and then summoned back to Richmond on the eve of the war. Mary Richards used the alias "Mary Jones," and Mary Jones was the only free black servant listed in the 1860 census record of the Van Lew family. She may well have been the free black "Mary" whose marriage to Wilson Bowser took place at St. John's Church in 1861, and the "Mary" whom Elizabeth refers to in her May 14, 1864, journal entry.

Moreover, we can establish that Mary Jane Richards worked for the Richmond underground. In 1867, Reverend Crammond Kennedy of New York interviewed Richards in Georgia; his subsequent article in the *American Freedman* reported that "while appearing as a slave, [Richards] was in the secret service of the U.S." during the war. He added, "she could write a romance from her experience in that employment." Richards herself, in an April 7, 1867, letter to a Freedmen's Bureau official, writes that during the war she was "in the service . . . as a detective." After the war, Richards married a man named Garvin—a name Annie R. (Van Lew) Hall might have confused with the name "Carter." As for the earlier marriage of Mary and Wilson Bowser, the nature and fate of that union remain a mystery. A Wilson Bowser is listed in the Richmond 1869 city directory, as a "factory hand," but no mention is made there of a Mary Bowser. If Mary Richards had indeed wed Wilson Bowser, the marriage was short-lived.[29]

In light of this evidence, it is unlikely, although not impossible, that Mary Bowser and Mary Richard were two distinct individuals. According to Van Lew descendant Dorothy Grant, family lore credits one African American Mary, not two, with having received a Northern education and worked as a Union agent.[30]

In other words, the details of Mary Richards's life lend credence to the irresistible legend of "Mary Bowser": those details allow us to confirm that the Van Lews did educate an African American servant in the North, that she did return south, and that she did work for the Union underground. While no hard documentary evidence from the war years has surfaced proving that Richards—or any other Van Lew servant—actually spied in the Confederate White House, her life story suggests that if the Union underground infiltrated the Davis mansion, it was through the skilled manipulation of aliases and multiple identities. Mary Richards, practiced in the art of leading a double life, may have used the name Bowser or some alias during the war to conceal her unconventional past from Southern authorities—and even to win their confidence.[31]

With Van Lew fearing that her mother's mansion was liable at any time to be searched or placed under surveillance by Confederate authorities, she developed security measures to be used within the house itself. She hid dispatches and other sensitive communications in a secret place in the library. As her executor John Reynolds explained, "It was done in this way: at each side of the fireplace was a pilaster, or column, that reached about two thirds of the way towards the mantle shelf. These were surmounted by two small bronze figures of some animal, in crouching postures. . . . They were quite small, . . . [and] hollow and made in halves. The crack where the halves come together opens enough to easily admit a letter. Here it was, then, that she deposited, as in a United States mail box, her letters for Union generals. . . . She could put them in there while alone in the room and no matter if she were watched, it would never be known what she was doing." Her African American servants could, the account continues, "stir round the fireplace and remove the mail" and hasten it on its way to Sharpe, without running the risk of being spotted conferring with or exchanging documents with Van Lew.[32]

By August of 1864, this complex interracial network of agents was functioning so smoothly that Sharpe could boast to Major General Andrew A. Humphreys, chief of staff of the Army of the Potomac, "if the commanding general desires any specific information I should be glad to have my attention directed to it." Van Lew's agents were able to send Sharpe an average of three intelligence reports a week. George Sharpe's intelligence reports to his colleagues and superiors in the Army of the Potomac—based on what he was learning from Richmond agents—constitute a revealing record of Virginia Unionists' espionage findings.[33]

During the first phase in the Petersburg siege, lasting from June until October of 1864, General U. S. Grant had a three-pronged strategy: to increase the strength and supply base of his army; to starve Richmond by cutting off its railway links to the South; and to strike at Lee's army with what historian James I. Robertson Jr. has called a "pendulum action," assailing Lee first on one end of his siege line and then on the other. This strategy produced some fearful battles in the summer and fall of 1864, most notably the ignominious Union defeat at the "crater" on July 30. But even defeats ultimately advanced Grant's plan, for he knew his side could sustain the losses in manpower while the Confederacy could not. With the two armies hammering away at one another, Richmond Unionists sent Sharpe a wealth of intelligence on Richmond's defenses; the condition of Lee's army; and, most important, the movement of troops and matériel back and forth between the Petersburg-Richmond corridor and the Shenandoah Valley. Sharpe generally passed such information on to Meade's chief of staff, Andrew A. Humphreys, and to Grant's aide Colonel Theodore S. Bowers.[34]

On the subject of Richmond's defenses, agents regularly sent word about the strength of the picket posts and fortified lines that girded the city. Some of that information was intended to help prepare the Federals for launching offensives. For example, on the eve of the second Battle of Deep Bottom (August 13–20), one of the Union attacks against the northern part of Lee's siege line, an agent freshly returned from a trip to Richmond reported to Sharpe that "there was a camp of seven regiments of infantry . . . in the neighborhood of Deep Bottom" and that "work was being done to the fortifications on the north side of the city [Richmond]." A month and a half later, on the eve of the more successful Union drives at Chaffin's Farm and New Market Heights (September 29–30), agents from Richmond reported to Sharpe that "eight guns have been sent to Chaffin's farm to be put in position, and there were signs all day long of great uneasiness in the city; so when the firing yesterday morning was distinctly heard in Richmond, one of the city battalions was immediately ordered out and sent down to Chaffin's Farm. Hampton's cavalry still remains on New Market Hill." The Federal assault on Chaffin's Farm resulted in the capture of Confederate Fort Harrison and the establishment of a new trench line along Richmond's southern defenses.[35]

With Grant committed to the destruction of Lee's army, the Federal high command craved insights into the state of Southern troops. The Richmond underground obliged with information such as that received by Sharpe on September 6, 1864: after making a series of inquiries his Richmond agent had learned that Lee had ordered the men of Richmond's Fire Brigade to go through the city rounding up able-bodied men to be sent to Petersburg; these men were examined so poorly and processed so quickly that "it was reported one blind man had been forwarded with the others." The agent went on to assert that "no sugar or coffee has been issued to the troops since our occupation of the Weldon railroad" and that there was "a great dearth of soft iron, so much so, that it is said that no more is to be had for the manufacture of heavy ammunition." Ten days later Sharpe learned from a Richmond agent he described as "an intelligent man, having more than ordinary facilities" that in the factory of Joseph R. Anderson, the largest iron manufacturer in Richmond, "no iron suitable for making nails or spikes has been on hand for two weeks past." While such intelligence did not have immediate tactical applications, it surely lifted morale at Federal headquarters, for it confirmed that Grant's plan to wear down the rebels was working.[36]

Most important of all the military intelligence gathered by the underground were its reports on the whereabouts and condition of Jubal Early's Army of the Valley. Entrusted by Lee with ridding the Shenandoah Valley of Federal troops and threatening Washington, D.C., thereby diverting Grant and the Army of the Potomac from their Richmond-Petersburg siege, Early led a successful raid across the Potomac to the northwestern perimeter of the Federal capital in the second week in July. In August, with Early's army once again ensconced in the valley, Grant called on cavalry legend Phil Sheridan to root him out, and to lay waste the crops in the so-called breadbasket of the Confederacy. The contribution Richmond Unionists made to this effort was to keep Grant informed of the flow of reinforcements back and forth between Early's army and Lee's, and of the rumors circulating in Richmond about Early's plans. A mid-August report to Sharpe by a Richmond agent, for example, revealed that Lee had sent reinforcements from Longstreet's First Corps to bolster Early in the valley; "Great secrecy was observed in the movement, and the troops were taken through the city mostly in the night." The agent also saw a long train of artillery pass through Richmond, and "was told by Mr. Barnes, a prominent merchant, that they were going to the Valley." As historian William B. Feis has explained, Grant responded to the news that Early was being reinforced by ordering an attack against the Richmond defenses (resulting in the aforementioned second clash at Deep Bottom) "to remind Lee that sending troops away would be costly."[37]

During the second half of August, the Richmond underground worked hard to divine the intentions of the Confederate high command by following the movement of men and matériel between the two fronts. On August 25, for example, Sharpe wrote to Babcock that "our information from Richmond the day before yesterday was to the effect that one Division of Cavalry was to be recalled from Early." A few days later, Sharpe learned from his Richmond sources that the flow of Confederate supplies to Early had run dry: "No supplies are being sent to General Early whatever. It is understood that Early must subsist himself or starve." Of special concern to the Federal high command was the disposition of General Joseph B. Kershaw's division, which had earlier been detached from Longstreet's corps; rumor had it that Kershaw was to return from the Valley to the Richmond-Petersburg front and help Lee recapture the vital Weldon rail junction. The stakes were high: should Lee recall Kershaw, Union General Phil Sheridan was poised to seize the moment and pounce on Early. Unionist spies struggled to evaluate the various rumors, well aware that the Confederate government might circulate misinformation to throw them off the trail; a September 7 report from a Richmond agent revealed that "the Government is sending out reports in order to conceal [Early's] real movements." After "making inquiry from different sources," the agent could attest only that Kershaw's division had not recently passed through Richmond on the way to the Petersburg lines.[38]

Finally in mid-September, the Federals had a long-awaited breakthrough, as intelligence from the valley confirmed that Kershaw had been sent east to Lee. Even as Kershaw made his way to Richmond, Unionists in the city reported that the Confederate high command was desperately divided over how to deploy its remaining chess pieces. Somehow—perhaps through the offices of Van Lew servant Mary—the underground had gleaned insights into what transpired at a "council of general officers . . . at Mr. Davis' house" attended by "all the prominent generals from General Lee's army and in Richmond":

> It was said that General Early insisted upon more men being sent to him if he was ordered to hold the Valley; that General Lee also very strenuously pressed the fact that without re-enforcements he would be unable to hold his lines or meet the expected extension of the Union lines; that it was admitted that a part of the rebel lines are mere skeletons; that at Chesterfield particularly the line had been weakened to such an extent, in order to strengthen the enemy's right, as to make it a common subject of conversation. It was said to be agreed that Early should not return from the Valley unless necessitated to do so by an attack here which could not be repelled, and that if Early should not be able to get down in time they were then to fall back to the new line between Petersburg and Richmond.

Such reports from the Unionist spy network, detailing as they did the narrowing of the Confederates' tactical options, served as yet another confirmation that the time was ripe for an advance. On September 19, a few days after the Confederate officers' meeting, Sheridan launched a series of attacks at Winchester and Fisher's Hill that left Early reeling, and forced Lee to send him precious reinforcements—indeed, to quote Feis, Lee opted to send Kershaw, "who had not yet reached the capital, *back* to the valley."[39]

With Kershaw "in transit between the two theaters," Feis explains, Grant "battered Confederate lines north and south of the James, resulting in the capture of Fort Harrison, a formidable redoubt outside Richmond." Early, for his part, could not hold off Sheridan, and with the Confederate defeat at Cedar Creek (October 19), the Union was in firm control of the valley.

Feis has demonstrated that Sheridan's and Grant's victories can be attributed in no small part to the efforts of agents in Richmond and the valley: "Utilizing quality intelligence, Grant and Sheridan had effectively isolated Kershaw . . . denying both Early and Lee the services of a veteran division at a critical time."[40]

In October of 1864, as Grant's army struck Lee's lines again, the underground sent word to Sharpe and his aides, John McEntee and John C. Babcock, about such matters as the location of Lee's headquarters, the movement of Confederate conscripts to the front, and the debate within Richmond about whether or not the Southern government should conscript—and grant freedom to—slaves. Just as William Rowley had formally recruited Van Lew into Butler's secret service, Van Lew now recruited stalwart Unionist Samuel Ruth for a dangerous mission—that of using Ruth's RF and P railroad as a channel of communication between Richmond and City Point. Van Lew was following instructions she received in the form of an October 1864 letter from intelligence chief George Sharpe. As Ruth recalls the encounter, "I was approached by Miss Van Lew, she showing me the letter, which I read and recognizing the handwriting at once agreed to undertake the business." Ruth would go on to meet Charles Carter "regularly once or twice a week." When Confederate authorities grew suspicious of travelers from Charles City County to Richmond and threatened to arrest some of the county's residents, Carter relied on "a colored man"—another brave black courier whose identity is a mystery—to meet with Ruth. Ruth himself relied on a cadre of unsung heroes, such as fellow railroad employees Thomas Dodamead, Wiiliam Day, and William Piemont, to obtain information. In the last year of the war, to quote historian Edwin Fishel, spymasters Van Lew and Ruth developed "overlapping rings of agents"; Charles Carter was the key link between the two rings.[41]

Richmond loyalists were especially eager to provide insight into whether Lee, in the wake of Sheridan's decisive victories, would now retrieve Early's men from the valley. In late November, Sharpe's agents determined that Kershaw's division had indeed returned to Richmond; as if to show how close these Richmond informants were to the action, one report sent to General Grant by his chief of staff noted that "The markets in Richmond yesterday were filled with Kershaw's men, and one of our agents, a market man, had his stall robbed by them." Later that winter, the underground would reveal that additional divisions had been recalled from the valley to

Richmond, leaving Early with "only scattered remnants of assorted commands"; armed with this information, Sheridan was able to finish off Early
in March of 1865. Richmond agents also engaged in some counterintelligence, alerting McEntee that General Lee had trained two youths to serve
as his spies; posing as newsboys, they had managed to give Lee "all manner
of information."[42]

Sheridan's destruction of the valley's foodstuffs and other resources was
felt keenly in Richmond, where living conditions and morale were fast eroding. Van Lew and her fellow Unionists knew that Grant relied on them not
only for military intelligence but also for assessments of the political atmosphere and of living conditions in the besieged capital. Taken together, their
reports provide a picture of increasing desolation—of business suspended;
of rampant inflation ("all kinds of meat" cost $2 per pound); of deserters
being herded into forced labor at the Tredegar Iron Works to free up the
factory workers for military duty; of public bitterness at the fall of Atlanta
to Sherman on September 2; and of constant rumors that Richmond was
to be evacuated. Unionist accounts of this demoralization are confirmed by
the laments of many a Confederate Richmonder; writing of the reverses of
the fall of 1864, Sallie Brock invoked the proverb, "Troubles never come
alone, but in battalions."[43]

In November of 1864, the underground reported that the public was
much demoralized by the "late Northern elections" in which Abraham Lincoln had resoundingly won a second term and by Sherman's progress in
Georgia. For example, Sharpe conveyed to Major General Humphreys the
following insight gleaned from the Richmond network: "All thoughts are
directed to the situation in Georgia. The Government, from time to time,
claims to have dispatches of a favorable kind, but this is not believed by the
community; and our friends send us word, as the best indication of the want
of confidence felt, that gold has been steadily rising since Sherman commenced his march, and has now touched the mark of 4,000 per cent." A
month later, scouts sent an update—in the wake of Sherman's capture of
Savannah, "the prospective evacuation of Richmond" was again a popular
rumor "among the plain classes in the town."[44]

Such reports emboldened and sustained Grant and his staff. The reminiscences of Grant's military secretary, Adam Badeau, permit us to conjure
up how Richmond intelligence was received at Grant's City Point headquarters: "When night came, all the officers on duty at the head-quarters

"Conversation was the sole amusement." *Grant's staff at City Point, Va.* (LIBRARY OF CONGRESS).

were accustomed to gather round the great camp fire, and the circle often numbered twenty or thirty soldiers. Grant always joined it, with his cigar, and from six or seven o'clock till midnight, conversation was the sole amusement. The military situation in every quarter of the country was of course the absorbing theme; the latest news from Sheridan or Sherman, the condition of affairs inside of Richmond, the strength of the rebel armies, the exhaustion of the South; the information extracted from recent prisoners, or spies, or from the rebel newspapers."[45]

Although she could take pride in the productivity of her intelligence network and take heart in the progress of Grant, Sheridan, and Sherman, Elizabeth Van Lew had her own troubles in the fall of 1864, as Confederate authorities conducted a formal investigation of her family. Whether or not a specific tip or act of betrayal prompted the investigation is not clear; with the likes of Charles Carter, James Duke, and other Union agents calling on the Van Lew mansion, the family was always vulnerable to exposure by false friends or suspicious neighbors. What is clear is that recently appointed Provost Marshal Thomas Doswell initiated the investigation, and sought to build a case against the Van Lew women by getting their friends and relatives to testify against them. Elizabeth's papers contain her extensive ruminations on this episode. Seething with indignation, she steps outside the circle of her own family and writes about it as though she were a concerned friend bearing

witness to its persecution. Her mother, who as head of the family was the initial target of the investigation, Van Lew refers to as "a lady upwards of sixty
years of age whose standing and character were irreproachable."[46]

Van Lew begins her account of Doswell's investigation by declaring that
it exemplified the "system of espionage and treachery which prevailed" in
Richmond at the time; in other words, she hurls the accusation of spying
back at the Confederates. She then writes, "A loyal family I well know on
learning that Thomas W. Doswell was made Provost Marshal of Richmond
congratulated themselves saying 'we know him; he has visited at our house
& he no doubt will be friendly to us.' Yet this man went himself to a lady
whom he knew to be intimate with the family and tried to persuade her to
come forward and give testimony against them, telling her it was her duty.
From her own lips I learned this."

Included in Van Lew's papers is a transcription of a note sent on September 27, 1864, from Detective W. W. New to a "Miss King," reading, "Captain
T. W. Doswell requests that you will come to Comissioner Sands Office on
10th St. between Broad & Capitol to give testimony against Mrs. Eliza Van
Lew." The detective reassured King that she would not see Mrs. Van Lew at
the commissioner's office nor would her name be mentioned to the Van
Lews.[47]

"This lady was afterwards taken from her home and made to answer such
questions they pleased to propound but she was true to friendship and they
learned nothing from her," Van Lew continues. When Doswell called in
family friend Reverend Philip B. Price, and he, too, "could think of nothing
to betray the mistress of the house," he was told to "refresh his memory."
Such interrogations were, in Elizabeth's opinion, assaults on the civil liberties
of innocent people. And her own mother, in her mind, was the very embodiment of innocence and purity. The following characterization of Eliza
Van Lew serves as a window into Elizabeth's moral universe. Her mother
was, "one who never did 'aught' against their 'dear young government' and
was ever kind to their people in whose home, for humanity's sake, the Confederate *private* ever found a friend. I should remember the pale face of this
dear lady, her feeble health and occasional illness from anxiety; her dread
of Castle Thunder for her arrest was constantly spoken of and frequently
reported on the street and some never hesitated to say she should be hung."
Where the corrupt were in power, Elizabeth concluded, her mother's "pure
life was an offence."[48]

It might strike the reader as curious, and even hypocritical, for Elizabeth Van Lew to express such righteous indignation at Doswell's investigation when her mother's house was in fact the nerve center of the Richmond underground. But her reaction bespeaks something other than hypocrisy. First, it reveals the resilience of conventional notions of femininity—while Elizabeth Van Lew had rejected the ideal of the Southern lady as a model for her own life, she paid it a kind of obeisance in her reverence of her mother. In this instance, Elizabeth was adopting a posture much like that of the famous fictional symbol of the Civil War South, Scarlett O'Hara, who worshipped her mother Ellen as a moral paragon even as she herself flouted conventional morality. It must have been psychologically comforting for Elizabeth to take solace in the unimpeachable purity of her mother when her family was subject to insults and suspicion. And expedient, too—perhaps one of the reasons that the Van Lews' cover of respectability remained intact even under Confederate scrutiny is that Elizabeth truly believed her family, as represented by her mother, to be respectable.[49]

Second, Elizabeth's reaction illuminates her understanding of patriotism. Elizabeth could take credit for her courageous efforts and decry the opposition's unfair treatment of her in the same breath because of a kind of political absolutism. Van Lew did not think, as many a modern-day observer might, that Union intelligence gathering and Confederate counterintelligence measures were analogous—the sort of "dirty work" each side must do to win a war. Rather, she rejected the label of "spy" altogether and saw her own actions as a kind of moral resistance to oppression, motivated by "true patriotism," and necessitated by the "reign of terror" perpetrated by her enemies. The conduct of Doswell and other officials toward civilians was but one emblem of the depravity of the Confederate regime. Ironically, Elizabeth was adopting a posture like that of Rose O'Neal Greenhow, her counterpart among Confederate spies, who proclaimed her own "innocence" and decried Northern "depravity" when investigated by the Federal government.[50]

Van Lew moved, then, in a maze of ideas about female purity and partisanship. As we have seen, Confederate opinion makers hoped to give women direction by positing that they could serve as apolitical "ministering angels" and partisan "Spartan mothers" all at once. But as the war took its twists and turns, women found themselves on uncharted ground. Elizabeth blazed a trail as a partisan for the Union cause even as her mother hewed to the path of the ministering angel. Fortunately for Elizabeth, her captors were caught in the same maze as she. Thanks to surviving records in the files of the Confederate Adjutant and Inspector General's Office, we can juxtapose Elizabeth's account of the September 1864 investigation with the words and findings of her accusers. On September 27, the same day that Detective New called on Miss King, Elizabeth's sister-in-law Mary C. Van Lew swore in the following deposition to Commissioner Alexander H. Sands, "That she is well acquainted with Mrs. Eliza L. Van Lew and Miss Elizabeth L. Van Lew—that she resided with them mostly from 1854 to 1857—that she has frequently visited them since the war commenced, and often heard them express ardent desire for the success of Federal arms and the failure of the Confederate States to establish its independence—that they are strong abolitionist—that they sent a negro woman North to be educated—that John N. Van Lew has gone North on account of his preference for that Government—that she don't want her children sent off with the Van Lews— that she has no interest in their estate. And further this deponent saith not."[51]

The deposition is revealing on many levels. It offers one more angle on the story of Bowser/Richards: Mary C. Van Lew clearly viewed her in-laws' special treatment of the servant they sent North as proof of their disloyalty to the South. And yet her deposition failed to reveal the identity of this "negro woman." This silence may itself testify to the skilled tradecraft—the ability to dissemble and even to "disappear"—of Elizabeth Van Lew's educated servant.[52]

Mary C. Van Lew's deposition is equally valuable for what it tells us of the inner life of the family during the war. While Elizabeth's account of the badgering of Miss King and Reverend Price raises the possibility that this testimony was coerced, Mary C. Van Lew had longstanding personal grievances against her mother-in-law and sister-in-law that may have motivated this betrayal. Elizabeth's brother John Newton Van Lew and Mary Carter West were married in 1854. John was 16 years older than his bride. As Mary's testimony reveals, the couple resided on and off in the Church Hill mansion; their second daughter, Annie, was born there. Indeed, they were residing there on the eve of the war, in 1860, according to the census records. One can surmise that it was trying for Mary C. Van Lew to live under the watchful eyes of Elizabeth and Eliza Van Lew, and that she came to resent the way that John Newton revered and deferred to his sister and mother. Moreoever, according to the great-granddaughter of John and Mary Van Lew, Dorothy Grant, the estrangement between the two can be traced to the feeling of Mary's family—the elite Carters of Virginia—that her betrothal to John was "marrying down" into the nouveau riche class.[53]

From Elizabeth Van Lew's perspective, the problem with the marriage was not John's social standing but Mary's poor behavior, particularly in fulfilling her duties as mother to the couple's daughters, Eliza and Annie. Mary C. Van Lew during the war left the Church Hill mansion and took up residence at a dwelling on Canal Street, between Second and Third Steets. On July 21, 1862, according to an entry in Elizabeth's journal, John Van Lew and several other gentlemen took young Eliza and her nurse away from Mary's home, as she had "forsaken" the sick child to go out for a night of "awful sin." Eliza was brought to the Van Lew mansion where Elizabeth and the widow Van Lew could take care of her. Elizabeth wrote in her journal in August that "the little creature has improved very much in a month—I trust I may be *enabled* to do my duty to her—and that she may grow up to be a good woman." Eliza was joined by Annie and the two girls remained in the custody of Elizabeth Van Lew and their grandmother.[54]

While she does not name the awful sin that Mary Van Lew committed on July 21, 1862, Elizabeth implies in her account of that night that Mary's behavior was part of a broader pattern of negligence. John Van Lew's decision to entrust the care of his children to Elizabeth was the culmination of his gradual estrangement from his wife, an estrangement that reflected not only Mary's misgivings about the Van Lews' social status and their misgivings about her parenting skills, but also political tensions. Mary was a staunch Confederate, and according to Dorothy Grant, Elizabeth and John Van Lew wanted to insulate the children from her influence and neutralize any threat that Mary, by witnessing the inner life of the Church Hill household, may have posed to the Richmond underground. John Van Lew and Elizabeth sought to keep Eliza and Annie not only at a physical remove from their mother, but a psychological one, as well; they discouraged the girls from asking about, or talking about, Mary C. Van Lew. While there are no surviving sources that corroborate the charge that Mary was a negligent mother, we can confirm that Annie and Eliza were deeply devoted to their aunt, Elizabeth Van Lew, and grateful for her loving care of them. Annie, who married John J. Hall of Richmond and then settled with him in Massachusetts, has left us admiring accounts of Elizabeth and of the work of the

Richmond underground. Eliza never married; indeed she lived at the Church Hill mansion her entire life, as Elizabeth Van Lew's closest companion.[55]

In light of this family history, Mary C. Van Lew's testimony against Elizabeth in September of 1864 may have been a bid to regain custody of her children. Mary was evidently aware that the likely punishment for disloyalty by elite women would have been a sentence of exile from the South. She had the status of her children in mind when she specified to Sands that she did not want them "sent off with the Van Lews" if the Confederate tribunal were to banish the family to the North. In order to make it clear that her motives were not mercenary, Mary also disavowed any interest in the Van Lews' property, should the sentence be confiscation.[56]

A few weeks after this deposition was taken, Provost Marshal Isaac Carrington sent a copy of it to the Adjutant and Inspector General's Office, asking "shall other evidence be taken with a view to the removal of these parties from [the Confederacy]?" and noting that "they are people of wealth and position." The reply Carrington received to his query about the Van Lews sheds more light than any other extant document on why Elizabeth Van Lew got away with her espionage activities. Charles M. Blackford of the Adjutant General's Office, having gleaned over the course of the investigation that Elizabeth and not her mother was the proper target of the Confederate probe, stipulated that "Miss El. Van Lew of this city is very unfriendly in her sentiments toward the Govt." But, he went on, "it does not appear that she has ever done anything to infirm the cause—Like most of her sex she seems to have talked freely—and in the presence of female friends, who have informed on her. The question is whether she shall be sent beyond the lines because of her opinion?" Blackford's superiors were evidently persuaded by the argument that Elizabeth had not actually "done anything" disloyal: the ultimate finding in her case was "no action to be taken."[57]

While those sympathetic to the Confederacy might be tempted to conclude based on Van Lew's case that the Southern government let her slip because it was too committed to the principle of female innocence and too committed to the practice of punishing dissenting action rather than dissenting belief, such a conclusion does not hold up. As we have seen, women languished in Castle Thunder as did men. And historian Mark Neely has demonstrated that disloyal talk did land countless Southerners in prison; in over 13 percent of the habeas corpus cases he has studied, "political opinion was the key to the prisoner's arrest." Isaac Carrington, one of the Confederate "habeas corpus commissioners" empowered by the War Department to conduct military investigations of civilians charged with disloyalty, had ruled in an August 1864 case that it was "inexpedient" to let men who uttered disloyal sentiments to "go at large."[58]

It was Confederate prejudices, not principles, which served to insulate Van Lew. The salient characteristics imputed to Elizabeth by those judging her were the "wealth and position" of her family, and her bad habit—a conventionally feminine one, or so they asserted—of talking too much and too freely. In other words, elitism and sexism disinclined Confederate authorities to believe a frail spinster lady capable of politically significant acts of disloyalty. Moreover, the men on record as judges in the Van Lew case— Charles M. Blackford and Isaac Carrington—may have had personal reasons for underestimating Van Lew. Blackford's mother, Mary Berkeley Minor Blackford, had been a strong Unionist during the secession crisis, and though she outwardly supported the "Cause" once the war broke out, she never hid from her family her view that the dissolution of her beloved Union had been a terrible tragedy. Charles Blackford, in rendering his assessment of Van Lew, might well have had his mother in mind; if Van Lew's laments for the Union were treasonous, then what of Mary Blackford's? Carrington, for his part, may have known that the Van Lews were longtime friends of members of his extended family, the Carringtons of Church Hill. If Elizabeth Van Lew was guilty of disloyalty, was her confidante Eliza G. Carrington guilty by association?[59]

One wonders how well the Confederate disinclination to believe Van Lew capable of treason would have held up if the authorities had gained access to some hard evidence incriminating her, rather than the easily discounted grumblings—and possibly coerced testimony—of women such as Mary C. Van Lew. The fact that the Confederates did not unearth hard evidence is as much a credit to Van Lew's shrewdness as to her opponents' shortsightedness. Van Lew's working assumption from the very outset of the war was that the Confederate authorities would do anything to deceive her into a misstep; she believed deeply, as we have seen, that there was no act of immorality or double-dealing of which the rebels were incapable. She assumed herself to be under constant surveillance: "Visitors apparently friendly were treacherous. . . . I have turned to speak to a friend and found a detective at my elbow. Strange faces could sometimes be seen peeping around the columns and pillars of the back portico," she wrote. Clearly, she made sure her deputies were well aware of the these threats—her servants had turned away the Libby escapees in February of 1864 for fear that they were not who and what they seemed to be. Van Lew, in other words, was wise enough to overestimate her enemies, even as they foolishly underestimated her. Ultimately, it was the disciplined nature of her spy tradecraft—her system of encrypting messages, of deploying couriers with various covers, and of using bribery to turn enemies into sources—that enabled her to stay out of the reach of her pursuers.[60]

There is no more potent evidence of the efficacy of her intelligence operation than the fact that in the midst of all this scrutiny, Van Lew continued to dispatch her operatives through the lines. On November 17, 1864, for example, Van Lew sent Butler information through a Confederate deserter who was in her confidence; her message was that "the enemy are planting torpedoes on all roads leading to the city." Remarkably, the reach of the Unionist underground extended far beyond Richmond. Thanks to Samuel Ruth's well-placed connections, he was able to send Sharpe information pertaining to Federal operations in North Carolina. In early December of 1864, General Butler initiated a month-long assault on Fort Fisher, which guarded the strategically vital port of Wilmington, North Carolina. According to Ruth's postwar petition for recognition of his services, his network of operatives was able to inform the Federal high command "of the exact number of troops sent by General Lee to Wilmington to re-enforce the forts below the town, on the Cape Fear River, when General Butler went to attack it." Unfortunately, as had happened before in Butler-led operations, the intelligence contribution by Richmonders came to naught, as Confederates beat back the Union advance. It wasn't until Butler was replaced by Brigadier General Alfred H. Terry, in mid-January of 1865, that the Federals were able to capture Fort Fisher, and in so doing, close the South's last seaport on the Atlantic.[61]

The Unionist network of couriers functioned not only to channel intelligence to the military but also to enable Richmond loyalists to communicate with family and friends behind Union lines. As of November of 1864, Burnham Wardwell had, like William Fay and James M. Humphreys before him, left the city and joined the Federal forces; he served as lieutenant colonel and provost marshal in Butler's army. The *Richmond Examiner* got wind of this defection and lamented "we understand that Wardwell's wife and children live here in Richmond [and] that he communicates with and sends gold and greenbacks to them constantly." This claim is lent credibility by what we know of Elizabeth Van Lew's own clandestine correspondence with her brother. John Van Lew, it will be recalled, had fled the Confederate conscript agents and headed north. After settling in Philadelphia, he established communication with his family in Richmond through the kind auspices of William Fay, whom, as we have seen, was one of the couriers who ventured back and forth from the city to Federal lines. "You are very kind to offer to send letters to my people for me," John wrote Fay on October 31, 1864. "I enclose you a letter directed to Miss Emma G. Plane, which is the name I write to sister, or her alias." Shortly thereafter, John had Fay convey to "Emma" a request for money: "If I had about 2000 Dollars in greenbacks I might soon make it 10,000. People here having money are not at all disposed to lend it." The tone of the letter reveals that John very much depended on and deferred to his older sister, and lacked confidence in his own ability to cope. His closing line reassured her, "I will under no circumstances hazard one cent of any money you may send me for I am old enough to know what I am about."[62]

When the money he requested failed to arrive, John panicked, and confided to Fay his fear that a letter containing the funds had fallen into the wrong hands. A very revealing December 20, 1864, missive from John to Fay attempted to retrace such a letter's course—Elizabeth might have sent it to Union lines in the hands of one of the "servant men" of the Van Lew family, he reasoned, noting that "Peter and Jim" were the most likely candidates as they were the "two youngest and most active men belonging to us." John suspected that these servants were instructed to hand the letter over to Fay or Wardwell but that Sharpe's chief scout Judson Knight had intervened and seized it. John's suspicion of Knight grew when the chief scout claimed to have "lost" the letter Elizabeth intended for her brother. Whether John was telling the truth about Knight's actions is unclear; it is possible that Knight intercepted the correspondence to do a little prudent checking up on the Van Lew family. But we do know that John eventually received his money from Elizabeth—and a good thing it was, as he was unemployed well into the spring of 1865.[63]

John Van Lew and Judson Knight's mutual suspicion only serves to highlight what a nerve-wracking game Richmond's Union network was playing. One had to take countless leaps of faith, hoping against hope that seeming allies were true to their words. The specter of Castle Thunder always loomed on the horizon, as Van Lew and her compatriots were reminded when their cherished associate, James Duke, was arrested and incarcerated there in November of 1864. "Through the influence of friends & by using a good deal of money," Duke got out of prison in January of 1865. But there was not much time for celebration, for a series of arrests in late January and early February would strike at the very heart of the Richmond underground.[64]

8

"A Flaming Altar"

THE FALL OF RICHMOND AND ITS AFTERMATH

THE FIRST TWO MONTHS OF 1865, THOUGH RELATIVELY QUIET ALONG THE TRENCH line from Petersburg to Richmond, was a time of great danger for the Richmond underground. January began promisingly enough with Ruth and his circle sending George H. Sharpe encouraging information on the Confederate rail network's state of disrepair. Based on such intelligence, Sharpe sent Meade the following anecdote about the "depression" of Confederate spirits: "At a meeting of the board of directors of the railroad company, of which one of our friends is superintendent and was present, the president of the road, being the father of General Breckenridge's acting assistant adjutant general, came in and met his son there. The first question was 'What is the news?' to which the officer replied, 'Damned bad. If Sherman cannot be stopped, there is an end to the business.' Our friends quite naturally send us word that Union sentiment is largely on the gain." Sherman, of course, had undertaken his legendary March to the Sea. Setting out from Atlanta in November of 1864 (they had occupied the city in September), Sherman and some 62,000 troops had slashed their way toward Savannah on the Atlantic coast of Georgia. Along the way, they laid waste to countless farms and plantations, tore up rail lines, seized private property such as cattle and horses, and succeeded in demoralizing and enraging Confederate civilians. The principal purpose of the march, as Sherman saw it, was to impress upon white Southerners that the Confederate army could no longer protect them. When Savannah fell into Union hands on December 21, 1864, Northern morale soared. "I beg to present you, as a Christmas gift, the city of Savannah," Sherman wrote Lincoln, in a memorable line that was soon splashed across Northern newspapers. As the next stage in his campaign, Sherman would head north through the Carolinas. His destination was Virginia—and a rendezvous with Grant's army.[1]

Fearing that Richmond Unionists would be emboldened by the favorable turn of events, Confederates ratcheted up their counterintelligence efforts. On January 20, 1865, the rebel authorities struck simultaneous blows at the loyalist network, arresting F. W. E. Lohmann, John Hancock, and James Duke, along with Duke's sons Moses, Thomas, and William, in Richmond, and John H. Timberlake and Isaac Silver in Spotsylvania County.[2]

The Confederates were acting on a tip from Elizabeth P. Dade, an elite woman living in King George County, who had heard rumors that Richmond refugees were escaping to Union lines through Fredericksburg. The authorities trapped a group of such refugees at James Duke's tavern in east Richmond and got them to reveal the identities of those facilitating their flight. Lohmann and Hancock were then arrested at Lohmann's house; three days later, detectives called on Samuel Ruth at the RF and P office on Eighth and Broad Streets and took him into custody. The Union men were thrown into Castle Thunder.[3]

Although the government asked the newspapers to refrain from publicizing these arrests, for fear of alerting other potential culprits to the impending danger of capture, the Richmond dailies could not resist breaking the dramatic story. The fate of the arrested men provides yet more evidence of how social connections functioned as a political shield. Lohmann and Hancock were presumed guilty by the dailies; the fact that incriminating documents—giving the Federal army information about Confederate deployments on the James—had allegedly been found on Hancock was all the evidence the papers needed. Ruth, by contrast, was presumed innocent by the press; the *Richmond Sentinel* declared that he had "been long and favorably known in this city as a most efficient railroad officer, and a respectable, prudent and cautious man." Official verdicts on the men followed suit: Lohmann and Hancock languished in prison until the evacuation of Richmond. (Hancock tried to effect his escape by "playing dead," but was recaptured by the Confederates.) Ruth, by contrast, was "honorably discharged" by habeas corpus Commissioner Sydney S. Baxter on February 1, 1865. "There was not the slightest shadow of evidence against him," the *Richmond Whig* explained, discounting Miss Dade's charges as "trumped up." Ruth would later ask for remuneration from the Federal government for the $2,500 he had spent in effecting his acquittal; whether the money went toward legal fees or bribes is unclear. Connections evidently came to the aid of Duke and Timberlake, as well—Duke was awarded a writ of habeas corpus for his release on February 1, 1865, and Timberlake, who as a policeman was in the army's jurisdiction, was acquitted by a court-martial on February 10.[4]

Given the rash of arrests, one can understand why Elizabeth Van Lew's "heart sank" when Federal scout Judson Knight visited her in February to report that a new agent, an Englishman, was going to be brought through the lines to Richmond and planted there—while working as an engineer and posing as a "Southern sympathizer," he was to serve as a source of intelligence for Elizabeth's network. "Here was another avenue of danger," Van Lew thought upon hearing of this plan. Her sense of foreboding was justified, as the Englishman, named Pole, proved traitorous to the Union cause: upon arriving in Richmond he went to the provost marshal's office and fingered the two loyalists, Lemuel Babcock and William White, whom Knight had designated to help him. Babcock, no stranger to Confederate harassment, soon found himself in one of the "dungeon cells" of Castle Thunder. He "suffered greatly in prison and feared he would be hung," Elizabeth wrote; Babcock would remain under lock and key until the eve of Confederate surrender. White, himself an Englishman, was new to the espionage game but had won Elizabeth's admiration by his brave conduct in the wake of Pole's treachery—when confronted by a Confederate detective demanding "tell all you know or I'll blow your brains out," White had defiantly replied "Blow away." His defiance landed him in Castle Thunder till war's end. Pole, for his part, paid dearly for his double dealing. The Confederates did not believe him trustworthy and sent him to Castle Thunder, though not to "a cell and solitary confinement" like Babcock and White.[5]

As the Confederates intensified their efforts to expose and punish Unionism, Van Lew and the underground, in what by now is a familiar pattern, chose to ratchet up rather than scale down their activities. The months of February and March 1865 would see the loyalist intelligence operation at its most productive; "Scouts and spies were more active than ever before," Lieutenant Colonel Horace Porter of Grant's staff has written about the war's final spring. With Lohmann, Hancock, Babcock, and White locked away in Confederate jail cells, those operatives remaining at large had to shoulder an extra burden. Ruth, Carter, and Van Lew, in particular, rose to the challenge. Ruth and Carter can be credited with significant contributions to two successful Union engagements. In late February, Ruth learned that the

Confederates planned to ship 400,000 pounds of tobacco to Hamilton's Crossing, to be hauled to the Potomac and illicitly exchanged for bacon. He immediately passed along this information to Carter, who in turn conveyed it to Union headquarters. "The result is well known," Ruth would later attest. "Nearly the whole fell into the possession of the United States." Indeed, Ruth's intelligence prompted General Grant to organize a massive raid on Fredericksburg on March 5–8, 1865, during which Union forces not only seized the black-market tobacco but also destroyed railroad bridges in the area and took over 400 rebels prisoner.[6]

Later in March, Ruth gave the Federal government advance notice of the attack Lee planned to make on Fort Stedman, informing them it would come "as soon as the ground was dry enough to move artillery." Lee's last desperate attempt to break Grant's siege line, the March 25 assault was a bloody and heartbreaking failure for the Confederates. This was but the culmination of a long campaign by Ruth to bedevil Lee. Along with his practice of slowing railroad operations at key moments, Ruth had devised the idea that Northern newspapers promise the payment of large premiums to "engine-runners, machinists, blacksmiths, molders, and other mechanics" who deserted the rebel service to work for the Union. "This suggestion was acted upon," Ruth would note proudly in his postwar claim. The newspaper advertisements were "distributed to the Army and passed over by the pickets," with the result that "large numbers deserted," threatening the entire suspension of the railroad during the critical last months of the war.[7]

With desertion and death eating away at the tattered remnants of Lee's army, public anxiety in Richmond crested. According to a February 11 dispatch from Sharpe to Meade, courtesy of "friends in Richmond," rumors of "alarming disasters to the Confederate cause" were swirling ominously about, setting civilians on edge: "It was reported from mouth to mouth in Richmond yesterday morning and night before last that Charleston was being evacuated, and our friends say that they have reason to believe that the War Department has information to that effect. Night before last the alarm bells were rung in Richmond, and everybody turned out upon the streets. The cause of the alarm could not be distinguished, except in the unsettled state of the public mind." A few weeks later, at the end of February, Sharpe told Meade of Confederate efforts to control the mood in the city: "Our friends tell us that there is an entire prohibition of all news to such an extent that the people are not allowed even to talk upon the streets about what is a happening in North Carolina," where Sherman continued his famed march, heading north to reinforce Grant in Virginia.

Just how much U. S. Grant valued insight into Richmonders' morale is revealed by staff officer Horace Porter, who wrote in his memoir *Campaigning with Grant* that in early March, "One of our scouts returned from a trip to Richmond, and was brought to headquarters in order that the general in chief might question him in person." To Grant's satisfaction, the scout reported that "a barrel of flour now costs over a thousand dollars, and a suit of clothes about twelve hundred"; he added that counterfeiting of the fast depreciating Confederate dollars was so rampant that the people "don't pretend to make any difference between good and bad money."[9]

The very same inflation and shortages that plagued Confederate Richmonders hit Unionists hard, too. In mid-March, Van Lew wrote to City Point, "May God bless and bring you soon to deliver us. We are all in an awful situation here. There is great want of food." Despite the hardships, Unionists remained firm in their resolve. Van Lew undoubtedly agreed with the sentiments expressed by John Minor Botts in a February 1865 letter to Charles Palmer: only when the South made an "absolute & unconditional recognition of the authority, & supremacy of the United States govt" and of the "Constitution & the enforcement of the laws of the US every where within its original limits" would peace be possible.[10]

By the middle of March, measures were being taken in the rebel capital to prepare for the long-rumored evacuation of its inhabitants. U. S. Grant informed Meade on March 14 that he had seen "a letter from a lady in Richmond" revealing that Confederate troops had been ordered down the Danville road; that warehouses of tobacco, cotton, and other goods had been turned over to the provost marshal; and that "citizens were ordered to be organized, no doubt to prevent plundering in the city when it is evacuated." To Grant, this information clearly betrayed the enemy's intention to fall back, southwest to Lynchburg.[11]

Deliverance soon came. In the wake of Lee's costly Fort Stedman attack, Grant counterpunched, with a forceful blow at Lee's right flank. Grant intended this action to cut the last functioning railroad out of Petersburg and to prevent Lee's army from escaping to the west. On April 1, Federal soldiers hammered at the Confederate-entrenched position at Five Forks, which Lee had ordered General Pickett to hold "at all hazards." Despite valiant Confederate resistance, the line gave way, and by nightfall Five Forks was in Union hands. This final major clash of the long siege—dubbed by one Southerner the "Waterloo of the Confederacy"—was the beginning of the end. In the words of historian James Robertson, "Grant now unloosed the full might of his army. Federal artillery, from the Appomattox River to Five Forks, spent the night of April 1–2 blasting Lee's position with the heaviest bombardment of the entire war. Flashing guns and shell explosions turned the night into day; the ground trembled all the way to Richmond."[12]

The morning of Sunday, April 2 brought a massive Federal attack that encircled Petersburg and forced Robert E. Lee to recommend to the War Department that Richmond be abandoned. Jefferson Davis was attending services at St. Paul's Episcopal Church when he received the grim news of the collapse of Lee's army. The Confederate president left his fellow parishioners to their praying and promptly assembled his cabinet for its last session. He directed government officials to prepare to depart Richmond for Danville, to the southwest, via the last working rail line; Davis himself would leave the beleaguered capital on the 7 P.M. train. With Confederate statesmen on the run, control over the city devolved upon the municipal authorities.[13]

The fall of Richmond, the subject of so many stirring eyewitness reports, is one of the most dramatic scenes in all of American history. By juxtaposing the reactions of the defeated Confederates and conquering Northerners with Van Lew's own lyrical account, we can come to understand the special meanings victory had for Southern Unionists. For Confederates, the fall of Richmond was nothing less than an apocalypse, one shot through with searing irony, as it was the conduct of Confederate officials rather than of the occupying Union army that brought about the destruction of the city. Following through on a plan that had been in place since the fall of Savannah that winter, the Confederate army set fire to a wide range of resources, to prevent their capture by the Federals: tobacco warehouses and flour mills, arsenals and ironclads, bridges and depots, all came under the torch, giving rise, as the winds kicked up at night, to an uncontrolled and rapidly spreading conflagration. To make matters worse, the Richmond city council put into effect its own ill-considered decision to destroy all the liquor in the city, hoping to prevent the intoxication of either the armies or civilians. Unfortunately, the plan literally backfired; alcohol released from storehouses ran

through the gutters of the burning city, becoming a conduit for the stream-
ing flames, to the dismay of desperate soldiers and civilians who sought to
lap up the liquor and save it for their own consumption.[14]

By the morning of April 3, the *Richmond Whig* reported, the city "presented a spectacle that we hope never to witness again. . . . The air was lurid
with the smoke and flame of hundreds of houses sweltering in a sea of fire."
Law and order had ceased to exist. As one Confederate captain tells it, a
"mob of men, women, and children, to the number of several thousands,"
descended upon the now unguarded government commissary depots and
threw open the doors, unleashing a "demonical [sic] struggle for the countless barrels of hams, bacon, whisky, flour, sugar, coffee, etc. etc." For Sallie
Brock, who had been such a careful chronicler of the Confederate spirit, the
destruction of Richmond spoke of millennial judgment: "All the horrors of
the final conflagration, when the earth shall be wrapped in flames and melt
with fervent heat, were, it seemed to us, prefigured in our capital." Union
troops under the command of General Godfrey Weitzel began to enter the
city at around 8 A.M.; when they reached Capitol Square, they raised the
American flag to the strains of the "Star-Spangled Banner." "It was a req-
uiem for buried hopes," Brock wrote of hearing the national anthem for the
first time in four long years.[15]

⁓

The Federal soldiers who entered Richmond on April 3 watched the spectacle
unfold with a mixture of jubilation, pity, and disgust. Edward H. Ripley,
commander of one of the occupying brigades, exalted as he stood on the
threshold of the city that "the cruel war was at last over, and that the peace
we had so longed and prayed for, triumphant peace, hovered over us and
that I should never again haunt the flank of a marching column with a heart
steeled against all its natural sympathies." But his elation was soon clouded
when he witnessed firsthand the desperate state of Richmond's citizens. For
Ripley, the fall of Richmond was not an apocalypse but a near "holocaust,"
as he put it, brought on by the "ruthless barbarity" of the Confederate
authorities to the Southern people. "The Confederacy," he reflected, "like a
wounded wolf, died gnawing at its own body in insensate passion and fury."
To that barbarism he contrasted the courageous behavior of Union troops
who, at the command of Weitzel, threw themselves into the work of saving

"The final conflagration."
*Richmond in ruins, April
1865* (LIBRARY OF
CONGRESS).

Richmond from the flames. "Had it been for their own homes and firesides their fight could not have been more heroic."[16]

For Van Lew, the Union occupation of Richmond represented redemption and vindication. Her account of the events of April 2–3—supplemented by a remarkable letter written by her niece Annie—dramatizes what a strange and complex position Southern Unionists found themselves in at war's end. The Van Lews empathized with, and even assisted, Confederate Southerners in their hour of despair, and at the same time proudly gloried in the end of slavery and of the Confederacy. Right until the very moment of deliverance, Van Lew kept up her double life, maintaining her image as a respectable lady even as she worked clandestinely for her beloved Union.

Toward the end of the day on Sunday, April 2, as Elizabeth's account begins, she went to the front door of a neighbor to discuss the news of the evacuation. In an effort to comfort the obviously distressed woman, who had a son in the army at Petersburg, Van Lew said "The war will end now. . . . The young men's lives will be saved." When the neighbor replied that she would rather have her son die than lose the war, Van Lew silently retreated in disbelief. Later that night, Elizabeth offered comfort of a more substantial sort to the last in the long stream of Union fugitives who had taken refuge with her. As the city was evacuated, prisoners at Castle Thunder were rounded up by Confederate authorities to be transferred to points south, out of the reach of the oncoming Federal army. Among those inmates were three Van Lew associates—John Hancock, William White, and F. W. E. Lohmann—all of whom managed to escape their Confederate guard as they were being marched through the burning city. (The *Whig*, which broke the story of this escape on April 6, claimed that the guard had let the prisoners slip when he "stopped to drink some whisky running in the gutters.") Two of the three men made their way under cover of darkness to Van Lew's house. They were "gladly welcomed" by the women, "but with the terror yet upon us," Van Lew explains, "we were afraid to have a light in the room they were in." A surviving letter from Van Lew's niece, Annie, to her aunt Anna Klapp in Philadelphia reveals that one of the fugitives secreted at the Church Hill mansion was "John Handcock," as Annie put it; the girl recalls Hancock helping the family to store "ours and the neighbors silver in the dark closet," to prevent it being seized by looters or soldiers. Van Lew has written of the family's efforts on the night of April 2–3 that "our wheel barrow was borrowed; plate, papers, gold, jewelry forced in upon us for security," confirming that fellow denizens of Church Hill suspected that the Van Lews's Northern roots would insure them respectful treatment by the occupying army.[17]

The Federal army's entrance into Richmond on the morning of April 3 represented a moment of literal deliverance for Van Lew, deliverance from wartime fears that she had shared with her fellow Richmonders—the fear of impoverishment, of hunger, of the loss of loved ones, and of the destruction of the city itself—and from the special dangers of ostracism, exile, and imprisonment that she had courted as a Union spy. Annie Van Lew's letter of April 3 permits us an intimate, child's eye glimpse (she was ten years old at the time) into the household that morning, and reveals how the young girl regarded her formidable aunt.

> We rose about 5 o'clock, I was but half dressed when I happened to glance out of the window, and saw a large part of the city in flames. I did not stop to dress, but with sister [Eliza] ran to the top of the house. We came down finished dressing, then we went into the parlor to see the prisoners. Beds having been made for them there, we had just seated ourselves at the breakfast table, when we heard the tune Yankee Doodle. Sister and I ran to the bottom of the garden and were overjoyed to see the Yankees marching up Main Street. But I must not forget to mention, that the Rebels threatened to set our house on fire. Auntie went out on the front porch and said if this house goes every house in the neighborhood should follow.

Remarkably, Annie alternated this image of Elizabeth as defiant protector of the household with an altogether softer, conventionally feminine one. After breakfast, the child relates, she and her sister accompanied Elizabeth into the heart of the city. On Main Street, they encountered Union soldiers; Van Lew, Annie wrote with a hint of bemusement, "spoke to many of them and even hugged the horses. I will never forget how she looked with that huge bonnet on which we thought was very fashionable."[18]

Elizabeth Van Lew's own account of April 3 seeks both to provide salient facts and to transcend experience, conveying the broader meaning of the day's events. Of the practical aspects of the Union troops' arrival in the city she wrote,

> There were wild bursts of welcome from the negroes and many whites as they poured in. In an incredibly short space of time, as by magic, every part of the city was under the most kind and respectful of guards.
>
> The Federal soldiers, immediately on entrance, went to work to arrest the progress of the flames. Had it not been for them, the whole city would have been a map of smouldering ruins. The loss of public and private property was immense. Our beautiful flour mills, the largest in the world and the pride of our city, were destroyed. Square after square of stores, dwelling houses and factories, warehouses, banks, hotels, bridges, all wrapped in fire, filled the sky with clouds of smoke as incense from the land for its deliverance.

While many other Richmonders shared Van Lew's gratitude to the blue-clad soldiers who served as fire fighters, very few Southern whites shared the interpretive framework into which Van Lew set the Union conquest. For her, it represented not only liberation from war and its dangers but, more important, the vindication of her entire world-view. The fact that Richmond was set to the torch by the very Southern men who had pledged to defend it was altogether fitting—the "consummation of the wrongs of years," she wrote.[19]

In attempting to capture in words the broader meanings of the Union army's conquest, Van Lew rose above the personal, and thundered in righteous tones, "What a moment! Avenging wrath appeased in flames! The chains, the shackles fell from thousands of captives, and thousands of arms fell powerless to wield the Christianizing lash. Civilization advanced a century. Justice, truth, humanity were vindicated. Labor was now without manacles, honored and respected. No wonder the walls of our houses were swaying; the heart of our city a flaming altar, as this mighty work was done. Oh, army of my country, how glorious was your welcome!" Van Lew concluded her account of Richmond's fall with the most moving, profound, and prescient passage in her journal—a passage that shows how far she had traveled from the ideological middle ground that she had staked out before the war. Van Lew confronted the truth that so many white Americans, Northern and Southern, could not bring themselves to face: that though the war was at last coming to an end, the work of reckoning with racism had only just begun. As a Southerner, Van Lew had borne witness to corrosive depravity of the slave system. But, she was at pains to make clear, only African Americans themselves could tell the true story of American slavery. The Southern social order had been designed to silence blacks, and that veil of silence would prove difficult to cast off. Just what the moment of deliverance from slavery meant, she wrote, "They feel but cannot tell you, but when eternity shall unknot the records of time, you will see written for them by the Almighty their unpenned stories, then to be read before a listening universe. Bottled are their tears on His ear." Elizabeth Van Lew's Civil War narrative ends, then, with an expression of empathy toward African Americans that doubles as a rebuke to whites. It will be a long time, she seems to say, before the world understands what we have done to them.[20]

꩜

Unfortunately, few of those entrusted with shaping the peace shared Van Lew's sensitivity or vision. From the start of Reconstruction, the restoration of order and the reconciliation of whites, rather than justice for blacks, was the priority of the men in power. Lincoln's promise of "malice toward none and charity for all" and Grant's lenient offer of peace to Lee at Appomattox on April 9 sparked the hope in many a Confederate that the Union would be magnanimous in victory—but also sparked a fear among diehard Southern Unionists that the defeated rebels would be able to cling to power. For Van Lew and other progressive Virginians who had opposed the Confederacy, postwar Reconstruction would be a time of stark contrasts, of sweet yet fragile victories and bitter setbacks—a time to marvel at and glory in the profound and very real transformations that Union victory and emancipation wrought in the

South, and a time to confront, in a rearguard action, those who were intent on restoring as much of the old order as possible.

To be sure, there were many sweet victories for Van Lew to relish in the first heady days of peace. The Federal army acted quickly to put an armed guard around the Church Hill mansion, and Union officials soon called on the family to pay their respects—Colonel Ely S. Parker and Colonel D. B. Parker, two of General Grant's staff officers; Major General Marsena Patrick, soon to be provost marshal of the city; and Jedediah Paine, a staff officer of Major General E. O. C. Ord, were among those who sought out the Van Lews. According to D. B. Parker's reminiscences, General Grant himself had handed down the order that "all of Miss Van Lew's wants [be] supplied." Visitors from the Federal army found the Van Lew mansion "filled with many Union people," to quote Parker, including none other than Erasmus Ross, the embattled Libby clerk who had so skillfully disguised his allegiance to the Union. A few months after the surrender, Van Lew had the honor of hosting Grant himself. Grant's wife Julia remembers that "she accompanied General Grant on his first visit to Richmond . . . and he said he must call on Miss Van Lew, [for] she had rendered valuable service to the Union."[21]

Official recognition of Van Lew's services came in a second form in the immediate aftermath of the Federal occupation: on April 5, Benjamin Butler sent a letter to the War Department asking that John Van Lew and Arnold Holmes, both of whom had taken refuge in Philadelphia, be permitted to return to Richmond. Butler's plea vouches for the loyalty and services of the two Union men but reserves its most fulsome praise for his "secret correspondent," Elizabeth, who "furnished valuable information during the whole campaign." Thanks to Butler, Elizabeth was soon reunited with John, and many other reunions were to follow, as Burnham Wardwell, William Fay, John Minor Botts, and other prominent Union men made their way home to Richmond.[22]

Along with the opportunity to demonstrate her fellowship with her compatriots openly, Van Lew could take some pleasure, in the weeks after the city's surrender, in the myriad transformations of its physical and political landscape. The Union army set to work on clearing the rubble and repairing the transportation and communications networks that had been devastated by the fires. And it took control of one after another locus of Confederate power: Major General Weitzel made his headquarters at Jefferson Davis's mansion, while other Union commanders set up shop in the governor's mansion, Custom House, and city hall. Aptly, the Confederate officials Van Lew regarded as most culpable for the ill treatment of Union prisoners were themselves arrested and thrown in prison—Commissioner of Exchange Robert Ould landed in Libby Prison while Provost Marshal Carrington was consigned to Castle Thunder. Even Richmond's cemeteries were transformed by the Union presence, as relatives and friends of deceased Federal soldiers came to Richmond to remove their bodies from places such as Oakwood and take them home to the North for reburial.[23]

In a move symbolic of the transfer of power in Richmond and of Van Lew's penchant for collecting what she considered to be important historical documents, Elizabeth obtained in the days after the surrender some of the papers of abolitionist martyr John Brown. These had presumably been seized by Virginia authorities in the wake of Brown's failed revolt of 1859 and had been stored at the State Capitol in Richmond. Van Lew gained access to the records in April of 1865, and took a few documents, such as a printed copy of "John Brown's Constitution"—a manifesto that condemned slavery as "barbarous, unprovoked, and unjustifiable"—home with her to preserve among her own papers.[24]

Van Lew also witnessed her friends and associates receive official recognition and gain public authority. Late in April F.W.E. and John Lohmann were appointed as detectives in the office of Federal Provost Marshal Marsena Patrick; their duties included tracking down escaped convicts and searching for stolen goods. By June of 1865, a host of other members of Van Lew's wartime network—Alexander Myers, John Hancock, D. W. Hughes, and Philip Cashmeyer—were on the payroll as Federal detectives. Within the year, Richmond underground members had come to fill a variety of federal, state, and municipal offices. Burnham Wardwell was a port inspector; John M. Higgins a member of the Hustings Court; and Arnold Holmes was the superintendent of the state penitentiary. In May of 1866, Wardwell and William Fay were chosen to represent Richmond Unionists as members of the Grand Jury that handed down an indictment of treason against Jefferson Davis in Norfolk, Virginia.[25]

Van Lew's cherished servant Mary Richards assumed a position of authority of a very different kind, joining forces with the Union army and Christian Commission to promote the education of the freedpeople: she worked for the Baptist Home Missionary Society, offering instruction to nearly 200 black children at a newly established school in the Ebenezer Baptist Church.[26]

However gratifying such developments were for Elizabeth, they were juxtaposed with a series of troubling and even ominous events, the most important of which was the assassination of Abraham Lincoln on April 14. Lincoln had visited Richmond on April 4, boating up the James from City Point and landing not far from Libby Prison. In a move laden with symbolism, Lincoln made the White House of the Confederacy the "destination of his march through the ruins" of the city. Richmond's blacks hailed him as their messiah. "Each step of his way" through the rebel capital, historian Nelson Lankford has written, Lincoln "attracted more followers. The freedmen crowded around to shake the president's hand or just touch him." When he finally reached the Confederate White House, Lincoln turned to the admiring crowd and respectfully bowed, acknowledging his debt to the loyal Union people, and particularly to the African Americans, of the South. Black reporter Thomas Chester wrote that "it seemed as if the echoes [of Lincoln's gesture] would reach the abode of those patriot spirits who had died without witnessing the sight."[27]

With Lincoln's stirring visit so fresh in their minds, blacks in Richmond were outraged and despondent when they learned that their liberator had been murdered by a Southern fanatic. They "hung mourning clothes from their shacks and cabins, attended memorial services, and rightfully feared that with his death the government's concern and protection of them would end." While Elizabeth Van Lew has not left us any record of how she regarded Lincoln's assassination, it is safe to assume that she shared the sentiments eloquently expressed by her associate Burnham Wardwell in a letter he sent to Benjamin Butler on April 19. Wardwell despaired that the tide seemed already to be turning in favor of the rebels: "Vile murderers walk our streets at will. Our hateful ministers occupy the same desks they used to, and still continue to mock God and insult men. Women exult over the death of President Lincoln." A strong Federal leader was needed to assert control over the resurgent Confederates, Wardwell suggested, begging Butler "General, can you not come to us?"[28]

Van Lew in the days after the assassination made her own bid to exercise a kind of public leadership in Richmond. She penned an address "To the Federal Army," that expanded upon her journal entry about the liberation

of Richmond, and she attempted to persuade one of her friends among the
Federal troops, Jedediah Paine, to get the Richmond papers to publish it.
Her address read:

> I feel a welcome which I cannot write. When our beautiful Flag was
> lost to sight I folded it with my heart and I have there sacredly guarded
> it with every thought, word and action. It was too holy—too sacred
> an emblem to wave over us in our bloody, execrable work of desola-
> tion, oppression and every wrong that could be perpetrated under the
> most merciless, relentless, vindictive of despotisms. Such a tyranny—
> such a terror all hearts true to their blessed birthright, that no pen can
> portray no one without conceive it. Oh, how can we welcome you our
> deliverers?—Was ever so glorious a cause entrusted to any army—to
> any people! Not only the salvation the redemption of our country—
> but as you forward marched, the dust in your pathway had been laid
> by the tears of generations—the air filled for years with the voiceless
> unlipped prayers of those who watched for your coming—who
> groaned being burdened—for whom no earthly future beamed—
> whose Sun rose and set under the dark cloud of unremitting—unrec-
> ompensed labor. The cotton plant had been watered and purified with
> the tears—the blood of these martyrs.

Appended to the address was a note to Paine revealing that Van Lew was
perfectly willing to adopt a posture of deference to men whom she felt
worthy; "You are a man and privileged to give your bodily presence to form
part of our glorious army," she wrote as if to explain why she had felt it
necessary to write the piece, "and I—why I am privileged to enjoy the
blessings you have brought us." In a 1912 letter to Van Lew biographer
William Beymer, Paine explains that he could not induce the Richmond
papers to publish the address, and General Ord did not feel that the army
could force the papers to do it, much to Van Lew's disappointment.[29]

That Van Lew sought to go public with views she knew would be considered radical by most whites reveals just how determined she was that her
fellow Richmonders face up to the truth of the war's origins and meaning.
But Van Lew was struggling not only to tell the truth but to find a place
for herself in the postwar order. Although her bid for publicity failed this
time around, she would frequently, in the years to come, use the press as a
vehicle for her political views, claiming, sometimes implicitly and sometimes

explicitly, that her position as a Southern Unionist gave her special insight into the political problems of the age. The problem of Confederate defiance got ever more acute as Lincoln's successor, Andrew Johnson, asserted his will in national affairs, implementing a policy of leniency toward ex-Confederates, indifference toward Southern Unionists, and outright hostility to the freedmen.

The men charged with charting Virginia's course under the new administration of Johnson proved a severe disappointment to the likes of Van Lew and Wardwell. President Johnson quickly recognized the Pierpont government, which had spearheaded the establishment of West Virginia and represented the Union-occupied sections of the state from a base in Alexandria, Virginia during the war. Led by Francis H. Pierpont of West Virginia, a convention of the Commonwealth's loyalists had disfranchised Confederates and abolished slavery in 1864. On May 9, 1865, Andrew Johnson endorsed Pierpont's bid to establish his headquarters in Richmond and extend his authority as governor over the entire state. Once in charge of Virginia, Pierpont embarked on a policy of leniency to former Confederates, restoring suffrage to secessionists and therefore permitting conservatives to seize control of the state legislature. Pierpont had hoped he could guide and control these men but he proved wrong: the general assembly rejected his requests that it pay the state debt and establish free schools, and instead, against his wishes, passed a harsh "black code" that required African Americans to carry passes or to be liable for "vagrancy." The man Pierpont had unwisely appointed as mayor of the city, former mayor Joseph Mayo, energetically enforced this black code with the help of the Richmond city police, arresting hundreds of blacks for not possessing the required passes.[30]

When blacks protested these conditions as a throwback to slavery, Pierpont removed Mayo from office and President Johnson replaced General Ord, who had succeeded Weitzel as commander of Union forces in the city, with General Alfred Terry. Although Terry declared void the vagrancy law and pledged that the Union army would protect black civil rights, he could not hold back the rising tide of conservatism in the state. As conservatives swept the field in the July 1865 elections for mayor and other municipal offices, Wardwell again wrote Ben Butler to complain: "In fact all the officers of any importance who were elected were violent secessionists, many of them having been commissioned officers under the Confederate or Mob Government. Now, I am most anxious to know whether we are to go back into the hands of those who caused all our troubles, or not. . . . No one has any use for a Union man here. In fact many of our Union men are discouraged, worn out. Is there any hope of our having a Military Governor, or any assistance from the Government we lost all the property we had in defence of, or must we submit to the rule of those scoundrels who so wickedly treated us and all others who dared do or say a word in favor of our Government?"[31] Wardwell's sense of disbelief and despair would become more acute as the October 1865 state and congressional elections saw the reactionaries triumph. Though the United States Congress refused to seat the members of the Virginia delegation, several of whom would not take the required test oath of allegiance to the Union, the conservative state legislators who filled the general assembly were free to flex their power. They promptly passed a series of compulsory labor laws aimed at giving former slaveowners control over black labor power: a new statute that punished "vagrants" who were not under contract to white employers, and another that punished anyone who "enticed" a contract laborer away from his employer.[32]

Members of Van Lew's circle of unconditional Unionists cried foul. Wardwell, John Minor Botts, and Charles Palmer, among others, attended Unionist conventions and signed petitions to protest the reactionary turn in state politics. While Van Lew had not yet fashioned a public, political role for herself in the postwar order, she did attempt to submit her own protest to the government. In the papers of Senator James R. Doolittle of Wisconsin, one of Andrew Johnson's conservative allies, are preserved two February 7, 1866, letters from Van Lew—the first a short cover letter addressed specifically to Doolittle and the second a much longer letter addressed generically to "Dear Friend." We can infer from the contents of both that they were part of a letter-writing campaign—that Van Lew sent the longer letter to a number of different congressmen, along with a personalized cover letter explaining her intentions. Van Lew's cover letter to Doolittle announces that the longer enclosure will describe the persecution of Richmond's loyalists, and she begs the senator to "read & circulate" such information in Congress. Van Lew also clearly specifies her motives: she had "no desire to bring [herself] forward in any way—simply to show things as they are and do justice to a class entirely overlooked and deeply injured." The loyal whites of the South, she explained, were nearly as deserving of Congress's attention as African Americans were; indeed those loyal whites could prove "very useful in caring for and protecting the Freedman."[33]

While the cover letter adopts a posture of humility and deference, the longer letter finds Van Lew in rhetorical high gear, marshaling sarcasm, irony, and didacticism to drive her points home. She had been loyal, she begins, because in her "ignorance and sincerity" she had "thought it best for the whole South to be so." "I cannot do things by halves," she states bluntly, in an apt and honest assessment of her own personality. She now wishes, she confesses, with tongue in cheek, that she could be a "real out and out Secessionist." Why? "Witness every thing around us," Van Lew explains. "Who receives all favors? Who is powerful? Who has made money and kept it? Who legislates for us? Who preaches to us? . . . The Secessionists." Meanwhile, she continues, "Who are the true Pariahs—wanting food—raiment—employment—office—snubbed by women—scorned by men—ignored by Govt.?" The loyal people of the South, who, like blacks, bore "unpardonable marks of low caste" in the eyes of the white majority. To Van Lew's bitter disappointment, the social dynamic that she had so long railed against had not changed: loyal whites and blacks were still the "scapegoats on which [Southerners] lay all their sins!"[34]

It is indecent for the nation to be so ungrateful, Van Lew argues, to a group that had suffered so much on its behalf. In an effort to conjure for her readers the wartime horrors of Castle Thunder and Salisbury and the other prison pens that had caged Unionist civilians, Van Lew evokes images of "old men—of spotless lives—and purest character—in densely crowded prison cells—without even a stool bench or table—living on the bare floor with the festering flesh falling from their poor backs." Confederates were even crueler to such Unionist civilians than to military POWs, Van Lew declares. "Noble Army of martyrs are the glorious Union dead of the South!"[35]

Those loyal union men who passed through this baptism by fire and are still alive, Van Lew informs the reader, could be a great asset to the Federal government, if only it would stretch out its hand toward them. In a rhetorical turn that would not have won points with the conservative Doolittle but may have appealed to his more progressive colleagues, Van Lew makes clear that among the Unionist whites in Richmond are many "radical men," with progressive views on the "Negro Question." Van Lew concludes her letter with a question and a warning: "Will Congress pass over them? God help us if they do!"[36]

No records have come to light revealing how Van Lew's letter was received by Doolittle or his colleagues. If it had been made in isolation, such a gesture as Van Lew's would have been ineffectual: congressmen were not inclined to follow the advice of female constituents, especially ones who wrote in such an unguarded, and, in the parlance of the times, "emotional" fashion. But Van Lew's plea was part of a much broader wave of loyalist protests, one that did eventually help to turn the tide of national politics. As historian Eric Foner has written, "the persistent complaints of persecution forwarded to Washington by Southern blacks and white loyalists altered the mood in Congress by eroding the plausibility of Johnson's central assumption—that the Southern states could be trusted to manage their own affairs without federal oversight." Especially important, Foner continues, was the loyalist testimony gathered by Congress's Joint Committee on Reconstruction in the first months of 1866. Unionist men such as John Minor Botts "criticized Johnson's amnesty policies for encouraging white intransigence" in the former Confederacy.[37]

Thanks in part to such testimony from Southern Unionists, congressional opposition to Andrew Johnson mounted, resulting in the passage—over Johnson's vetoes—of the Civil Rights Bill in April 1866 and Freedmen's Bureau Bill in July, 1866. Both bills were intended to extend the protection of the law and the courts to former slaves. As auspicious as these developments were, they did not dramatically alter the balance of power in Virginia, where the conservatives remained firmly in control for the remainder of the year; "All our papers, little and big traitors, are all loud in their praise of Andrew Johnson," Wardwell wrote to Butler in 1866, concluding "I think Southern Union men and negroes have but little to hope for." Wardwell had good reason to be bitter, as conservative papers heaped vituperation upon him, on Botts, and on other loyalists. After Wardwell addressed a crowd of freedmen on July 4, 1866, declaring his admiration for Abraham Lincoln and for the black Union soldiers who had fought "so gallantly" for freedom, the *Richmond Examiner* excoriated Wardwell for pandering to "niggers" and called his speech an "insult to the Southern community." The paper suggested that he owed his popularity among blacks to the fact that he plied them with whiskey. Wardwell was sent a letter in July of 1866 by some "Rebels of the C. S. Army" informing him that if the Union army were not present to protect him, he would be "hung up to a tree in less than twenty-four hours."[38]

Finding the local press hostile to them, Richmond blacks used other channels to communicate their distress, sending letters and reports to sympathetic Northern papers such as the *Christian Recorder*, the organ of the African Methodist Episcopal Church, and William Lloyd Garrison's *The Liberator*. A correspondent going by the initials "S. M. O." wrote the *Recorder* from Richmond in September of 1866 on behalf of his fellow blacks: "It is truly heart-rending, for us, native born citizens, unconditionally loyal, and who always have been loyal, to walk through the streets of our native city, in which we are required to pay every species of tax that a white man is required to pay; a city whose honor and welfare we take pride in promoting, and see others, who have been disloyal, and are disloyal," voting, prospering, and wielding power.[39]

At the same time that they protested the control of unreconstructed rebels over state politics, Richmond's Union circle also confronted the United States government's stubborn unwillingness to offer them appropriate monetary compensation for their wartime services. In January of 1866, Samuel Ruth, F. W. E. Lohmann, and Charles M. Carter submitted petitions to the War Department, detailing their intelligence contributions and asking for remuneration. Despite the fact that their claims were enthusiastically endorsed by U. S. Grant and by General George Sharpe, who was "unwilling to name a less sum than forty thousand dollars" as adequate for paying the three men, Secretary of War Stanton disallowed them, on the grounds that the severance pay the men had received in June of 1865 ($500 each for Carter and Ruth and $200 for Lohmann) had compensated them in full for their work.[40]

The betrayal of Richmond's unconditional Unionists by the Pierpont and Johnson administrations was made all the more galling by the fact that it stood in stark contrast to the treatment such loyalists were receiving at the hands of the grateful Northern press. As reporters came South to cover political affairs, they inevitably began to uncover and then to publicize the stories of the wartime heroism and sacrifices of Van Lew's circle. Charles Palmer, F. W. E. Lohmann, Samuel Ruth, and Van Lew herself all were the subject of laudatory articles in Northern newspapers and magazines in 1865 and 1866. Upon learning that Charles Palmer was gravely ill in July of 1865, the *Philadelphia Inquirer* described him as a heroic "rebel to the Rebellion" whom "the nation should shrine in its heart and hold there as a treasure forever." The following month, the *Inquirer* and other Northern dailies ran a story that had first appeared in the *Richmond Republic* on August 5, bringing to light the role the loyalist underground had played in the exhumation and reburial of Ulric Dahlgren. It detailed how Lohmann, Lipscomb, Rowley (incorrectly referred to as "Rowlett"), and "Orrick" (sic) had pulled off their subterfuge, and revealed that after the evacuation of Richmond the Lohmanns had disinterred the body from Orrock's farm and had it sent to Washington, D.C., where Admiral Dahlgren at long last took possession of it. In the fall of 1865, *Harper's Weekly* ran an article on the Richmond, Fredericksburg, and Potomac Railroad, saying of its superintendent Samuel Ruth, "Not only is this gentleman highly prized for his most affable manners by all the traveling public, but he has ever been a strong Unionist, and indeed, for conscience' sake, had a taste of Libby hospitality."[41]

Nine months later, in July of 1866, *Harper's* would feature a long celebratory story on Elizabeth and her mother. The level of detail in the article suggests that the author conducted a long interview with Elizabeth, and that she showed him passages of her wartime "occasional journal"; the article therefore provides fascinating insights into how Elizabeth wanted to be perceived by the public at this stage in Reconstruction. Next to a large illustration titled "View of the Residence of Mrs. John Van Lew, on Church Hill, Richmond, Virginia," the *Harper's* piece begins with the words, "Among the many points of interest to be shown to every man visiting Richmond there is, perhaps, no one more deserving of notice than the one selected for illustration on this page. The late war called forth many heroic characters, whose deeds have been proclaimed through the civilized world; but there are many whose works, although unobtrusive, and hitherto unheralded, have been such as to do honor to the American name—indeed, to the human race; and we know of none more deserving of a nation's gratitude and applause than the estimable lady and her daughter who form the subject of these remarks."[42]

The ensuing "remarks" cast Eliza and Elizabeth Van Lew in the mold of "ministering angels" such as Florence Nightengale, praising them for attending to the needs of the poor, suffering prisoners at Libby and Belle Isle. No mention whatsoever is made of Elizabeth's spy network or espionage efforts. Instead the Van Lews are held up as exemplars of the "moral courage of Woman" for having maintained their "almost romantic" attachment to the Union in the face of "slanderous abuse" in the public papers. The *Harper's* article quotes at length the 1861 *Richmond Dispatch* piece that had chastised Van Lew and her mother for their attention to wounded Yankees, suggesting that "the writers of such paragraphs, if still living, must blush at

a reperusal of them in calmer and more sober moments!" The Van Lew
ladies "are now living in most peaceful retirement," the *Harper's* piece concludes, "and spending their means—painfully reduced through the war—as
they have always done, in quiet acts of individual charity."[43]

While we will never know for sure, it seems likely that *Harper's Weekly*
was silent on the subject of Van Lew's spy work because Elizabeth chose to
withhold that part of her wartime experience from the press. She was well
aware that spies, particularly female ones, were vulnerable to the charge of
self-interest, of capitalizing on war by selling their services to the government. More important still, she knew that to go public with details of her
spy operations was to invite reprisals from ex-Confederates. It was undoubtedly less risky to stay on the moral high ground, by portraying herself and
her mother as victims of a repressive regime, motivated by the unimpeachable—and feminine—impulse of charity.

The fact that Van Lew's benevolence toward Union prisoners won her
admiration in the North is testified to by her 1866 exchange with former
Massachusetts governor John A. Andrew. She wrote Andrew early that year
on behalf of a Richmond friend, Thomas Upshur, who was applying for a
political appointment, as Virginia's "Commissioner for Massachusetts."
Judging by his response, Andrew, who had been a staunch advocate for
emancipation during the war, knew Van Lew personally and was aware of
her efforts on behalf of Massachusetts men in rebel prisons: he forwarded
Van Lew's letter to the current governor, Alexander H. Bullock, with a note
explaining, "Miss Van Lew is one of the most devoted, hearty, intelligent
friends of the Union, and & of the freedmen & of the Anti-slavery cause, I
ever knew. For her help to our poor fellows when sick & in rebel prisons I
would gladly do her any favor."[44]

Unfortunately for Van Lew, such good publicity and praise did little to
solve the pressing problem—alluded to in *Harper's*—of the family's financial
straits. Van Lew was in a bind. To tell the story of the Richmond underground was potentially to endanger those of its members still living in the
unrepentant South. But only by telling—and documenting—that story
could she lay her hands on the monetary and political rewards she believed
were due her. In the summer of 1866, Van Lew briefly flirted with the idea
of publishing a memoir of the war, based on her personal journal. When
the Richmond press got wind of this scheme, however, Van Lew was exposed
to bitter attacks and unwanted publicity. In September, the conservative

Richmond Times ran an article accusing Van Lew of trying to hawk her memoirs to a Boston publishing house. (Boston "was a more congenial clime to her," the article surmised.) Her account of the war was going to heap "bitter abuse" upon Jefferson Davis, Robert E. Lee, and other Confederate heroes, according to the *Times*. The Radical Republican organ in the city, the *Richmond New Nation*, quickly took up Van Lew's banner, quoting the *Harper's Weekly* story on her, and describing Elizabeth as a "native Virginian, of high moral and religious character, devotedly attached to the cause of human freedom." But while the *Harper's* article cast Van Lew as stoic sufferer, the *New Nation* cast her as an avenging angel. Van Lew had stayed true to the Union "for four long years," the *New Nation* crowed, and "she dares and defies [Confederates] today." She would publish her book "regardless of rebel slander or traitor's threats."[45]

As it turned out, Van Lew's prospective memoir was never published. Whether publishers rejected it or Van Lew withdrew the project after the press attack is unclear. Years later, in 1887, Van Lew would rebuff attempts by a Mr. Brace in the North (most likely from Harcourt and Brace publishing house) to get her to publish her story; she wrote a letter to unnamed "gentlemen" saying "I desire Mr. Brace to know that I objected to writing of myself and my parentage" because "I thought it in coarse taste."[46]

Van Lew was concerned about preserving her family's safety as well as obeying the dictates of good taste. Like Burnham Wardwell and other Unionists, she received direct threats of violence. Preserved among Van Lew's papers is a chilling note, adorned with a skull and crossbones, from white supremacist vigilantes calling themselves the "White Caps." Although the note is undated, it in all probability is traceable to the postwar period when, thanks to the *Harper's* article, Van Lew's Unionism became a matter of public record. The note ominously warns the Van Lews: "White Caps are around town. They are coming at night! Look out! Look out! Look out! Your house is going at last. FIRE."[47]

By the fall of 1866, with her brother John Newton struggling to keep the hardware business afloat, her family's need for income was so great that Van Lew felt compelled to take her case to the Federal government, whatever the attendant risks of exposure. Like her associates Ruth, Carter, Lohmann, and others, Van Lew had received money from the government during the war, to offset her expenses, and at the end of the war General Grant had authorized a payment of $2,000 to the family. But she was convinced that she deserved more. In order to document her claim, Van Lew requested on December 12, 1866, that the War Department give over to her all the papers it possessed relating to her espionage operations. It obliged her, and Van Lew proceeded to build a case that the United States should offer her pecuniary assistance in reward for her loyalty.[48]

Van Lew had powerful supporters in this bid. In January of 1867, George Sharpe led a campaign to convince Congress to appropriate $15,000 for the Van Lews, penning the extensive letter on her services that has been quoted so frequently above. He recounted in detail her efforts on behalf of prisoners, summing up her contributions with the startling observation that "for a long, long time, she represented all that was left of the power of the U.S. government in the city of Richmond." He concluded by calling Van Lew's "the most meritorious case I have known during the war" and by declaring that Generals Grant, Butler, and Patrick, among other notable men, could also vouch for Elizabeth's loyal service. Despite Sharpe's vehemence, Congress granted Van Lew only one-third of what she wanted. As this $5,000 proved inadequate to provide for the family, Van Lew pressed on, lobbying and appealing to powerful men to take up her cause. In the spring of 1867 she wrote Benjamin Butler to request his help. His response was long on praise but short of promises: "There is no lady in the country whom I rather would meet than yourself. I retain a lively sense of your patriotism and fidelity to the Country in her darkest hours."[49]

That winter Van Lew met Freedmen's Bureau Commissioner General O. O. Howard, and asked him to appoint her to a position in the organization. She was well aware that the Freedmen's Bureau, which provided relief, promoted education, adjudicated labor disputes, and generally embodied the Federal government for Southern blacks, was an embattled and controversial institution. She thus tried to reassure Howard that she fully supported the Bureau's aims and did not believe conservative slanders against it. She was looking for "any public position which will afford me the means of living." Howard turned the case over to Bureau education superintendent J. W. Alvord, who then contacted General Orlando Brown, assistant commissioner of Virginia's Freedmen's Bureau. Alvord's February 13, 1868, letter to Brown asked him to "employ Miss Van Lew in some industrial school for the freedmen in Richmond." Alvord also passed along General Howard's praise for Elizabeth, writing that Howard's "repeated in-

terviews with Miss Van Lew have made an impression in favor of her apti-
tude for some such work."[50]

Virginia commissioner Orlando Brown was no stranger to Van Lew; she
had contacted him in 1867 to ask the Bureau to transport Maria Parrish, "a
mulatto woman, aged about sixty, of excellent character," to the house of
her brother-in-law Joseph Klapp of Philadelphia. Parrish, Van Lew explained,
had badly injured her arm and was without a home; Brown complied with
her request. Brown thought Van Lew worthy of hiring—on February 19 he
wrote to Howard announcing his intention to appoint Van Lew as a clerk
in the Richmond headquarters of the Freedmen's Bureau. Two days later,
Van Lew's appointment was made official; she was to earn $100 a month.
Elizabeth was disappointed that she had received a clerkship rather than a
teaching position. She wrote to Brown that she would have preferred a post
that gave her the opportunity to help African Americans directly, or as she
put it, to be "serviceable to these poor creatures and . . . [carry] out the real
purposes of the Bureau." But Van Lew evidently found ways to imbue her
clerkship with some public authority. According to a letter by Richmonder
Elizabeth Saunders to her cousin Betty in Franklin, Virginia, "Miss Van Lew"
used her clerkship as a bully pulpit to "[urge] on all wickedness" to former
Confederates. "It helps them to get money to tell her lies," Saunders continued. For unreconstructed rebels like Saunders, the Freedmen's Bureau was
a subversive force, as it encouraged "impudence" among blacks and raised
the specter of racial "amalgamation."[51]

Even as it angered whites, Van Lew's outspoken support for black civil
rights endeared her to Richmond's African Americans. Thanks to a surviving
letter from militiaman William Evins, we know that as early as the fall of
1867 Van Lew had acquired a reputation among blacks as a heroine. Evins's
letter thanks Van Lew for lending to his militia unit a special flag she had
been given by the Union high command. As the militia marched with it in
a Petersburg parade, Evins recounted to Van Lew, "we thought of you." Van
Lew's own reminiscences reveal how proud she was of this recognition. The
militia had "stopped before our house in a body," to pick up the flag, she
wrote, and "thanked me for it, calling me the Goddess of Liberty."[52]

While Van Lew negotiated the political terrain of postwar Richmond, her
former slave Mary J. R. Richards (she added the initial "R." to her name
after the war) charted a perilous new course in her capacity as a teacher to

the freedpeople in Georgia. After teaching stints in Richmond, Manchester, and Norfolk, Richards made her way south to Florida, where she taught in Jacksonville; she then headed north to Georgia when she learned that there was a crying need for freedmen's schools there. Richards's remarkable correspondence with G. L. Eberhardt, Georgia's Assistant Superintendent of Schools, confirms Van Lew's sense that teachers served as the front line in the battle against southern racism—and reveals a great deal about how life in the Van Lew household shaped Richards.[53]

Richards first wrote Eberhardt on February 22 of 1867, introducing herself and asking for basic supplies such as textbooks and chalk boards. Eberhardt was a native of Pennsylvania and veteran of the Union army. By way of establishing her credentials, Richards explained that she "opened some of the first schools in Richmond" after the war. She was drawn to the community of St. Mary's, Georgia, just over the border from Florida, by the rumor that the freedpeople there were anxious to support a school; she quickly learned that they were "perfectly unable to pay for the schooling of their children." She resolved to stay on nonetheless, out of a profound sense of obligation. "I felt that I had the Advantage over the most of my Race both in Blood and Intelligence, and that it was my duty if possible to work where I was most needed," she confided to Eberhardt. Just what Richards meant by an "advantage in blood" is unclear. Van Lew's prewar letter to the colonization society indicated that Richards was "born a slave in our family." Given the prevalence of sexual coercion of black women by white men, it may very well be that her father was a white man, perhaps a member of the Van Lew family or their Lynchburg cousins, the Richardses.[54]

Richards next wrote Eberhardt on March 10, 1867. She was proud to report that she had a regular attendance at her school of over 50 children, and that she taught an additional 75 souls, adults and children, at her weekly Sabbath school. Richards also reported that she had just been visited by the Reverend Crammond Kennedy of the American Freedmen's Union Commission, who gave her "a great deal of encouragement." Thanks to an article he wrote for the *American Freedman*, we have a record of Kennedy's perspective on this meeting with Richards. "She has a wonderful history," Kennedy began, noting that Richards had been educated in New Jersey and then went to Liberia for four years. "On returning," he continued, "she went to Richmond, and while appearing as a slave, was in the secret service of the U.S." Kennedy was accompanied on this trip by none other than Harriet

Beecher Stowe; Richards brought tears to Stowe's eyes as she recounted her incredible story.[55]

The most intriguing and puzzling part of Kennedy's article is his assertion that Richards's "mother is a white lady, and her father was a mixture of the Cuban-Spaniard and negro." Is it possible that Elizabeth Van Lew was herself the "white lady" in question, and that she was Richards's mother? Such a scenario is highly unlikely, for a number of reasons. First, according to Southern law, a child born of a free mother was free, and both Van Lew's 1859 letter to the ACS and the St. John's baptism record of 1846 indicate that Richards was born a slave. Second, and perhaps more important, Elizabeth was steeped from childhood in the prevailing notion that a "true woman" should be pious and pure; not only did she revere her mother Eliza, who embodied such qualities, but she was, as a young adult, under Eliza's watchful scrutiny. Third, at the time of Mary Richards's birth in the early 1840s, Elizabeth still shared the racism of her native region. She felt a sentimental and patronizing sympathy for blacks like Richards but there is no indication that she yet regarded them as social equals and would have risked her reputation and respectability by entering into an intimate relationship with a black man. Finally, even if, despite all the countervailing forces, Van Lew had given birth to Richards, it is inconceivable that she would have chosen to stay in Richmond under such circumstances rather than relocating to the relative safety of the North. Although we may never be certain, odds are that Richards was the daughter of a black mother and white father, and that she either dissembled to Kennedy or that he got her lineage wrong.[56]

While it is difficult to establish Richards's genetic relationship to the Van Lews, it is easy to establish her ideological kinship with Elizabeth. Richards's April 7, 1867, letter to Eberhardt features her chilling account of how racist white Southerners threatened her and her school. Richards lamented to Eberhardt "I wish there was some law here or some protection." And then she explained why. "I know these southerners pretty well, and their present appearance is not at all favorable. [I have] been in the service so long as a detective that I still find myself scrutinizing them closely. There is little of the open bragadocio [sic] that generally characterizes them, but there is that sinister expression about the eye and the quiet but bitterly expressed feeling that I know portends evil. . . . Their apparent good feelings, and acquiescence, are only a vail [sic] to hide their true feelings." Richards begged Eberhardt not to think her cowardly; "any one that has spent 4 months in Richmond prison does not be so easily frightened," she asserted. The posture Richards adopts in this letter—that of the insider, the infiltrator, who can see things as they really are—is remarkably similar to the posture Elizabeth Van Lew adopted after the war. The Van Lew family provided Richards not only with the formal education that made it possible for her to write such sophisticated prose to Eberhardt, but also with schooling in how to "read" the faces, and the souls, of white Southerners.[57]

Mary J. R. Richards wrote her last letters to Eberhardt in June of 1867, announcing that she had married a man named Garvin and was planning to shut down her school. She simply could not sustain it financially; although teachers were supposed to make $47 a month, Richards had only been able to collect a salary of $10 a month from the African Americans of St. Mary's. Richards's repeated requests for monetary support ran headlong into Eberhardt's own belief that freedpeople's schools had to be self-sustaining. In July of 1867, as a result of bureau infighting, Eberhardt was removed from office. After she signs off her correspondence with Eberhardt, Mary J. R. Garvin disappears from the historical record.[58]

Van Lew's and Richards's quest for financial stability and a public voice took place against a backdrop of dramatic political developments on the state and national level. In January of 1867, the same month George Sharpe penned his laudatory testimonial for Van Lew, the Virginia General Assembly rejected the Fourteenth Amendment, which Congress had passed in June of 1866 to bestow citizenship on the freedmen and to reduce the congressional representation of states that did not permit black men to vote. This act of defiance brought to an end the first phase of Virginia's reconstruction, which had been characterized by leniency toward former Confederates, and ushered in the second: in March, Congress imposed on the Old Dominion the 1867 Reconstruction Act, nullifying the general assembly, reorganizing the state as "Military District Number One," and laying out the requirements for readmission to the Union. Virginia, along with the other intransigent Confederate states, was required to call a new constitutional convention of delegates elected by universal—white and black—manhood suffrage; adopt a new constitution that enfranchised African American men; and ratify both this constitution and the Fourteenth Amendment. Only once these conditions were fulfilled would the state be readmitted to the Union and its representatives recognized by Congress.[59]

As General Schofield, military commander of Virginia, set about regis-
tering voters for the upcoming elections of delegates to the constitutional
convention, loyal Virginians worked to organize a state Republican party.
From the very start, that party was rent by factions, divided into conservative, centrist, and radical wings. Associates of Van Lew's could be found
in each category. The relatively conservative faction among Republicans,
represented by men such as Franklin Stearns, opposed black suffrage and
any harsh proscriptions against former Confederates. Moderate republicans
such as John Minor Botts and Horace L. Kent accepted black suffrage but
did not countenance social equality between the races. The Radical Republicans, championed by such men as Burnham Wardwell, demanded not only
black suffrage but the disfranchisement of all Confederates, confiscation of
some rebel property, and the establishment of a tax-supported free school
system open to both races. Initially, Radical Republicans had the upper hand.
Under the leadership of James W. Hunnicutt, a clergyman/editor from Fredericksburg, and Judge John C. Underwood, a Northern-born farmer, they
dominated the first Republican state convention, held in Richmond on April
17, 1867. Attended by some 210 delegates, including 160 blacks, the convention passed resolutions thanking Congress for the passage of the Reconstruction Act, and asserting that all men were free and equal. Radicals also
took heart from the establishment in May of 1867 of an interracial grand
jury, under the auspices of Judge Underwood, to indict Jefferson Davis for
treason. The jury included Burnham Wardwell, and John Newton Van Lew,
along with African American leaders such as Lewis Lindsay and Joseph
Cox.[60]

While two of Van Lew's collaborators in the Richmond underground—
Wardwell and Martin Meredith Lipscomb—participated in the April convention, others of her allies, most notably Botts and Stearns, rejected it as
too radical and tried to craft an alternative strategy of "cooperation," namely
restoring political and civil rights to all former Confederates who were willing to declare their loyalty to the Union, save for the former leaders of the
rebel state. Deeply divided, the Republican party nonetheless pressed forward
and presided over the Constitutional Convention in Richmond in December
of 1867; with radical delegates outnumbering moderates, the convention
produced a constitution that provided for black male suffrage, established
free public schools for both races, and disfranchised men who had held civil
or military office in the rebel government. Although the constitution rep-

"Military District Number One." *The grand jury convened to hear the case against Jefferson Davis (Burnham Wardwell is on the left-most end of the first row, and John Newton Van Lew is second from the right in the second row)* (VALENTINE RICHMOND HISTORY CENTER).

resented a compromise of sorts between radical and moderate Republicans—radicals such as Hunnicutt had hoped for harsher proscriptions against ex-Confederates—reactionary Democrats declared the Constitution an illegitimate aberration, the product of a convention of "illiterate vagabonds," "vandals," "kangaroos." These anti-Republican forces had an unexpected ally in the person of General Schofield, who was hostile to the radical agenda and postponed elections for the constitution's ratification in order to buy time for its opponents to mount a counterattack.[61]

The counterattack was cleverly designed by Alexander H. H. Stuart, who proposed through the medium of the Richmond newspapers a formula for compromise between Republicans and Democrats: universal suffrage in return for universal amnesty. Black men, in other words, would vote but so too would former Confederates. After winning over a cadre of prominent men in the state, Stuart contemplated the next step: persuading the president and Congress of the wisdom of his proposal. Fortunately for Stuart, political developments on the national stage seemed favorable to compromise. In 1867 and 1868, as Republicans in Virginia had labored to win readmission for their state, the national party had effected the disgrace of Andrew Johnson, who was impeached by Congress and nearly removed from office, and the ascendancy of Ulysses S. Grant as party leader and candidate in the 1868 presidential contest. A man of unimpeachable bravery and heroism, Grant struck a chord with his "Let Us Have Peace" campaign motto, easily defeating Democrat Horatio Seymour in the November contest. The fate of Virginia—and of Elizabeth Van Lew—was once again in Grant's hands.[62]

9

"A Fiery Ordeal"

THE TRIALS OF A FEMALE POLITICIAN

ON MARCH 17, 1869, JUST 13 DAYS AFTER HIS INAUGURATION, PRESIDENT U. S. GRANT nominated Elizabeth Van Lew as postmaster of Richmond, a lucrative and coveted civil service post, and one of the highest federal offices a woman could hold in the nineteenth century. Grant's nomination of Van Lew was one of his first official acts as president, and therefore a sign of how he might wield his powers of patronage and of whether his policies would reflect his conciliatory campaign motto. Two days later, the United States Senate, in executive session, confirmed Grant's nomination. Van Lew had explicitly asked Grant for the postmastership when he had visited her after the war.[1]

Grant's was a singularly controversial move. Formerly Confederate news-papers, in Virginia and elsewhere, expressed outrage at Grant's choice of Van Lew. The *Richmond Enquirer and Examiner* declared: "We regard the selec-tion of a Federal spy to manage our post-office as a deliberate insult to our people." The *Southern Opinion*, a Richmond paper "devoted to white su-premacy, state equality and Confederate memories," fumed, in a derogatory allusion to Van Lew's age (50, at the time of her appointment) and the fact that she was unmarried, that Grant had chosen a "dried up maid for Post-mistress" who would soon gather around her a "gossiping, tea-drinking, quilting party of her own sex."[2]

Northern papers that favored a lenient course of Reconstruction also con-demned Grant's choice. The (Washington, D.C.) *National Intelligencer*, for example, doubted "whether any one could have been appointed who is more offensive to the people of Richmond," and hoped that the "utterly mean and malignant spirit" that Grant demonstrated in Van Lew's case would not control other government appointments.[3]

Republican newspapers farther North cast Van Lew's appointment in a positive light. Thanks to prisoners' reminiscences and the 1866 *Harper's*

Weekly article, Van Lew's efforts on behalf of Union inmates was already well known to the public. But now, in the publicity surrounding her post-mastership, the details of Van Lew's espionage work came to light. The *Baltimore Sun* and a host of other Northern papers ran an article explaining that Van Lew "furnished most valuable information to general Grant relative to the forces, positions, &c. of the Confederates, including diagrams and valuable documents." The *Philadelphia Evening Telegraph* intoned that "the escutcheon of the woman who proved unfalteringly faithful among the faithless, and who braved all perils . . . to guide our armies to the true point of attack, is stainless; and most fitting is it that she should be rewarded and honored." The *Troy Times* agreed that "such devotion of loyalty was rare during the war, and deserves to be rewarded and recognized"; the *New York Times,* for its part, averred that Grant's appointment had "given the highest satisfaction to the country." Moreover, Union soldiers around the country came forward on behalf of Van Lew. The Seventy-ninth Regiment of Highlanders, Fourth Brigade, First Division, New York, for example, sent Grant a resolution commending him for bestowing the post office on one so worthy.[4]

In order to understand why Van Lew's appointment would stir up so much controversy, it is necessary to know something about the nature of postmasterships and about the political climate in 1869. The post office department had been, ever since Andrew Jackson's day, both the largest and the most politicized of federal agencies. Whichever political party was in power had the opportunity, in filling post office positions, to exercise patronage on a grand scale. The president appointed the postmaster general, a cabinet member who headed up the department in Washington, D.C.; he in turn appointed "deputy postmasters" to fill thousands of local offices around the country. The president also handpicked the deputy postmasters of such major cities as Richmond.[5]

Deputy postmasters could expect not only to draw an excellent salary (some, Van Lew included, earned as much as $4,000 a year) but also to exercise considerable political clout. Responsible for the hiring of clerks and mail carriers, postmasters could dispense patronage and thereby build a "sizable partisan army"; once their staffs were in place, they could use their time to "attend political conventions, organize political rallies, and collect money . . . for the party's treasury." Postmasters also controlled the dissemination of political information and had a monopoly on the flow of information in general. Proslavery postmasters in the antebellum South, for example, destroyed rather than processed abolitionist tracts that came through their offices. Like congressmen, postmasters possessed the franking privilege—the right to send out documents without paying for postage—and could therefore freely distribute speeches, newspapers, and government documents of their choosing. Finally, because of their prominence in community affairs, postmasters had the opportunity to advance their own political fortunes. Postmasterships were often stepping stones to elective office; the most famous example of a postmaster turned politican is none other than Abraham Lincoln.[6]

A bastion of partisanship, the postal service was also a bastion of male privilege. Post offices themselves were, historian Richard John has written, male spaces—men gathered there to discuss politics, catch up on the latest news, and conduct business. So "aggressively masculine" were post offices that "respectable ladies" were advised to avoid them and to send their servants to pick up the mail; post offices in major cities often featured "ladies' windows," where women could pick up their mail without coming into contact with unruly crowds of men.[7]

While female postmasters were not unheard of, they constituted, on the eve of the Civil War, less than 1 percent of the total number in office, and they tended to serve in small communities rather than major cities. During the war, with men off fighting, women assumed civil service positions, postmasterships included, in unprecedented numbers. The vast majority of these jobs reverted to men when the war ended—particularly in the South, as the Confederate government was dismantled. But women had nonetheless gained a foothold in the terrain of white-collar employment. It was unclear, at the time of Van Lew's appointment in 1869, whether or not women's wartime gains would lead to the large-scale integration of women into government service.[8]

Because Van Lew's appointment represented female encroachment on what had traditionally been a male domain, it became a point of contention between supporters and opponents of woman's suffrage. The organized struggle for woman's rights was some two decades old in 1869, and on the eve of a resurgence. That year would witness the founding of two new suffrage organizations: the American Woman Suffrage Association, under the leadership of Lucy Stone, and the National Woman Suffrage Association (NWSA), under Elizabeth Cady Stanton and Susan B. Anthony. Together, the two groups faced a protracted battle, one that would not culminate in victory until 1920. Opposition to woman's suffrage was particularly strong in the conservative South.[9]

Much of the commentary on Van Lew played itself out in the context of the woman's rights debate. An editorial in the *Philadelphia Evening Standard* praised Van Lew, but mused nervously that in appointing her Grant had given a "semi-endorsement" to woman's rights. The *New York Herald* saw Van Lew's appointment as evidence of how well women could do without the vote: "a fat office is better than a lean ballot," its editors opined. Though the NWSA was extremely critical of Grant and the Republican party for ignoring women in the voting provisions of the Fourteenth Amendment, it saw in Van Lew a potential standard bearer: the organization's official organ, the *Revolution*, edited by Elizabeth Cady Stanton, praised Van Lew's appointment in March of 1869 and followed her career closely in subsequent years. To the *Herald's* quip that a "fat office is better than a lean ballot" the *Revolution* replied pointedly, "the 'ballot' is not 'lean' in a man's hand, but the talisman that brings many fat things." When Susan B. Anthony visited Richmond in December of 1870 to help the fledgling Virginia State Woman Suffrage Association, she paid a visit to the home of Van Lew; Van Lew's nephew later wrote that Anthony was a "great admirer" of his aunt.[10]

Van Lew, then, entered upon her post office career under an intense public gaze and unusual pressure. How did she fare at her duties? Van Lew set up shop on the first floor of the imposing Custom House building, fronting Main Street between Tenth and Eleventh. As it also housed the offices of the collector of customs; the collector, assessor, and supervisor of internal revenue; the United States District Attorney for Richmond; and a federal courtroom and the offices of judges, the Custom House building was the central locus of government authority in the former Confederate capital. (The building had been headquarters of the Confederate Treasury Department during the war, and Jefferson Davis had had his office on the third story.) Van Lew was literally surrounded by figures of authority—all of them men.[11]

As postmaster, in some ways Van Lew was a success, presiding over the expansion and modernization of the Richmond post office. She instituted citywide delivery of letters (replacing post office boxes); enlarged the money order and registered letter facilities; and had boxes placed on the principal streets of the city for the dropping off of outgoing letters. In 1871 she even published a post office manual that the *Revolution* described as "the best in use." The manual, which provided Richmond post office patrons with useful information such as the hours the office was open, the rates of postage, and how to process money orders, was also an impressive piece of publicity for Van Lew and her employees. From 1869 until 1871, thanks to Van Lew's efforts to constantly upgrade the system of free delivery she had established, the number of letters delivered in the city had risen from 14,483 a month to 83,258 a month. Van Lew's pride in this accomplishment was evident. She explained, showing her didactic side, that "free delivery practically brings the Post Office to every man's door, and benefits all classes of people." From a historian's perspective, the most remarkable feature of Van Lew's postal manual is its tone—disregarding the gender conventions of her time, she speaks to her readers as an authority figure and a professional. Nothing about the document—it is signed "E. L. Van Lew, Postmaster"—reveals that it was written by a woman. Van Lew understood that her title conferred authority, and specifically requested that Virginia newspapers refer to her as "postmaster" and not as "postmistress."[12]

Following the script of countless male postmasters, Van Lew speedily made use of her powers of patronage. She expanded the number of postal clerks from 21 to 32; as any male postmaster would have done, she filled the positions under her control with associates whom she felt were competent and deserving. Among her hires were women, including Eliza G. Carrington. At least initially, such hires met with approbation from the Richmond press, which saw nothing wrong with the presence of "estimable ladies" in the post office. She also used her authority to intercede on behalf of office-seekers. Shortly after assuming the postmastership, for example, she dashed off a letter to President Grant, addressing him "not as the president but as a dear friend." She asked Grant to find a civil service position for her brother John, whom she assured Grant was a "faithful Republican." "I do not think you would want to humiliate my only sensible & beloved brother by overlooking him," Van Lew exhorted the president. Grant evidently did not provide John Van Lew with a desirable office. After a brief stint as United States Tobacco Inspector at the Richmond Custom House, John accepted a clerkship in his sister's post office.[13]

Her accomplishments notwithstanding, Van Lew soon found herself caught in the vortex of shifting political winds. Her first years in office were turbulent times in state politics, as they witnessed the formation and then rapid demise of a ruling coalition of Conservatives (the new party label for conservative former Whigs and Democrats) and moderate, or "true," Republicans. With President Grant's aid and blessing the coalition won control of the state government in July of 1869, and engineered the ratification of a new state constitution that, in the name of compromise, both enfranchised blacks and preserved the voting rights of ex-Confederates. To the dismay of Radical Republicans, who felt that Grant's conciliation of the moderates was a betrayal, Virginia was readmitted to the Union in January of 1870. The coalition soon broke down, and party lines hardened, with Conservative ranks filled primarily by ex-Confederates committed to white supremacy and Republican ranks filled by white Southern Unionists, Afro-Virginians, and white Northerners who had settled in Virginia. In Virginia, as elsewhere in the Reconstruction South, the Republican party was besieged by enemies willing to use the tools of fraud, intimidation, and violence to achieve their political ends.[14]

Virginia Republicans were also rent by factionalism. Moderates, who countenanced some compromise with Conservatives, were antagonistic to Radicals, who did not; many native Southern whites (dubbed "scalawags") were antagonistic to Northern "carpetbaggers"; and black Republicans often felt alienated from and misrepresented by white ones. Moreover, white Radical Republicans themselves were divided into factions, one led by Congressman Charles H. Porter and represented in the press by the newspaper the *National Virginian* and the other led by Senator John Lewis and Congressman James Henry Platt Jr. and represented by the Richmond *State Journal*.[15]

In this volatile atmosphere, Van Lew made efforts to position herself as someone who put principle above partisanship, and who was "friendly," as she put it, to the "good men" across the political spectrum. Such efforts won her praise from such divergent sources as the Conservative press and the woman's suffrage movement, but brought upon her the wrath of the men in her own party. Van Lew's troubles began a few months after she took office, when she was charged by the postmaster general for "insubordination"—for adjusting the salaries of her clerks without receiving permission to do so. The United States Marshal for Richmond, David B. Parker, was called to Washington, D.C., and interviewed by President Grant, who sought to get to the bottom of the controversy. Grant asked Parker, "How do the public regard her administration of the office?" and he replied "She is giving eminent satisfaction. There is no complaint on the part of the public." Shortly thereafter, Van Lew brought the salaries of her clerks back into compliance with postal regulations. But the taint of "insubordination" proved hard for Van Lew to shake.[16]

The problem, the conservative *Richmond Dispatch* explained in a November 1870 article, was that however satisfied the public may be with Van Lew's skills as a bureaucrat, she could never make the grade as a politician. Her fellow Republicans—particularly the "Custom House" ring led by Collector Joseph M. Humphreys—coveted Van Lew's office and believed that to have a woman as postmaster was a "waste of Government machinery." The *Dispatch*, which described Van Lew as a "prim, vigilant-looking lady," and cast her detractors as "office-hunting wolves," declared "we heartily wish Miss VAN LEW protection from these monsters."[17]

Confronted by a whisper campaign to discredit her, Van Lew went on the offensive. In January of 1871, the *Revolution* reported, Van Lew publicly objected to the fact that "certain Congressmen while at Washington franked alot of envelopes and sent them to their friends at Richmond to be used by them, thereby defrauding the United States of their revenue." When she refused to allow such franked letters to pass through her office, Van Lew implicated herself in the bitter feud between the Porter and Platt wings of the Republican party.[18]

For much of the winter and spring of 1871, she found herself under attack from Porter and his allies, who were determined to unseat her. Porter harbored animosity not only toward Van Lew but toward the federal office-holders of Richmond "as a class," most of whom, he charged, belonged to the rival faction of the state's Radical Republicans and were intent on destroying his own political reputation and career. In making a case against Van Lew, Porter's clique utilized a readily available ideological weapon—gender aspersions. They charged that Van Lew should be replaced by a man because "no lady can wield the political influence which the dignity and value of the office should command." In asserting that Van Lew lacked "influence," her detractors were drawing attention to her anomalous position. As postmaster, Van Lew had her own political platform and voice. But even so, she could not fulfill the vital function of speaking *for* men—lacking both the political experience and the legal standing of rank-and-file voters, she could never be accepted as a leader among them.[19]

Van Lew's woes made strange bedfellows of Virginia Conservatives and NWSA suffragists, both of whom rushed to her defense. The *Petersburg Daily*

"A prim, vigilant-looking lady."
Van Lew in the prime of her life
(VIRGINIA HISTORICAL SOCIETY).

Index accused the Porter clique of "great ungallantry" in its efforts to "stir up party opinion" against Van Lew. "Miss V. L. has done her duty," its Richmond correspondent averred, "and if she won't associate with the ragtag and bob-tail of her party, it only shows her good sense." The National Woman Suffrage Association, for its part, took up Van Lew's banner through articles in the *Revolution*. The journal described Van Lew as a "thoroughly incorruptible" model of efficiency, who rightly refused to let her post office be "used for political purposes." Such a characterization tapped into a powerful current in nineteenth-century discourse on female civic duty—the notion that women were morally superior to men. Female moral superiority was a malleable doctrine. Antisuffragists argued that enfranchisement would put women's virtue at risk by bringing them into competition with men. Suffragists, by contrast, argued that the vote was a tool that women could use to purify the public sphere. The NWSA believed that Van Lew served as a shining example of how women might operate within the male sphere of partisan politics without being tainted by it.[20]

In the first months of 1872, Van Lew again put principle above partisanship and further compromised her standing among Republicans. In March, a dozen of her mail carriers angrily resigned after she had dismissed a Mr.

Doughty, the chief of the carriers' department. Van Lew felt perfectly justified in her decision—she had asked Doughty to perform overtime duties to cover for a sick clerk, and he had refused. According to the striking employees, however, Van Lew had acted unjustly, and "on a whim." Once again, the Conservative press proved surprisingly sympathetic: the *Richmond Enquirer* deemed Van Lew's reasons for firing Doughty "sufficient" and reassured the public that since Van Lew had already filled the other vacancies, "there will be no interruption in the business of the office, and the mails will be received and sent off as usual."[21]

Van Lew survived Porter's challenge, and the Doughty flap, and counted on U. S. Grant to extend her term of office should he himself win a second term in 1872. She must have been both gratified, and in light of her battles, bemused, when the Republican party platform of that year included, for the first time, a plank that acknowledged women's contributions to the nation's political life: "The Republican party is mindful of its obligations to the loyal women of America for their noble devotion to the cause of freedom," the platform intoned. "Their admission to a wider field of usefulness is viewed with satisfaction, and the honest demand of any class of citizens for additional rights should be treated with respectful consideration." This gesture prompted disaffected suffragists such as Susan B. Anthony to return to the fold. The NWSA published an appeal to the women of the United States in 1872 that cast Grant as "favorable to increased rights for women," noting that "he has officially recognized their competency and given them many Government positions." Taking part in rallies, processions and other kinds of meetings, women in the North enthusiastically campaigned for Grant's reelection.[22]

In 1873, in the wake of Grant's triumph, the Republican State Central Committee officially recommended to the president that he replace Van Lew with a man, one William T. Bailey, who was Joseph Humphrey's Deputy Collector in the Custom House. After Van Lew called on Grant in Washington, D.C., to plead her case, the "brave and true" president bestowed upon her a second term; among Grant's most heroic qualities, Van Lew would later write, was that he was "faithful to his friends." The *Richmond Enquirer* and *Richmond Whig*, which had so vehemently opposed her 1869 appointment, applauded Grant for retaining Van Lew as postmaster. "Miss Van Lew is an efficient officer," the *Enquirer* averred, "equal to, if not more efficient, than perhaps any of the persons who would likely have been appointed to succeed her." The *Whig,* for its part, declared that "while the reasons of her original appointment may not have commanded our approval, the fact that, under her administration, the office has been in the main admirably conducted, renders her reappointment altogether satisfactory to us." In her second term, as in her first, Van Lew made gestures to demonstrate that she put service to her clients above partisanship. In February of 1874, for example, she sent a gift—a book—to the newly elected Conservative governor of the Commonwealth, James Lawson Kemper. He wrote her a cordial note in return, saying it would always afford him pleasure "to reciprocate her courteous attention."[23]

Unfortunately for Van Lew, the praise of Conservative journals and politicians proved to be hollow. For while ex-Confederates might, especially when it served to fan the flames of Republican factionalism, commend Van Lew's bureaucratic skills, they could not abide her escalating efforts to promote black civil rights. Even as Van Lew's political independence alienated her from Republicans, her racial politics inexorably alienated her from the conservative white majority in Richmond.[24]

From the start of her tenure in office, Van Lew positioned herself as a champion of racial equality, and took actions, both symbolic and concrete, to elevate the status of blacks. In April of 1870, for example, when Richmond blacks orchestrated a massive procession through the city to celebrate the ratification of the Fifteenth Amendment (that enfranchised African American men), Van Lew hung an American flag on the outside of her mansion to show her approval. The procession "gave rousing cheers" when it passed her house. Van Lew's action won the praise of the *New National Era,* the Washington, D.C., newspaper edited by eminent black abolitionist Frederick Douglass; hers was "one of the few houses upon which the flag of the Union was flying," the paper noted in its coverage of the event. Van Lew, for her part, kept an autograph of Frederick Douglass, which she may have obtained on one of his visits to the city, preserved among the treasures in her scrapbook.[25]

The cause of African American education was dear to Van Lew's heart, and she used the press as a vehicle for its advancement. In April of 1871, she published a stirring tribute to a Northern white woman, Mrs. Howe, who had devoted the last years of her life to educating freedpeople in Richmond. Van Lew addressed herself to "many a noble heart which differs from me politically," hoping to ignite a spark of sympathy in the opposition. Van Lew clearly identified with her subject, who had "walked our streets under the loathing scorn of ignorance . . . to do what she thought duty." Van Lew ended her short eulogy with a poignant plea to her fellow citizens: "[we] should cultivate a spirit of toleration and charity towards all from whom we differ—then would our community prosper." The conservative *Petersburg Daily Index* took disapproving note of Van Lew's tribute, calling it a "strange document" and chiding her for "commenc[ing] by a reference to politics."[26]

Van Lew also used the press to publicize the dire condition of race relations in Virginia. Conservative whites used a host of nefarious measures, legal and extralegal, to restrict black voting and officeholding. One of these measures, historian Michael Chesson explains, was the passage of a law making petty larceny grounds for disfranchisement; trumped-up charges were then made the pretext for depriving thousands of African Americans of the vote in the period 1870 to 1892. Van Lew was outraged at the treatment of black Republicans by white Conservatives, and made no secret of it. In an 1872 conversation with a correspondent of the *New York Tribune*, she declared that "there were at least 200 negroes now in the penitentiary for no crime except being Republicans." Because the *Richmond Dispatch* saw fit to reprint the *Tribune's* account of this conversation, Van Lew's critique was soon known to the public of her native city.[27]

While Van Lew's gestures and comments on race relations were disturbing to Conservatives, so too was her exercise of her patronage powers. For Van Lew hired blacks to work in the Richmond post office—and thereby struck a powerful blow at the South's racial caste system. Before the Civil War, the postal service had made a policy of excluding African Americans from employment, in the North as well as in the South. After the war, blacks were slowly integrated into the civil service; Van Lew and the Richmond post office were on the leading edge of this significant transformation. Van Lew not only employed blacks in the important and hitherto unattainable position of mail carrier but in lucrative clerkships that could be stepping stones to elective office. Among Van Lew's clerks were active black civic leaders, such as James H. Bowser and N. V. Bacchus. One of them, Josiah Crump, even went on to serve on Richmond's city council. Van Lew's efforts to promote African American officeholders extended beyond Richmond: in

"Representing all classes of the
people."
*Josiah Crump, postal clerk and city
councilman* (LIBRARY OF VIRGINIA).

1869, she secured the appointment, by lobbying powerful friends in Virginia,
of a "mulatto" man, George E. Stephens, to the post of Sheriff of Essex
County.[28]

Thanks to the survival of a richly detailed letter by celebrated orator Anna
Dickinson to her mother in 1875, we can establish that the presence of
African Americans in Van Lew's post office was striking to even the most
liberal observer. Dickinson was the preeminent Republican woman of the
Civil War era, an exception to the rule that women did not wield authority
within the party. A Pennsylvania Quaker, Dickinson had made a name for
herself giving antislavery speeches in the antebellum North and was tapped
by the Republican party to campaign on its behalf during the war. "In the
1870s," historian Melanie Gustafson has written, Dickinson "maintained a
place in the public eye by giving lectures, publishing books and plays, and
appearing on the stage." She traveled to Richmond in 1874, and was hosted
by the Van Lews. At Elizabeth's urging, Dickinson visited the post office,
where she "found nearly all of the clerks & attendants colored." Their
prominence Dickinson rightly understood to be profoundly significant.
"Miss Van Lew evidently believes in *representing all* classes of the people,"
she asserted. Among those employed at the post office, Dickinson added,
were some of the Van Lew's former slaves; one of them, Van Lew told her,

was the "best man in the place." She may have had in mind Peter Roane, whom Van Lew promoted from paid domestic servant in the Church Hill mansion to post-office clerk in 1871. After assuming the clerical job, Roane continued to reside at the Church Hill mansion.[29]

Even for such an antislavery crusader as Dickinson, Van Lew's egalitarianism was remarkable. "A black is evidently not only as good as a white, to her, but a good bit better," Dickinson wrote, adding "She treats her servants & employees as she would think of doing if they were white." But Dickinson was careful to note that Van Lew did not fit the mold of a "Northern strong minded woman." Instead, Elizabeth appeared to her fascinated visitor as a surprisingly traditional figure, a relic, in her temperament, if not in her politics, of a bygone time. Van Lew was "romantic & a bit sentimental . . . fond of novels & poetry, & quotations" and beset by "bad Southern taste." Even Van Lew's physical appearance seemed incongruent with her record of innovation and of courage. According to Dickinson, Elizabeth was, in her mid-fifties, a "little, wizened woman, skinny & parched. With a frazzle of curls, thin face, clear blue eyes, little claws of hands, & the most intense nervous organization & manner I *ever* saw."[30]

This seemingly frail woman, Dickinson learned over the course of her visit, was indeed a study in contradictions. When Van Lew learned that Dickinson was opposed to the Civil Rights Bill pending in Congress, which was championed by Benjamin Butler and intended to "safeguard what remained of Reconstruction," Van Lew nearly "picked [Dickinson's] eyes out." But ultimately, Van Lew was "too good a soul to fall out with," and she and her visitor had a heart-to-heart talk and rapprochement. "At last [Van Lew] took me into her little sticks of arms, & into her favor once more," Dickinson concluded.[31]

Despite Van Lew's evident competence as a bureaucrat, her respectful treatment of blacks had made Elizabeth "frightfully unpopular with the whites," Dickinson observed, "even with the Union people." Dickinson's assessment must be set against the backdrop of the Republican "retreat from Reconstruction" that unfolded during Van Lew's second term in office. In 1874, the resurgent Democratic Party recaptured the United States House of Representatives and, to quote David Blight, "in state after state overturned the Civil War era's political landscape." The Democrats' victories represented a public backlash against "Grantism"—against the economic depression that rocked the nation in 1873; against political scandals that reached into the upper echelons of Grant's administration; and, most ominously for Van Lew, against Reconstruction itself. Republicans in both the North and South, having paid a steep electoral price for supporting black civil rights, concluded that the party had done all it could for blacks and that the era of Federal intervention in Southern race relations should come to an end. Since Van Lew refused to join in this repudiation of Reconstruction, she found herself ever more isolated, socially and politically, and ever more vulnerable to attack.[32]

As the 1876 presidential election approached, the "Republican and Democratic parties faced each other for the first time since before the war as relative equals, represented in both sections." With the stakes so high, moderate and Radical Republican men alike made the case that Van Lew's presence in the post office would hurt the party's chances for victory. Virginia Republicans such as Alexander Rives and George K. Gilmer (a moderate former legislator who wanted the postmastership for himself) hoped that Van Lew could be pressured into resigning. Van Lew must be replaced by a man, Rives wrote Gilmer early in 1876, for Virginia Republicans could not do well in the upcoming presidential election with "one so disqualified by her sex if not other infirmities from exerting influence."[33]

Van Lew was well aware that many men in her party saw her as a liability. During the 1876 campaign season, she found herself "persecuted unrelentingly by both wings of the Republican party." She knew they believed that "Va. would be lost" if she were not replaced, and she marveled at their unscrupulousness. Her male critics even took issue with her hiring of female clerks, demanding "what are these women doing here—we want voters." For Van Lew, the demise of Reconstruction must have been a painful echo of the secession crisis. In 1860 and 1861, she had watched those whom she considered her political allies either co-opted by the opposition or driven from power. Now she watched as the men in her party abdicated their commitment to racial justice and to loyal Republican women.[34]

As she had so often done during the Civil War, however, Van Lew chose, in the face of critical scrutiny, to ratchet up rather than ratchet down her activism. In January of 1876, for example, she sponsored a library for Richmond's African Americans. A notice she sent to the *Richmond Dispatch* announced her intention to use the post office as a repository for donations of books, and reminded the "charitable" of "the thirst for knowledge among our colored citizens"—a provocative statement at a time when so many

Southern whites worked to undermine blacks' tenuous prerogatives as citizens. That summer, she appealed directly to Congressman James Garfield to attend an upcoming Republican meeting. "We desire to make this meeting a success and take it beyond our local politics and give it a national standing," she informed him, adding "many disaffected democrats will gladly hear you." Perhaps Van Lew hoped that if Garfield complied she could silence the critics who claimed she lacked influence; unfortunately, Garfield respectfully declined her invitation.[35]

Determined to exercise the authority that came with her office and to prove herself a worthy Republican, Van Lew in October of 1876 published a desperate and daring appeal "to Northern Democrats" in the *Washington Chronicle*, urging them to repudiate the Democrats/Conservatives of the South. The piece was reprinted in the *Richmond Dispatch*. Written just a few week before the presidential election, Van Lew's 1876 letter provides a window into her self-image as well as into race relations. She portrays herself, by turns, as a political insider and outsider, as powerful and disempowered. The letter began confidently, with Van Lew stating that as a "representative of loyalty to the Government," she had the duty to disabuse Northern men of their misconceptions about the South and give them "facts as they really are." White Southerners remained defiant in their contempt for Northerners and for Southern Unionists, she explained. "The proscription of Republicans here is something of which no idea can be formed by transient visits to the South," she chided her readers—"you have only a parlor view."[36]

By the middle of the letter Van Lew turned, reluctantly, to the subject of her own persecution. A martyr to the principles of Republicanism, she had been the victim of "constant and repeated gross personal insults," but had stood firm; there is "no political act for which I blush," she declared. When her mother died in September of 1875, "we had not friends enough to be pall-bearers." Her burial was "ridiculed and called the 'nigger funeral.' "[37]

Van Lew next told of the violence and fraud whites perpetrated against black Republicans, and noted with palpable horror that the "lash was used even upon the women." "I am not exaggerating," she noted. "A man (a conservative) told me we [Republicans] might have the votes—the majority—but that we could never carry an election here: that it was so arranged and would continue to be so." At the end of the letter, she confronted the political reality of women's disfranchisement. "As a woman, I have no power but through your vote," she implored. "Remember the ballot is the moral lever by which you put in place and power your officials."[38]

⌒

Van Lew's sense of her own powerlessness would deepen profoundly in the wake of the 1876 presidential election, as she battled to retain her office. With newly elected moderate Republican Rutherford B. Hayes promising to end Radical Reconstruction, men across the political spectrum seized the opportunity to rid the Richmond post office of Elizabeth Van Lew. To that end, they mounted a calculated and at times vicious campaign to slander Van Lew and undermine the administration's confidence in her. The *Richmond Enquirer* inaugurated the campaign shortly after Hayes took office, noting that although Van Lew had proved quite competent, there might yet be a chance to unseat her if only a "sufficient complaint" might be brought.[39] Van Lew, it turns out, was in for the fight of her life.

Van Lew campaigned for her reappointment on two fronts. In Richmond, she followed the standard practice among office seekers of submitting petitions to the public for its support. Her most influential backer among white Virginians was Judge Robert W. Hughes, a moderate Republican who had been the party's candidate in the 1873 Virginia gubernatorial race, and who, like Van Lew, was deeply devoted to Ulysses S. Grant. In a letter to Hayes on Van Lew's behalf, Hughes declared that the post office had been "more efficiently administered" during Van Lew's tenure than ever before, and averred that the "quiet people" of Richmond—as opposed to those clamoring for office—wanted Van Lew to retain her position. Hughes's favorable appraisal of Van Lew was seconded by a scattering of former Confederates, ranging from General William C. Wickham, a former member of the Confederate Congress, to "humble ex-soldier of the rebel army" P. T. Atkinson. The former wrote to Van Lew that he found her management of the post office "eminently satisfactory to the community here," while the latter wrote directly to President Hayes, testifying that "she is a good officer to all but the prejudiced and should not be cast off."[40]

Given the Hayes administration's stance on Reconstruction, it might have been politically expedient for Van Lew to repudiate her ties to the black community. To her credit, she refused to do so. Indeed, she submitted petitions to blacks for their support; among those who endorsed her were

Reverend W. B. Derrick of Richmond's Third Street Church, one of the city's principal African American congregations. In April, a group of 40 African American men, presided over by William C. Roane and including some of Van Lew's postal employees, called a meeting at the Third Street Methodist Church to draft a report to Hayes urging the retention of Van Lew. Their petition argued that "if any other person is appointed postmaster the colored people will have no chance whatever of getting employment in the office."[41]

Van Lew also campaigned in Washington, D.C., calling on Hayes in March; she was supported in that mission by a delegation of African American men from Richmond, who secured a "private interview" with the president to plead Van Lew's case. The Republican party's organ in Washington, D.C., the *National Republican*, editorialized on Van Lew's behalf, casting her a "good Union woman" who was being victimized by "intriguing politicians." To underscore her association with the former president, the paper reported that Van Lew "proposes fighting it out on the same line if it takes all summer," paraphrasing Grant's famous dictum about the Virginia campaign of 1864 through 1865. Grant himself weighed in, declaring that Van Lew had filled her office "with capacity and fidelity and is deserving of continued confidence by a Republican administration."[42]

Despite entreaties from Van Lew and her allies, President Hayes delayed making a decision on the Richmond post office, and thereby gave her opponents the time they needed to make a persuasive case against her. During her first term in office, when Radical Republicans were ascendant in national politics, white men in Richmond, on the left and the right, had deemed it best to deny Van Lew status as a "Radical," despite her ardent support for racial justice. Now that Radicals were in retreat, these same men made every effort to brand her as one. Conservatives argued that Van Lew represented the discredited regime of Radical Reconstruction and "pernicious social-equality doctrines" on which it was founded. Holding Hayes accountable for his promise to restore "self-rule" to the South, the white supremacist press argued that Van Lew was "objected to by the great mass" of Richmonders; they considered it a great strike against her that "Northern Radical politicians," "military men," and local African Americans constituted her base of support. "Can the most ardent friend of Hayes claim that the Southern question is disposed of while Elizabeth L. Van Lew sits immured in the Richmond Postoffice?" the *Richmond Enquirer* pointedly demanded as the president pondered his options.[43]

Van Lew's political enemies were especially enraged by her negative comments about Richmond in the Northern press; they repeatedly took her to
task for "reviling and abusing the people among whom she lives." The *Richmond State*, in direct reference to Van Lew's October 1876 letter to "Southern
Democrats," declared that "this postmistress delights in doing all in her
power to misrepresent [Virginia] among the people of other Common-
wealths." The *Alexandria Gazette* agreed, and printed a letter from an irate
Virginian chiding Van Lew for writing a "letter to the *Washington Republican*,
setting forth, in short that the people of Richmond were barbarous." The
Gazette editorialized that "women's letters have always been dangerous
things, to other people, but Miss Van Lew's letter . . . proves to have been
more dangerous to herself than to anybody else."[44]

As she had throughout her tenure in office, Van Lew also faced opposition
from within the Republican party. The United States Marshal in Richmond,
C. P. Ramsdell, headed up a faction that put forward the collector of customs, Dr. C. S. Mills, for Van Lew's post; the group called on Hayes early
in April to make the case for that candidate. (In 1870, Van Lew had recommended Mills to Grant as a "worthy citizen"; she now characterized him
to Hayes as a man of "small mental calibre.") A second and more formidable
Republican challenger was Van Lew's own assistant postmaster, J. A.
Jefferds.[45]

Jefferds's bid for her office was a terrible blow to Van Lew, as she had
considered him a friend and confidant. Indeed, just a few weeks before
Hayes took office, Jefferds had defended Van Lew in a bitter legal dispute
between her siblings. The dispute, which made its way to Richmond's Chancery Court in February of 1877, had to do with the disposition of Elizabeth's
father's will. John Van Lew, it will be remembered, died in 1843, and made
his wife Eliza his executrix. She, though well intentioned, had not properly
followed the provisions of the will, to the financial detriment of Elizabeth's
sister Anna Klapp of Philadelphia. Anna and her husband sought a remedy
that would divide the remaining estate more equitably, giving them a share
equal to the those of Elizabeth and of John Newton. Unfortunately, tempers
flared during the court proceedings, with the Klapps alleging that Elizabeth
and John Newton had colluded in unfairly living off their father's estate,
and Elizabeth charging that the whole affair represented an attack against
the character of her dearly departed mother. "I have wiped the tears from
my mother's eyes so many times in the silent night," Elizabeth testified of

her mother's grief at the internecine conflict. Elizabeth went so far as to say that the legal battle, which began brewing in 1875, "helped to kill" Eliza.[46]

The lengthy Chancery Court case of 1877 comprised not only a dispute over the estate but also over which lawyers were owed what fees; a Robert Stiles, Esq., who represented the Klapps, claimed that Van Lew, too, owed him money, for advice he tendered her and for work he did trying to mediate between the parties. At this point, Jefferds entered the picture, to speak to the merits of Stiles's claim. Jefferds explained that Van Lew had consulted him "both confidentially and freely" with regard to the family dispute, and that "scarce a day [had] elapsed" during which the affair was not the subject of conversation at the post office. Evincing sympathy with Van Lew, Jefferds testified that she was eager for an "amicable" settlement but would not agree to any resolution that would "impugn her mother's memory." Van Lew had never, to the best of Jefferds's knowledge, contracted with Stiles, and she therefore could not possibly owe him any money.[47]

The case itself dragged on for years before the siblings reached a mutually agreeable settlement. For our purposes, the February 1877 chapter of the dispute is important because it reveals why Van Lew was so angry over Jefferds's political bid for the postmastership: she had confided in him, and now he turned against her. Moreover, the 1877 case reveals that Van Lew was under considerable strain on the domestic front at the very same time her political battles were reaching a fever pitch.

Refusing to be outmaneuvered by Jefferds and his allies, Van Lew adopted, in April of 1877, a rather opportunistic tack. She portrayed herself, to the Hayes administration and the public, as the defenseless victim of a "carpetbagger" conspiracy of Northern men. In an April 10 letter to Hayes's secretary, Van Lew reported that her chief clerks had joined forces against her and were conducting a smear campaign, trying to undermine her reputation. "[T]hey say I am a sick & crass peculiar irritable old maid," she complained, adding "I am a woman and not able to protect myself for that reason." Van Lew was willing to fight fire with fire. She told the *National Republican* that her principal opponent, Jefferds, was "not identified with the people of Richmond" but was a "Boston carpetbagger." At the end of April she struck a still more potent blow at her enemies by discharging Jefferds and a clerk, Major Carruthers, who had supported him. Van Lew replaced Jefferds with one Thomas W. Brockenbrough, who had been a bookkeeper in the firm of Van Lew, Taylor, and Co.[48]

She defended these measures in a pair of revealing interviews with the *Richmond Enquirer*. When a reporter showed up at her doorstep inquiring about her firing of Jefferds and Carruthers, Van Lew at first hesitated to talk to him but then gave in and led him back to her private office to tell him her side of the story. She explained how the two had plotted against her and appealed to the reporter's empathy: "I submit that if you were postmaster you would desire to be surrounded by your friends rather than your enemies." All Van Lew wanted, she confessed, was fair treatment. "I am a Richmond woman," she tearfully told the *Enquirer* reporter, proudly showing him the respectful and admiring obituary of her father that had run in the paper some 33 years earlier. Though she had tried to "conciliate" the people of her beloved native city, she had been, Van Lew lamented, misunderstood and mistreated by them.[49]

Unfortunately for Van Lew, the *Enquirer* juxtaposed this April 29 interview with a scathing and mean-spirited attack from Carruthers. He lambasted Van Lew for having a "very peculiar temperament"—for being "erratic to say the least." When the reporter asked Carruthers, in response to this charge, "Can you prove it?" the disaffected clerk told a story about how when a patron was conducting some business with Jefferds, Van Lew interrupted the proceedings and declared "with abundant gesticulation, 'I am postmaster here.' " Van Lew's assertion of her authority may well have been prompted by the patron's sexist assumption that Jefferds was the head of the post office. Carruthers was not interested in the subtext of the incident. Rather he opined that Van Lew's manner was so "obnoxious" that the citizens of Richmond "entertain an absolute hatred for her."[50]

Van Lew had a chance to fire back, as the *Enquirer* ran a follow-up interview on May 1, 1877. In it, she took issue with Carruthers's characterization of her personality. "Major Carruthers told the ENQUIRER that I was erratic. It's a pity my eccentricity hadn't been manifested earlier," she asserted, in order to discredit Carruthers as a political opportunist. Indeed, Van Lew had a point. It is to the 1877 conflict over the postmastership that we can date the charge—one that would be repeated endlessly in the coming years—that Van Lew was mentally unstable. Democratic critics and Republican challengers had cast a wide range of aspersions against Van Lew over the years but those charges had centered on her politics. Only in the bitter battles of 1876 and 1877 did Van Lew's sanity come under question. Carruthers had, in effect, trapped Van Lew: since Elizabeth's assertiveness was "proof" of her instability, any efforts she made to defend herself could play into her enemies' hands.[51]

Not surprisingly, the *Enquirer* gave Carruthers the last word in the exchange, appending to Van Lew's comments his parting blow. Hoping to tap into public skepticism about women's competence to hold office, the ex-clerk suggested that Jefferds was the "actual postmaster"—he did the real work of running the office while Van Lew simply "paid exorbitant salaries" to her favorite clerks. Not only her personality but her personalism disqualified Van Lew from office.[52]

Van Lew's Southern opponents were not the only ones to cast her as a female interloper on the male terrain of political office. On May 2, 1877, the *New York World* ran a tendentious article entitled "Arrival of the Woman of the Future." "It seems that the coming woman has already got to Richmond, and she is making it pretty hot for the effete man," the article intoned. The "ability which [Van Lew] has displayed in the intrigue for her reappointment," was guaranteed to "strike terror into the heart of the average man." In a tone both humorous and ominous, the essay asked "Is it possible that the sphere of public office is to be taken from him?"[53]

A few weeks later, President Hayes answered that question in the negative when he appointed Colonel William W. Forbes, a native Virginian "of the moderate stripe," and a member of the Custom House ring, to replace Van Lew. (Van Lew described Forbes as a "Confederate colonel of loose character.") According to the *Richmond Whig*, the news of "the downfall of the masculine VAN LEW spread like wild-fire from one end of the city to the other," and caused "everybody . . . to be in unusual good humor." Although deeply hurt by the news, Van Lew refused to give her enemies the comfort of seeing her suffer. The *Whig* had to concede that "Miss Van Lew accepts her removal with quiet and becoming dignity." While she must have been appalled to see her nemesis Carruthers quickly reinstated by Forbes, she could take satisfaction that many of her other hires—including Mrs. C. C. Mera and African Americans James Bowser, Josiah Crump, and Peter Roane—had proven so competent that Forbes opted to keep them on.[54]

The reminiscences of novelist Ellen Glasgow, who grew up on Church Hill, feature a telling anecdote about one of the African American postmen who served her neighborhood during the 1880s, after Van Lew's ouster. One of the more memorable figures of her childhood, she recounts, was a "friendly very light colored letter carrier, named Forrester." Because he was a Republican, Forrester was "threatened with the loss of his place." But then the "children of the neighborhood rose in resentment, and circulated a petition." Glasgow remembers "rushing in and out of houses, and begging people, especially fathers, to sign [it.]" This letter carrier—Richard G. Forrester—had first been hired by Van Lew in 1873; the fact that he and other black clerks and mailmen won the respect, however grudging, of some white Richmonders illustrates just how Van Lew's pioneering hiring practices had changed the social landscape of Richmond.[55]

The *National Republican* criticized Hayes for putting political expediency above principle; its offices were flooded by letters from former Union soldiers defending Van Lew and her record. But that very record of wartime loyalty had become a political liability. Van Lew was one of hundreds of progressive Southern Republicans turned out of office by Hayes and replaced with moderates, even Conservatives and Democrats, many of them former Confederates. Post offices in Memphis, Tennessee, and other prominent locales went to Democrats; one observer estimated that in his first five months in office, Hayes bestowed one-third of all his appointments in the South on Democrats.[56]

Among Hayes's prominent appointments were women. Virginia Thompson of Louisville, Kentucky, who endeared herself to her townsmen by being an "intense Democrat," was named postmaster by Hayes in the very same year that Van Lew lost her office. Van Lew's ouster, although a personal setback, did not alter the trend of women's entrance into the civil service. By 1893, women held 6,335 postmasterships, nearly 10 percent of the national total.[57]

Van Lew was driven from office, then, not simply because she was a woman but because she was a former Unionist and Grant Republican, associated in the public mind with the Union conquest of Richmond, the era of Radical Reconstruction, and with the heretical doctrine of racial equality. A male postmaster of a similar political ilk as she would surely have found himself the subject of attacks and might have lost his job as well when Hayes replaced Grant. Van Lew's gender, however, determined the *kinds* of attacks to which she was subjected; it provided men with a language in which to express their opposition to her. When her male critics claimed she lacked influence or suggested that she was erratic they were tapping into time-tested images of female inferiority. Unfortunately for Van Lew, there was no readily available language in which to respond to these charges, no script for the

pioneering female politician to follow. Given Van Lew's pride in her education and in her powers of eloquence, it broke her heart that when it
mattered most, words failed her.

Van Lew's loss of her job was not only emotionally devastating but financially
ruinous, as it deprived her family of her considerable salary. She tried to
generate funds by selling off various properties the family owned, but that
proved "entirely unproductive." She also undertook some new ventures,
such as becoming partner in a Richmond foundry business, but these too
were insufficient. She had friends recommend her for other civil service
positions, such as that of Pension Agent for Virginia, but President Hayes
was unwilling to honor her even with that office. In desperation, Elizabeth
put the Church Hill mansion up for sale. Her ad for it in a local journal
included the ringing endorsement of her friend Honorable John M. Forbes,
an eminent Boston politician. He declared, "It is the finest old city home I
ever saw." But the offers Van Lew received for it she regarded as insulting,
and so the property remained in her hands.[58]

So Van Lew worked assiduously to ply the only trade she knew, and to
be reinstated as postmaster. When James Garfield replaced Hayes as president in 1881, Van Lew could again be found in Washington, lobbying for
her old job. She also sent missives, by turns pointed and poignant, to influential Republicans asking for their support. To her beloved U. S. Grant she
wrote, shortly before Garfield's inauguration, "I tell you truly and solemnly
that I have suffered. I have not one cent in the world." The social ostracism
she suffered was so great that she could not even get a fair mortgage on her
property. She asked Grant to influence Garfield to find her "a good office,"
reminding Grant, as if he needed it, that she would "be glad to be postmaster
because I understand that business."[59]

Grant evidently tendered his support, for in mid-March of 1881, as Garfield mulled over his options, Van Lew wrote to New York Republican leader
Thurlow Weed that she was an applicant for the Richmond postmastership
"strongly recommended by Genl. Grant." "I would be very glad to be recommended also by you," she continued. Van Lew's letter reveals what an
able politico she could be. She wrote that the current frontrunner for the
Richmond post office, a Mr. Pelouze, was neither a "true Republican" nor

a "gentleman." "If I get to office I propose to take care of your friends," she promised. But Van Lew also rose above the rhetoric of patronage to offer a cogent analysis of the recent political realignment in her state. In 1879, William Mahone's Readjuster Party had established dominance in Virginia politics by bringing together black and white Republicans and white Democrats who wanted to "readjust," or partially repudiate, the state's enormous debt. While Conservatives wanted to pay off, or "fund" that debt, and were willing to raise taxes and slash social services in order to do so, the Readjusters saw such a policy as elitist and inimical to the needs—particularly the need for decent public schools—of the common man. Led by unlikely reformer Mahone, a native Virginian who had owned slaves and served in the Confederate army, the Readjuster insurgency began among the white landowners in Virginia's western counties, who had longstanding antagonisms to eastern politicians. The movement soon attracted African Americans, as well, who felt betrayed by the state's Republican party. Although Mahone successfully "fused" local Democrats and Republicans under the "Readjuster" banner, he cast his lot in national politics with the Republicans, and through political maneuvering as United States Senator earned the right to distribute the thousands of patronage positions the party won with Garfield's 1880 election to the presidency.[60]

Van Lew understood that the old party bonds had "been broken" by Mahone, and that the Republican party in Virginia was therefore at a critical crossroads—if only it had able leaders, it could build on the Readjusters' success and attract "the laboring classes—the poor white man—& the man of moderate means" away from the Conservatives. She was such a leader, she averred, and knew just what the Republican party "should do"—that is, maintain a high presence in Virginia, through the press and public meetings, not only during campaign seasons but year round.[61]

Van Lew not only worked behind the scenes to be reinstated but appealed directly to the public. On March 26, 1881, she published a "card" in the *Washington Evening Star*, expressing her dismay at the fact that she had been declined an interview with Garfield and boldly averring that if the issue of who should be made postmaster were "left to the nation it would be decided in my favor."[62]

Van Lew's efforts were in vain. The post went to George Gilmer, a "prominent readjuster" who had Mahone's backing. To Van Lew's credit, she did not let her disappointment with this result cloud her assessment of political realities. The ascendant Readjusters were the "only hope of the negro for protection," she wrote President Garfield in June of 1881, to encourage him to support the Mahonites. In the "name of humanity and human freedom," Van Lew vowed to Garfield, "I shall do all I can to aid the readjusters." Van Lew realized that in their practice of bestowing public offices to blacks, the Readjusters built on her own legacy. "At the height of Readjuster power," historian Jane Dailey has shown, "black men constituted 27 percent of Virginia's employees in the Treasury Department, 11 percent in the Pensions Bureau, 54 percent in the Secretary's Office, and 38 percent in the post office." Van Lew's connection to the Virginia fusion movement was not only ideological but personal. Her allies William C. Roane and Josiah Crump were two of the leading black Readjusters in Richmond.[63]

In what must have seemed an all-too-familiar dialectic, the Readjusters' gains prompted a bitter Democratic backlash; the more black Readjusters asserted their equality, the better able Democrats were to play the "race card"—that is, to stigmatize the fusion coalition as a threat to white supremacy and as a vehicle for racial amalgamation. Democrats cast the 1883 elections in Virginia as a choice between "white government or negro," Jane Dailey explains, and "went door-to-door asking potential white voters, 'Are you going to vote with the whites, or niggers, this time?' "[64] Such language, along with the familiar tools of social ostracism and physical violence, enabled the Democrats to sweep the Readjusters out of power in 1883. Van Lew's nightmare—that Virginia would join the so-called Solid South in which Democrats reigned unchallenged—was becoming a reality.

There was no running away from this reality, Van Lew would soon learn. In 1883, during the presidency of Chester A. Arthur, Van Lew submitted an application for a post office clerkship to the Appointment Office in Washington, D.C. She took the required civil service examination and passed, Chief Post-Office Inspector David Parker recounts, "with the highest rating." The postmaster general, Judge Gresham, advocated that Van Lew fill a vacancy in the office of the third assistant postmaster general, a Mr. Hazen. Hazen demurred, arguing that Van Lew would be "troublesome and hard to get along with," as she was reputed to have been during her Richmond postmastership. Parker defended Van Lew, saying, "If she had been a soldier, she would be entitled to preference under the law. Surely she rendered services that ought to put her on par with soldiers." Hazen was outnumbered, and Van Lew was offered the clerkship.[65]

In order to take up her new duties, Van Lew left Richmond behind and moved to Washington, D.C. Her life in the nation's capital was nomadic—she rented a series of apartments in northwest D.C., changing address three times during her clerkship. It was also traumatic, as Van Lew found herself at the mercy of a cruel boss. As she explained in her journal, she worked in the post office department under a Tennessean named George A. Howard, a former clerk who, once promoted to supervisor, became drunk with power. He demanded that his employees dramatically increase the pace of their labors, and "there was no let up in him." Van Lew confided her displeasure to a fellow clerk, a Miss Best, saying Howard "acts as if he were driving slaves." Best replied "indeed he does," adding "he tries to impress you all the time with 'I am Chief.'" Another fellow clerk, a Mr. Kelly, told Van Lew that he was tired of submitting to Howard's "rudeness & hollering." Although hard on everyone, Howard reserved his special wrath for Van Lew herself. For he was an unreconstructed rebel. "I once heard him say the South had never done anything wrong," Van Lew wrote to an ally. Howard "sharply hates me," she continued, and "it is a political hate."[66]

Howard gave vent to this hate in 1887 when he had Van Lew transferred from the third assistant postmaster's office to the dead letter office. The demotion was punitive, and was interpreted by Van Lew as an effort to humiliate her. When she received notice of the transfer, Van Lew sought solace from fellow employees like Miss Best, who reassured her that she had indeed been a good clerk and that Howard's move was unwarranted. The transfer not only consigned Van Lew to what she called "a wretched place," but also reduced her salary from $1,200 a year to $720. While a few Republican newspapers tried to make political capital out of the demotion, seeing it as politically motivated attempt by the Grover Cleveland administration to disparage a Republican stalwart, the press was generally unsympathetic to Van Lew. The *Jersey City Argus*, for example, opined that, "As a matter of fact Miss Van Lew can live comfortably on $720 a year. There are thousands of men in this country who are rearing families, and no small ones, on less."[67]

Rather than accept the demotion, Van Lew, on July 28, 1887, resigned, and returned to Richmond. Her career as a civil servant—a career in which she had taken such deep pride—was over forever.[68]

10

The Myth of "Crazy Bet"

VAN LEW'S LAST YEARS BROUGHT WITH THEM BOTH A DEEPENING GENDER CON-sciousness and increasing social isolation. Looking back on her embattled civil service career, she concluded that her downfall as a politician lay not in her political views but in her gender. Van Lew had always been an "active and earnest Republican so far as a woman can be." In her day women could "subscribe freely to party purposes—get up torchlight processions—tell men what to say at meetings." But such exercises of indirect influence, she had come to realize, were ineffectual. She had "suffered unusual persecution from both parties," Van Lew confided to John M. Forbes, a prominent Bostonian with whom she maintained a correspondence, because "as a woman" she was "without the protecting ballot." The right to vote was the "moral lever," the "creative force" of the government. When her critics had charged that no one who lacked this fundamental right could wield meaningful political influence they, alas, had been correct. Van Lew summed up her political career with a seven-word epitaph: "I had not the power—the ballot."[1]

Van Lew felt keenly that it was not only her political contributions but her experience as a wage earner and property owner that entitled her to vote. In 1880, she sent a one-line letter to Elizabeth Cady Stanton, president of the National Woman Suffrage Association, laying out her views. "I am a property holder and taxpayer [who] ought of right to vote and wish[es] to do so," Van Lew wrote. She sent the same simple and blunt message to the municipal authorities in Richmond: in 1892, when Van Lew paid her annual tax to the city treasurer, she attached a note of "solemn protest," explaining that it was unjust to tax one who was "without representation" in the government.[2]

Unfortunately, Van Lew was not able to derive any comfort from the emergence, in the 1890s, of an indigenous suffrage movement among white Southern women. The rhetorical strategies favored by suffragists in the late nineteenth century were anathema to Van Lew: in a bid to prove their movement "respectable," many suffragists played the race card, arguing that white women should be enfranchised so that they could counteract the votes, and thereby undermine the power, of African American men. As Marjorie Spruill Wheeler has explained, the suffrage leaders of the New South—even relatively progressive ones such as Virginians Lila Meade Valentine and Mary Johnston—viewed the era of Reconstruction as a "dreadful period" characterized by "political ineptitude on the part of ignorant and gullible Southern blacks," and hoped that woman's suffrage would restore white supremacy. Back in the 1870s, woman's rights advocates had praised and courted Van Lew, seeing her as a representative of female competence and integrity; in the 1890s, with a new generation of suffragists working to cast off the taint of radicalism, Van Lew was no longer a useful symbol.[3]

The conservative turn in the suffrage movement was part of a broader trend in American political culture, in which whites, in the name of sectional reconciliation, repudiated Reconstruction and embraced the mythology of the "Lost Cause." Lost Cause mythology cast the South's part in the Civil War as noble and heroic. Confederates had courageously defended the righteous cause of states' rights and had lost only because of the "overwhelming numbers and resources" of the North; there was no shame, therefore, in fighting the war, and no shame in defeat. Most important, their moral righteousness and bravery linked Southern men to their battlefield foes. Soldiers on both sides had fought with honor, and now that the war was long over, the nation could commemorate it as a unifying event—as a stirring display of manly virtue, of which all Americans could be proud.[4]

Lost Cause mythology had both social and political roots. It reflected a generational transition—as veterans of the war entered old age, they invariably romanticized the glory days of their youth, and young Americans invariably sought to record and understand the experiences of those heroes who were passing from the scene. This powerful—and universal—impulse to glorify the past took on an added intensity during the 1890s, historian David Blight explains, because white Americans sought to "gird [themselves] against racial, political, and industrial disorder." The Lost Cause "became a tonic against fear of social change"; the Confederacy and the South came to represent "conservative traditions" to which the entire country could cling during the wrenching upheavals of the Gilded Age.[5]

The Lost Cause, Blight has shown, "also armed those determined to control, if not destroy, the rise of black people in the social order." The glorification of the Civil War as a noble display of manly valor obscured the centrality of slavery and emancipation to the conflict. African Americans such as Frederick Douglass worked hard to promote the "emancipationist" interpretation of the war. Douglass encouraged Americans to acknowledge African American patriotism, to repent the sins of the slavery, to glory in the righteousness of freedom, and to recognize that the battle against racism—the real root cause of the Civil War—was far from won. But such efforts were in vain. As one African American newspaper put it in 1890, "The poetry of the 'Blue and the Gray' is much more acceptable" to Americans "than the song of the black and the white."[6]

To Van Lew's dismay, her native Richmond was the hub of the Lost Cause cult. In a ceremony that made manifest the nation's fascination with and pride in the Confederacy, a giant statue of Robert E. Lee on horseback was unveiled in Richmond on May 29, 1890—Memorial Day weekend—to the delight of a crowd of more than 100,000 spectators. That day marked a turning point for Van Lew. Through the trials of sectionalism, secession, war, and Reconstruction, Elizabeth's resolve to remain in Richmond had never wavered. But the resurgence of Confederate sentiment was too much for her to bear. In her 1891 letter to John Forbes, she confessed that "ever since the Lee unveiling . . . I have felt that this was no place for me."[7]

Emboldened by the Lost Cause creed, white Richmonders, so it seemed to Elizabeth, conspired to isolate and humiliate her. In their eyes, she represented the era of Reconstruction and of Republican dominance. "We can never forget it nor ever forgive you," one prominent gentlemen told her. Even her few white Southern friends recommended that she leave Richmond. In this atmosphere of hostility, Elizabeth "[shrank] from every thing like a gathering of my fellow beings, church, concerts, everything." "The fearful effect upon my life and health," she wrote to Forbes, "you cannot conceive."[8]

Elizabeth's sense of isolation reflected the fact that outmigration and death had thinned the ranks of her companions and defenders. Burnham Wardwell and Arnold B. Holmes, among others, fled Virginia after Reconstruction for the more politically congenial climate of the North. Tragically for Van Lew, several of her close allies who stayed on in Richmond died prematurely. Three of her principal African American allies—James H. Bowser, Josiah

"No one will go with us
anywhere."
*Van Lew with her nieces,
brother John, and servant,
on the mansion grounds*
(NEW YORK PUBLIC LIBRARY).

Crump, and William C. Roane—passed away in the prime of their lives.
Bowser, whom Van Lew had hired to work in the Richmond post office,
died in 1881, at the age of 30, of tuberculosis. His obituary in the *Virginia
Star* praised him for his long, esteemed career as a postal clerk, and declared
his life "an example worthy of imitation." Three years later, William C.
Roane, the Readjuster lawyer who had led the campaign among Richmond
blacks to retain Van Lew in office in 1877, himself died at the age of 30,
also of tuberculosis. Like Bowser, he was a clerk in the Richmond post office
at the time of his demise. Josiah Crump, the postal clerk turned city councilman, passed away in 1890, at the age of 53. Crump had been regarded as
"one of Richmond's most respected colored citizens," renowned for using
his "influence for the best interests of the city, regardless of party." When
the city council met to eulogize him, councilman John M. Higgins—an old
member of the Richmond underground—gave a "glowing tribute to the
deceased."[9]

John Newton had settled with his second wife, Augusta, and their children
on his farm in Louisa County. His daughter Annie (from his first marriage)
was married to John J. Hall, one of Van Lew's former post office employees,
and living in Massachusetts. Thus Elizabeth's niece Eliza (Annie's sister) was
the only relative who still resided at the Church Hill mansion. The social
ostracism experienced by Elizabeth naturally had a "fearful effect" on Eliza
as well. "No one will walk with us on the street. No one will go with us
anywhere—and it gets worse and worse as the years roll on," Van Lew wrote
in 1891. Eliza had gone so far as to declare "if I had a child and it was a

republican I would kill it, aunty," rather than have it suffer as such rejection. Not surprisingly, the unnatural isolation they experienced took a toll on the relationship between Elizabeth and her niece. Eliza showed signs of nervous prostration. Elizabeth complained about her "mania for cleaning—doing the most drudged work." Whenever Van Lew tried to distract her niece from this obsession, Eliza lashed out in anger, and ordered Elizabeth to leave the house. Tired of fighting, Elizabeth often accepted this sentence of exile, and "wandered from one place to another," through the streets of the city.[10]

The Van Lew mansion, which had once symbolized the family's exalted social status and been a refuge for so many Unionists, was now a burden to Elizabeth. She confessed to John Forbes her desire to "sell this elephant soon," and thus make the money she needed to relocate to Boston or some other Northern city. But the property had lost its former luster. Because of Van Lew's financial woes, the gardens showed the effect of years of neglect, and the dwelling was in disrepair as well. Alexander Wilbourne Weddell, son of the rector of St. John's Church, visited the mansion in the 1890s. Its "shabbiness so approached squalor as to impress even my childish eye," he later wrote. Most important, the property was tainted by its association with Van Lew. No white Richmonder wanted to buy the home of a social pariah.[11]

Van Lew was caught, in her last years, in a vicious cycle. Fearful of rebukes and reprisals, she became a recluse; on those few occasions she braved the streets, she acted skittish and suspicious of others. Compounding the political prejudice against her was what we might now call "ageism"—Elizabeth in her seventies was no longer the "prim, vigilant-looking lady" the *Richmond Dispatch* had once praised. Rather, she was frail, nervous, and bedraggled. Looking at Van Lew—an old woman dressed in black, in the fashions of a bygone era—many Richmonders saw what timeless literary traditions and folklore and gossip primed them to see: a hag, a crone, a witch.[12]

Countless reminiscences by Richmonders testify to the demonization of the elderly Van Lew. People "shunned her like the plague," her family doctor, William H. Parker recalled. Children were encouraged by their parents to see her as a kind of bogeyman. Little boys "taunted her" while "girls were terrified of her," one Richmond paper claimed. One girl whose curiousity was stronger than her fear—Richmond's acclaimed novelist Ellen Glasgow—felt herself drawn to the infamous spy, as children often are to that which is mysterious and forbidden. One day while playing near the Van Lew man-

"Squalor as to impress even my childish eye." *The Van Lew mansion in the 1890s* (VALENTINE RICHMOND HISTORY CENTER).

sion Glasgow caught a "fleeting glimpse" of its notorious inhabitant. It was hard for Glasgow to believe that the "frail, shrunken, white-haired old lady" whom she beheld had such a "sinister reputation."[13]

As she had her whole life, Van Lew relied, in her last years, on African American friends to provide her with support. A handful of paid servants worked at the mansion, and they, too, were targets of public wrath and contempt. An interview with Church Hill resident Kitty Dennis, who as a very young child met Elizabeth, provides an African American perspective on the ostracism of Van Lew and her circle. Van Lew had a "very nice maid named Daisy," Dennis recalls, "and the other children called her Crazy Daisy." Her mother warned Kitty never to be so disrespectful, and allowed her to make social visits to the mansion. "Ms. Van Lew was very fond of my mother," Dennis proudly remembers. Kitty Dennis was evidently not taken in by the rumors that Van Lew was crazy and frightening. Instead she understood that the attacks on Van Lew were politically motivated. "Ms. Van Lew was made the northern post mistress for here in this area," Dennis would recall, in a revealing, if somewhat inaccurate, choice of words, and that is why "Virginians would not speak to her."[14]

Although she had suffered so at the hands of politicians, politics remained the great, abiding passion of Van Lew in her final years. In a comment that serves as an important corrective to the notion that the elderly Elizabeth had let slip her mental moorings, her physician William H. Parker described her as "lonely but not neurotic" and possessing a "bright mind." She was "much interested in politics," he recalled, and "loved to open a bottle of champagne and chat with me" about current affairs. Van Lew never lost her nerve when it came to appealing to the powerful. Sometime between 1897 and her death in 1900, she penned a letter to President William McKinley's wife, urging her to take interest in a "very important appointment soon to be made here"—namely the appointment of a new postmaster for the city. Showing her considerable savvy and understanding of the political climate, Van Lew positioned herself as a fellow Christian and fellow supporter of the temperance (antiliquor) movement. The man being pushed for postmaster by Richmond politicians, a Mr. Knight, Van Lew accused of being a drunkard. She suggested that the McKinley administration support a Mr. Otis H. Russell instead, noting that Russell's wife was a devoted temperance woman. Russell, a former collector of the port of Richmond, was a longtime friend of Van Lew's, one of the few white friends she had left in the city. "Please ask your husband to examine carefully all of Mr. Russell's testimonials," Van Lew urged, with the following statement of her own credentials: "I write to you as I am a lady myself, and I was for eight years Postmaster of this city under Genl. Grant, and I know what would please our People, both Republicans and Sound Money Democrats."[15]

Van Lew's appeal was in vain; she no longer had political patrons in the government. But she did have patrons of a different sort, in the form of a group of influential Bostonians who sustained her in her old age. Van Lew's wartime assistance to Massachusetts soldiers, most notably Colonel Paul J. Revere, had won her many admirers in the Bay State, and after the war Elizabeth frequently made social visits to the city. After losing her postmastership, Van Lew was in such financial straits that she appealed to one of her Boston connections, the sister of the late Colonel Revere, for help. Revere's sister, Mrs. Reynolds, directed her own son, John Phillips Reynolds Jr., to establish a subscription fund in Boston that could be paid out to Van Lew for her support. Beginning in 1883, an annual payment was made to Van Lew, thanks to a small group of donors, all of them eminent Bostonians: George Higginson, Colonel Henry Lee, J. Ingersoll Bowditch, Frederick L.

"Virginians would not speak to her." *Van Lew at her Church Hill home in her final years* (VALENTINE RICHMOND HISTORY CENTER).

Ames, F. Gordon Dexter, Honorable John M. Forbes, William Endicott, and Mrs. G. Howland Shaw. John P. Reynolds visited Richmond to make the payments, and he struck up a friendship with Van Lew. He found her to be fascinating but elusive. "At times she talked with me about the past," he has revealed, "but always in a very meagre way, as she was always reticent about herself and her accomplishments."[16]

If Van Lew's modesty was striking, so too was her generosity. Although her resources were limited, she could not resist the impulse to give what she could—namely old family possessions—to those who were kind to her or in greater need than she was. Her friend Otis Russell remembered that " 'Aunt Lizzie' had the heart of a child whenever suffering appealed. She was literally land poor, and every year was obliged to dispose of some of the original estate to keep the wolf from the door. Then piece by piece the old family silver plate went to the curio dealers . . . and then, sadder than all, the fine old bits of antique furniture, the pictures and the bric-a-brac followed. Aunt Lizzie continued to give right and left, and every little kindness she repaid with 'souvenirs' of the historic place, till almost everything of value was dispersed."[17]

The last five years of Van Lew's life were characterized by loss. In 1895, her beloved brother John Newton died, and shortly thereafter her sister Anna passed away, as well. The cruelest blow, however, was the sudden and unexpected death of her niece Eliza on May 10, 1900; although the two women's intimacy had frequently been a source of friction, Elizabeth had deeply cherished Eliza, and regarded her as a daughter. One local paper later reported that as Eliza lay dying, Van Lew begged her nurse, "Save her! Save her! I love her better than anything in the world. She is all that I have." According to the *Richmond Dispatch*, the "strength of the attachment" between Van Lew and her niece "may be imagined from the fact that [Elizabeth] never allowed the Christmas decorations to be removed from the walls of her house which her niece had placed there."[18]

Elizabeth may have clung to her memories of the Christmas of 1899 in fear that it was her last. That very winter, Elizabeth began to show signs of dropsy, a disease in which the body retains fluids, eventually filling the sufferer's lungs with water. For the first few months of 1900, Van Lew fought the illness back, and her "wonderful vitality so often asserted itself," so a local paper reported, "that it seemed as if her death were a very remote contingency." After Eliza's death in May, however, Elizabeth's health dramatically declined. She was tenderly nursed by her former slave Judy Johnson, and attended by three eminent physicians—Dr. Marcy, Dr. Ramon Garcin, and Dr. Emily Chenault Runyon. But there was nothing they could do to prevent the progress of the disease. In July of 1900, the *Richmond Evening Leader* ran a headline declaring "MISS VAN LEW VERY ILL." As a privileged Southern belle, Van Lew had once been looked on "as a young princess." Now, the newspaper continued, with more than a hint of satisfaction, she was living in "absolute seclusion, bereft of relatives, forsaken by friends."[19]

In late September, knowing the end was near, Van Lew summoned the daughters of her late sister Anna Klapp to come to Richmond. The two women, Mrs. B. F. Nicholls, of Philadelphia, and Mrs. C. A. Ricksecker, of Buffalo, promptly complied and were at their Aunt's bedside in her final days. Van Lew was also comforted by the Reverend Mr. Goodwin, pastor of St. John's Church. Word of Van Lew's rapid decline soon went public, and on September 25, 1900, the *Richmond Dispatch* announced that "Miss Van Lew was thought to be dying." She had a "sinking spell" on the September 24, the paper explained, and though she "rallied from this, and was able to walk, with assistance, [and] to drink some tea," she fell unconscious again before midnight. "Among the last things she did before losing consciousness," her benefactor John P. Reynolds Jr. later learned, "was to tell [her family] where the manuscript" detailing her wartime experiences was to be found. When her relatives produced it, Van Lew exclaimed "Why there is nearly twice as much more. What has become of it?" Reynolds, to whom the dying Van Lew entrusted the manuscript, was never able to locate the missing pages.[20]

Like Van Lew's nieces, Reynolds had been summoned to her bedside, but he did not arrive in time to bid her goodbye. At 4:10 A.M. on September 25, Elizabeth Van Lew died. Her relatives saw to it that her body was quickly embalmed, and it lay upon a temporary bier in the drawing room of the mansion, the room in which she died, while a gravesite was prepared in the family plot at Shockoe Cemetery. "The portraits of her ancestors adorn the walls about her," the *Dispatch* wrote of her temporary resting place, "and a lifesize portrait of herself at the age of 6 years looks down upon her." The impending funeral would be "as simple as possible, in deference to the wishes expressed by the deceased shortly before her death."[21]

Elizabeth Van Lew was buried in Shockoe Cemetery on Friday, September 28, 1900, right across from the graves of her mother Eliza and father John. Because the family plot had insufficient room, Van Lew's casket was placed in the ground vertically rather than horizontally. Her nieces Mrs. Nicholls and Mrs. Ricksecker were joined in mourning by a small circle of kin, including Van Lew's niece Annie, identified in the papers as "Mrs. John J. Hall, of Medford, Mass."; John Newton's widowed second wife Augusta Van Lew, and two of her daughters; and Elizabeth's Philadelphia brother-in-law, Joseph Klapp. The ten pall-bearers designated for the ceremony comprised old friends of Elizabeth's such as Franklin Stearns and postwar friends such as Otis Russell and Dr. Marcy.[22]

After Van Lew was laid to rest, her family gathered together for the reading of her will. It surely surprised no one that Van Lew bequeathed her property to Annie Randolph Hall, John Newton's daughter by his first wife Mary. Annie and her sister Eliza had been raised at the Van Lew mansion, and functioned as surrogate daughters for Elizabeth. The first copy of her will that Elizabeth had drawn up, in February of 1900, had divided the estate equally between these two nieces; after Eliza passed away that May, Van Lew had the will modified to make Annie her sole beneficiary. The only piece of Van Lew's estate designated for someone other than Annie was Van Lew's precious manuscript account of her life story, which she left to her Boston benefactor and friend John P. Reynolds, Jr.[23]

Reynolds collaborated with Otis Russell to obtain a memorial stone for Van Lew's grave that would be worthy of her stature as a war hero. Given her connection to Boston, Reynolds thought it appropriate that Elizabeth's memorial stone should be from Massachusetts, and he arranged for a giant pudding stone from the grounds of the State House in Boston to be shipped to Richmond. While the costs of the transfer were covered by a collective of Boston admirers of Van Lew, it is Reynolds who deserves the credit for designing the bronze tablet that is secured to the face of the stone. Its inscription reads:

ELIZABETH L. VAN LEW

1818   1900

SHE RISKED EVERYTHING THAT IS DEAR TO MAN—FRIENDS—

FORTUNE—COMFORT—HEALTH—LIFE ITSELF—ALL FOR THE

ONE ABSORBING DESIRE OF HER HEART—THAT SLAVERY

MIGHT BE ABOLISHED AND THE UNION PRESERVED. THIS BOULDER

FROM THE CAPITOL HILL IN BOSTON IS A TRIBUTE

FROM MASSACHUSETTS FRIENDS

The stone was installed at Shockoe Cemetery, with Russell superintending the work, in July of 1902. Reynolds worried that the bronze tablet would be "pried off and destroyed"; years later he expressed satisfaction that "Southerners have always respected it and left it as it was delivered."[24]

Van Lew's death occasioned an outpouring of press coverage, with the *New York Times*, *Boston Herald*, and scores of other newspapers joining the Richmond dailies in featuring lengthy obituaries and overviews of Van Lew's life. These stories invariably highlighted the Libby outbreak, Dahlgren reburial, and espionage for Grant as the principal points of interest in Elizabeth's story; the significance of her postmastership escaped the attention of the press. The coverage of Van Lew's death in conservative Richmond papers was a characterized by grudging respect for her accomplishments, "morbid curiousity" (to quote Van Lew's nieces) about her finances and estate, and belittling aspersions against her personality. "One of Miss Van Lew's peculiarities," the *Richmond News Leader* opined, for example, "was a very pronounced opposition to paying taxes." Van Lew, as we have seen, was not opposed to paying taxes, but objected to not having a vote even though she was a taxpayer. Her principled support of woman's suffrage was thus reduced by the *News Leader* to just more evidence of her "contrariness." The only local paper that gave Van Lew a reverent obituary was the African American *Richmond Planet*. Lamenting the passage of "one of the great figures of the late war," the *Planet* intoned that Van Lew "was zealous and true and as a representative of the Union won the respect and esteem of her bitterest enemies."[25]

⁓

Ultimately, it was Boston newspapers, not Richmond ones, which did the most to shape Van Lew's legacy and fix her image in the public eye. For in the Northern press coverage of her death, Van Lew's strange afterlife as "Crazy Bet" began. On September 26, 1900, John P. Reynolds Jr. wrote a note to the editor of the *Boston Evening Transcript* announcing Van Lew's demise. Reynolds, we have seen, had organized the charitable efforts of Van Lew's Boston benefactors and had been given possession of her manuscript papers. In keeping with his duty to perpetuate Van Lew's memory, Reynolds constructed, in his September letter, a narrative of her life. The dominant theme of that narrative was that Van Lew had succeeded in her spy work because she feigned craziness. "For a long time, if not continuously," Reynolds wrote, "she pretended to be a little light-headed and would go singing through the streets, perhaps a basket of fruit on her arm, as if she were a peddler, and so she soon was known as harmless, or 'Crazy Van Lew.' " She thus "was allowed to pass the guard and go into Libby prison." Her "sharp piercing little eyes saw farther and saw more than a dozen of her detractors," Reynolds declared, with admiration, and her "acute woman's instinct" kept her alert to possible dangers. Though he admitted to the press that he had not actually looked at the Van Lew manuscripts in his possession yet, Reynolds's narrative proved irresistible. Other newspapers paraphrased his September 26 letter; the *Boston Morning Journal*, for example, ran a story that said of Van Lew: " 'Crazy Bet' the townspeople [of wartime Richmond] called her, and guards let her pass freely into all sorts of places."[26]

The label "Crazy Bet" became a staple of Van Lew lore, thanks in large part to the influence Reynolds was able to exert over a scholar named William Gilmore Beymer, who in 1911 would publish the first extensive biographical piece on Van Lew in the popular journal *Harper's Monthly*. Beymer's own personal papers contain his revealing correspondence about Van Lew with Reynolds. Beymer first wrote Reynolds in 1908, seeking access to the Van Lew manuscripts that Reynolds, as executor, had in his possession. Reynolds responded that while he had met with Van Lew on a number of occasions in her waning years, she had revealed very little about her wartime activities. Reynolds went on to offer up his opinion about the personal papers Van Lew had willed to him: he declared them "perfectly valueless for purposes of publication, as [they] contain long chapters on her views on slavery, woman's rights, and all sorts of other uninteresting things."[27]

In response to Beymer's cajoling, Reynolds eventually sat down with the papers in the Van Lew estate and read them, and in doing so he became convinced that they were not "perfectly valueless" as he had originally declared but rather a treasure trove, the chronicle of a true American heroine. This revelation made Reynolds more proprietary than ever about Van Lew's story, and he tried to dictate, chapter and verse, what Beymer should write in his article. Reynolds pushed the idea that Van Lew, as he put it, "took her own eccentric manners and exaggerated them until she was almost thought light-headed" and when Beymer sent him an initial draft of the *Harper's* article, Reynolds took him to task for not emphasizing enough that Van Lew affected eccentricity; Reynolds scribbled in the margins of his letter to Beymer that Van Lew was known as "Old Crazy Bet." Beymer relented, and his *Harper's* article features the theme of "Crazy Bet" prominently. That article has become the single most frequently quoted secondary source on Van Lew.[28]

The notion that Van Lew was Crazy Bet has been embellished upon again and again in the modern scholarly literature on her, resulting in claims that she "commonly dressed in odd clothes," that she frequently could be seen about the streets of Richmond smiling her "vacant smile," and that "most people considered her a silly, hysterical woman." By cultivating this image as a crazy person, so the dominant argument runs, Van Lew was able to broadcast her Unionism without fear of reprisal, and was even allowed to "wander about within the [Confederate] prisons almost at will." Many a treatment of Van Lew implies that the role of "Crazy Bet" came easy to her because she was, in fact, a "nervous," "tense," and "eccentric" individual. As an article from *Civil War Times Illustrated* has put it, "Elizabeth Van Lew was a strange little woman. . . . How many of her peculiarities were assumed to hoodwink the Confederate authorities and how many were real is difficult to tell." The notion that key to Van Lew's spy tradecraft was her ability to appear daft has become so ingrained in the public memory that virtually every published work on Van Lew for the last 100 years has adopted the concept of "Crazy Bet" as its tag line, title, theme, or thesis.[29]

To remember Van Lew as Crazy Bet is misleading, counterproductive, and indeed, unjust. For the Crazy Bet myth flatly contravenes the historical record. Van Lew, as we have seen, was never allowed to enter Libby prison, and lived in terror of being detected by the Confederates. She did indeed resort to a number of ruses to avoid detection. On several occasions she dressed in odd garb—"coarse clothes, with a sunbonnet on my head & a basket on my arm"—but the purpose of such play acting was to conceal her identity as Elizabeth Van Lew, not to give the impression that she had gone crazy. As we have seen, Van Lew's favorite role to play during the war was that of the loyal Confederate, whose sympathies to Union soldiers were merely extensions of the noblesse oblige ethic of the elite Christian lady. It strains credulity to think that Van Lew, who was keenly aware that her family's respectability was her most important asset, would taint her reputation by persistently acting the madwoman. Instead, Van Lew astutely capitalized on the blindness of Confederate authorities—on their unwillingness to believe that a woman of her social standing could be a dangerous Union agent.

Moreover, not one of Van Lew's compatriots—Lohmann, Rowley, Sharpe, et al.—ever alludes to her feigning craziness. Neither do the rebel authorities. Surely, if there had been a widespread belief in wartime Richmond that Van Lew was crazy, it would have surfaced in the Confederate investigation of her in the fall of 1864. Just as surely, Van Lew's political enemies would have seized on such a reputation when they sought to discredit her in 1869, as she assumed her postmastership. It was not until Van Lew's bitter battle to retain her office that the first public charges of mental instability were leveled against her—and they were politically motivated charges about her "erratic" behavior in office, not her comportment during the war.

Ultimately, the biggest problem with the Crazy Bet myth is that it overshadows other more plausible and better documented explanations for Van Lew's success as a spy. That success owed to her careful and deliberate tradecraft: the way she used money to turn enemies into informants; the way she painstakingly encrypted her dispatches in code; and the way she chose her couriers and coordinated their efforts. The survival of the Unionist underground depended on the willingness of total strangers—African American Unionists, Federal scouts, and prisoners themselves, among others—to trust Van Lew, and literally to put their lives in her hands. A purported madwoman could not have inspired that trust.

If wartime and Reconstruction sources do not support the theory that Civil War Richmonders regarded Van Lew as crazy, then why did Reynolds and subsequent chroniclers seize on the notion? Reynolds, it must be remembered, made Van Lew's acquaintance after Reconstruction, when she was in her late sixties. Her political troubles and family tensions had taken a toll both on her nerves and on her public reputation. Reynolds did not see the Van Lew who had cannily manipulated the likes of General Winder or who had inspired the devotion of William Rowley and F. W. E. Lohmann; he did not see the Van Lew whose professionalism in the post office had won the grudging praise even of Richmond's most conservative papers. Rather he saw a frightened, paranoid old woman who was shunned by the "good" people of her city and obsessed with the theme of her own persecution. Like so many others did, Reynolds projected what he knew of the elderly Van Lew back into the past. The image of the bedraggled, nervous, poverty-stricken crone—of Crazy Bet—effaced the image of the articulate, razor sharp, and efficient spymaster and politician.

Van Lew's Ghost

IN RICHMOND, WHERE THE ELDERLY VAN LEW HAD BEEN REGARDED BY MANY AS A kind of witch, the dead Crazy Bet, according to a popular urban legend, rose from her grave as a ghost. In 1901, after her death, Van Lew's mansion was purchased by the Virginia Club, a civic organization. According to an article in the *Richmond Evening Journal*, the "negroes" who worked at the mansion "believed that it was haunted, [and] even the president of the club admitted that there were some strange noises there." When the basement was renovated, the story went on, "there started out upon the wall the outline of the spy's face and figure, terrifying a negro engaged in shaving ice"; he cried out in horror "I done hear Miss Lizzie walkin' 'bout. I knowed all 'long she was here." The notion that the Church Hill mansion was haunted persisted during the time it was owned by Dr. William H. Parker, Van Lew's former physician, who in 1908 converted the dwelling into a sanatorium. Not surprisingly, the public made no objection when the city condemned the mansion in 1911 and had it torn down the following year. A public school—the Bellevue School—was constructed on the site and stands there to this day. The image of "Crazy Bet" as a bogeyman or ghost outlived the mansion itself. According to Richmonder Hyman Schwartzberg, curator of the Richmond National Battlefield Park and the Maggie L. Walker National Historic Site, his father Max, who was born in 1905, was told by his parents that "Crazy Bet would get him" if he did not behave.[1]

Indeed, Van Lew continued to haunt Richmond, metaphorically if not literally, long after her death. Three stories will suffice to illustrate the city's enduring fascination with Crazy Bet. In 1909, renowned novelist Ellen Glasgow published a novel entitled *The Romance of a Plain Man*. Glasgow it will be remembered, had grown up on Church Hill and defied her parents' warnings to stay away from the grounds of the Van Lew residence. A brilliant social critic, harbinger of the Southern Literary Renaissance, and standard bearer of Virginia's fledgling woman's suffrage movement, Glasgow represented a new generation of white Southern progressives. Her novel *Romance* is set in Richmond in the period 1875 to 1908; its central plot line is the story of a how a Horatio Alger-like figure, Ben Starr, rises from obscurity to wealth, only to suffer a spiritual crisis along the way and be redeemed by the love of his wife, Sally. Although it is hardly one of her best novels, *Romance* is noteworthy because it contains her most outspoken and radical female protagonist—a character plainly based on Elizabeth Van Lew.[2]

Named Mataoca Bland, that character is an "old maid" living on Church Hill, and the surrogate mother to her niece Sally. A supporter of woman's suffrage, Mataoca was "one of those unhappy women . . . who suffered from greater mental activity than was usually allotted to females," Glasgow has her narrator, Ben Starr, wryly declare. Mataoca was widely believed by respectable people in the city to be "crazy," and a "Yankee abolitionist." Why? Because she had had the nerve to go to the state legislature and ask that a woman's suffrage measure be passed. As the presidential election campaign approached, Mataoca worked herself into a state of nervous prostration writing prosuffrage letters to the local papers. When they failed to garner support, she resorted to a desperate gambit: she marched right into the midst of a large Democratic party procession that was winding through the streets and literally unfurled her suffrage flag. Glasgow clearly had the legendary Crazy Bet in mind when she described Mataoca's daring, and final act: "There she was, in her poke bonnet and her black silk mantle, walking primly at the straggling end of the procession, among a crowd of hooting small boys and gaping negroes. Her eyes, ever wide and bright, like the eyes of one who is mentally deranged, were fixed straight ahead, over the lines of men marching in front of her, on the blue sky above the church steeples. Under her poke bonnet I saw her meekly parted hair and her faded cheeks, flushed now with a hectic color. In one neatly gloved hand her silk skirt was held primly; in the other she carried a white silk flag, on which the staring gold letters were lost in the rippling folds."[3]

The mental and physical strain of entering the male domain of the parade proved too much for Mataoca, and she collapsed in the street and died of heart failure. "I always thought her sense of honour would kill her," Mataoca's old acquaintance, Dr. Theophilus, muttered at her deathbed.[4]

Glasgow's portrayal of Mataoca Bland bespeaks the ambivalence progressive white Virginians had toward Van Lew early in the century. Glasgow clearly sympathizes with her character's plight and endorses her principles. But she just as clearly rejects Mataoca's—and, by extension, Elizabeth's—methods. It *is* crazy, and ineffectual, Glasgow seems to say, for women to stand in such open defiance of social conventions and to forsake the support and company of men.

While in Glasgow's vision, Van Lew's very radicalism rendered her vulnerable and powerless, conservative commentators continued to view Van Lew's story as a cautionary tale about what happens when women wield too much power. In August of 1911, just two months after the publication in *Harper's Monthly* of William Gilmore Beymer's biographical article on Van Lew, the "Confederate column" of the *Richmond Times-Dispatch* featured a story intended to counter Beymer's tales of heroism and to "set the record straight." Van Lew, the article reminded its readers, was guilty of the cardinal sin of having promoted black officeholders. The "unwritten chapter" of her life was the story of how she "foisted ... these harpies on us in the dark days immediately after the war." Her death as a forsaken outcast was her just reward, the article concluded. "The world recoils at the name of a Judas, a Benedict Arnold ... and a Van Lew."[5]

Van Lew continued to be regarded as a "traitor" by conservative white Richmonders well into modern times. In 1959, to give the richest of many examples, the *Richmond News Leader* ran a four-part series entitled "View of a Vixen: Van Lew Spying Value Questioned." The newspaper coverage was designed to publicize a play, "The Lone Vixen: The Story of Elizabeth Van Lew," sponsored by the Friends of Historic Richmond Foundation in order to raise funds for the restoration and preservation of Church Hill. The *News Leader* articles trafficked in many old myths about Van Lew—such as the notion that "she made no secret in Richmond of her abolitionist leanings"—but also added a new spin. Projecting the loneliness of her very last years back into the war era, the paper declared that from the moment of secession, Van Lew found herself utterly isolated. "Visitors ceased coming" to the Church Hill mansion, and her fabled espionage work Van Lew carried out singlehandedly. The fall of Richmond to Union troops was thus a "moment of lonely triumph for Miss Elizabeth Van Lew. Indeed it was her only one." The play, it turned out, was a success: all three performances of it were sold out, and "Mrs. John J. Pershing, an active member of the [Historic Richmond Foundation] Board, made a notable hit in a comedy role as Miss Van Lew's maid."[6]

Van Lew's legendary loneliness, like her "craziness," served a political purpose—it had the effect of erasing the history of Virginia's loyalists, black and white. For those clinging in the twentieth century to the Lost Cause version of the Confederate past, it was comforting to regard Van Lew as an aberration rather than as the center of widespread network of committed Unionists. Moreover, the notion that Van Lew acted alone served to absolve the Confederacy from the taint of incompetence: who could blame the rebel authorities for letting a "lone vixen" slip through their net?

It is only in the past three decades—that is to say, in the aftermath of the Civil Rights revolution of the 1960s—that Van Lew's reputation has been somewhat redeemed. The advent of women's history and African American history as established fields of inquiry has led to efforts, by the public and historical professionals alike, to recover the experiences of Southern Unionists, suffragists, and other dissenters. Two honors recently bestowed on Van Lew are symptomatic of these efforts. When, in the late 1980s, the Virginia Business and Professional Women's Clubs established a "Women of Virginia Historic Trail," they included Van Lew and the fabled Mary Elizabeth Bowser among their initial group of inductees. Similarly, the Bellevue school, which constitutes the Van Lew site on the trail, took measures to honor Van Lew's memory—and her crucial role as a mentor to the city's black leaders—by creating a "Maggie Walker Museum" in the school lobby. The displays therein not only note that Walker was born in the Van Lew mansion, they also include several portraits and news clippings of Van Lew, and an homage to Bowser.[7]

Unfortunately, for every careful treatment of Van Lew in recent years there seems to be another that perpetuates falsehoods and stereotypes. In 1987, the airing on CBS of a made-for-TV movie called "A Special Friendship" occasioned a new series of articles on Van Lew in the Richmond press. The movie purported to be the story of Van Lew and Bowser, but as the local reviews indignantly pointed out, many liberties were taken with the facts. Van Lew, played by actress Tracy Pollan, is a "lovely young TV movie creature" who is fed false information, jailed, and then interrogated by the young Confederate officer to whom she had been engaged; only the ingenuity of the Bowser character permits Van Lew/Pollan to go free and obtain reliable information for the Union. While reviewers railed against the inaccurate plot line of the movie, they could not resist perpetuating in its stead the image of Van Lew as the despised, eccentric, lone spinster, who "by some accounts . . . may have become the 'Crazy Bett' that she pretended to be during the war."[8]

Van Lew, thus, has continued to elude us, much as she eluded her potential captors during the war. For we, like they, have been blinded by our fantasies and our prejudices. It is a bitter irony of the Crazy Bet myth that Van Lew saw herself as more sane, not less, than those around her. It was for her rationality that Van Lew wanted to be remembered; the central theme running through her writings is the conviction that she was a pillar of reason in a world gone mad. Interestingly, at the very same time that John P. Reynolds Jr. was circulating his stories of "Crazy Van Lew," Elizabeth's oldest friend, Eliza Griffin (Carrington) Nowland, was trying in vain to publish her own account of Elizabeth's life. "In a few brief pages I propose to portray the patriotic and philanthropic characteristics of Elizabeth Van Lew," Eliza began her manuscript, which was rejected by a Boston publisher. "Possessed of a logical mind. . . ." Carrington continued, Van Lew "believed slavery to be a blot on the nation. . . . When Patrick Henry stood in historic old St. John's Church and shouted 'Give me liberty or give me death,' the walls of the Old Van Lew mansion . . . echoed . . . and Elizabeth Van Lew's heart caught up the refrain and cried 'Give them liberty or give me death.' . . . Love for her family sustained her in her trials through her life. . . . I have never known as noble a woman."[9] We owe it to this noble woman to put the myth of "Crazy Bet" in its proper context, and to listen to the real Elizabeth Van Lew—a woman whom we should remember not only for her ability to conceal the truth, but for her ability to tell it.

LIST OF ABBREVIATIONS

BRFAL   Bureau of Refugees, Freedmen, and Abandoned Lands

EVL   Elizabeth Van Lew

EVLP   Elizabeth Van Lew Papers, microfilm edition, Library of Virginia, Richmond (original manuscript is held at the New York Public Library). Because many pages in Van Lew's papers have no page numbers or multiple, conflicting page numbers that do not correspond to the order of the documents themselves, I have assigned a number to each microfilm frame and provided such frame numbers in the endnotes. In cases in which there is a clear page number on a given page, I provide that number in the citation, followed by the frame number. In cases in which there are conflicting page numbers or no page numbers at all, I provide only the frame number.

JMCB   Chancery Court Records, John Marshall Courts Building, Richmond, Va.

LC   Library of Congress, Washington, D.C.

LVA   Library of Virginia, Richmond

NA   National Archives, Washington, D.C., College Park, Md., and Waltham, Mass.

O.R.   *Official Records of the War of the Rebellion*

UTA   Center for American History, University of Texas at Austin

UVA   Special Collections, Alderman Library, University of Virginia, Charlottesville

VHS   Virginia Historical Society, Richmond

W&M   Swem Library, College of William & Mary, Williamsburg, Va.

NOTES

PROLOGUE

1. For an inventory of the contents of the Church Hill mansion at the time of Elizabeth's death, see Elizabeth Van Lew, Fiduciary Account, 1900, JMCB. For obituaries, see for example *Richmond Dispatch*, September 25, 26, 1900; *Richmond News Leader*, September 25, 1900; *Boston Globe*, September 26, 1900; *Boston Evening Transcript*, September 26, 1900.
2. *Richmond Enquirer*, April 29, 1877; *Richmond Times-Dispatch*, September 23, 1937.
3. Van Lew, Fiduciary Account, 1900, JMCB; the Grant portrait is preserved among the papers of William Gilmore Beymer, a scholar who published an influential and widely read article on Van Lew in *Harper's Monthly* in 1911. William Gilmore Beymer Papers, UTA.
4. On Botts, see Daniel W. Crofts, *Reluctant Confederates: Upper South Unionists in the Secession Crisis* (Chapel Hill: University of North Carolina Press, 1989); on Andrew and Sumner, Thomas O'Connor, *Civil War Boston: Homefront & Battlefield* (Boston: Northeastern Press, 1997); on Grant and Lincoln, see James M. McPherson, *Ordeal by Fire: The Civil War and Reconstruction* (New York: Knopf, 1982).
5. *Richmond News Leader*, September 25, 1900; *Richmond Dispatch*, September 25, 1900.
6. EVL to John A. Andrew, February 28, 1866, Executive Dept. Letters, vol. 97, 107a, Massachusetts State Archives, Boston, and "Telegram from my Dear Friend, Governor Andrew," n.d., Elizabeth Van Lew Papers, W&M; Eric Foner, *Reconstruction: America's Unfinished Revolution* (New York: Harper & Row, 1988), 230, 496.
7. EVL, "Personal Narrative," EVLP, Frame 14; John P. Reynolds Jr. to William Gilmore Beymer, December 14, 1908, December 6, 1910, Beymer Papers, UTA.
8. EVL, "Notes on Being Called a Spy," EVLP, Frames 137–39.

CHAPTER ONE
"AN AWFUL RESPONSIBILITY": THE MAKING OF A DISSENTER, 1818–1860

1. EVL, "Notes on her Ancestry," EVLP, Frames 240–45.

2. EVL, "Notes," EVLP, Frames 240–41; William Henry Egle, M.D., "The Federal Constitution of 1787. Sketches of the Members of the Pennsylvania Convention," *Pennsylvania Magazine of History and Biography*, 10 (1886), 450; Eliza Griffin (Carrington) Nowland, "Elizabeth L. Van Lew," EVLP, 9–10, Frames 186–87; Pennsylvania Abolition Society Papers, List of Members, 1784–1819, Historical Society of Pennsylvania, Philadelphia; David Brion Davis, *The Boisterous Sea of Liberty: A Documentary History of America from Discovery through the Civil War* (New York: Oxford University Press, 1998), 353.

3. EVL, "Notes," EVLP, Frames 240–45.

4. Lewis W. Burton, *Annals of Henrico Parish, Diocese of Virginia, and Especially of St. John's Church, The Present Mother of the Parish, from 1611 to 1884* (Richmond: Williams Printing Company, 1904), 233; *Richmond Enquirer*, January 15, 1818.

5. Marie Tyler-McGraw, *At the Falls: Richmond, Virginia, and Its People* (Chapel Hill: University of North Carolina Press, 1994), 77–79.

6. Tyler-McGraw, *At the Falls*, 90–91, 97; Gregg D. Kimball, *American City, Southern Place: A Cultural History of Antebellum Richmond* (Athens: University of Georgia Press, 2000), 3–8.

7. Tyler-McGraw, *At the Falls*, 110–12; Kimball, *American City*, 16–18.

8. Kimball, *American City*, 37; Midori Takagi, *"Rearing Wolves to Our Own Destruction": Slavery in Richmond, Virginia, 1782–1865* (Charlottesville: University Press of Virginia, 1999), 16–17.

9. Business Drafts, Thomas M. Randolph of Tuckahoe to John Van Lew, May 31, September 27, October 4, 1826, John Van Lew Manuscript, Library Company of Philadelphia, Historical Society of Pennsylvania; John Van Lew to Charles Richards, February 13, 1840, Richards Family Correspondence, LVA; *Richmond Whig*, September 6, 1836. On U.Va., see for example John Van Lew & Company to Arthur Spicer Brockenbrough, February 28, March 5, April 10, 17, June 7, 1821, in the Modern English Collection at the University of Virginia, Electronic Text Center, http://etext.virginia.edu.

10. John Van Lew to Richards, February 13, 1840, Richards Family Correspondence, LVA; Marguerite Crumley and John G. Zehmer, *Church Hill: The St. John's Historic District* (Richmond: Council of Historic Richmond Foundation, 1991), 52–57; Bryan Clark Green, Calder Loth & William M. S. Rasmussen, *Lost Virginia: Vanished Architecture of the Old Dominion* (Charlottesville: Howell Press, 2001), 48–49.

11. Ritchie, as quoted in EVL, "For Sale: The Van Lew Homestead," *A.O.H.*

Journal (October 1879), 3; Louis H. Manarin and Clifford Dowdey, *The History of Henrico County* (Charlottesville: University Press of Virginia, 1984), 211–12.

12. Ritchie, as quoted in EVL, "For Sale," 3.

13. Crumley and Zehmer, *Church Hill*, 52–57.

14. EVL, "For Sale," 3.

15. Crumley and Zehmer, *Church Hill*, 52–57; Eliza Griffin (Carrington) Nowland, "Elizabeth L. Van Lew," EVLP, 10–11, Frames 187–88; Burton, *Annals*, 184. Eliza Carrington is listed as the widow of Thomas Nowland in *Sheriff & Co's Richmond City Directory, 1875/76* (Richmond: West, Johnston & Co.), 150. Because she wrote her piece on Van Lew after her marriage, she will be referred to as (Carrington) Nowland in the notes, but as Carrington when I describe events prior to her marriage.

16. (Carrington) Nowland, "Elizabeth L. Van Lew," EVLP, 10–11, Frames 187–88; "Pass Granted to Mrs. E. L. Van Lew to Visit Chaffin's Farm," July 6, 1864, Elizabeth Louisa Van Lew Album, VHS; Elizabeth R. Varon, *We Mean to Be Counted: White Women and Politics in Antebellum Virginia* (Chapel Hill: University of North Carolina Press, 1998).

17. Burton, *Annals*, 266; Fourth U.S. Census, 1820, Richmond City, Henrico County, Va., 194; Fifth U.S. Census, 1830, Richmond City, Henrico County, Va., 456; Sixth U.S. Census, 1840, Richmond City, Henrico County, Va., 157.

18. *Richmond News-Leader*, September 25, 1900; *Richmond Whig*, June 16, 1840; *Richmond Dispatch*, September 25, 1900.

19. EVL, "Notes," EVLP, 5, Frames 243–44; Fiduciary Accounts, Eliza Van Lew, 1876, JCMB.

20. EVL, "Notes," EVLP, 5, Frames 243–44.

21. (Carrington) Nowland, "Elizabeth L. Van Lew," EVLP, 10–11, Frames 187–88; John Albree Jr., lecture, n.d., Elizabeth Van Lew Papers, W&M.

22. (Carrington) Nowland, "Elizabeth L. Van Lew," EVLP, 10–11, Frames 187–88; EVL to Richards, August 2, 1838, Richards Family Correspondence, LVA.

23. EVL to Richards, August 2, 1838, Richards Family Correspondence, LVA.

24. Ibid.

25. (Carrington) Nowland, "Elizabeth L. Van Lew," EVLP, 12–13, Frames 189–90; Author's Interview with Dorothy Grant, March 31, 2002; Dorothy Lewis Grant, "Lady of Refinement: The Spy Called 'Crazy Bet,' " *The Torch* 70 (Spring 1997), 22–26.

26. (Carrington) Nowland, "Elizabeth L. Van Lew," EVLP, 12–13, Frames 189–90; on Virginia women's benevolence, see Varon, *We Mean to Be Counted*.

27. *Richmond Enquirer*, September 29, 1843.

28. Will of John Van Lew, Henrico County Will Book no.11, 266–73, LVA.

29. Ibid.

30. Burton, *Annals*, 282; First African Baptist Church Minutes, 1841–1930, November 12, 1843, and July 12, 1856, LVA.

31. "Van Lew Ex. & Smith," May 25, 1845, Henrico County Deeds (HCD), Book 49, 61; Indenture, "Van Lew Ex. & Talbott," February 26, 1847, HCD, Book 50, 588; "Van Lew Ex. & Rix," April 29, 1847, HCD, Book 51, 222; "Van Lew Ex. & Rix," September 3, 1848, HCD, Book 54, 248, all at LVA; Henrico County Register of Free Negroes and Mulattoes, 1831–65, volume for 1831–43, 39; volume for 1844–52, 8, LVA.

32. Suzanne Lebsock, *The Free Women of Petersburg: Status and Culture in a Southern Town, 1784–1860* (New York: W. W. Norton, 1984), 112, 138.

33. Bonnie S. Anderson, *Joyous Greetings: The First International Women's Movement, 1830–1860* (New York: Oxford University Press, 2000), 104; Margaret H. McFadden, *Golden Cables of Sympathy: The Transatlantic Sources of Nineteenth-Century Feminism* (Lexington: University Press of Kentucky, 1999), 44, 75.

34. Frederika Bremer, *Homes of the New World; Impressions of America, Vol. II* (New York: Harper & Brothers, 1853), 509–10.

35. Albree, lecture, n.d., and interview with Anna I. Whitlock, n.d., Van Lew Papers, W&M.

36. Sixth U.S. Census, 1840, Richmond City, Henrico County, Va., 157; Seventh U.S. Census, 1850, Richmond City, Henrico County, Va., 246; U.S. Census Slave Schedule, 1850, Richmond City, Henrico County, Va., 4; Personal Property Tax Records, Richmond City, Henrico County, Va., 1850 and 1860; "Van Lew Ex. & Ege," June 7, 1856, HCD, Book 68, 308, LVA.

37. For a long time, scholars have accepted uncritically an assertion made in the first lengthy biographical article on Van Lew, William Beymer's 1911 essay in *Harper's Monthly*. In it, Beymer claims that Elizabeth "gave freedom to nine of the Van Lew slaves; others were bought that they might be reunited with a husband or a wife already in the Van Lew possession." This claim has been repackaged again and again in the Van Lew literature, usually taking the form of the assertion that Van Lew persuaded her mother to free the family's bondpeople after John Van Lew's death. Beymer, *Harper's Monthly* (June 1911), 86–7; David D. Ryan, ed., *A Yankee Spy in Richmond: The Civil War Diary of "Crazy Bet" Van Lew* (Mechanicsburg, Pa.: Stackpole Books, 1996), 5–6; Duane Schultz, *The Dahlgren Affair: Terror and Conspiracy in the Civil War* (New York: W. W. Norton, 1998), 63–6.

38. While the census records do not provide names for these slaves, they do locate them within age ranges (i.e., age 10–23), allowing us to deduce that at least five of the individuals Eliza held in bondage in 1850 had not been in the family's possession ten years earlier, and that some four to six of the slaves John had held in 1840 had disappeared off the census rolls by 1850. Sixth U.S. Census,

1840, Richmond City, Henrico County, Va., 157; Seventh U.S. Census, 1850, Richmond City, Henrico County, Va., 246.

39. On William Sewell, see First African Baptist Church Minutes, September 30, 1843, LVA, and John P. Reynolds Jr. interview transcript with Annie Randolph Hall, December 9, 1910, Beymer Papers, UTA. On Oliver Lewis see "Pass granted to Bob & Oliver, July 12, 1864," Van Lew Album, VHS, and First African Baptist Church Minutes, November 12, 1843, LVA. On the Roanes, see First African Baptist Church Minutes, October 30, 1842, and July 12, 1856, LVA; "Record for Peter Roane," no. 2439, February 2, 1871, Richmond City, Henrico County, Va., Freedmen's Savings and Trust Company Registers, NA; John Van Lew to "Emma Plane" [Elizabeth Van Lew], December 20, 1864, William Fay Papers, LVA; EVL, "Notes," EVLP, Frames 244–45; Ninth U.S. Census, 1870, Richmond City, Henrico County, Va., 506; and "Receipt for Purchase of Louisa," January 1, 1863, Van Lew Album, VHS. On Nelson see EVL, "Personal Narrative," May 14, 1864, EVLP, 661–63, Frames 52–53, and Ninth U.S. Census, 1870, Richmond City, Henrico County, Va., 506; on Anderson see "Commonwealth v. Eliza Van Lew" Hustings Court Minutes, Minute Book no. 27 [1860–62], 200, LVA; on Caroline see, "Hiring Agreement between Eliza Van Lew and Richard H. Lorton, January 1, 1852," Van Lew Album, VHS; on Judy Johnson see (Carrington) Nowland, "Elizabeth L. Van Lew," EVLP, 13–14, Frames 190–91 and Ninth U.S. Census, Richmond City, Henrico County, Va., 1870, 506; on Elizabeth Draper Mitchell, see Maggie Lena Walker Historical Site, National Park Service, http://www.nps.gov/malw/details/htm.

40. Luther Porter Jackson, *Free Negro Labor and Property Holding in Virginia, 1830–1860* (New York: D. Appleton-Century Co., 1942), 6.

41. Takagi, *"Rearing Wolves to Our Own Destruction,"* 22, 38–39; Jackson, *Free Negro Labor and Property Holding,* 181.

42. Hiring Agreement between Eliza Van Lew and Richard H. Lorton, January 1, 1852, Van Lew Album, VHS. On Wright and Goodall, see Judith Wright to EVL, October 26, 1857, Richmond City Hustings Deeds, Book 70A, 252, LVA; Ninth U.S. Census, 1870, Richmond City, Henrico County, 31; "Record for Mary Goodhall," no. 4369, March 12, 1872, Richmond City, Henrico County, Va., Freedmen's Savings and Trust Company Registers, NA.

43. *Richmond Dispatch,* May 17, 1861; "Commonwealth v. Eliza Van Lew," Hustings Court Minutes, Minute Book no. 27 [1860–62], 200, LVA.

44. Marion M. Thompson Wright, *The Education of Negroes in New Jersey* (New York: Teachers College, Columbia, 1941), 114; "The Bark Lamartine," *African Repository* (February 1856), 57–59.

45. Varon, *We Mean to Be Counted,* 41–70.

46. Kimball, *American City,* 118–19.

47. EVL to William McLain, April 20, September 29, October 2, 1854, April 24,

1857, December 2, 1858, April 21, 1859, American Colonization Society Papers, LC; Robert T. Brown, *Immigrants to Liberia, 1843–1865: An Alphabetical Listing* (Philadelphia: Institute for Liberian Studies, 1980), 50; "The Bark Lamartine," *African Repository* (February 1856), 57–59; "Intelligence from Liberia," *African Repository* (May 1856), 135–38; "Latest Intelligence from Liberia," *African Repository* (June 1856), 162.

48. EVL to Mr. Williams, September 10, 22, 1859, ACS Papers, LC. Thanks to Marie Tyler-McGraw for furnishing the background on Anthony D. Williams.

49. Ibid.

50. "Return of the Stevens," *African Repository* (April 1860), 116.

51. Kimball, *American City*, 71–73; *Richmond Whig*, August 21, 30, 1860.

52. *Richmond Whig*, August 21, 30, September 11, 1860. According to EVL's cousin Anna Whitlock, the hired cook Caroline "was the mother of Mary Bowers [sic]." No sources establishing a connection between Caroline and M. J. Richards have come to light. Anna I. Whitlock to John Albree, April 25, 1913, Van Lew Papers, W&M.

53. Eighth U.S. Census, 1860, Richmond City, Henrico County, Va., 110; Hustings Court Minutes, Hustings Court Minute Book no. 28, [1862–63], 302, LVA; Burton, *Annals*, 248.

54. "Letter from Rev. Crammond Kennedy," *American Freedman* 2 (April 1867), 205.

55. (Carrington) Nowland, "Elizabeth L. Van Lew," EVLP, 13–14, Frames 190–91, and Ninth U.S. Census, Richmond City, Henrico County, Va., 1870, 506; "Receipt for Purchase of Louisa," January 1, 1863, Van Lew Album, VHS; Albree, lecture notes, n.p., Van Lew Papers, W&M.

56. On Elizabeth Draper Mitchell, see Maggie Lena Walker Historical Site, National Park Service, www.nps.gov/malw/details/htm. Author's interview with Dorothy Grant, March 31, 2002; author's interview with Hyman Schwartzberg, curator, Richmond National Battlefield Park, July 29, 2002.

57. Anna E. Dickinson to Mary Dickinson, January 9, 1875, Family Correspondence, Anna E. Dickinson Papers, LC. The author would like to thank Dickinson biographer J. Matthew Gallman for bringing this letter to her attention, and for determining that an undated excerpt in Dickinson's papers (container 4) was a misfiled part of the January 1875 letter, which is preserved in container 3 of Dickinson's correspondence. *Richmond Enquirer*, May 1, 1877.

58. "Van Lew Ex. & Tait," May 24, 1847, HCD, Deed Book 51, 289, LVA; "Van Lew Ex. & Tait," February 19, 1852, HCD, Book 60, 263; Kimball, *American City*, 112.

59. Philip Schwarz, *Migrants Against Slavery: Virginians and the Nation* (Charlottesville: University Press of Virginia, 2001), 103; on the trip to Europe see "Klapp &c. v. Van Lew &c.," February 2, 1877, Chancery Court Cases ended File

131, Richmond City, Va., JCMB; on one of Van Lew's trips to Philadelphia, see Mary S. Hull to Mrs. Henry Merrit, Hull Family Papers, August 9, 1847, VHS.

CHAPTER TWO
"MY COUNTRY! OH MY COUNTRY!": VIRGINIA LEAVES THE UNION

1. EVL, "Personal Narrative," EVLP, 19, Frame 110.
2. Crofts, *Reluctant Confederates*, 46–48.
3. Ibid., 44, 156–63.
4. John Minor Botts, *The Great Rebellion: Its Secret History, Rise, Progress, and Disastrous Failure* (New York: Harper & Brothers, 1866), xi–xii, 67; *Richmond Whig*, October 3, 1860; Varon, *We Mean to Be Counted*, 156–57.
5. John McCardell, *The Idea of a Southern Nation: Southern Nationalists and Southern Nationalism, 1830–1860* (New York: W. W. Norton, 1979); Charles B. Dew, *Apostles of Disunion: Southern Secession Commissioners and the Causes of the Civil War* (Charlottesville: University Press of Virginia, 2001).
6. Varon, *We Mean to Be Counted*, 138–39.
7. EVL, "Chapter 1—The beginning of the war," EVLP, 1–3, Frame 112.
8. Ibid., 4–5, Frames 113–14.
9. *Richmond Enquirer*, October 1, 5, 1860; *Richmond Whig*, August 29 and October 3, 1860.
10. Varon, *We Mean to Be Counted*.
11. EVL, "Chapter 1," EVLP, 5, Frame 114; Crofts, *Reluctant Confederates*, 106, 138; William W. Freehling, "Why Virginia's (Reluctant) Decision to Secede: Menace to Slavery or to States Rights or to??" Paper delivered at "Virginia's Civil War and Aftermath: The Douglas Southall Freeman and Southern Intellectual History Conferences," University of Richmond, February 2002, 5.
12. Crofts, *Reluctant Confederates*, 208–13, 248–51, 415.
13. Crofts, *Reluctant Confederates*, 262; *Richmond Dispatch*, March 5, 1861.
14. EVL, "Chapter 1," EVLP, 6–7, Frames 114–15.
15. *Richmond Enquirer*, February 5, 1861.
16. Crofts, *Reluctant Secessionists*, 316; Varon, *We Mean to Be Counted*, 158–61; EVL, "Chapter 1," EVLP, 7–8, Frames 115–16.
17. Crofts, *Reluctant Secessionists*, 273–76.
18. Crofts, *Reluctant Secessionists*, 290–96; McPherson, *Ordeal by Fire*, 144.
19. McPherson, *Ordeal*, 144–45.
20. EVL, "Chapter 1," EVLP, 8, Frame 116; Freehling, "Why Virginia's (Reluctant) Decision to Secede."
21. Crofts, *Reluctant Secessionists*, 320–21; Emory M. Thomas, *The Confederate State of Richmond: A Biography of the Capital* (Baton Rouge: Louisiana State

University Press, 1971), 5; Ernest B. Furgurson, *Ashes of Glory: Richmond at War* (New York: Alfred A. Knopf, 1996), 17.

22. EVL, "Chapter 1," EVLP, 9, Frame 117; Freehling, "Why Virginia's (Reluctant) Decision to Secede," 17.

23. Freehling, "Why Virginia's (Reluctant) Decision to Secede," 17–18; *Richmond Enquirer*, May 31, 1861. The allegedly official—and oft-cited—figures for the ratification vote were 125,950 for and 20,373 against. But as historian Edward Steers Jr. has revealed, those figures, based on estimates by Governor Letcher, did not properly account for the antisecession vote of western counties in the state; Steers's own figures—141,837 for secession to 43, 089 against—accurately reflect both the eastern and western tallies. Edward Steers Jr., "Montani Semper Liberi: The Making of West Virginia," *North & South* 2 (January 2000), 21.

24. EVL, "Chapter 1," EVLP, 9–10, Frame 117.

25. *Richmond Dispatch*, September 25, 1900; Testimony of John F. Lewis and of Horace Kent, in Claim of Horace Kent, Records of the U.S. Court of Claims, RG 123, Henrico County, Va., Case no. 564, 1872, NA; Claim of Joseph Segar, Southern Claims Commission, Allowed Claims, RG 217, Elizabeth City County, Va., Case no. 12131, 1874, NA; Claim of James Sharp, Southern Claims Commission, Allowed Claims, RG 217, Charles City County, Va., Case no. 17108, 1879, NA.

26. Stephen V. Ash, *When the Yankees Came: Conflict & Chaos in the Occupied South, 1861–1865* (Chapel Hill: University of North Carolina Press, 1995), 108–9.

27. Marjorie Spruill Wheeler, *New Women of the New South: The Leaders of the Woman Suffrage Movement in the Southern States* (New York: Oxford University Press, 1993), 58.

28. EVL, "Personal Narrative," EVLP, 262, Frame 19.

29. Ibid., 262–63, Frames 19–20.

30. Ibid., 263–64, Frame 20, and 454, Frame 75.

31. Ibid., 12–14, Frame 111.

32. On Mary C. Van Lew, see Testimony of Mary C. Van Lew, Letters Received by the Confederate Adjutant and Inspector General, 1861–65, October 15, 1864, NA. On the Bakers, see Albree transcription of interview with Anna Whitlock, Van Lew Papers, W&M; on McCreery, see Seventh U.S. Census, Richmond City, Henrico County, Va., 246 and John Van Lew McCreery Recollections, 1862–63, VHS.

33. Ibid., Frames 41–42, 113.

34. EVL, "Notes on her Ancestry," EVLP, Frame 244.

35. EVL, "Personal Narrative," EVLP, 311, Frame 27, and Frame 42.

36. Ibid., 11–12, Frame 118.
37. Ibid.

CHAPTER THREE
"OUR FLAG WAS GONE": THE WAR'S FIRST YEAR

1. *Richmond Enquirer*, April 25, 27, 1861, May 10, 1861.
2. *Richmond Daily Dispatch*, June 5, 7, 12, 1861, August 6, 1861. Brock first published her memoir, in 1867, under the rubric "A Richmond Lady." Brock married Richard F. Putnam after the war, in 1882, and the edition of her book currently in print appears under her married name. Sallie Brock Putnam, *Richmond During the War: Four Years of Personal Observation* (1867 Reprint: University of Nebraska Press, 1996), xxi, 29. She is referred to as Brock in the text, and will be cited as Brock Putnam in the notes.
3. Brock Putnam, *Richmond During the War*, 24; *Richmond Enquirer*, April 23, 1861.
4. EVL, "Personal Narrative," EVLP, 21, Frame 111.
5. Ibid.
6. *Richmond Enquirer*, June 18, 1861; EVL, "Personal Narrative," EVLP, 36, Frames 89 and 17, Frame 95.
7. EVL, "Personal Narrative," EVLP, 17, Frame 95.
8. James I. Robertson Jr., *Civil War Virginia* (Charlottesville: University of Virginia, 1991), 34; Chesnut as quoted in David J. Eicher, *The Longest Night: A Military History of the Civil War* (New York: Simon & Schuster, 2001), 100.
9. Brock Putnam, *Richmond During the War*, 65; William H. Jeffrey, *Richmond Prisons, 1861–1865* (Johnsbury, Vt.: The Republican Press, 1983), 29–30; Lonnie R. Speer, *Portals to Hell: Military Prisons of the Civil War* (Mechanicsburg, Pa.: Stackpole Books, 1997), 20; Sandra V. Parker, *Richmond's Civil War Prisons* (Lynchburg, Va.: H. E. Howard, 1990), 4.
10. Parker, *Richmond's Civil War Prisons*, 4; Speer, *Portals*, 20–21.
11. Alfred Ely, *The Journal of Alfred Ely, A Prisoner of War in Richmond*, ed. Charles Lanman (New York: D. Appleton and Company, 1862), 36, 77, 96; Michael Corcoran, *The Captivity of General Corcoran* (Philadelphia: Barclay & Co., 1862), 29; Blakey, *General John H. Winder*, 58–59.
12. EVL, "Personal Narrative," EVLP, 17–18, Frames 94–96.
13. For a definitive biography of Winder, see Arch Fredric Blakey, *General John H. Winder, C.S.A.* (Gainesville: University of Florida Press, 1990).
14. *Richmond Dispatch*, June 12, 1861; EVL, "Personal Narrative," EVLP, 19, Frame 96; Blakey, *General John H. Winder*, 1.
15. Speer, *Portals*, 21–22; Corcoran, *The Captivity of General Corcoran*, 27–30;

William C. Harris, *Prison-Life in the Tobacco Warehouse at Richmond* (Philadelphia: George W. Childs, 1862), 31–32.

16. EVL, "Personal Narrative," EVLP, 350, Frame 40, Frame 103; Ely, *The Journal of Alfred Ely*, 163; Harris, *Prison-Life*, 35.

17. EVL, "Personal Narrative," EVLP, Frame 109; *Richmond Enquirer*, July 29, 1861.

18. *Richmond Dispatch*, July 31, 1861.

19. Brock Putnam, *Richmond During the War*, 67; Ryan, ed., *A Yankee Spy*, 33; For more on Ricketts, see C. Vann Woodward, ed., *Mary Chesnut's Civil War* (New Haven: Yale University Press, 1981), 136–37.

20. *Charleston Mercury*, August 12, 1861; William R. Robinson, *Justice in Grey: A History of the Judicial System of the Confederate States of America* (Cambridge: Harvard University Press, 1941), 229.

21. Edwin C. Fishel, *The Secret War for the Union: The Untold Story of Military Intelligence in the Civil War* (Boston: Houghton Mifflin, 1996), 58–68.

22. Elizabeth D. Leonard, *All the Daring of a Soldier: Women of the Civil War Armies* (W. W. Norton & Company, 1999), 39–41.

23. *New York Herald*, August 26, 1861.

24. *Richmond Examiner*, August 30, 1861; *Richmond Dispatch*, December 11, 1861.

25. *Richmond Dispatch*, August 14, 24, 1861.

26. John B. Jones, *A Rebel War Clerk's Diary*, ed. Earl Schenk Miers (Baton Rouge: Louisiana State University Press, 1958), 47–48; Robinson, *Justice in Grey*, 244, 385; *Journal of the Congress of the Confederate States of America, 1861–65. Volume 1* (Washington, D.C.: Government Printing Office, 1904), 403, 798; Mary A. DeCredico, "Confiscation," *Encyclopedia of the Confederacy* (New York: Simon & Schuster, 1990), vol. I, 389.

27. (Carrington) Nowland, "Elizabeth L. Van Lew," EVLP, 14, Frame 191; "Testimony of Lewis Francis," *Report of the Joint Committee on the Conduct of the War* (Washington, D.C.: Government Printing Office, 1863), 477–78.

28. Ely, *Journal of Alfred Ely*, 158–63.

29. Ibid., 166–68.

30. EVL, "Personal Narrative," EVLP, Frame 105.

31. Ibid.

32. Ely, *Journal of Alfred Ely*, 210–16; William M. Robinson Jr., *The Confederate Privateers* (New Haven: Yale University Press, 1928), 49–57, 144–48.

33. *National Tribune*, August 20, 1891; Pauline Revere Thayer, *A Memorial of Paul Joseph Revere and Edward H. R. Revere* (Clinton, Mass.: W. J. Coulter, 1913), 83; EVL, "Personal Narrative," EVLP, Frame 100.

34. W. Raymond Lee to EVL, January 29, 1862 and A. M. Wood to EVL, January 30, 1862, Van Lew Papers, W&M. The original scrapbook is preserved at the

Virginia Historical Society as the Elizabeth Van Lew Album; the Van Lew papers at W&M contain a typescript, prepared at the behest of John Albree, of the text contents of the scrapbook.

35. EVL, "Personal Narrative," September 27, 1864, EVLP, 66, Frame 91; M. A. Revere to John P. Reynolds Jr., February 10, 1901, EVLP, Frames 203–4; *Richmond Whig*, April 29, 1862.

36. Brock Putnam, *Richmond During the War*, 92; John Winder to EVL, December 12, 1861, Van Lew Album, VHS; Owen B. Hill to EVL, January 23, 1862, and A. G. Bledsoe to EVL, January 24, 1862, EVLP, Frames 85–87, 152; EVL to Judah P. Benjamin, January 23, 1862, Letters Received by the Confederate Secretary of War, 1861–1865, NA.

37. EVL, "Personal Narrative," EVLP, Frames 77, 87; Revere to Reynolds Jr., February 10, 1901, EVLP, Frames 203–4; Furgurson, *Ashes of Glory*, 80.

38. William Harris, *Prison-Life*, 41–44.

39. *Richmond Enquirer*, February 28, 1862; Harris, *Prison-Life*, 117; Ely, *Journal*, 191–92; *Charleston Mercury*, March 4, 1862.

40. McPherson, *Ordeal by Fire*, 366; Furgurson, *Ashes of Glory;* 112–13; Edward Younger, ed., *Inside the Confederate Government: The Diary of Robert Garlick Hill Kean* (Baton Rouge: Louisiana State University Press, 1957), 23; *Richmond Enquirer*, March 4, 1862.

41. Brock Putnam, *Richmond During the War*, 101.

42. Blakey, *General John H. Winder*, 49–50.

43. Furgurson, *Ashes of Glory*, 101, 113–15; Blakey, *General John H. Winder*, 132–33; *New York Herald*, March 6, 1862; *Richmond Examiner*, March 6, 1862; *Richmond Dispatch* March 6, 1862.

44. W. S. Ashe to Jefferson Davis, February 28, 1862, Letters Received by the Confederate Secretary of War, 1861–1865, RG 109, NA.

45. On Wardwell and Palmer see Meriwether Stuart, "Colonel Ulric Dahlgren and Richmond's Union Underground, April 1864," *Virginia Magazine of History and Biography* 72 (April 1964), 178–79, 189–91; on Higgins, see *Washington Chronicle*, May 8, 1865; on Fay, see *Richmond Examiner*, March 6, 1862 and Accounts and Receipts, 1854–1884, William Fay Papers, LVA.

46. John Minor Botts, *The Great Rebellion*, 283–87.

47. On Palmer's release see *Richmond Enquirer*, March 7, 1862. On Botts see Miss M. M. Blair to President Davis, March 22, 1862, *O.R.*, ser. 2, vol. II, 1546; Rosalie Botts to John B. Baldwin, April 4, 1862, and Baldwin to George W. Randolph, April 7, 1862, Letters Received by the Confederate Secretary of War, 1861–1865, RG 109, NA; George Henry Sharpe to C. B. Comstock, January 1867, EVLP, Frames 129–35; Stuart, "Colonel Ulric Dahlgren," 181. On Stearns, see Nance & Williams to G. W. Randolph, April 25, 1862, Letters Received by

the Confederate Secretary of War, RG 109, NA; *Richmond Dispatch*, April 26, 1862; "Summary of Franklin Stearns File," M 346, NA.

48. P. Cashmeyer to Colonel N. P. Chipman, October 12, 1865, *O.R.*, ser. 2, vol. VII, 764–65; Abraham Lincoln to Edwin Stanton, September 18, 1862, *O.R.*, ser. 2, vol. IV, 528; Mrs. B. Wardwell to John G. Williams, June 5, 1862, Letters Received by the Confederate Secretary of War, 1861–1865, RG 109, NA.

49. *Richmond Examiner*, March 10, 1862; *Richmond Dispatch*, May 1, 1862.

50. Brock Putnam, *Richmond During the War*, 77; Blakey, *General John H. Winder*, 51–52.

51. Fishel, *The Secret War*, 84–86.

52. Ibid., 87.

53. Donald E. Markle, *Spies and Spymasters of the Civil War* (New York: Hippocrene Books, 1994), 146–47; Fishel, *The Secret War*, 148–49; *Richmond Examiner*, April 3, 4, 1862.

54. Thomas G. Dyer, *Secret Yankees: The Union Circle in Confederate Atlanta* (Baltimore: Johns Hopkins University Press, 1999), 92–93, 147–48.

55. *Richmond Examiner*, April 30, 1862.

56. EVL, "Personal Narrative," EVLP, Frame 99; *Charleston Mercury*, November 18, 1862; Fishel, *The Secret War*, 101.

57. Allan Pinkerton, *The Spy of the Rebellion* (New York: G. W. Carleton & Co., 1883), 549–550; *Richmond Examiner*, April 23, 1862.

CHAPTER FOUR
"THE BRIGHT RUSH OF LIFE": THE MAKING OF THE RICHMOND
UNDERGROUND

1. McPherson, *Ordeal by Fire*, 236–37; Fishel, *The Secret War*, 149–50.

2. EVL, "Personal Narrative," June 20, 1862, EVLP, 541, Frame 72; Mary Elizabeth Barlow to Beymer, June 22, 1911, Beymer Papers, UTA.

3. EVL, "Personal Narrative," June 21, 1862, EVLP, 541–43, Frame 73.

4. Stephen W. Sears, *To the Gates of Richmond: The Peninsula Campaign* (New York: Ticknor & Fields, 1992), 199–209; John B. Jones, *A Rebel War Clerk's Diary*, 85; Ryan, ed., *A Yankee Spy*, 141; "Permission is granted Miss E. G. Carrington . . . ," Van Lew Album, 12, VHS; Mark E. Neely Jr., *Southern Rights: Political Prisoners and the Myth of Confederate Constitutionalism* (Charlottesville: University Press of Virginia, 1999), 2–6, 81.

5. EVL, "Personal Narrative," June 26, 1862, EVLP, 544–45, Frame 74.

6. McPherson, *Ordeal by Fire*, 248; Mrs. Roger A. Pryor, *Reminiscences of Peace and War* (New York: Macmillan Co., 1904), 188.

7. EVL, "Personal Narrative," EVLP, 244–46, Frames 83–4.

8. EVL, "Personal Narrative," EVLP, 244–46, Frames 83–4; Ladies Aid and Defense Association Minutes, Museum of the Confederacy, Richmond, Va.

9. The summer of 1862 is when the elusive and controversial Thomas McNiven claims to have recruited Van Lew to work in his already active Federal spy ring. McNiven's story comes to us thirdhand: allegedly, he related his wartime exploits to his daughter Jeannette who in turn related them to her nephew Robert W. Waitt, who many years later (in 1952) typed up a transcript of those details that Jeanette could recall. The authenticity of McNiven's "Recollections" is hotly debated in Civil War circles. I regard the source as unreliable. The main problem with McNiven's claim to have been a leader of the Richmond underground is that none of the other major players—Van Lew, Rowley, Lohmann, and others—ever mentions McNiven, although they repeatedly refer to one another. A second problem is that many of his claims about Van Lew—that her code name was "Babcock"; that she masterminded the 1864 Libby outbreak; and that she learned of Ulric Dahlgren's burial spot from a Confederate official nicknamed "Bull-head"—are not supported by extant sources (as I will demonstrate below). Finally, McNiven's claim that he was a Federal agent in 1862 is contradicted by the meticulous work of Edwin Fishel, who shows that Richmond Unionists did not start making regular intelligence reports to the Federal army until early in 1864. Indeed, Fishel's work in the extensive records of the Bureau of Military Intelligence turned up no mention of McNiven. My hunch is that McNiven was indeed a Unionist and was acquainted with Van Lew and others, but was a peripheral figure, whose story was embellished upon by his descendants. Robert W. Waitt, "Recollections of Thomas McNiven and his Activities in Richmond during the American Civil War," LVA; Fishel, The Secret War, 552. On inaccuracies in McNiven's recollections, see also William B. Feis, Grant's Secret Service: The Intelligence War from Belmont to Appomattox (Lincoln: University of Nebraska Press, 2002), 241.

10. Stuart, "Colonel Ulric Dahlgren," 183–85, 188–89; Charles Palmer to M. Collings, August 17, 1865, Consolidated File, Quartermaster General, C.S.A., RG 92, NA; William Lohmann to Joseph Segar, June 20, 1868, Office of the Secretary of War, Registered Letters Received, 976: 1873, RG 107, NA; Eighth U.S. Census, Richmond City, Henrico County, Va., 266, 644, 650; Richmond City, Henrico County, Va., Personal Property Tax Records, 1859; Klaus Wust, The Virginia Germans (Charlottesville: University Press of Virginia, 1969), 218–20; Christian B. Keller, "Pennsylvania and Virginia Germans during the Civil War: A Brief History and Comparative Analysis," Virginia Magazine of History and Biography 109 (January 2001), 75–76.

11. Stuart, "Colonel Ulric Dahlgren," 177–83; Claim of William S. Rowley, Southern Claims Commission Records, Allowed Claims, RG 217, Surry County, Va., Case no. 2160, 1872, NA; EVL to U. S. Grant, Oct. 2, 1869, EVLP, Frames 158–60.

Meriwether Stuart has argued that Rowley and his son Merritt used the code-names John Y. Phillips and Charles H. Phillips during the war, but as his case rests on the testimony of an unreliable source (a northern minister named Hemenway who visited Richmond after the war and fabricated many tales about the underground), it is not fully persuasive. Meriwether Stuart, "Of Spies and Borrowed Names: The Identity of Union Operatives in Richmond Known as 'The Phillipses' Discovered," *Virginia Magazine of History and Biography* 89 (1981), 308–27.

12. Stuart, *Colonel Ulric Dahlgren*, 177–85. The spectrum of incomes of Unionists ranged from that of Franklin Stearns, who in 1860 had real estate valued at $155,000 and personal property at $200,000, to Eliza Van Lew, who had real estate valued at $90,000 and personal property at $27,000, to F. W. E. Lohmann, who had real estate valued at $10,000 and personal property at $1,000, to Burnham Wardwell, with real estate of $1,500 and a personal estate of $2,000, to William Fay and Rowley, each of whose personal property was valued at $100. Eighth U.S. Census, 1860, Richmond City, Henrico County, Va., 2, 366, 710, 839, 869.

13. Edwin Fishel, *The Secret War*, 147, 623 ff38; Stuart, "Colonel Ulric Dahlgren," 188–89.

14. Libby received its first inmates on March 26, 1862. Speer, *Portals to Hell*, 91; *Richmond Enquirer*, July 1, 1862; Willard W. Glazier, *The Capture, the Prison Pen and the Escape* (Hartford, Conn.: H. E. Goodwin, 1869), 45–46; EVL, "Personal Narrative—The Libby," EVLP, 137–38, Frame 85.

15. United States Sanitary Commission, *Narrative of the Privations and Sufferings of United States Officers and Soldiers While Prisoners of War in the Hands of the Rebel Authorities* (Philadelphia: King and Baird, 1864), 162–63.

16. Speer, *Portals*, 93–95; Joseph Ferguson, *Life-Struggles in Rebel Prison: A Record of the Sufferings, Escapes, Adventures and Starvation of the Union Prisoners* (Philadelphia: James M. Ferguson, 1865), 39–40; Confederate States of America, *Evidence Taken before the Committee of the House of Representatives, Appointed to Inquire into the Treatment of Prisoners at Castle Thunder* [n.p., 1863?], 25–31, LVA; EVL, "Personal Narrative," EVLP, Frames 97–102.

17. G. E. Sabre, *Nineteen Months a Prisoner of War* (New York: American News Company, 1865), 59.

18. EVL, "Personal Narrative—The Libby," EVLP, 137, Frame 85; Sharpe to Comstock, January 1867 and Thomas Pratt Turner to EVL, February 15, 1863, EVLP, Frames 129–35, 150.

19. Claim of Horace Kent, U.S. Court of Claims, RG 123, NA.

20. H. H. Bigelow, *I Want Justice Here and Now: Burnham Wardwell Vindicated in His Work for Humanity* (n.p.: Aldine Book Co., 1921), 5; Burnham Wardwell to William Fay, October 27, 1871, Fay Papers, LVA.

21. Sharpe to Comstock, January 1867, EVLP, Frames 129–35; *Charleston Mercury*, December 13, 1862; William H. Jeffry, *Richmond Prisons, 1861–1862* (St. Johnsbury, Vt.: Republican Press, 1893), 87; Claim of Horace Kent, RG 123, 33–34; Stuart, "Colonel Ulric Dahlgren," 187–88; Eighth U.S. Census, 1860, Richmond City, Henrico County, 110; Ninth U.S. Census, 1870, Richmond City, Henrico County, 506.

22. John F. Hill, "To and from Libby Prison," in Frank Moore, comp., *The Civil War in Song and Story. 1860–1865* (New York P. F. Collier, 1889), 272; Glazier, *The Capture, the Prison Pen, and the Escape*, 69; Sabre, *Nineteenth Months*, 41, 61.

23. *New York Herald*, August 14, 1862; *New York Times*, August 17, 1862; *Richmond Dispatch*, July 1, 1862; *Richmond Enquirer*, August 8, 1862.

24. *New York Times*, September 4, 1862.

25. Lounsbury as quoted in David B. Parker, *A Chautauqua Boy in '61 and Afterward: Reminiscences of David B. Parker* (Boston: Small, Maynard & Company, 1912), 54–64; *Richmond Dispatch*, July 17, 1883.

26. John P. Reynolds Jr., "Article or Address on Elizabeth L. Van Lew," EVLP, 3, Frame 195.

27. Lounsbury as quoted in Parker, *A Chautauqua Boy*, 54–64; *Richmond Dispatch*, July 17, 1883.

28. Transcription of Albree's August 15, 1904 interview with Captain W. H. Bricker and Captain E. L. Schroeder, Van Lew Papers, W&M.

29. William R. Hartpence, *History of the Fifty-First Veteran Volunteer Infantry* (Cincinnati, Ohio: R. Clarke Co. 1894), 170–74; "Mrs. Abby Green," *House of Representatives Report #115*, Thirty-ninth Congress, First Session, July 28, 1866, 1, VHS; "Report to Accompany Bill S. No. 550," *Senate Report # 129*, Fortieth Congress, Second Session, June 15, 1868, NA; Abby Green letter, January 25, 1867, House of Representatives, Fortieth Congress, "Accompanying Papers File," RG 233, NA.

30. Claim of William H. Brisby, Southern Claims Commission Records, Allowed Claims, RG 217, New Kent County, Va., Case no. 19204, 1875, NA.

31. Lounsbury as quoted in Parker, *A Chautauqua Boy in '61*, 54–64; *Richmond Dispatch*, July 17, 1883; Sharpe to Comstock, January 1867, EVLP, Frames 129–35.

32. Speer, *Portals*, 102; Hesseltine, *Civil War Prisons*, 172–78; *New York Times*, August 9, 11, 15, 17.

33. Sharpe to Comstock, January 1867, EVLP, Frames 129–35.

34. Mary Elizabeth Barlow to Beymer, June 22, 1911, Beymer Papers, UTA; EVL, "Personal Narrative," August 19, 1862, EVLP, Frame 82.

35. Stuart, "Colonel Ulric Dahlgren" 163, 187–90; Sharpe to Comstock, January 1867, EVLP, Frames 129–35; Claim of Christian Burging, Southern Claims

Commission Records, Disallowed Claims, RG 233, Henry County, Va., Case no. 3299, 1872, NA; Palmer to Collings, August 17, 1865, RG 92, NA; Lohmann to Segar, June 20, 1868, RG 107, NA.

36. John P. Reynolds Jr., Typescript of December 9, 1910 interview with Mrs. Annie R. Hall, Beymer Papers, UTA; Henrietta R. Winfrey statement, June 18, 1964, VHS; Claim of William Brisby, RG 217, NA.

37. *New York Times*, August 8, 18, 23, 25, September 30, 1862; *Charleston Mercury*, June 28, 1861; Wm. Henry Hurlbut to Charles Palmer, August 14, 1862; W. Henry Hurlbut to F. J. Cridland, August 14, 1862, Fay Papers, LVA.

38. Ibid.

39. Meriwether Stuart, "Samuel Ruth and General R. E. Lee: Disloyalty and the Line of Supply to Fredericksburg," *Virginia Magazine of History and Biography* 71 (January 1963), 35–72; Stuart, "Colonel Ulric Dahlgren," 184.

40. Fishel, *The Secret War*, 255, 258, 273, 276, 287, 291, 295, 336, 557.

41. *New York Herald*, October 4, 7, 1862; William C. Harris, "After the Emancipation Proclamation: Lincoln's Role in the Ending of Slavery," *North & South* 5 (December 2001), 48–53.

42. Noel C. Fisher, *War at Every Door: Partisan Politics & Guerrilla Violence in East Tennessee, 1860–1869* (Chapel Hill: University of North Carolina Press, 1997), 112–13; Ash, *When the Yankees Came*, 116, 120.

43. Speer, *Portals*, 104–5; McPherson, *Ordeal*, 455; *New York Times*, January 19, 1863. Although the policy of executing white officers leading black troops was not carried out by the Confederacy, numerous atrocities were committed by the Confederate soldiers against black Union troops. The most notorious example is the Fort Pillow massacre of April 1864 in Tennessee, in which black prisoners and their white officers, possibly more than 200 men in all, were shot in cold blood while attempting to surrender. Eicher, *The Longest Night*, 656–57.

44. Speer, *Portals*, 122; U.S. Sanitary Commission, *Narrative of Privations and Sufferings*, 31, 39, 40; EVL, "Personal Narrative," EVLP, 622, Frame 17; Van Lew diary extract in Maria Lydig Daly, *Diary of a Union Lady, 1861–65*, ed. Harold Early Hammond (Lincoln: University of Nebraska Press, 2000), 364–65.

45. "Castle Thunder Prison," *Encyclopedia of the Confederacy* (New York: Simon & Schuster, 1993), vol. I, 265–66; Neely, *Southern Rights*, 136–37.

46. Fishel, *The Secret War*, 249; EVL, "Personal Narrative," EVLP, 279, Frame 50.

47. *Richmond Enquirer*, July 25, 1863; Leonard, *All the Daring*, 252–62.

48. Reuben Bartley Papers, 40, VHS; Elizabeth D. Leonard, *Yankee Women: Gender Battles in the Civil War* (New York: W. W. Norton, 1994), 138–42.

49. *Report of Brigadier General John H. Winder, Headquarters Department Henrico, Feburary 13, 1863*, Beinecke Library, Yale University, New Haven, Conn.; *Richmond Enquirer*, July 25, 1863.

50. EVL, "Personal Narrative," EVLP, 121, Frame 88.

51. Thomas, *The Confederate State of Richmond*, 117–118; Furgurson, *Ashes of Glory*, 189–193.

52. Thomas, *The Confederate State*, 119–120; Furgurson, *Ashes of Glory*, 193–94; Statement of James Craig, transcribed in letter from Colonel George H. Sharpe to Major General Butterfield, April 10, 1863, Miscellaneous Letters, Reports and Lists Received, Army of the Potomac, 1861–1865, RG 393, NA; Michael Chesson, "Harlots or Heroines? A New Look at the Richmond Bread Riot," *Virginia Magazine of History and Biography*, 92 (1984), 131–75.

53. *Richmond Examiner*, April 4, 1863; Furgurson, *Ashes of Glory*, 195; Thomas, *The Confederate State*, 121–22; George C. Rable, *Civil Wars: Women and the Crisis of Southern Nationalism* (Urbana: University of Illinois Press, 1989), 110; *New York Herald*, April 17, 1863.

54. EVL, "Personal Narrative," January 24, 1864, EVLP, 620–21, Frames 16–17. The Thomas McNiven typescript contains the startling and cryptic observation that "A lot of dollars American went into organizing the riots"; no other source has surfaced, to date, connecting the underground and the events of April 2, 1863. McNiven, "Recollections," 5; *Richmond Examiner*, April 13, 1863.

55. Leonard, *All the Daring of a Soldier*, 80–81; Furgurson, *Ashes of Glory*, 220–21; *Richmond Examiner*, July 20, 23, December 21, 1863, February 4, 11, 20, October 28, December 19, 1864; *Charleston Mercury*, July 22, 1863.

56. Dyer, *Secret Yankees*, 108–111.

CHAPTER FIVE
ELIZABETH AND "THE BEAST": BUTLER FINDS HIS SPY

1. McPherson, *Ordeal by Fire*, 268; Trefousse, "Butler, Benjamin Franklin," *American National Biography*, eds. John A. Garraty and Mark C. Carnes (New York: Oxford University Press, 1998), 91–92.

2. McPherson, *Ordeal by Fire*, 380; Trefousse, "Butler," 91–92; Benjamin F. Butler, *Butler's Book* (Boston: A. M. Thayer & Co., 1892), 414–19; William Best Hesseltine, *Civil War Prisons: A Study in War Psychology* (Columbus, Ohio: Ohio State University Press, 1998), 84–86.

3. *New York Times*, November 7, 1863; Drew Gilpin Faust, *Mothers of Invention: Women of the Slaveholding South in the American Civil War* (Chapel Hill: University of North Carolina Press, 1996), 210; Butler, *Butler's Book*, 421.

4. Faust, *Mothers of Invention*, 210.

5. Frank Moore, *Women of the War; Their Heroism and Self-Sacrifice* (Hartford, Conn: S. S. Scranton & Co., 1866), 506–7; Frank Moore, comp, "A Noble Richmond Girl," in *The Civil War in Song and Story*, 402; H. S. Howard Deposition, January 25, 1866; William S. Rowley to Edwin Stanton, December 12, 1865; William S. Rowley statement, n.d.; and Burnham Wardwell to Benjamin Butler,

January 10, 1866, all in Secret Service Accounts, RG 110, NA; *Richmond Dispatch*, January 28, 1864; Glazier, *The Capture, the Prison Pen, and the Escape*, 60–61; Samuel Ruth to Edwin M. Stanton, December 21, 1865, William Hillyer Papers, UVA; Stuart, "Of Spies and Borrowed Names," 313.

6. On the Holmes family, see Seventh U.S. Census, 1850, Warren Co., Ohio, 677 and Eighth U.S. Census, 1860, Philadelphia Co., Pa., 596.

7. Moore, *Women of the War*, 506–7; Moore, comp., "A Noble Richmond Girl," 402; H. S. Howard Deposition, January 25, 1866; Rowley to Stanton, December 12, 1865; Rowley statement, n.d; and Wardwell to Butler, January 10, 1866, in Secret Service Accounts, RG 110, NA; *Richmond Dispatch*, January 28, 1864; Glazier, *The Capture, the Prison Pen, and the Escape*, 60–61; Ruth to Stanton, December 21, 1865, Hillyer Papers, UVA.

8. Trefousse, "Butler," 92; Butler, *Butler's Book*, 617.

9. Butler to Charles O. Boutelle, December 19, 1863, and Butler to EVL, January 18, 1864 in *Private and Official Correspondence of General Benjamin F. Butler Volume III February 1863–March 1864* (privately issued, 1917), 228–29, 319; Butler, *Butler's Book*, 348.

10. Butler to EVL, January 18, 1864, in Butler, *Private and Official Correspondence*, 319; H. S. Howard Deposition, January 25, 1866; Rowley to Stanton, December 12, 1865; Rowley statement, n.d., Secret Service Accounts, RG 110, NA; John P. Reynolds Jr. Statement, November 21, 1900, EVLP, Frames 208–209.

11. See for example Ryan, ed., *A Yankee Spy*, 12; Feis, *Grant's Secret Service*, 239.

12. Rowley to Stanton, December 12, 1865; Rowley statement, n.d., Secret Service Accounts, RG 110, NA; George C. Meade to Mr. Babcock, February 4, 1864, EVLP, Frame 176; Ryan, ed., *A Yankee Spy*, 58; Meade to Babcock, December 16, 1864, John C. Babcock Papers, LC; Fishel, *The Secret War*, 544–57.

13. Howard Deposition, January 25, 1866, Rowley to Stanton, December 12, 1865, and Rowley statement, n.d., Secret Service Accounts, RG 110, NA; Ruth to Stanton, December 21, 1865, Hillyer Papers, UVA; Stuart, "Colonel Ulric Dahlgren," 198–99.

14. EVL to Butler, January 30, 1864, *O.R.*, ser. 1, vol. XXXIII, 519–21; EVL to Butler, January 25, 1864, and Butler transcription of February 4 conversation, in Butler, *Private and Official Correspondence Vol. III*, 381–82. The versions in the official record and Butler's correspondence differ slightly in punctuation but are identical in substance—but for the curious discrepancy in dates. Given that both sources date Butler's report to Stanton as having been sent on February 5, 1864, the discrepancy is without consequence.

15. EVL to Butler, January 29, 1964, *O.R.*, ser. 1, vol. XXXIII, 519–21; EVL to Butler, January 25, 1864 and Butler transcription of February 4 conversation, in Butler, *Private and Official Correspondence Vol. III*, 381–82. On the identities

of "Quaker" and the "boy," see Stuart, "Colonel Ulric Dahlgren," 187 and Stuart, "Of Spies and Borrowed Names," 310–11. Long after the war, the claim would surface in the Thomas McNiven typescript that "Quaker" had been McNiven's code name, but there are no extant sources that corroborate such a claim. McNiven, "Recollections," 3.

16. Speer, *Portals*, 259; Butler to Stanton, February 5, 1864, *O.R.*, ser. 1, vol. XXXIII, 519; Butler, *Private and Official Official Correspondence Vol. III*, 380–81; Butler, *Butler's Book*, 620; Schultz, *The Dahlgren Affair* 63–66.

17. Isaac J. Wistar to Colonel S. P. Spear, February 5, 1864, *O.R.* ser. 1, vol. XXXIII, 521–22.

18. George R. Agassiz, ed., *Meade's Headquarters, 1863–65: Letters of Colonel Theodore Lyman from the Wilderness to Appomattox* (Boston: The Atlantic Monthly Press, 1922), 68–70; Frances H. Kennedy, ed., *The Civil War Battlefield Guide* (Boston: Houghton Mifflin, 1998), 260.

19. Wistar to Butler, February 7, 9, 1864, *O.R.*, ser. 1, vol. XXXIII, 145–48.

20. R. C. Shiver to "Hon. Sec. Of War," January 29, 1864, Letters Rec'd by the Confederate Secretary of War, RG 109, NA.

21. Samuel J. Martin, *Kill-Cavalry: The Life of Union General Hugh Judson Kilpatrick* (Mechanicsburg, Pa.: Stackpole Books, 2000), 147–48; Reports of Major General Benjamin F. Butler, February 6–8, 1864, Expedition from Yorktown against Richmond, and Wistar to Butler, February 9, 1864, *O.R.* ser. 1, vol. XXXIII, 143–48.

22. Captain Frank E. Moran, *A Thrilling History of the Famous Underground Tunnel of Libby Prison* (New York: The Century Company, 1889), 3–6; Captain I. N. Johnston, *Four Months in Libby, and the Campaign Against Atlanta* (Cincinnati: R. P. Thompson, 1864), 55–58.

23. Moran, *A Thrilling History*, 6; Johnston, *Four Months in Libby*, 58–59. Johnston's account claims that it took 15 nights to access the cellar through the chimney, while Hamilton remembers that it took 12 nights. Andrew G. Hamilton, *Story of the Famous Tunnel Escape from Libby Prison* (Chicago: S. S. Boggs, 1893).

24. Moran, *A Thrilling History*, 7–9; Johnston, *Four Months in Libby*, 60–64. Again there are some discrepancies in the various principal accounts of the escape; Johnston and Moran recount 3 unsuccessful attempts before a viable tunnel was dug while Hamilton tells of 2 not 3 false starts; Moran states that the three failed efforts swallowed up 39 days while Hamilton says 38. Hamilton, *Story of the Famous Tunnel Escape*.

25. EVL, "Personal Narrative," EVLP, Frames 66–70; Abby Green Statement, January 25, 1867, and A. D. Streight to G. M. Van Buren, December 31, 1867, RG 233, NA.

26. Moran, *A Thrilling History*, 10; Johnston, *Four Months in Libby*, 65–70.

27. Moran, *A Thrilling History*, 11; Johnston, *Four Months in Libby*, 72; Charles F. Bryan Jr. and Nelson D. Lankford, eds., *Eye of the Storm: A Civil War Odyssey* (New York: Free Press, 2000), 167.

28. "Narrative of Captain John F. Porter Jr.," in Linus Pierpont Brockett, *The Camp, the Battlefield, and the Hospital: or, Lights and Shadows of the Great Rebellion* (Philadelphia: National Publishing Co, 1866), 280–82; "Mrs. Abby Green," *House of Representatives Report No. 115*, 1866; *New York Herald*, February 15, 1864; Albert D. Richardson, *The Secret Service, the Field, the Dungeon, and the Escape* (Philadelphia: Jones Bros., 1865), 379, 391–96. Richardson also tells the stories of two other Union men, a spy named George W. Hudson and soldier named Robert Slocum, who were aided in their escapes from prison by the Richmond underground.

29. *Richmond Sentinel*, April 18, 1864; *Richmond Dispatch*, February 7, 1888; "Mrs. Abby Green," *House of Representatives Report No. 115*, 1866.

30. Moran, *A Thrilling History*, 11–12; Johnston, *Four Months in Libby*, 72–79; James M. Wells, *With a Touch of Elbow; or Death Before Dishonor* (Philadelphia: John C. Winston Co., 1909), 134–61.

31. Hamilton, *Story of the Famous Tunnel Escape*; Johnston, *Four Months in Libby*, 82–89; Moran, *A Thrilling History*, 13–15

32. Johnston, *Four Months in Libby*, 90; Harrison Hobart, "Libby Prison—The Escape" from the papers read before the Wisconsin MOLLUS vol. I (1891), 394–409; Glazier, *The Capture, the Prison Pen and the Escape*, 83–86.

33. *Charleston Mercury*, February 16, 1864; *Richmond Examiner*, February 11, 1864; *Richmond Daily Enquirer*, February 11, 1864; Frank L. Byrne, ed., "A General Behind Bars: Neal Dow in Libby Prison" in *Civil War Prisons*, ed. William B. Hesseltine (Bowling Green: Kent State University Press, 1962), 69–73. On the treatment of those recaptured see Moran, *A Thrilling History*, 20; F. F. Cavada, *Libby Life: Experiences of a Prisoner of War in Richmond* (Philadelphia: Lippincott, 1865), 176; Glazier, *The Capture, the Prison Pen and the Escape*, 87.

34. Abby Green Statement, January 25, 1867, RG 233, NA.

35. Glazier, *The Capture, the Prison Pen and the Escape*, 87; *Richmond Examiner*, February 11, 15, 1864. On Streight's reputation and conduct in prison see "Letters from Libby," *National Tribune*, December 29, 1891; *New York Herald*, May 18, 1863; *Charleston Mercury*, September 8, 1863; Junius Browne, *Four Years in Secessia* (Hartford, Conn.: O. D. Case & Company, 1865), 269; Richardson, *The Secret Service*, 370; Joseph Ferguson, *Life-Struggles in Rebel Prisons* (Philadelphia: James M. Ferguson, 1865), 41; A. D. Streight to James A. Seddon, August 30, 1863, *O.R.*, ser. 2, vol. VI, 241–42.

36. EVL, "Personal Narrative," EVLP, Frames 67–70.

37. EVL, "Personal Narrative," EVLP, Frames 67–70; Albree notes on interview with Whitlock, n.p., Van Lew Papers, W&M.

38. EVL, "Personal Narrative," EVLP, Frames 67–70; Stuart, "Colonel Ulric Dahlgren," 160.

39. EVL, "Personal Narrative," EVLP, Frames 67–70; Stuart, "Colonel Ulric Dahlgren," 160. John tried to dodge heavy duties by pleading illness. An army doctor who examined him in March of 1864 conceded that Van Lew was "of a delicate appearance" but concluded nonetheless that he was fit for active duty. "Med Exam Board," March 14, 1864, Owen Thweatt Papers, VHS.

40. "Mrs. Abby Green," *House of Representatives Report No. 115*, 1866; A. C. Roach, *The Prisoner of War and How Treated* (Indianapolis: Railroad City Publishing House, 1865), 108–9; *Richmond Dispatch*, July 17, 1883, February 7, 1888; EVL, "Personal Narrative," February 15, 1864, EVLP, 259–60, Frames 18–19; Ryan, ed., *A Yankee Spy*, 144–45; Stuart "Colonel Ulric Dahlgren, 204.

41. EVL, "Personal Narrative," February 15, 1864, EVLP, 260–65, Frames 18–21.

42. Wistar to Colonel J. W. Shafter, February 15, 1864, *O.R.*, ser. 1, vol. XXXIII, 565; *New York Times*, February 16, 1864; *Richmond Sentinel*, February 20, 1864.

43. EVL, "Personal Narrative," February 15, 1864, EVLP, 262–65, Frames 19–21; *Richmond Examiner*, May 2, 1864; Phoebe Yates Pember, *A Southern Woman's Story: Life in Confederate Richmond*, ed. Bell I. Wiley (St. Simon's Island, Ga.: Mockingbird Press, 1988), 134–35.

44. Ibid.

45. *Richmond Dispatch*, February 7, 1888; *New York Herald*, March 1, 1864; *New York Times*, March 4, 1864.

46. Wistar to Shafter, February 15, 1864, *O.R.*, ser. 1, vol. XXXIII, 565; Hobart, "Libby Prison—the Escape" 394–409; Charles Warrington Earle, M.D., *The Capture, The Imprisonment in Libby, and the Escape by Tunnel* (Chicago: P. F. Pettibone & Co., 1889), 35–37; "The Escape from Libby Prison," *Harper's Weekly*, March 5, 1864, 151; Johnston, *Four Months in Libby*, 104, 108–9, 112; "Escaping Union Officers Succored by Slaves," *Harper's Weekly*, March 12, 1864.

47. *Richmond Dispatch*, July 17, 1883.

48. Van Lew diary extract in Daly, *Diary of a Union Lady 1861–65*, ed. Hammond, 364; Frank L. Byrne, "Belle Isle Prison," *Encylopedia of the Confederacy*, vol. I, 155; Furgurson, *Ashes of Glory*, 211.

49. Stephen Sears, "Raid on Richmond," in *Controversies and Commanders: Dispatches from the Army of the Potomac* (Boston: Houghton Mifflin, 1999), 234.

CHAPTER SIX
"THIS PRECIOUS DUST": THE CLANDESTINE REBURIAL
OF COLONEL ULRIC DAHLGREN

1. EVL, "Personal Narrative," EVLP, 302, Frame 22; Schultz, *The Dahlgren Affair*, 127–31.

2. EVL, "Personal Narrative," EVLP, 302, Frame 22.

3. Sears, *Controversies and Commanders*, 230–34.

4. James O. Hall, "The Dahlgren Papers: A Yankee Plot to Kill President Davis," *Civil War Times Illustrated* 22 (November 1983), 31–32; Sears, *Controversies and Commanders*, 235.

5. Samuel J. Martin, *Kill-Cavalry: The Life of Union General Hugh Judson Kilpatrick* (Stackpole, 2000), 159–60; Sears, *Controversies and Commanders*, 238–39.

6. Martin, *Kill-Cavalry*, 154–55; Sears, *Controversies and Commanders*, 237–39.

7. Hall, "The Dahlgren Papers," 31; Sears, *Controversies and Commanders*, 240; Kennedy, ed. *The Civil War Battlefield Guide*, 260.

8. J. Kilpatrick to A. Pleasonton, March 3, 1864, *O.R.*, ser. 1, vol. XXXIII, 182; Sears, *Controversies and Commanders*, 241; Hall, "The Dahlgren Papers," 31; *Richmond Examiner*, March 5, 1864.

9. Hall, "The Dahlgren Papers," 31–35; *Richmond Examiner*, March 8, 1864.

10. Reuben Bartley Memoir, ca. 1868–69, VHS, 17–18.

11. Hall, "The Dahlgren Papers," 35; Sears, *Controversies and Commanders*, 243; *Harper's Weekly*, March 26, 1864.

12. Hall, "The Dahlgren Papers," 36–37.

13. Hall, "The Dahlgren Papers," 37–38; Sears, *Controversies and Commanders*, 245–26. Duane Schulz looks at evidence on both sides of the Dahlgren papers debate and concludes that the authenticity issue "is a mystery that may never be resolved." Schulz, *The Dahlgren Affair*, 240–57. I agree with Sears that Hall's analysis is conclusive.

14. EVL, "Personal Narrative," EVLP, 315–17, Frames 29–30.

15. EVL, "Personal Narrative," EVLP, 302–4, Frames 22–23.

16. *Richmond Examiner*, March 8, 1864; *Richmond Whig*, March 8, 1864.

17. EVL, "Personal Narrative," EVLP, 306, Frame 24.

18. Drew Gilpin Faust, "The Civil War Soldier and the Art of Dying," *Journal of Southern History*, vol. LXVII 1 (February 2001), 10, 14, 17.

19. Stuart, "Colonel Ulric Dahlgren," 167–69; Narrative of F. W. E. Lohmann, Richmond, Va., October 17 1865, in Letters Received by the Secretary of War, 976–1873, RG 107, NA; Affadavit of Lohmann, Secret Service Accounts, RG 110, NA. McNiven claims that Van Lew found out from a highly placed informant that the Confederates were going to bury Dahlgren at Oakwood, and that McNiven and Christopher Taylor hid nearby and actually witnessed the burial. This claim is flatly contradicted by Van Lew's own memoirs, which state that "Several endeavored to trace [the buried corpse] and Mr. F. W. E. Lohmann succeeded in doing so." EVL, "Personal Narrative," EVLP, 306, Frame 24 and Frame 40; McNiven, "Recollections," 3. On Lipscomb, see John T. O'Brien, " 'The People's Favorite': The Rise and Fall of Martin Meredith Lipscomb," *Virginia Cavalcade*, 31 (1982), 216–33.

20. M. M. Lipscomb to William P. Palmer [n.d], Palmer Family Papers, VHS; EVL, "Personal Narrative," EVLP, 307–8, Frames 25–26.

21. Lipscomb to Palmer, Palmer Family Papers, VHS; Narrative of F. W. E. Lohmann, RG 107; Affadavit of Lohmann, RG 110; McNiven, "Recollections," 3.

22. Affadavit of Lohmann, RG 110; Lipscomb to Palmer, Palmer Family Papers, VHS; Stuart, "Colonel Ulric Dahlgren," 173, 194–95; EVL, "Personal Narrative," EVLP, 307–8, Frames 25–26.

23. Faust, "The Civil War Soldier," 23; EVL, "Personal Narrative," EVLP, 307–8, Frames 25–26.

24. Stuart, "Colonel Ulric Dahlgren," 171; Narrative of Lohmann, RG 107; EVL, "Personal Narrative," EVLP, 307–10, Frames 25–26.

25. EVL, "Personal Narrative," EVLP, 311–13, Frames 27–28.

26. Stuart, "Colonel Ulric Dahlgren," 195–97, 201; EVL, "Personal Narrative," EVLP, 314–15, Frames 28–29.

27. S. J. Wardwell to Stanton, January 9, 1866, Secret Service Accounts, RG 110; EVL, "Personal Narrative," EVLP, 314–15, Frames 28–29; Stuart, "Colonel Ulric Dahlgren," 196–97. The McNiven typescript provides a second theory—that the two women were the widows Johannah von Hoffman and Louisa Delarue, who were staying at the Orrock's for a "holiday" (or so was their cover); McNiven contends that Delarue and von Hoffman were integral to the underground but no evidence corroborating this claim has surfaced. McNiven, "Recollections," 3.

28. Butler to Robert Ould, March 11, 1864, O.R., ser. 2, vol. VI, 1034–35; Stuart, "Colonel Ulric Dahlgren," 158–159. According to McNiven, Van Lew had sent a note to Butler via the Carringtons informing him of the reburial. McNiven, "Recollections," 3.

29. "Scouts, March 15, 1864," Miscellaneous Letters, Reports, and Lists Received, 1861–65, Files of the Bureau of Military Information, RG 393, NA; Meade to Henry Halleck, March 16, 1864, O.R., ser. 1, vol. XXXIII, 681–82; Butler to Rowley, March 22, 1864, Private and Official Correspondence, Vol. III, 564–65; Butler to James Allen Hardie, April 5, 1865, EVLP, Frames 153–56.

30. Abby Green vouchers, March 25, 1864, Secret Service Accounts, RG 110; Baltimore American, April 6, 1864; Stuart, "Colonel Ulric Dahlgren," 204.

31. Butler to Mr. Bigelow, February 15, 1882, in Bigelow, I Want Justice Here and Now, 3–4; "A Visit to General Butler and the Army of the James," Fraser's Magazine for Town and Country (April 1865), 443.

32. Richmond Examiner, March 9, 10, 12, 19, 28, 1864.

33. On the Cashmeyer incident, see EVL, "Article in response to a newspaper article entitled 'Men and Monopolists" ca. 1885–1890, EVLP, Frames 210–18.

34. Richmond Examiner, April 14, 1864; Stuart, "Colonel Ulric Dahlgren," 155.

35. EVL, "Personal Narrative," EVLP, Frames 76–78; Dyer, Secret Yankees, 160–61.

CHAPTER SEVEN
"THE SMOKE OF BATTLE": GRANT MOVES ON RICHMOND

1. EVL, "Personal Narrative," May 6, 1864, EVLP, 660–61, Frames 51–52; Mc-
   Pherson, *Ordeal by Fire*, 410–412; Furgurson, *Not War But Murder*, 13.

2. EVL, "Personal Narrative," May 6, 1864, EVLP, 660–61, Frames 51–52; Kennedy, *The Civil War Battlefield Guide*, 282–83.

3. Gordon C. Rhea, *To the North Anna River: Grant and Lee, May 13–25, 1864*
   (Baton Rouge: Louisiana State University Press, 2000), 41–61; McPherson, *Ordeal by Fire*, 413; Ryan, ed., *A Yankee Spy*, 150; Butler, *Butler's Book*, 640–41.

4. EVL, "Personal Narrative," May 14, 1864, EVLP, 661–63, Frames 52–53.

5. Robertson, *Civil War Virginia*, 152–53; McPherson, *Ordeal by Fire*, 413, 420;
   EVL, "Personal Narrative," May 27, 1864, EVLP, 663, Frame 53.

6. Robertson, *Civil War Virginia*, 153; McPherson, *Ordeal by Fire*, 422–26.

7. *National Tribune*, April 20, 27, May 4, 1893; Sharpe to Comstock, January 1867,
   EVLP, Frames 125–36; Stuart, "Colonel Ulric Dahlgren," 177.

8. Jean Edward Smith, *Grant* (New York: Touchstone, 2001), 367.

9. Robertson, *Civil War Virginia*, 153; McPherson, *Ordeal by Fire*, 422–26; William
   S. McFeely, *Grant: A Biography* (New York: W. W. Norton, 1981), 174–75.

10. McFeely, *Grant*, 175; Fishel, *The Secret War*, 545–46; Feis, *Grant's Secret Service*,
    216; Sharpe to Comstock, January 1867, EVLP, Frames 125–36; EVL, "Letter
    in response to 'Men and Monopolists,'" EVLP, Frame 215.

11. Sharpe to Comstock, January 1867, EVLP, Frames 125–36; Ryan, ed., *A Yankee
    Spy*, 122.

12. Fishel, *The Secret War*, 551–52.

13. Fishel, *The Secret War*, 553; Feis, *Grant's Secret Service*, 237; EVL, "Genl. Geo.
    H. Sharpe," EVLP, Frame 172; *Richmond Dispatch*, July 17, 1883. On the Van
    Lew's small farm, see Van Lew v. Duke, Chancery Court Cases, File 15, 1869,
    JMCB.

14. On Fay, see G. F. Clark to B. F. Smith, June 1, 1864, Miscellaneous Letters,
    Reports and Lists Received, 1861–1865, RG 393, NA; Claim of Major Marable,
    Southern Claims Commission Records, Disallowed Claims, RG 233, Charles
    City County, Va., Case no. 7728, 1877, NA. On Hancock, see Stuart, "Colonel
    Ulric Dahlgren," 185; J. L. Burrows, "Recollections of Libby Prison," *Southern
    Historical Society Papers* 11 (1883), 83–92; Stuart, "Samuel Ruth," 98.

15. On Hughes and Duke, see Claim of James Duke, Southern Claims Commission
    Records, Allowed Claims, RG 217, Henrico County, Va., Case no. 14990, 1875,
    NA.

16. On Myers and Sharp, see Claim of James Sharp, Southern Claims Commission
    Records, Allowed Claims, RG 217, Charles City County, Va., Case no. 17108,
    1879, NA. On Major and Marable, see Claim of Charles J. Major, Southern

Claims Commission Records, Allowed Claims, RG 217, Charles City County, Va., Case no. 19460, 1877, NA; Claim of Major Marable, RG 233, NA.

17. Claim of L. E. Babcock, Southern Claims Commission Records, Allowed Claims, RG 217, Charles City County, Va., Case no. 21160, 1875, NA.

18. Stuart, "Samuel Ruth," 81–82; *Petition for the Relief of Samuel Ruth, F. W. E. Lohman, and Charles M. Carter,* House Report No. 792, Forty-third Congress, First Session, June 22, 1874; Fishel, *The Secret War,* 551–52.

19. For Duke's testimony, see Claim of James Sharp, RG 217, NA.

20. Claim of Sylvanus J. Brown, Southern Claims Commission Records, Allowed Claims, RG 217, Charles City County, Case no. 7724, 1878, NA.

21. *Richmond Dispatch,* March 18, 1869 and July 17, 1883; *Richmond News Leader,* September 25, 1900; Ella Forbes, *African American Women During the Civil War* (New York: Garland, 1998), 42; "Pass for Bob and Oliver," July 12, 1864, Van Lew Album, VHS; John Van Lew to Fay, December 20, 1864, Fay Papers, LVA.

22. "Pass for Mrs. E. L. Van Lew, 2 ladies & driver," July 6, 1864, and Albree transcript of interview with Anna Whitlock, Van Lew Papers, W&M; "Pass for Bob and Oliver," July 12, 1864, Van Lew Album, VHS; EVL, "Ancestry," EVLP, Frame 244.

23. *Richmond Evening Leader,* July 27, 1900.

24. John P. Reynolds Jr., "Biographical Sketch of Elizabeth L. Van Lew," EVLP, Frames 254–57; Reynolds Jr., December 9, 1910 interview with Mrs. Annie R. (Van Lew) Hall, Beymer Papers, UTA; Varina Jefferson Davis to Miss Isabelle Maury, April 17, 1865, Davis Family Collection, Eleanor Brockenbrough Library, Museum of the Confederacy, Richmond, Va.

25. Reynolds Jr., "Biographical Sketch of Elizabeth L. Van Lew," EVLP, Frames 254–57; John P. Reynolds Jr., December 9, 1910 interview with Hall, Beymer Papers, UTA.

26. Reynolds Jr., December 9, 1910 interview with Hall, Beymer Papers, UTA; *Burton, Annals,* 248.

27. William Gilmore Beymer, "Miss Van Lew," *Harper's Monthly* (June 1911), 90.

28. Of all the Richmond loyalists, only the unreliable Thomas McNiven makes mention of the White House spy. According to the typescript account of his alleged exploits, Van Lew's "colored girl Mary was the best [source] as she was working right in Davis' home and had a photographic mind. Everything she saw on the Rebel President's desk she could repeat word for word. Unlike most colored, she could read and write. She made a point of always coming out to my wagon when I made deliveries at the Davis' home to drop information." McNiven, "Recollections," 1.

29. Mary J. R. Richards to G. L. Eberhardt, April 7, June 1, and June 27, 1867, Registered Letters Received, Georgia Superintendent of Education, vol. I, 1865–

1867, Education Records, Bureau of Refugees, Freedmen and Abandoned Lands (BRFAL), NA; Eighth U.S. Census, 1860, Richmond City, Henrico County, Va., 110; "Letter from Rev. Crammond Kennedy," *American Freedman* 2 (April 1867), 205; *Boyd's Directory of Richmond City* (Richmond: West & Johnston, 1869), 53. Recently, two other theories have surfaced about Bowser's identity and fate. Ervin L. Jordan Jr. asserts that Bowser is the Davis servant "Betsy" who fled to Union lines in 1864 with a slave named Jim Pemberton; based on a passage in Mary Chesnut's famous diary, he claims that Betsy and Pemberton tried to burn down the Davis mansion before they fled. Jordan's assertion is problematic on two levels—he offers no evidence that Van Lew's "Mary" and Davis's "Betsy" are the same person. Morever, Jordan's theory has Betsy/Bowser leaving Richmond in January 1864—before the Union underground had geared up its espionage operations for Butler and Grant. A second theory is that Bowser is one and the same as Ellen Bond, a Davis servant who provided an account, published in the *Philadelphia Inquirer*, of Jefferson Davis's capture by the Union army in 1865. Unfortunately, there is no hard evidence substantiating this claim. Ervin L. Jordan Jr., *Black Confederates and Afro-Yankees in Civil War Virginia* (Charlottesville: University Press of Virginia, 1995), 285; Forbes, *African American Women*, 41, 48.

30. Author's interview with Dorothy Grant, March 31, 2002.
31. Drawing on family lore, and connecting Van Lew's mention in her journal of a visit to the Davis residence with the Bowser story, Grant's published article on Van Lew asserts that during a social call to Varina Davis, Elizabeth Van Lew, observing the poor performance of Varina's own servants, offered her the use of Mary as an "excellent house servant who never faltered in the dining room or parlor." Grant, "Lady of Refinement," 22–26.
32. John P. Reynolds Jr., "Biographical Sketch of Elizabeth L. Van Lew," EVLP, 6, Frame 255.
33. Sharpe to Andrew A. Humphreys, August 29, 1864, *O.R.*, ser. 1, vol. XLII/2, 568.
34. Robertson, *Civil War Virginia*, 164–165.
35. Sharpe to Theodore S. Bowers, August 13, 1864, and Sharpe to A. Humphreys, September 25, 1864, *O.R.*, series 1, vol. XLII/2, 144–45 and 1010–11.
36. Sharpe to A. Humphreys, September 7 and 17, 1864, *O.R.*, ser. 1, vol. XLII/2, 734–36, 881–83.
37. Sharpe to Bowers, August 13, 1864, *O.R.*, ser. 1, vol. XLII/2, 144–45; Feis, *Grant's Secret Service*, 241–43.
38. Sharpe to Babcock, August 25, 1864, John C. Babcock Papers, LC; Sharpe to A. Humphreys, August 29 and September 7, 1864, *O.R.*, ser. 1, volume XLII/2, 568, 734–36.
39. Sharpe to A. Humphreys, September 7 and September 19, 1864, *O.R.*, ser. 1,

vol. XLII/2, 734–36, 912–13; Roberston, *Civil War Virginia*, 158–61; Feis, *Grant's Secret Service*, 246–47.

40. Feis, *Grant's Secret Service*, 246–47.

41. Ruth to Stanton, December 21, 1865, Hillyer Papers, UVA; Fishel, *The Secret War*, 551–555; Stuart, "Samuel Ruth," 84–86.

42. McEntee to A. Humphreys, October 14, 1864; McEntee to Bowers, October 20, 1864; McEntee to A. Humphreys, October 31, 1864; McEntee to A. Humphreys, November 1, 1864; J. A. Rawlins to Grant, November 20, 1864; Sharpe to A. Humphreys, November 23, 1864, *O.R.*, ser. 1, vol. XLII/3, 226, 282, 445, 472, 665, 686–87; Feis, *Grant's Secret Service*, 256–58.

43. Sharpe to A. Humphreys, September 7, 17, and 24, 1864; Sharpe to Babcock, September 22, 1864; *O.R.*, ser. 1, vol. XLII/2, 734, 881, 964, 989; Putnam, *Richmond during the War*, 334.

44. McEntee to A. Humphreys, November 13, 1864; Sharpe to A. Humphreys, November 26, 1864; Sharpe to S. Williams, December 31, 1864, *O.R.*, ser. 1, vol. XLII/3, 613–14, 710, 1107–8.

45. Adam Badeau, *Military History of General Ulysses S. Grant, from April, 1861 to April, 1865 Volume II* (New York: D. Appleton, 1881), 243.

46. EVL, "Personal Narrative," EVLP, 63–65, Frames 90–91.

47. EVL, "Personal Narrative," EVLP, 63–65, Frames 90–91; W. W. New to "Miss King," September 27, 1864, EVLP, Frame 148.

48. EVL, "Personal Narrative," EVLP, 63–66, Frames 90–91.

49. Ibid.

50. On Greenhow, see Leonard, *All the Daring*, 35–44.

51. Testimony of Mary C. Van Lew, Letters Received by the Confederate Adjutant and Inspector General, 1861–1865, October 15, 1864, RG 109, NA.

52. Ibid.

53. Author's Interview with Dorothy Grant, March 31, 2002; Eighth U.S. Census, 1860, Richmond City, Henrico County, Va., 110.

54. EVL, August 19, 1862, EVLP, Frame 82; Author's Interview with Dorothy Grant, March 31, 2002; *Richmond Examiner*, March 23, 1864.

55. Ibid.

56. Ibid.

57. Order of Charles Blackford, October 18, 1864, Letters Received by the Confederate Adjutant and Inspector General, 1861–1865, RG 109, NA.

58. Neely, *Southern Rights*, 90–91.

59. On Blackford, see Varon, *We Mean to Be Counted*, 151–152, 154, 167.

60. EVL, "Personal Narrative," EVLP, 69–70, Frames 93–94.

61. J. Jourdan to General Weitzel, November 17, 1864, *Private and Official Correspondence of General Benjamin F. Butler Vol. 5*, 354–55; Kennedy, ed., *The Civil War Battlefield Guide*, 401–2; *Petition for the Relief of Samuel Ruth, F. W. E.*

Lohman, and Charles M. Carter, House Report No. 792, Forty-third Congress, First Session, June 22, 1874.

62. *Richmond Examiner*, November 19, 1864; John N. Van Lew to Fay, October 31 and November 4, 1864; Wm. L. Plane [John] to Emma G. Plane [Elizabeth], November 4, 1864, Fay Papers, LVA.

63. John Van Lew to Fay, December 20, 24, 31, 1864, March 8, 1865, Fay Papers, LVA.

64. Claim of James Duke, RG 217, NA.

CHAPTER EIGHT
"A FLAMING ALTAR": THE FALL OF RICHMOND AND ITS AFTERMATH

1. Sharpe to Meade, January 13, 18, 1865, *O.R.*, ser. 1, vol. XLVI/2, 114, 170; Stuart, "Samuel Ruth," 91–95; McPherson, *Ordeal by Fire*, 459–63.

2. Silver, as we have seen, who was brother-in-law of Unionist Robert Orrock, had helped H. S. Howard through the lines, and had served as a reliable scout for Sharpe and Meade. The role of Timberlake, a Fredericksburg policeman, in the Unionist operation has proven difficult to pinpoint. Stuart, *Colonel Ulric Dahlgren*, 197–98.

3. Petition of Samuel Ruth and F. W. E. Lohmann, January 12, 1866, Letters Received by the Secretary of War, U.S.A., 976–1873, RG 107, NA; Stuart, "Samuel Ruth," 91–95.

4. Stuart, "Samuel Ruth," 92–99 and "Colonel Ulric Dahlgren," 185; *Richmond Sentinel*, January 26, 1865; *Richmond Whig*, February 2, 1865. On Hancock's escape attempt, see Burrows, "Recollection of Libby Prison," 83–92.

5. EVL, "Personal Narrative," EVLP, 1–8, Frames 60–64.

6. U.S. House of Representatives, *Samuel Ruth, F. W. E. Lohman, and Charles Carter*, House Report no. 792, forty-third Congress, First Session, June 22, 1874; Stuart, "Samuel Ruth," 101–3; Horace Porter, *Campaigning with Grant* (New York: Konecky and Konecky), 402.

7. Stuart, "Samuel Ruth," 79–81; U.S. House of Representatives, *Samuel Ruth, F. W. E. Lohman, and Charles Carter*, 1874.

8. Sharpe to Meade, February 11, 26, 1865, *O.R.*, ser. 1, vol. XLVI/2, 525, 706.

9. Porter, *Campaigning with Grant*, 392.

10. EVL message, March 15 [1865], RG 393, entry 3980. Sharpe quoted Van Lew in his March 22 letter to Major General Ord of the Army of the James; Sharpe to Ord, March 22, 1865, *O.R.*, ser. 1, vol. XLVI/3, 78–79. Botts to Palmer, February 5, 1865, Palmer Family Papers, VHS.

11. Grant to Meade, March 14, 1865, *O.R.*, ser. 1, vol. XLVI/2, 963.

12. Time-Life Books, *Illustrated Atlas of the Civil War* (Alexandria, Va.: Time Life, 1998), 180; Eicher, *The Longest Night*, 808–9; Kennedy, ed., *The Civil War Battlefield Guide*, 417; Robertson, *Civil War Virginia*, 167.

13. For the definitive account of the fall of Richmond, see Nelson Lankford, *Richmond Burning: The Last Days of the Confederate Capital* (New York: Viking Press, 2002).

14. *Richmond Whig*, April 4, 6, 1865; Furgurson, *Ashes of Glory*, 322–40.

15. *Richmond Whig*, April 4, 1865; Clement Sulivane, "The Fall of Richmond," Robert U. Johnson and Clarence C. Buel, eds., *Battles and Leaders of the Civil War*, vol. 4 (New York: Century, 1887–1888), 725–26; Brock Putnam, *Richmond During the War*, 366–67, 375.

16. Edward Ripley, "Final Scenes at the Capture and Occupation of Richmond, April 3, 1865," NY MOLLUS, vol. III, 1907, 472–502.

17. EVL, "Personal Narrative," April 2, 3 1865, EVLP, 730–33, Frames 54–55; Stuart, "Colonel Ulric Dahlgren," 185.

18. Annie Randolph Van Lew to Aunt Anna, April 3, in Willard Van Liew, *Van Lew-Lieu-Lew Genealogical and Historical Record* (Upper Montclair, N.J.: n.p., 1956), 77–78.

19. EVL, "Personal Narrative," April 2, 3 1865, EVLP, 730–33, Frames 54–55.

20. Ibid.

21. Marsena Patrick, *Inside Lincoln's Army: The Diary of Marsena Rudolph Patrick*, ed. David Sparks (New York: Thomas Youseleff, 1964), 488; *Richmond Dispatch*, July 17, 1883; Jedediah Paine to Beymer, February 12, 1912, Beymer Papers, UTA; M.E.C. to Mr. Carpenter, April 2, 1901, EVLP, Frame 201.

22. Butler to Hardie, April 5, 1865, EVLP, Frames 153–56; *Richmond Whig*, April 10, 1865; *Philadelphia Inquirer*, June 7, 1865.

23. Tyler-McGraw, *At the Falls*, 164–65; *Richmond Whig*, April 6, 27, May 4, 16, 1865.

24. Albree lecture on Van Lew and "John Brown's Constitution," Van Lew Papers, W&M.

25. N. Smith to John C. Babcock, June 13, 1865; Babcock to General Turner, June 14, 1865; and Captain E. A. Ellsworth to Babcock, August 14, 1865, Scouts, Guides, Spies and Detectives, Records of the Provost Marshal General's Office, RG 110, entry 31, NA; Cashmeyer to Babcock, August 28, 1865, Scouts, Guides, Spies and Detectives, Records of the Provost Marshal General's Office, RG 110, entry 36, NA; *Richmond City Directory 1866* (Richmond: E. P. Townsend, 1866), 165, 203; *Richmond Whig*, May 14, 1866.

26. *Freedman's Record*, vol. 1 (July 1865), 119, and vol. 2 (April 1867), 205.

27. Lankford, *Richmond Burning*, 161–63.

28. Tyler-McGraw, *At the Falls*, 161–62; Jordan, *Black Confederates and Afro Yankees*, 295–96; Wardwell to Butler, April 19, 1865, *Private and Official Correspondence of Benjamin F. Butler, Vol. V*, 598.

29. EVL to Jedediah Paine, April 18, 1865, Paine to Beymer, February 12, 1912, Beymer Papers, UTA.

30. Tyler-McGraw, *At the Falls*, 166.

31. Wardwell to Butler, July 26, 1865, *Private and Official Correspondence Vol. V*, 645–46.
32. Alrutheus Ambush Taylor, *The Negro in the Reconstruction of Virginia* (Washington, D.C.: The Association for the Study of Negro Life and History, 1926), 16–22.
33. EVL to James R. Doolittle, February 7, 1866, Doolittle Papers, Wisconsin Historical Society.
34. Ibid.
35. Ibid.
36. Ibid.
37. Eric Foner, *Reconstruction: American's Unfinished Revolution, 1863–1877* (New York: Harper & Row, 1998), 246–47.
38. *Harper's Weekly*, September 16, 1865; *Richmond Enquirer*, May 18, 1866; Wardwell to Butler, February 26, 1866, *Private and Official Correspondence Vol. V*, 701–2; Taylor, *The Negro in the Reconstruction of Virginia*, 22; *Richmond Examiner*, July 6, 1866; *Richmond New Nation*, July 19, 1866.
39. *Christian Recorder*, October 13, 1866.
40. Stuart, "Samuel Ruth," 81, 101–3; Sharpe to Stanton, March 3, 1866, Registered Letters Received by the U.S. Secretary of War, 1873:976, RG 107, NA.
41. *Philadelphia Inquirer*, July 25, August 8, 1865; *Harper's Weekly*, October 14, 1865.
42. *Harper's Weekly*, July 14, 1866.
43. Ibid.
44. EVL to Andrew, February 28, 1866, Massachusetts State Archives.
45. *Richmond Times*, August 8, 1866; *Richmond New Nation*, September 20, 1866.
46. EVL to "Gentlemen," July 11, 1887, EVLP, Frames 141–42.
47. "Warning to Mrs. Van Lew from the White Caps," EVLP, Frames 205–7.
48. Ryan, ed., *A Yankee Spy*, 133; Stuart, "Colonel Ulric Dahlgren," 199, Sharpe to Comstock, January 1867, EVLP, Frames 129–35. Much of the material the War Department forwarded to Van Lew was subsequently lost or destroyed by her, and thus surviving examples of intelligence dispatches in her own hand are few in number. She may have been motivated to destroy certain documents to protect fellow Unionists who were still living in Richmond.
49. Sharpe to Comstock, January 1867, EVLP, Frames 129–35; Zeinert, *Elizabeth Van Lew*, 128; Butler to EVL, May 14, 1867, Van Lew Album, VHS.
50. J. W. Alvord to Orlando Brown, February 13, 1868 and EVL to Orlando Brown, February 23, 1868, Registered Letters and Telegrams Received, Records of the Asst. Comm. for the State of Va., BRFAL, NA.
51. Alvord to Brown, February 13, 1868; EVL to Brown, November 2, 1867 and February 23, 1868, Registered Letters and Telegrams Received, Records of the Asst. Comm. for the State of Va., BRFAL, NA; Elizabeth Lewis (Dabney) Saunders to Betty Saunders, n.d., Saunders Family Papers, VHS.

52. Tyler-McGraw, *At the Falls*, 167; Wm. Evins to EVL, October 17, 1867, Van Lew Papers, W&M.

53. Mary J. R. Richards to G. L. Eberhardt, February 22, 1867, Registered Letters Received, Georgia Superintendent of Education, vol. I, 1865–1867, Education Records, BRFAL, NA.

54. Richards to Eberhardt, February 22, 1867, Registered Letters Received, Georgia Superintendent of Education, vol. I, 1865–1867, Education Records, BRFAL; Paul A. Cimbala, *Under the Guardianship of the Nation: The Freedmen's Bureau and the Reconstruction of Georgia, 1865–1870* (Athens: University of Georgia Press), 106–7, 127–28.

55. Richards to Eberhardt, March 10, 1867, Registered Letters Received, Georgia Superintendent of Education, vol. I, 1865–1867, Education Records, BRFAL; "Letter from Rev. Crammond Kennedy," *American Freedman* 2 (April 1867), 205.

56. Ibid.

57. Richards to Eberhardt, April 7, 1867, Registered Letters Received, Georgia Superintendent of Education, vol. I, 1865–1867, Education Records, BRFAL.

58. Richards to Eberhardt, June 1, 27, 1867, Registered Letters Received, Georgia Superintendent of Education, vol. I, 1865–1867, Education Records, BRFAL; Cimbala, *Under the Guardianship of the Nation*, 106–7, 127–28.

59. Michael Chesson, *Richmond After the War, 1865–1890* (Richmond: Virginia State Library, 1981), 88–95.

60. Chesson, *Richmond After the War*, 109–110; Taylor, *The Negro in the Reconstruction of Virginia*, 208–221; *New York Times*, May 14, 1867. After many delays and postponements, the Federal government opted not to try Davis for fear that "such a trial would inflame the restive South." Tyler-McGraw, *At the Falls*, 171–176.

61. Jane Dailey, *Before Jim Crow: The Politics of Race in Postemancipation Virginia* (Chapel Hill: University of North Carolina Press, 2000), 19–20.

62. William Gillette, *Retreat from Reconstruction, 1869–1879* (Baton Rouge: Louisiana State University Press, 1979), 81.

CHAPTER NINE
"A FIERY ORDEAL": THE TRIALS OF A FEMALE POLITICIAN

1. U. S. Grant to the Senate of the United States, March 17, 1869, Records of the U.S. Senate, RG 42, NA; *Richmond Whig*, March 20, 1869; EVL, "Article in response to 'Men and Monopolists,' " EVLP, Frames 210–18.

2. *Richmond Enquirer and Examiner*, March 23, 1869; Richmond *Southern Opinion*, March 27, 1869. Ironically, only a single or widowed woman possessed the legal standing to assume the role of postmaster, with its assumption of financial culpability, in Virginia; since the Old Dominion had not yet granted

married women property rights, they were not able to keep their own wages, to sue or be sued, make contracts, and conduct business in their own names. The Virginia General Assembly did not guarantee married women property rights until 1877. Suzanne D. Lebsock, "Radical Reconstruction and the Property Rights of Southern Women," in Catherine Clinton, ed., *Half Sisters of History: Southern Women and the American Past* (Durham: Duke University Press, 1994). For examples of Virginia women who were "disqualified by marriage" to hold postmasterships, see *Richmond State Journal*, July 9, November 4, 1870.

3. *National Intelligencer* (Washington, D.C.), March 18, 1869. Grant has not left a record of the reasoning behind his appointment of Van Lew; indeed the appointment seems inconsistent with the conciliatory course of action he would soon adopt in Virginia (see below). His nomination of Van Lew is consistent however with his habit of letting personal loyalty dictate his patronage choices. Gillette, *Retreat from Reconstruction*, 21.

4. *Baltimore Sun* as quoted in *Richmond Whig*, March 19, 1869; *Troy Times*, March 17, 1869; *New York Times* as quoted in *Richmond Enquirer* and *Examiner*, March 23, 1869; James D. Horan, *Desperate Women* (New York: G. P. Putnam's Sons, 1952), 162; "Resolutions of the 79th Regiment of Highlanders," May 17, 1869, EVLP, Frames 169–70; *Philadelphia Evening Telegraph*, March 20, 1869.

5. Wayne E. Fuller, *The American Mail: Enlarger of the Community Life* (Chicago: University of Chicago Press, 1972), 288–89, 294–95. While most postmasters were appointed by the postmaster general, those with salaries over $1,000 were appointed by the president with the advice and consent of the Senate. Dorothy Ganfield Fowler, *Unmailable: Congress and the Post Office* (Athens: University of Georgia Press, 1977), 13, 24.

6. William E. Nelson, *The Roots of American Bureaucracy, 1830–1900* (Cambridge: Harvard University Press, 1982), 24–25; Fuller, *The American Mail*, 294–95; Richard John, *Spreading the News: The American Postal System from Franklin to Morse* (Cambridge, Mass.: Harvard University Press, 1995), 124.

7. John, *Spreading the News*, 112, 138–39, 164–66.

8. John, *Spreading the News*, 139; Rable, *Civil Wars*, 265–88.

9. Sara Evans, *Born for Liberty: A History of Women in America* (New York: Free Press, 1989), 124; Elna C. Green, *Southern Strategies: Southern Women and the Woman Suffrage Question* (Chapel Hill: University of North Carolina Press, 1997).

10. *Philadelphia Evening Standard*, March 20, 1869; *New York Herald*, March 19, 1869; *Revolution*, March 25, 1869; Sandra Gioia Treadway, "A Most Brilliant Woman: Anna Whitehead Bodeker and the First Woman Suffrage Association in Virginia," *Virginia Cavalcade*, 43 (Spring 1994), 166–77; *Richmond Times-Dispatch*, September 23, 1937.

11. *Visitors Guide to Richmond and Vicinity* (Richmond: Benjamin Bates, 1871), 16–17.

12. *Richmond Dispatch*, April 2, 1869; *Richmond Enquirer and Examiner*, April 2, 1869; *Revolution*, April 22, 1869, February 23, 1871; E. L. Van Lew, *Post Office Manual* (Richmond: Evening State Journal Steam Printing House, 1871), 11–12; *Williamsburg Virginia Gazette*, April 15, 1869.

13. EVL to Grant, April 6, 1869, EVLP, Frames 166–68; *Register of Officers and Agents, Civil, Military, and Naval, in the Service of the United States* (Washington, D.C.: Government Printing Office, 1870), 768; *Register of Officers and Agents, Civil, Military, and Naval, in the Service of the United States* (Washington, D.C.: Government Printing Office, 1874), 402–3; *Boyd's Directory of Richmond City* (Richmond: Bates & Waddy Bros., 1870), 226; *Richmond City Directory* (Richmond: B. W. Gillis, 1871), 2; *Richmond Dispatch*, April 2, 1869.

14. Richard Lowe, *Republicans and Reconstruction in Virginia, 1856–70* (Charlottesville: University of Virginia Press, 1991); Jack P. Maddex, *The Virginia Conservatives, 1867–1879: A Study in Reconsrtuction Politics* (Chapel Hill: University of North Carolina Press, 1970); Gillette, *Retreat from Reconstruction*, 80–85. According to one Virginia newspaper, as of 1877, there were some 1,458 post offices in the state; 18 of Virginia's postmasterships were designated as presidential appointments; the rest fell under the appointment powers of the postmaster general. *Alexandria Gazette*, May 10, 1877.

15. On the divisions within Republican ranks, see Lowe, *Republicans and Reconstruction*, 168–69, 172–77, 185–89 and his article "Local Black Leaders during Reconstruction in Virginia," *Virginia Magazine of History and Biography*, 103 (April 1995), 181–206; William D. Henderson, *The Unredeemed City: Reconstruction in Petersburg, Virginia, 1865–1874* (Washington, D.C.: The University Press of America, 1977), 235–240; Comments of James Henry Platt Jr., *Congressional Globe*, Forty-first Congress, Third Session, Pt. II (Washington, D.C.: F. & J. Rives and George A. Bailey, 1871), 881; Speech of Honorable C. H. Porter, *Congressional Globe*, Forty-first Congress, Third Session, Pt. III (1871), 291–294; Speech of James Henry Platt Jr., *Congressional Globe*, Forty-second Congress, Second Session, Appendix (1872), 196–98.

16. *Richmond Enquirer and Examiner*, April 2, 1869; Parker, *A Chautauqua Boy*, 59–61; EVL, "Article in response to 'Men and Monopolists' " EVLP, Frames 216–18.

17. *Richmond Dispatch*, November 9, 1870. Joseph M. Humphrey's assistant collector of customs was James M. Humphreys, who had seen a scout for Ben Butler and member of Van Lew's spying during the war. *Boyd's Directory of Richmond City* (Richmond: West and Johnston, 1869), 120.

18. *Revolution*, January 26, 1871; *Petersburg Index*, April 5, 6, 7, 1871; *Richmond Dispatch*, January 25, 28, 1871; *Alexandria Gazette*, April 7, 1871; Maddex,

Virginia Conservatives, 74–75, 82, 87–88. Congressmen and postmasters alike had the franking privilege. John, *Spreading the News*, 58–59, 123–24.

19. *Revolution*, January 26, 1871; *Petersburg Index*, April 5, 6, 7, 1871; *Richmond Dispatch*, January 25, 28, 1871; *Alexandria Gazette*, April 7, 1871.

20. *Petersburg Index*, April 5, 6, 7, 1871; *Revolution*, December 22, 1870, January 12, 1871.

21. *Richmond Dispatch*, March 13, 1872; *Richmond Enquirer*, March 13, 18, 19, 1872.

22. Melanie Susan Gustafson, *Women and the Republican Party, 1854–1924* (Urbana: University of Illinois Press, 2001), 48–49.

23. *Richmond Enquirer*, March 6, 9, 11, 15, 1873; *Richmond Whig*, March 12, 1873; J. L. Kemper to EVL, February 24, 1874, Van Lew Papers, W&M.

24. EVL to General Brown, November 2, 1867, in Register of Letters and Telegrams Received by the Assistant Commissioner for Va., January 1 to December 31, 1867; and EVL to Brown, February 23, 1868, Letters Received by the Assistant Commissioner for Va., from January 1, 1868 to June 30, 1868, in BRFAL, NA; Beymer, "Miss Van Lew," 98.

25. *New National Era* (Washington, D.C.), April 28, 1870; Van Lew Album, VHS.

26. *Richmond Dispatch*, April 21, 1871; *Petersburg Index*, April 22, 1871.

27. *Richmond Dispatch*, January 5, 1872; Chesson, *Richmond After the War, 1865–1900*, 182–83.

28. John, *Spreading the News*, 140–43; on Bowser, see *Freedman's Record*, 4 (April 1868), 64; on Bacchus, *Richmond Whig*, October 16, 1873; on black mail carriers see *Richmond Dispatch*, March 13, 1872; for the names of the clerks Van Lew hired, see *Official Register*, 1869, 768; 1871, 358–59; 1873, 402–3; 1875, 498–99; on Josiah Crump see Eric Foner, "Crump, Josiah" in *Freedom's Lawmakers: A Directory of Black Officeholders during Reconstruction* (New York: Oxford University Press, 1993), 54–55 and Virginius Dabney, *Richmond: The Story of a City* (Charlottesville: University Press of Virginia, 1976), 237; on Stephens, *Richmond Times-Dispatch*, August 27, 1911.

29. Anna E. Dickinson to Mary Dickinson, January 9, 1875, Family Correspondence, Anna E. Dickinson Papers, LC; Gustafson, *Women and the Republican Party*, 24–33, 74; on Peter Roane, see Ninth U.S. Census, 1870, Richmond City, Henrico County, 506; and *Richmond City Directory* (Richmond: B. W. Gillis, 1871), 2; "Record for Peter Roane," no. 2439, Freedmen's Savings Bank Deposit Ledger, Richmond Va., NA.

30. Ibid.

31. Anna E. Dickinson to Mary Dickinson, January 9, 1875, Dickinson Papers, LC; Foner, *Reconstruction*, 553.

32. David W. Blight, *Race and Reunion: The Civil War in American Memory* (Cambridge, Mass.: Harvard University Press, 2001), 130–32.

33. EVL, "Article in response to 'Men and Monopolists,'" EVLP, Frames 210–18;

Alexander Rives to George K. Gilmer, January 31, 1876, George K. Gilmer Papers, VHS; Ryan, ed., *A Yankee Spy*, 155. Gilmer finally succeeded in winning appointment as Richmond postmaster, in 1880. *Richmond Dispatch*, March 8, 1881.

34. EVL, "Article in response to 'Men and Monopolists'" EVLP, Frames 216–18.

35. *Richmond Dispatch*, January 8, 1876; EVL to General James Garfield, June 20, July 5, 7, 1876, James Garfield Papers, LC.

36. EVL, "To Northern Democrats. An Appeal Which Should Not Go Unheard," October 27, 1876, newspaper clipping, EVLP, Frame 7; *Richmond Dispatch*, November 1, 1876.

37. Ibid.

38. Ibid.

39. *Richmond Enquirer*, March 18, 1877.

40. R. W. Hughes to Rutherford B. Hayes, April 6, 1877, Rutherford B. Hayes Papers, LC.; William C. Wickham to EVL, February 24, 1877, EVLP, Frames 173–74; P. T. Atkinson to Rutherford B. Hayes, April 27, 1877, Van Lew Album, VHS.

41. *Alexandria Gazette*, March 14, 27, 1877; *Richmond Whig*, April 14, 1877; On William C. Roane see "Record for William C. Roane," no. 940, Freedmen's Savings Bank Deposit Ledgers, Richmond, Va, NA.

42. *National Republican* (Washington, D.C.), March 13, April 11, 14, 23, 1877; *Richmond Enquirer*, March 13, 1877; Copy of U. S. Grant letter, February 26, 1877, EVLP, Frame 172.

43. *Richmond Enquirer*, April 11, May 3, 6, 1877.

44. *Alexandria Gazette*, March 17, 22, April 6, 1877; *Richmond State*, March 22, 1877.

45. *National Republican* (Washington, D.C.), April 6, 24, 1877. John Y. Simon, ed., *The Papers of Ulysses S. Grant, Volume 20: November 1, 1869–October 31, 1870* (Carbondale and Edwardsville: Southern Illinois University Press, 1995), 347; EVL to Mr. Rogers (Hayes's secretary), April 10, 1877, EVLP, Frames 161–65.

46. Klapp &c v. Van Lew &c., February 1877, Chancery Court of Richmond, Cases Ended File 131, JMCB.

47. Ibid.

48. EVL to Rogers, April 10, 1877, EVLP, Frames 161–65; *National Republican* (Washington, D.C.), April 30, 1877; *Richmond Whig*, April 27, 1877.

49. *Richmond Enquirer*, April 29, 1877.

50. Ibid.

51. *Richmond Enquirer*, May 1, 1877.

52. Ibid.

53. *New York World*, as reprinted in *National Republican* (Washington, D.C.), May 2, 1877.

54. *Richmond Whig*, May 21, 22, June 30, July 2, 1877.

55. Ellen Glasgow, *The Woman Within: An Autobiography* (Charlottesville: University Press of Virginia, 1994), 21; *Official Register*, 1873, 452.

56. *Richmond Enquirer*, May 20, 1877; EVL to George Howland, June 16, 1877, EVLP, Frames 258–60; *National Republican* (Washington, D.C.), May 23, 25, 1877; C. Vann Woodward, *Reunion and Reaction: The Compromise of 1877 and the End of Reconstruction* (New York: Oxford University Press, 1966), 225–26.

57. Marshall Cushing, *The Story of Our Post Office: The Greatest Government Department in all its Phases* (Boston, Mass.: A. M. Thayer & Co., 1893), 11, 442–51. On Virginia Thompson, see *Nation*, June 7, 1877, 336–37.

58. Agreement between C. W. Jenkins and E. L. Van Lew, September 29, 1877, Chaffin Family Papers, VHS; J. V. Reddy to R. B. Hayes, May 26, 1877, Dept. of the Interior Field Office Papers, Entry 15, Box 712, RG 48 NA, EVL, "For Sale," 3.

59. EVL to U. S. Grant, February 1, 1881, James Garfield Papers, LC; *Richmond Dispatch*, March 17, 1881.

60. For an excellent study of the Readjusters, see Jane Dailey, *Before Jim Crow: The Politics of Race in Postemancipation Virginia* (Chapel Hill: University of North Carolina Press, 2000).

61. EVL to Thurlow Weed, March 16, 1881, EVLP, Frames 261–67.

62. *Evening Star* (Washington, D.C.), March 26, 1881.

63. EVL to James Garfield, June 8, 1881, James A. Garfield Papers, LC; Dailey, *Before Jim Crow*, 89; *Richmond Whig*, March 31, 1881.

64. Dailey, *Before Jim Crow*, 142–51.

65. Parker, *A Chautauqua Boy*, 61–64.

66. EVL, "An account of her transfer to the dead letter office," EVLP, Frames 219–23; EVL to Mr. Howe, July 13, 1887, EVLP, Frames 144–46. Van Lew lived at 326 4½ Street N.W. in 1884, at 622 E. Street, N.W. in 1885, and at 906 I Street, N.W. in 1887. *William H. Boyd, Boyd's Directory of the District of Columbia* (Washington, D.C.: Adams and Ballantyne, 1884), 825; *Boyd's*, 1886, 814; *Boyd's*, 1887, 835.

67. EVL, "An account of her transfer to the dead letter office," EVLP, Frames 219–23; EVL to Mr. Howe, July 13, 1887, EVLP, Frames 144–46; *Richmond State*, July 11, 1887; *Richmond Dispatch*, July 8, 1887.

68. M. O. Chance to Albree, April 17, 1908, Van Lew Papers, W&M.

CHAPTER TEN
THE MYTH OF "CRAZY BET"

1. EVL to Mr. Forbes, March 20, 1891, EVLP, Frame 226; EVL, "Article in response to 'Men and Monopolists,' " EVLP, Frames 210–18; Ryan, ed., *A Yankee Spy*, 130.

2. EVL to the National Woman Suffrage Association, May 29, 1880, The Papers of Elizabeth Cady Stanton and Susan B. Anthony, NWSA Collection, Yale University, New Haven, Ct.; EVL to John Childress, November 28, 1892, EVLP, Frame 236.

3. Wheeler, *New Women of the New South*, 102–11.

4. Blight, *Race and Reunion*.

5. Ibid., 266.

6. Ibid., 298.

7. Blight, *Race and Reunion*, 267; EVL to Mr. Forbes, March 20, 1891, EVLP, Frames 230–32.

8. EVL to Mr. Forbes, March 20, 1891, EVLP, Frames 224–34.

9. Bigelow, *I Want Justice; Virginia Star* (Richmond), April 30, 1881; Bureau of Vital Statistics Death Register, City of Richmond, 1881 and 1884, LVA; *Richmond Planet*, February 22, 1890; *Richmond Times-Dispatch*, May 8, 1921.

10. *Official Register*, 1873, 452; EVL to Mr. Forbes, March 20, 1891, EVLP, Frames 224–34; EVL letter, n.d., EVLP, Frames 267–72; Tenth U.S. Census, 1880, Louisa County, Va., 133; Author's interview with Dorothy Grant, February 9, 2003.

11. EVL to Mr. Forbes, March 20, 1891, EVLP, Frames 224–34; *Richmond News Leader*, January 6, 7, 8, 1959.

12. *Richmond Dispatch*, January 9, 1870.

13. *Richmond News Leader*, January 7, 1959; Ellen Glasgow, *A Certain Measure: An Interpretation of Prose and Fiction* (New York: Harcourt, Brace and Company, 1938), 65–66.

14. Interview with Kitty Dennis, August 25, 1982, Church Hill Oral History Project, Virginia Black History Archives, James Branch Cabell Library, Virginia Commonwealth University, Richmond.

15. *Richmond News Leader*, January 8, 1959; EVL to Mrs. McKinley, Van Lew Papers, W&M; Van Lew obituary, newspaper scrap, EVLP, Frame 5.

16. EVL to Fay, August 1, 1884, Fay Papers, LVA; Reynolds to Beymer, December 14, 1908, December 6, 1910, Beymer Papers, UTA.

17. Van Lew obituary, newspaper scrap, EVLP, Frame 5.

18. *Richmond Dispatch*, September 25, 1900; Miss Gilberta S. Whittle, "Miss Van Lew's Spies in the Davis Household," *Richmond Evening Journal* clipping, n.d., EVLP, Frame 3.

19. *Richmond Dispatch*, September 25, 1900; *Richmond Evening Leader*, July 27, 1900; Reynolds to Emily Chenault Runyon, ca. 1900, VHS; (Carrington) Nowland, "Elizabeth L. Van Lew," EVLP, Frames 177–93.

20. *Richmond Dispatch*, September 25, 26, 1900.

21. Reynolds to Beymer, December 14, 1908, December 6, 1910, Beymer Papers, UTA; *Richmond Dispatch*, September 26, 1900.

22. *Richmond Dispatch*, September 27, 28, 1900.

23. Will of Elizabeth Van Lew, Richmond Chancery Court Records, Will Book no. 7, 419, JCMB.

24. *Richmond Dispatch*, July 29, 1902; Reynolds to Beymer, December 6, 1910, Beymer Papers, UTA.

25. *New York Times*, September 26, 1900; *Boston Herald*, September 25, 1900; *Richmond Dispatch*, September 26, 1900; *Richmond News Leader*, September 25, 1900; *Richmond Planet*, September 29, 1900.

26. *Boston Evening Transcript*, September 26, 1900; *Boston Morning Journal* clipping, n.d., EVLP, Frame 4.

27. Reynolds to Beymer, December 14, 1908, Beymer Papers, UTA.

28. Reynolds to Beymer, April 22, 29, 1910, UTA.

29. Ryan, ed., *A Yankee Spy*, 59; Leonard, *All the Daring*, 55; William Gilmore Beymer, *Harper's Monthly* (June 1911), 89–91; Harnett T. Kane, *Spies for the Blue and Gray* (Hanover House, 1954), 232; Clifford Dowdey, *Experiment in Rebellion* (New York: Doubleday, 1946), 91; Alan Axelrod, *The War Between the Spies: A History of Espionage During the American Civil War* (Boston: Atlantic Monthly Press, 1992), 104; Richard Weinert, "Federal Spies in Richmond," *Civil War Times Illustrated* (February 1965), 28, 30.

EPILOGUE
VAN LEW'S GHOST

1. Green et al., *Lost Virginia*, 48–49; Whittle, "Miss Van Lew's Spies in the Davis Household," *Richmond Evening Journal* clipping, n.d., EVLP, Frame 3; Author's phone interview with Hyman Schwartzberg, July 24, 2002; *National Tribune* (Washington, D.C.), July 4, 1901.

2. Ellen Glasgow, *The Romance of a Plain Man* (New York: Macmillan, 1909).

3. Glasgow, *Romance*, 174–76, 208–10, 215, 227–29.

4. Ibid., 230.

5. *Richmond Times-Dispatch*, August 27, 1911.

6. *Richmond News Leader*, January 6, 7, 8, 1959; Crumley and Zehmer, *Church Hill*, 124.

7. James W. Loewen, *Lies Across America: What Our Historic Sites Get Wrong* (New York: The New Press, 1999), 300–301.

8. *Richmond Times-Dispatch*, March 29, 1987; *Richmond News Leader*, March 28, 1987. Van Lew is still regarded as a villain by some Richmonders. In 1994, for example, one of the editors of the *Richmond Times-Dispatch* took historian Marie Tyler-McGraw to task for including long and laudatory passages on Eliz-

abeth in her newly published history of Richmond, *At the Falls.* The editor described Van Lew succinctly as "that dreadful woman." *Richmond Times-Dispatch*, December 4, 1994.

9. (Carrington) Nowland, "Elizabeth L. Van Lew," EVLP, 1–4, 16, Frames 180–82, 186–87.

INDEX

abolitionist movement, 10, 18, 24
abolitionists, 32, 37–38, 39, 50
Adams, Richard, 15, 22
Adams, John, 12, 15
Adams, George W., 22
Adler, Adolphus, 88–89
African-American press, 244, 253
African Americans, 101, 144, 162, 195,
    231–32; arrest of, 30–31; black code
    and, 200; civil rights of, 5, 200, 209,
    225, 229; education of, 28, 31, 165,
    168, 197–98, 209–12, 223–26; flogging
    of, 83–85; Freedmen's Bureau and, 208–
    12; as fugitives from confederacy, 95;
    hiring of, 226–28, 236–37; Lincoln's
    death and, 198; postwar distress of, 203–
    4; as prisoners, 101; in Readjuster
    Party, 239–40; Republican party and,
    226, 230; as soldiers, 99, 111; in spy
    network, 159, 162–68, 173; suffrage
    for, 213–14, 221, 225; as Union guides,
    90–93, 131, 138, 173; as Unionists, 64,
    83–85, 88, 91–93, 128, 131–32; as Van
    Lew allies, 5, 159, 209, 225, 231–32,
    236, 240, 244–45, 247, 253; Van Lew
    servants, 32–34, 126, 155, 159, 163–69,
    183. See also free blacks; slavery
African colonization scheme, 28–29, 31
Aiken's Landing, 93
Albree, John Jr., 24, 91
Alexander, George W., 78, 84, 100
Alexandria Gazette, 233
Alien Enemies Act (CSA), 61, 63
Allan, (Mrs. Pat) Mary Caroline, 102, 105
Allan, Patterson, 105
allegiance, 136; oath of, 61, 70, 73, 201.
    See also disloyalty; loyalty

Alvord, J. W., 208
American Colonization Society (ACS),
    28, 29
American Freedman, 167, 210
amnesty, postwar, 203, 214–15
Anderson, Joseph R., 170
Anderson (slave), 25, 27, 164
Andersonville Prison, 57, 115
Andrew, John A., 4, 5, 206
Anthony, Susan B., 4, 218, 219, 224
antislavery organizations, 27. See also
    abolitionists
Appomatox, Lee's surrender at, 195
Army of the James, 111, 154, 157, 162
Army of the Potomac, 70, 155, 157, 171;
    Meade and, 113, 149, 153
arrests of Unionists, 70–73, 94, 102, 105,
    161, 186–87
Arthur, Chester A., 240
Ash, Stephen V., 47
Ashe, W. S., 71
Atkinson, John Wilder, 143, 144, 151
Atkinson, P. T., 231
Atlanta, Georgia, 105–6, 174, 185

Babcock, John C., 97, 113, 171, 173
Babcock, Lemuel, 159, 161–62, 187
Babcock, Orville, 33
Badeau, Adam, 174
Bailey, William T., 224
Baker, Hilary (grandfather), 10, 47
Baker, Hilary (uncle), 12
Baker, William A. (cousin), 49, 164
Baldwin, John B., 43, 72
Baltimore, Maryland, 51; newspapers, 52,
    150, 217
Banks, Nathaniel, 153

Baptist Home Missionary Society, 198
Bartley, Reuben, 102, 139–40
Bates, E. L., 121
battles: Bethel Church, 54; Bull Run/
    Manassas, 55, 61–62; Cedar Creek, 172;
    Cold Harbor, 156; Deep Bottom, 169–
    70; Oak Grove, 78; Seven Days, 78, 79–
    80; Seven Pines, 77; Wilderness, 153–
    154
Baxter, Sydney S., 186
Beauregard, Pierre Gustave T., 61, 155,
    157
Bell, John, 39
belle, Van Lew as, 18–20
Belle Isle prison, 100, 115, 133
Belleville School, 257, 260
Belvidere Hill Baptist Church, 103
Benjamin, Judah P., 64, 65, 96, 117, 140
Best, Miss (postal worker), 241
Beymer, William Gilmore, 166–67, 199,
    254–55, 259, 268n.37
black code, 200
Blackford, Charles M., 180, 181
Blackford, Mary Berkeley Minor, 181
black labor, 201. See also slavery
black market, 85, 188
Bland, Mataoca (Romance of a Plain
    Man), 258–59
Bledsoe, A. G., 64
Blight, David, 228, 243–44
Bob (slave), 25, 164
Bolton, Augusta, 148
Bolton, Christopher, 147
Bostonian friends, 248
Boston newspapers, 253, 254
Bottom's Bridge, 116–17, 138
Botts, John Minor, 4–5, 78, 79, 129, 189;
    arrest of, 70–71, 72; black suffrage and,
    213; postwar criticism of, 203; return
    to Richmond, 196; secession crisis and,
    4, 39, 40, 46, 49; as slaveholder, 4, 33;
    as Unionist standard bearer, 36–37,
    201; as Whig, 5, 17, 36, 81
Boutelle, Charles O., 111, 112
Bowers, Theodore S., 169
Bowser, James H., 226, 236, 244–45
Bowser, Mary Elizabeth, 31, 165–168,
    170, 178, 290n.29. See also Richards,
    Mary Jane

Bowser, Wilson, 166, 167–68
Boyle, William, 117
Breckenridge, James, 39
Bremer, Frederika, 23–24
bribery, 182; of prison guards, 85, 86, 87,
    89, 114, 125, 126
Brisby, William H., 92–93, 95
Brock, Sallie Ann, 52, 53, 55, 60, 174,
    191, 273n.2
Brockenbrough, John W., 41
Brockenbrough, Thomas W., 234
Brown, John, 37–38, 197
Brown, Orlando, 208, 209
Brown, Spencer Kellogg, 101
Brown, Sylvanus, 159, 162–63
Bullock, Alexander H., 206
Bureau of Military Intelligence, 113, 138,
    277n.9
Burging, Christian, 81, 94
Burnside, Ambrose, 97
Butler, Benjamin, 106, 107–9, 111, 138,
    196; Civil Rights bill and, 228;
    Dahlgren affair and, 148, 149; failed
    raid on Richmond and, 117; on
    postwar compensation, 208; spy
    network and, 150, 157, 159; threat to
    Richmond by, 153, 154; Van Lew's
    dispatches to, 112–13, 114–15, 120, 154–
    55, 182
Butt, Martha Haines, 56

Campaigning with Grant (Porter), 189
Caphart, John, 84–85
Caroline (slave), 26, 27
Carrington, Eliza Griffin, 14–15, 17, 32,
    63, 181; as companion to Van Lew, 78,
    164; as postal worker, 220; on Van Lew
    as "belle," 18, 20
Carrington, Isaac, 164, 180, 181, 197
Carrington, Littleberry, 15, 17
Carrington family slaves, 159, 164
Carruthers, Major, 235–36
Carter, Betty, 27
Carter, Charles M., 159, 162, 173, 175,
    187–88, 204
Carter family, 179
Cashmeyer, Philip, 73, 150–51, 197
Castle Godwin prison, 71, 72, 78, 84, 89,
    160; Union spies in, 73, 75, 76

Castle Thunder prison, 83–85, 92, 100–102, 197, 202; escapes from, 114, 192; Unionists in, 150, 160, 161, 184, 186, 187; women in, 102

casualties, 78, 79, 135, 154, 156; civilian, 51, 64–65, 103; Confederate, 54, 55, 157. *See also* deaths; execution

Catlin, Harry, 109. *See also* Howard, Harry S.

CBS television, 260

Chaffin's Farm, 164, 170

Chancellor Bibb (steamer), 111

Chancery Court, 233–34

charity work, 16, 20, 56, 94, 206; with Union prisoners, 59–60, 64, 66, 83. *See also* female benevolence; generosity

Charles City County, Virginia, 159, 160, 161, 173

Chesson, Michael, 226

Chester, Thomas, 198

Chesnut, Mary, 55

childhood, 9, 12

Christian Recorder, 204

Church Hill ladies, 53, 60

Church Hill mansion, 3, 4, 12–14, 168–69, 178, 247; armed guard around, 130, 196; attempted sale of, 238; escaped prisoners hiding in, 89–91; gardens of, 13, 246; haunting of, 257

Church Hill neighborhood, 16, 259

City Point, Virginia, 90, 157, 163, 174–75

civilians: casualties, 51, 64–65, 103; in Confederate prisons, 55–56. *See also* underground; Unionists

Civil Rights Bill (1866), 203, 228

civil service, 226, 241; women in, 218, 237. *See also* postmastership

Civil War Times Illustrated, 255

Clark, Terrence, 120

Clark, George F., 160

Clay, Henry, 17, 28, 36

clergy, 49, 85–86

Cleveland administration, 241

Committee on War Claims, 158

Confederacy, 7; as "Lost Cause," 243–44, 260; loyalty to, 53–54, 67, 75, 76, 96. *See also* ex-Confederates

Confederate army, 44, 52, 67, 190, 280n.43; casualties of, 54, 55, 157;

desertions from, 95, 127–28, 188; food seizure by, 103; high command, 139, 171, 172; home guard, 135, 138; importance of railroad to, 96–97; pickets, 78–79, 94, 131, 146–47; recruitment for, 49; Richmond attack scheme and, 116, 117

Confederate authorities, 66, 93, 108, 150, 255; postwar arrests of, 197; bread riots and, 104; counterintelligence by, 186–88; fall of Richmond and, 190, 191; Libby prison breakout and, 125; treatment of women by, 62–63, 76; Unionist spy network and, 156, 161, 162, 163, 173. *See also* investigation of Van Lew

Confederate government, 72, 73, 75, 101, 180; Congress, 61, 63, 99; misinformation from, 171–72

Confederate prisons, 82, 94, 99, 145, 255; overcrowding in, 57, 83, 100–101, 115. *See also* prisoners, Union; *and specific prisons*

Confederate White House, 165–66, 167, 168, 198, 289n.28

Confiscation Act (1861), 107

Congress, U.S., 39, 41, 107, 201–3, 208; Reconstruction and, 212–13, 215, 228

conservatism, 200–202, 203, 243, 259

Conservatives, 221, 226, 232, 238, 239; support for Van Lew by, 222, 224, 225

conspiracy charges, 72. *See also* treason

Constitutional convention, 212, 213–14, 221

Constitutional Union Party, 36, 39

Corcoran, Michael, 59, 71

courage, 48, 177, 228

courts, 27, 31, 72, 105, 197

Cox, Joseph, 213

Craig, James, 103

Crazy Bet myth, 247, 253–56, 257, 258, 261

Cridland, F. J., 96

Crofts, Daniel, 41, 43

Crump, Josiah, 226, 227, 236, 244–45

Cumber, Warren, 92

Curtis, Mrs., 63

Custom House Building, 219

Dade, Elizabeth P., 186
Dahlgren, John A., 137, 141, 148–49, 205
Dahlgren, Ulric, 135–46, 204–5; aborted
    mission of, 135–37; burial, 142–43,
    286n.19; death of, 135–36, 138;
    documents found on, 139–42, 143;
    Unionist reburial of, 143–49, 151
Dailey, Jane, 240
Daisy (Van Lew maid), 247
Daniel, Peter V., Jr., 97
Davenport, John I., 157
Davis, Jefferson, 65, 69, 107, 143, 152;
    bread riots and, 104; Butler and, 108;
    execution threats of, 66, 99; plot to
    capture/kill, 115, 136, 139, 140;
    postwar trial of, 197, 213; Richmond
    evacuation and, 190; spies in home of,
    167, 172, 290n.29; Tennessee invasion
    and, 69, 70
Davis, Varina Howell, 76, 165–66,
    290n.31
death, 198, 244–45; ideal, 143, 146; in
    Van Lew family, 3, 20–21, 230, 245,
    250, 251–53. See also casualties;
    executions
Delarue, Louisa, 287n.27
Democratic Party, 16, 129, 214; postwar
    resurgence of, 228, 230, 237, 240;
    secession crisis and, 35, 37, 39, 40, 45
Dennis, Kitty, 247
Derrick, W. B., 232
Dickinson, Anna, 4, 32, 227–28
disease, 10, 29, 164, 250–251
disloyalty, 53–55, 70, 76, 78, 204; arrests
    of Unionists for, 71, 94, 102, 160; Van
    Lew investigation for, 178, 180–81; in
    visiting Union prisoners, 56; of women,
    106, 108–9. See also allegiance; loyalty
Dix, Morgan, 105
Doolittle, James R., 201, 202
Doswell, Thomas, 175–77
double life, 53–55, 192
Doughty, Mr. (postal worker), 224
Douglas, Stephen, 39
Douglass, Frederick, 225, 244
Dow, Neal, 125
Draper, Elizabeth. See Mitchell, Elizabeth
    Draper
Drewry's Bluff fort, 154

Duke, James, 159, 160, 161, 175, 184, 186
Dyers, Thomas G., 105

Earle, Charles W., 132
Early, Jubal, 170–72, 173, 174
Ebenezer Baptist Church, 198
Eberhardt, G. L., 210, 211, 212
economic growth, 35–36
economic inflation, 174, 189
economic recession, 228. See also
    financial straits
education, 17–18, 20, 214; of blacks, 28,
    31, 165, 168, 197–98, 209–12, 225
elite, 34, 36, 48–49; families, 12, 15, 33;
    women, 40, 60, 69, 80, 105–6, 180–81
Ely, Alfred, 55, 56, 59, 64, 65, 69
emancipation of slaves, 5, 18, 26–27, 195.
    See also free blacks; manumission
Emancipation Proclamation, 98–99
encoded dispatches, 112–13, 114–15, 149,
    182
espionage, 61–63, 73–75, 217; arrests for,
    96; by women, 61–62, 206. See also
    intelligence gathering
Evins, William, 209
Ewell, Richard, 116
ex-Confederates, 200, 204, 209, 221, 239;
    amnesty for, 203, 213, 214–15; Van
    Lew's postmastership and, 225, 231,
    237
executions, 65, 66, 99, 107, 138; of John
    Brown, 37–38; of Union spies, 75, 101

family: brother's desertion and, 127–28;
    childhood, 9, 12; deaths in, 20–21, 230,
    245, 250; dispute in, 233–34; education
    of blacks and, 212; Elizabeth as
    household head, 67; financial support
    for, 86–87; hardware business of, 12,
    156, 207; parents, 9–10, 17, 48;
    Richmond ties of, 33–34; sister-in-law's
    deposition, 178–80; unique culture of,
    47–48. See also specific Van Lews
family home. See Church Hill mansion
Farragut, David, 107
Faust, Drew Gilpin, 108, 143
Fay, William, 71, 86, 96, 159, 183, 196,
    197; imprisonment of, 72, 160
Feis, William B., 113, 171, 172–73

female benevolence, 16, 20, 52–53, 80; to Union prisoners, 63, 65, 67, 69, 206. *See also* charity work; generosity
female spies, 61–62, 74, 75, 76
feminism, 23. *See also* woman's rights movement
Ferguson, Joseph, 126
Fifteenth Amendment, 225
financial straits, 86, 206, 212, 237–38, 248
First African Baptist Church, 22, 25, 27
Fishel, Edwin, 74, 113, 173, 277n.9
Fislar, John C., 120
Fitzsimmons, George, 119
Five Forks, 189–90
flag-of-truce boats, 111–12, 113
flour mills, 11, 194
food for prisoners, 64, 85, 86, 90, 100
food shortages, 102–3, 174, 189
Forbes, William W., 236
Forbes, John M., 238, 242, 244, 246
Ford, Robert, 92, 120, 122, 125, 128
forged documents, 139–41, 143
Forrester, Richard G., 236–37
Fort Fisher, 182
Fort Harrison, 170, 172
Fort Monroe, 77, 111, 148
Fort Stedman, 188, 189
Fort Sumter issue, 43, 44
Fourteenth Amendment, 212, 219
Fox, Thomas, 92
Francis, Lewis, 64
Fredericksburg, Virginia, 188
Frederick's Hall Station, 138
free blacks, 11, 22–23, 26, 28, 162; arrests of, 30–31; education of, 197–98
Freedmen's Bureau, 203, 208–9
freedom, 173; purchase of, 27. *See also* emancipation; manumission of slaves
freedom of speech, 49

Gallagher, John, 119
Garcin, Raymond, 251
Garfield, James, 230, 238, 239, 240
Garrison, William Lloyd, 204
Garvin, Mary J. R., 168, 212. *See also* Richards, Mary Jane
generosity, 132, 250. *See also* charity; female benevolence
Georgia, 174, 185, 210

German Unionists, 81, 94–95, 147, 148
Gibbs, George C., 65
Gillum, Nelson, 25, 155, 164
Gilmer, George K., 229, 239
Glasgow, Ellen, 236, 246–47, 257–59
Glazier, Willard, 111, 124
Godwin, Colonel, 73, 79
Goodhall, Cornelius, 27, 34
Goodwin, Rev., 251
Grant, Dorothy, 20, 32, 168, 179
Grant, Julia, 196
Grant, Ulysses S., 4, 69, 188, 189, 196, 219; in final battles, 156–57; intelligence dispatches to, 163, 173, 174–75; and payment for wartime service, 204, 207; Petersburg seige and, 169; as president, 215; reelection of, 224; surrender of Lee and, 195; Van Lew postmastership and, 3, 216–17, 220, 221, 232, 238, 296n.3; Van Lew's war correspondence with, 157; war strategy and, 153
Greanor Prison, 88
Great Rebellion, The (Botts), 72
Green, Abby, 90, 92, 120, 125, 132, 150; aid to prison escapees by, 122, 128–29
Greenhow, Rose O'Neal, 61–62, 74, 177
Gresham, Judge, 240
Gustafson, Melanie, 227

habeas corpus cases, 70, 181, 186. *See also* courts
Hairston, J. W. T., 86
Halbach, Edward, 139
Hall, Annie Randolph (niece), 95, 113, 166, 252; on fall of Richmond, 192, 193–94; marriage of, 245; as oral historian, 20, 32, 179; on prison escapees, 89–90, 193
Hall, James O., 141
Hall, John J., 245
Halyburton, James D., 105
Hamilton, Andrew G., 118–20, 123
Hampton, Wade C., 117, 137, 138, 170
Hancock, John, 159, 160, 186, 192, 193, 197
Harper's Ferry raid, 37
Harper's Monthly, 166, 254–55, 259, 268n.37

Harper's Weekly, 132, 140, 205–6, 207, 216–17
Harris, William, 59, 68–69
Hatch, Colonel, 88
Hayes, Rutherford B., 231–32, 234, 236, 237, 238
Hazen, Mr., 240
Henley, Mary Jane, 31. *See also* Richards, Mary Jane
Henrico County, Virginia, 13, 160–61
Henrico County Jail, 66, 67
Henry, Patrick, 11
Higginbotham, Edward, 64, 68
Higgins, John M., 71, 73, 197, 245
Hill, John F., 87
Hill, Owen B., 68
Hinton, Mary, 106
Hobart, Harrison C., 120, 123, 131
Holmes, Arnold B., 109–10, 115, 159, 196, 197; death of, 244
Holmes, Elmira, 145
Holmes, Josephine, 109–10
Homes of the New World (Bremer), 23
Hooker, Joseph, 97
Horne, J. W., 29
hospital visits, 80, 85
Houdon, Jean-Antoine, 11
Howard, O. O., 208
Howard, George A., 241
Howard, Harry S., 109, 111, 112, 114
Howe, Mrs., 225
Hughes, D. W., 159, 160, 161, 197
Hughes, Robert W., 231
Humphreys, James M., 162, 183
Humphreys, Joseph M., 222, 224
Humphreys, Andrew A., 169, 174
Hunnicutt, James W., 213, 214
Hurlbut, William Henry, 95–96
Huson, Calvin, Jr., 55, 64–65, 83
Hustings Court, 27, 31, 197

immigrants, as Unionists, 81, 82, 94–95
intelligence gathering, 93, 97–98, 114–15, 157–74; by blacks, 159, 162–68; final battles and, 170–74; payments for, 149, 150, 158, 186, 207–8; rendevous for, 159–60; Van Lew role in, 111–12, 113, 158–59. *See also* espionage; Sharpe, George Henry

investigation of Van Lew, 175–82, 256; disloyalty charges and, 178, 180–81; mother's innocence, 176–77; self-defense, 176–77; sister-in-law's deposition, 178–80; surveillance following, 181–82
iron foundries, 11, 80, 103, 170, 174

Jackson, Andrew, 16
Jackson, Thomas J. "Stonewall," 55
Jackson, Luther, 27
Jackson, Mary, 103, 104
James River, 13, 138, 156, 157
Jefferds, J. A., 233, 234–36
Jefferson, Thomas, 15
Jefferson Davis (privateer), 65
Jersey City Argus (newspaper), 241
John, Richard, 218
Johnson, Andrew, 200, 203, 215
Johnson, Judy, 25, 32, 34, 250
Johnson, Laura J., 102
Johnston, I. N., 119, 121, 122, 124, 132
Johnston, Joseph, 63, 77, 153
Johnston, Mary, 243
Jones, John B., 74, 78
Jones, Mary, 31, 167. *See also* Richards, Mary Jane
Jordan, Thomas, 61
Josselyn, Mr., 65

Kean, Robert, 69
Kemper, James Lawson, 225
Kennedy, Crammond, 31, 167, 210–11
Kent, Horace, 46, 86, 213
Kershaw, Joseph B., 171, 172, 173
Kilpatrick, H. Judson, 135–37, 138
King, Miss, 176, 178
Klapp, Anna, 233. *See also* Van Lew, Anna Paulina
Klapp, Joseph, 209, 252
Knight, Judson, 156, 159, 161, 183, 184, 187
Know Nothing Party, 36

Ladies Aid and Defense Association, 80
Lafayette, Marquis de, 11
Lankford, Nelson, 198
LaTouche, Lt., 125
Lawton, Hattie, 74, 75, 76, 101

Lebsock, Suzanne, 23
Lee, William Raymond, 66
Lee, Robert E., 140, 153, 155, 174, 182;
  assault against McClellan by, 77; attack
  on Fort Stedman by, 188, 189; capture
  of John Brown by, 37; General Early
  and, 172; Grant's army and, 157, 173;
  Petersburg seige and, 169; railroad lines
  to, 96–97; surrender of, 195
Letcher, John, 44–45, 56, 99, 272n.23;
  bread riot and, 103, 104
Lewis, John F., 17, 46, 221
Lewis, Oliver, 22, 25, 164
Lewis, Pryce, 74–75
Libby Prison, 85, 89, 94, 197, 255;
  overcrowding in, 83, 100
Libby Prison breakout, 90, 91–92, 109,
  118–33; plan for, 118–21; recapture of
  escapees, 125–26, 131; Unionist safe
  houses for, 120, 126–32
Liberator (newspaper), 204
Liberia, 28–31
Lincoln, Abraham, 4, 63, 111, 116, 136,
  218; administration of, 65; African
  colonization and, 28; death of, 198;
  election of, 39; emancipation
  proclamation of, 5, 98, 99; Grant and,
  153; peace and, 195; privateersmen
  and, 66, 93; reelection of, 174;
  secession and, 41–42, 43
Lindsay, Lewis, 213
Lipscomb, Martin Meredith, 144–45, 205
Littlepage, William, 139
Lohmann, Frederick William Ernest, 81,
  94–95, 107, 192, 204, 256; arrest of,
  186; Dahlgren reburial and, 144–45,
  146, 205, 286n.19
Lohmann, Herman, 81, 149
Lohmann, John A., 81, 145, 146, 197
Lohmann brothers, 81, 96, 147, 148
"Lone Vixen, The" (play), 259
Longstreet, James, 171
Lost Cause myth, 243–44, 260
Lounsbury, William H., 89–90
loyalists, 82, 83, 99, 117, 151. See also
  underground; Unionists
loyalty: to Confederacy, 53–54, 67, 75, 76,
  96; to Union, 7, 81, 213, 217. See also
  allegiance; disloyalty; patriotism

Lyman, Theodore, 116
Lyons, James, 105

Maddox, Joseph H., 98
Magruder, John B., 77
Mahone, William, 238, 239
Major, Charles, 159, 161
male sphere, 61, 218, 222, 223, 235–36
Manning, Frederick, 157
manumission of slaves, 9, 28; deeds of,
  25, 26–27; Van Lew secret, 32–34
Marable, Major, 159, 161
Marcy, Dr., 251, 252
Marshall, John, 11, 15
martial law, 68, 70
Martin, Samuel J., 137
Mary (Van Lew servant), 155, 172,
  289n.28. See also Richards, Mary Jane
Massachusetts soldiers, 248
Masters, Lt., 88
Matthews, Fanny, 102
Mayo, Joseph, 104, 200
McAvery, David, 88
McClellan, George, 70, 77–78, 79, 88, 153
McConigle, Miss, 78, 94, 95
McCreery, John Van Lew (cousin), 49
McCullough, John R., 109, 111
McDonald, Bedan B., 120, 122, 128, 129,
  131
McEntee, John, 97, 173, 174
McKinley administration, 248
McNiven, Thomas, 277n.9, 286n.19,
  287n.27, 289n.28
Meade, George, 136, 140, 149, 188; Army
  of the Potomac and, 113–14, 134, 153
Mechanicsville, Virginia, 78
Memminger, Christopher G., 56, 65
memoirs/manuscript, 6–7, 206–7, 251,
  252, 253–54
mental instability, 235, 256, 258. See also
  Crazy Bet myth
military installations, 45. See also Forts
military service act, 75
Mills, Dr. C. S., 233
Mines, John F., 64
Missouri Compromise, 41
Mitchell, John F. B., 138
Mitchell, Elizabeth Draper, 26, 32
Mobile, Alabama, 153

money, 183, 189; for wartime service, 204, 206. *See also* bribery; financial straits; remuneration
Moore, Thomas, 85–86
morale, 152, 170, 174, 185, 188–89
Moran, Frank, 119
Mount Vernon Association, 80
Murphy, F., 88, 89
Myers, Alexander, 159, 161, 197

National Republican, 232, 234, 237
National Virginian, 221
National Woman Suffrage Association, 218, 222, 224, 242
Neely, Mark E., Jr., 101, 180
Nelson, T. A. R., 99
New, W. W., 176
New National Era, 225
New Orleans, Louisiana, 107–8
New York Herald, 62, 88, 131, 141, 219
New York Times, 96, 108, 130, 217, 253; on prison escapes, 88, 93
New York Tribune, 163, 226
New York World, 236
Nicholls, Mrs. B. F., 252
North Carolina, 182, 189
Northern carpetbaggers, 221, 234–36
Northern press, 95, 104, 188, 204, 216–17
Nowland, Eliza G. C. *See* Carrington, Eliza Griffin
Nuckols, Elias, 160

Oakley, J. M., 88
Oakwood Cemetery, 143–44, 151, 197, 286n.19
O'Hara, Scarlett, 177
Ord, E. O. C., 104, 196, 199
Orrock, Robert, Jr., 146, 147–48, 205
ostracism, 46, 238, 240, 245–47. *See also* social isolation
Ould, Robert, 148, 149, 197

Paine, Jedediah, 196, 199
Palmer, Charles, 33, 86, 96, 201, 204; arrest of, 71, 72, 94; Dahlgren reburial and, 145; in spy network, 115; Whig background of, 17, 81
Palmer, William P., 72
Parker, Ely S., 196

Parker, David B., 129, 132, 196, 221, 240; on Van Lew's network, 90, 93, 163
Parker, William H., 246, 248, 257
Parrish, Maria, 209
partisanship, 218, 221, 223, 225. *See also specific political parties*
passport system, 30, 31, 78–79, 92, 200
Patrick, Marsena, 196, 197
patriotism, 76, 106, 177, 208, 244; of black Unionists, 131; of women, 42, 52–53, 80–81. *See also* allegiance; loyalty
patronage, 216, 217, 220, 226, 239
Pember, Phoebe Yates, 130
Peninsula Campaign, 77, 82, 153
Pennsylvania Abolitionist Society, 10
Petersburg Index, 222–23, 225
Petersburg (Virginia) seige, 156–57, 169, 190
Pettigru, James, 38
Philadelphia, Pennsylvania, 10, 18, 33, 110
Philadelphia Evening Telegraph, 217, 219
Philadelphia Inquirer, 204
Pickett, George, 190
Pierpont, Francis H., 200, 204
Pinkerton, Allan, 62, 74–75, 76, 77, 97
Platt, James Henry, Jr., 221, 222
Pleasanton, Alfred, 137–38
Pole (English spy), 187
political climate, 11, 217–18
political influence, 16, 61. *See also* postmastership
political parties, secession and, 35–37, 40. *See also* partisanship; *and specific party*
Pollan, Tracy, 260
Pollard, James, 138
Porter, John F., Jr., 121, 122, 128
Porter, Charles H., 221, 222, 224
Porter, Horace, 187, 189
postmastership, 3–4, 218–39; accomplishments in, 219–20; blacks and, 225–28, 231–32, 236; family dispute and, 233–34; franking privilege and, 218, 222; Grant and, 3, 216–17, 220, 221, 232, 238, 296n.3; insubordination charge and, 221–22; male sphere and, 218, 222, 223, 235–36; politics and, 218, 220–25, 242, 247–48; reappointment campaign, 231–33, 234–36, 238–39; women's suffrage and, 218–19, 221, 222–23

press, 73; African American, 244, 253; Northern, 95, 104, 188, 204, 216–17. *See also* Richmond press

Price, Philip B., 176, 178

prisoner exchange, 60, 93, 99–100, 107–8

prisoners, Union, 55–60, 63–69, 82–94, 98, 116, 137, 140; Atlanta underground and, 105; bribing of guards by, 85, 86, 87, 89, 114, 125, 126; food for, 64, 85, 86, 90, 100; officers and civilians, 55–56; planned rescue of, 117–18; punishment of, 83, 84–85, 100, 125; Van Lew mansion as refuge for, 89–91; Van Lew's charity toward, 59–60, 66–67, 78, 206; women as, 101–2. *See also* Confederate prisons; *and specific prison*

prison escapees, 87–93, 109; black Unionist aid to, 91–93; Van Lew home as refuge for, 89–91, 192–93. *See also* Libby Prison breakout

privateers, 65, 66, 93

propaganda, 93, 106

property rights, 21, 63, 296n.2

property sale, 22–23, 25, 238, 250

prostitution charges, 108

Pryor, Sarah, 79

punishment: of prisoners, 83, 84–85, 100, 125; of slaves, 50

Putnam, Sallie Ann Brock. *See* Brock, Sallie Ann

Quarles, John H., and family, 90, 122, 128

racial equality, 225, 228, 232, 237

racial politics, 225–28, 230

racial solidarity, 37

racism, 9, 51, 195, 210, 211, 244. *See also* white supremacy

Radical Republicans, 5, 111, 213, 221, 229, 232. *See also* Republican Party

railroads, 11, 96–97, 173, 185, 188, 189, 205

Ramsdell, C. P., 233

Randolph, George W., 72, 105

Randolph, Thomas, 12

Readjuster Party, 239–40

Reconstruction, 5, 195–96, 212–15, 231, 232, 243; demise of, 228–29; Joint Committee on, 203

remuneration, 149, 150, 158, 186; for wartime service, 207–8. *See also* money

Republican Party, 4, 43, 227, 239, 242; antislavery stance of, 37, 40, 48, 50; blacks and, 226, 230; Reconstruction and, 213, 215, 228–29, 232; threat to racial hierarchy by, 81; Van Lew and, 223, 224, 230, 233, 237; woman's rights and, 219, 221, 222, 224. *See also* Radical Republicans

respectability, 5, 67, 177, 192, 255

Revere, M. A., 67, 68

Revere, Paul Joseph, 66, 67, 165, 248

Revolutionary War heroes, 10, 11, 47

Revolution (suffragette journal), 219, 220, 222, 223

Reynolds, John Phillip, Jr., 6, 165, 166, 168–69, 250, 256; Crazy Bet myth and, 253–54, 261; Van Lew funeral and, 251, 252

Rice, Lucy A., 128–30, 132, 150

Richards, Mary Jane, 25, 29–32, 34, 178; aliases of, 31, 165–68; arrest and trial of, 30–31; education of, 28, 31; teaching by, 197–98, 209–12; in Liberia, 28, 29–30

Richardson, Albert D., 121, 126

Richmond, Virginia: 1863 bread riot in, 102–5; evacuation of, 189; fall of, 3, 190–95; fires in, 190–91, 194; home defense brigade, 135; Lost Cause cult and, 244; martial law in, 68, 70; pre-Civil War growth of, 10–12; Union schemes to attack, 115–17, 135–36; Union spies in, 74; Van Lew's ties to, 33–34

Richmond, Fredericksburg, and Potomac (RF&P) Railroad, 11, 96–97, 173, 205

Richmond Dispatch, 110, 205, 222, 226, 229, 250; on female patriotism, 53; on Lincoln inaugural, 42; on spy network, 163; on treatment of women, 62, 63; on Unionist disloyalty, 71; on Van Lew charity, 60

Richmond Enquirer, 10, 13, 20, 33, 70, 98; on female prisoners, 102; on mobilization for war, 52; on secession, 43, 45; on Van Lew as postmaster, 216, 224–25, 231, 235–36; on Van Lew's prison visits, 59–60, 69

Richmond Evening Journal, 257

Richmond Evening Leader, 165

Richmond Examiner, 71, 73, 105, 183, 203, 216; on bread riots, 104; on Dahlgren affair, 139, 142, 151; on spy execution, 75

Richmond loyalists. *See* loyalists underground; Unionist Underground

Richmond News Leader, 253, 259

Richmond press, 49, 76, 141, 214, 220, 253; on arrest of Unionists, 186; attack on Van Lew by, 206–7; on Dahlgren affair, 139, 140; on female patriotism, 52–53; on Libby Prison breakout, 125, 131; Van Lew letter to, 199. *See also specific newspaper*

Richmond Prison Association, 59

Richmond Republic, 204

Richmond Sentinel, 130, 186

Richmond State Journal, 221, 233

Richmond Times-Dispatch, 207, 259

Richmond underground. *See* Unionist underground

Richmond Whig, 31, 43, 186, 191, 236; on Dahlgren affair, 142, 146; on Van Lew as postmaster, 224–25

Ricksecker, Mrs. C. A., 252

Ricketts, James B., 60

Ricketts, Fanny, 60, 67, 76

Riddle, William, 88

Riggs, Marion C., 84

Ripley, Edward H., 1917

Rives, Alexander, 229

Rives, William C., 41

Rix, Virgina and Mary Ann Rix, 22–23

Roach, A. C., 129

Roane, Hannah, 25

Roane, James, 25, 164, 183

Roane, Louisa, 26, 32

Roane, Peter, 25, 26, 32, 164, 183, 227, 228

Roane, William, 22, 25, 50, 164

Roane, William C., 232, 240, 245

Robertson, James I., 156, 169, 190

Robinson, Martin, 138

Rockwood, George W., 66

Romance of a Plain Man (Glasgow), 257–59

Rose, Thomas E., 118–20, 123, 125

Ross, Erasmus, 89, 92, 121, 122, 196

Rowley, Merritt, 115

Rowley, William S., 81–82, 95, 112, 156, 256; aid to fugitives by, 90, 110; Dahlgren reburial and, 145, 146–47, 148, 205; as Dunkard, 115, 156; postwar payments to, 149–50; in spy network, 113, 114, 159, 173, 278n.11

Ruffin, Edmund, 38

Runyon, Emily Chenault, 95, 251

Russell, Otis H., 248, 250, 252

Ruth, Samuel, 96–97, 147, 173, 204, 205; aid to fugitives by, 110; arrest of, 186; in spy network, 114, 187–88

St. John's Episcopal Church, 11, 14, 15, 16, 22, 167

St. Mary's, Georgia, 210

Salisbury (NC) prison, 72–73, 160, 202

Sands, Alexander H., 178

Saunders, Elizabeth, 209

Savannah, Georgia, 174, 185

Savannah (privateer), 65

Schofield, George M., 213, 214

Schwartzberg, Hyman, 257

Scobell, John, 74, 75

Scott, Anne E., 73, 75

Scott, Robert, 45

Scully, John, 74–75

Searce, William, 128, 131

Sears, Stephen, 141

secession crisis, 5, 35–51, 81; Brown's raid and, 37–38; Lincoln's threat and, 41–42, 43; militant "fire-eaters" and, 37, 39, 45, 46; slavepower and, 48–51; Southern nationalism and, 36, 39, 42; Unionists and, 35–37, 39, 40, 43, 45, 46–47; vote in Virginia and, 272n.23; women and, 40, 42–43

Seddon, James A., 41, 126

Seddon, Mrs. James A., 140

Sedgewick, John, 116, 117

Segar, Joseph, 42, 46

Sequestration Act (CSA), 63

Seven Pines, 77

Seward, William, 43

Sewell, William, 25, 95

Seymour, Horatio, 215

Sharp, James, 46, 161, 162

Sharpe, George Henry, 93, 94, 156, 188, 204, 256; Babcock and, 113; and bread

riot, 103; intelligence dispatches and, 114, 169, 170, 173, 182, 185; on postwar compensation, 208; as spymaster, 97, 157–58, 159; on Van Lew's prison charity, 85, 86. *See also* intelligence gathering
Shenandoah Valley, 153, 155, 170–72
Sheridan, Philip H., 154, 171, 172, 173, 174
Sherman, William, 153, 174, 185, 189
Shockhoe Cemetery, 251, 253
Sigel, Franz, 153, 155
Silver, Isaac, 114, 147, 186
slaveholding, 3, 28, 81, 82; hiring out and, 26–27; mutual dependence in, 32–34; by Van Lew family, 16, 21–22, 24–28, 30–33, 64, 67, 164–68, 268n.38
slavery, 22, 39, 130, 195, 197; emancipation proclamation and, 98–99; end of war and, 194–95; in prewar Richmond, 11–12, 23–24; hopes for gradual reform of, 9, 34, 49, 51; secession crisis and, 48–51; Unionists and, 36, 38–39, 99; Virginia loyalists' abolition of, 200
slaves, runaway, 95, 99, 101, 107
Slidell, John, 140
Smith, George W., 17
Smith, Letitia (great aunt), 10, 47
social isolation, 9, 229, 242, 244, 259–60; ostracism, 46, 238, 240, 245–47. *See also* Crazy Bet myth
South: devotion to, 34; woman's rights in, 219
South Carolina, 43, 44; soldiers from, 52, 53
Southern Claims Commission, 158
Southern Opinion, 216
Southern rights, 37, 44–45. *See also* secession crisis
Southern whites, slave power and, 48–51. See also white supremacy
Spear, S. P., 116
"Special Friendship, A" (film), 260
Spotsylvania Court House, 154
spy network, 7, 101, 206. *See also* espionage; intelligence gathering; Unionist network
Stanton, Elizabeth Cady, 218, 219, 242
Stanton, Edwin, 99, 115, 141, 204

Stearns, Franklin, 89, 145, 213, 252; arrest of, 71, 72; as Whig, 17, 81
Stephens, George E., 227
Sterling, John, 120, 128, 131
Stiles, Robert, 234
Stockton, Betsy, 28
Stone, Cyrena, 105–6, 152
Stone, Lucy, 218
Stowe, Harriet Beecher, 28, 211
Streight, Abel D., 125–26, 128, 129–30, 131, 150
Stuart, Alexander H. H., 214, 215
Stuart, J. E. B., 154
Stuart, Meriwether, 96–97, 115, 128, 148, 278n.11
suffrage. *See* voting rights; woman's rights movement
Summers, George W., 40–41, 46, 49
Sumner, Charles, 4, 5
Sweet Springs Resort, 18–19, 24

Tait, Bacon, 33
taste, 12, 207, 228
tax protests, 242, 253
temperance movement, 248
Tennessee, 69–70, 98, 99, 280n.43
Terry, Alfred H., 104, 182
Third Street Methodist Church, 232
Thompson, Virginia, 237
Timberlake, John H., 186–87
tobacco factories, 11, 23–24; as prisons, 55, 57, 64, 84, 88. *See also specific prison*
Todd, David H., 56, 59, 65
treason, 102, 105. *See also* disloyalty
Tredegar Iron Works, 80, 103, 174
Tucker, Beverly, 16
Turner, Dick, 83, 92
Turner, Thomas Pratt, 83, 85, 125
Tyler, John, 41
Tyler-McGraw, Marie, 207n.48, 302n.8

Underwood, John C., 213
Underwood, Margaret, 101
Union army, 9, 50–51, 196, 203, 280n.43; Army of the James, 111, 154, 157, 162; Army of the Potomac, 70, 155, 157, 171; casualties of, 54, 78, 79, 156; Dahlgren mission and, 137; high command, 116, 159, 170, 182; occupation of Richmond

Union army (*continued*)
by, 191–92, 193, 194; Richmond attack
scheme and, 116–17; tributes to Van
Lew by, 217
Unionist underground, 80–82, 114, 134,
169, 182–84, 185, 256, 260, 277n.9; aid
to fugitive blacks by, 95–96; aid to
prison escapees by, 121–22, 126–32; aid
to prisoners by, 83, 86, 109–10, 121,
124; arrests of, 160–61, 184, 186–87;
counterintelligence and, 186–88;
Dahlgren affair and, 136, 142, 143, 144–
49, 151, 204–5; emancipation
proclamation and, 98, 99; failed raid
on Richmond and, 117; final days of
war and, 170, 173; German immigrants
in, 81, 94–95, 147, 148; in Atlanta, 105–
6; intelligence reports from, 170–72,
277n.9; morale of, 152, 170; postwar
employment of, 197; postwar
conservatism and, 200–203; recruitment
as spies, 111, 160; Sharpe and, 173,
182. *See also* Unionists
Unionists, 48, 75, 79, 200, 230, 255; flight
of, 95–96; aid to Union prisoners by,
59, 83, 88, 89–93; arrests of, 30–31, 70–
73, 94, 102, 105; bread riot and, 104–5;
Confederate punishment of, 63;
Dahlgren affair and, 141, 142; defense
of Richmond by, 135; emancipation
proclamation and, 99; fall of
Richmond and, 190; imprisonment of,
68–69, 150, 161, 186, 197; loyalty and,
76; Reconstruction and, 195–96;
secession crisis and, 39, 40–41, 43, 45,
46–47; Virginia politics and, 35–37;
women as, 61, 64, 69, 105–6, 109–10,
121–22. *See also* loyalists; Unionist
underground
Union prisoners. *See* prisoners, Union
University of Virginia, 12
Upshur, Thomas, 206

vagrancy law, 104, 201
Valentine, Lila Meade, 243
Van Buren, Martin, 16
Van Lew, Anna Paulina (sister), 16, 21,
33, 233
Van Lew, Annie. *See* Hall, Annie
Randolph

Van Lew, Augusta (sister-in-law), 245, 252
Van Lew, Eliza Louise Baker (mother), 9–
10, 15–16, 67, 176–77; death of, 230
Van Lew, Eliza (niece), 179, 245–46, 250
Van Lew, John (father), 9–10, 12, 18, 35;
death of, 20–21; will of, 21–22, 26, 233
Van Lew, John Newton (brother), 16, 67,
149, 161, 213, 220, 233; desertion from
army by, 127–28; family business and,
12, 156, 207; marriages of, 178–79, 245;
northern exile of, 156, 160, 183–84,
196
Van Lew, Mary Carter (sister-in-law), 49,
178–80
Van Lew family. *See* family
Van Lew servants, 155, 159, 163–64, 169,
183; secret freedom for, 32–34
Velasquez, Loreta Janeta, 101
violence, 207, 240. *See also* punishment
Virginia Club, 257
Virginia Colonization Society, 29
Virginia Legislature, 98, 200, 212, 296n.2;
secession crisis and, 38, 40–41
Virginia Star, 245
Virginia State Woman Suffrage
Association, 219
von Hoffman, Johannah, 287n.27
voting rights: for black men, 213, 214,
221, 225; for women, 48, 218–19, 221,
223, 230, 242–43

Walker, Mary, 101–2
Walker, George W., 69
Walker, Maggie Lena, 26, 32, 260
Wardwell, Burnham, 117, 150, 196, 197,
207; aid to fugitives by, 90, 110; arrest
of, 71, 72, 145; Conservative hostility
and, 200–201, 203; death of, 244; on
Lincoln's death, 198; prison visits by,
86; in spy network, 159, 183; voting
rights and, 213
Wardwell, Sarah J., 73, 145, 148
Washington, D.C., 74, 241
Washington, George, 11
Washington press, 110, 230, 233, 239
Webster, Timothy, 74, 75–76
Weddell, Alexander Wilbourne, 246
Weed, Thurlow, 238
Weitzel, Godfrey, 191, 196
Wells, James, 122–23

Wheeler, Marjorie Spruill, 48, 243
Whig Party, 16–17, 35–36, 40, 47, 81, 82
White, William, 187, 192
White Sulfur Springs, 18, 38
white supremacy, 81, 207, 221, 232, 240, 243
Whitlock, Anna I., 24, 127, 164
Wickham, William C., 231
Williams, John G., 73
Williams, Anthony D., 29, 30
Wilmington, North Carolina, 182
Winder, John H., 55, 63, 64, 69, 85, 256; arrests of Unionists and, 70–73, 147; treatment of prisoners by, 56; Union agent in office of, 150–51; Van Lew and, 56–57, 68, 127, 128
Winder, William, 70
Winder, William Andrew, 57, 74
Winder, William Sidney, 57
Wise, Henry A., 38, 44–45
Wistar, Isaac J., 116–17, 130, 136, 138
Woman in Battle (Valesquez), 101

women, 60–63, 102–6, 259; in civil service, 218, 237; disloyalty of, 106, 108–9; elite, 40, 60, 69, 80, 105–6, 180–81; imprisonment of, 101–2; innocence of, 60–61, 177; patriotism of, 42, 52–53, 80–81; property rights of, 21, 63, 296n.2; secession crisis and, 40, 42–43; Southern ideal, 15–16, 177, 242–43; as spies, 61–62, 74, 75, 76; as threat to social order, 61; Unionist, 61, 64, 69, 105–6, 109–10, 121–22; vote for, 223, 230; wartime treatment of, 62–63; in working-class riot, 102–5. *See also* female benevolence; woman's rights movement
Women of Virginia Historic Trail, 260
woman's rights movement, 61, 48, 218–19, 221, 224, 242–43, 253, 258; male sphere and, 218, 222
Wood, Alfred M., 66
Wust, Klaus, 81
Wyatt, Henry L., 54

DATE DUE

MAR 0 6 2004		
FEB 2 8 2005		
JUN 0 9 2005		
GAYLORD		PRINTED IN U.S.A.